CIVIL WARS, INSECURITY, AND INTERVENTION

CIVIL WARS, INSECURITY, AND INTERVENTION

Edited by Barbara F. Walter and Jack Snyder

COLUMBIA UNIVERSITY PRESS   NEW YORK

COLUMBIA UNIVERSITY PRESS
Publishers Since 1893
New York, Chichester, West Sussex
Copyright © 1999 by Columbia University Press

Library of Congress Cataloging-in-Publication Data
Civil wars, insecurity, and intervention / edited by Barbara F. Walter
    and Jack Synder.
        p.   cm.
    Includes bibliographical references and index.
    ISBN 0-231-11626-8 (alk. paper). — ISBN 0-231-11627-6 (pbk.)
    1. Civil war.   2. Low-intensity conflicts (Military science)
    3. Ethnic relations.   4. World politics—1989–   I. Walter, Barbara
    F.   II. Snyder, Jack L.
U240.C584   1999
355.02'18—dc21   99-22812
                                                                         CIP

Casebound editions of Columbia University Press books are printed on permanent
and durable acid-free paper.

Printed in the United States of America

c 10 9 8 7 6 5 4 3 2 1
p 10 9 8 7 6 5 4 3 2 1

Contents

Acknowledgments

We are grateful to the Ford Foundation for supporting this project through a grant to the Institute of War and Peace Studies at Columbia University, and especially to Geoffrey Wiseman at Ford, who helped us to crystallize our conception of the project. Among the many critics who provided helpful ideas, we would especially like to thank Fiona Adamson, Yael Aronoff, Richard Betts, Michael Brown, Neta Crawford, Timothy Crawford, Kurt Dassel, Steven David, Page Fortna, V. P. Gagnon, Virginia Gamba, Sumit Ganguly, Russell Hardin, Colin Kahl, Radha Kumar, Jodi Nelson, Barry Posen, Gideon Rose, John Ruggie, Said Samatar, Timothy Sisk, Stephen Stedman, Anders Stephanson, Shashi Tharoor, Leslie Vinjamuri, Jon Western, Warren Zimmerman, and the reviewers for Columbia University Press. Kay Achar, Ingrid Gerstmann, Jana Harrison, Audrey Rosenblatt, and the rest of the staff at War and Peace did their usual marvelous job with the conferences and every stage of the project. Most important, Barbara and Jack express their gratitude to Zoli and Nina for being understanding when the contributors to the volume (not its editors!) inexplicably chose to hold one of our conferences on Valentine's Day.

Barbara F. Walter
Jack Snyder

CIVIL WARS, INSECURITY, AND INTERVENTION

Introduction

Barbara F. Walter

This book is about how fear and uncertainty can combine to promote and prolong civil wars. In it we explore three questions. To what extent do mutual security fears contribute to the outbreak of civil war? To what extend do these fears discourage groups from negotiating settlements, even if they would prefer to avoid continued war? Under what conditions is outside intervention likely to ameliorate these fears and help end violence? Our aim is to uncover the conditions under which high levels of uncertainty and fear are likely to emerge within a country, to explain why these fears might then lead to war, and to offer some suggestions on how outside intervention might or might not help manage these issues.

Over the last fifty years the number of civil wars has increased to the point where civil wars now exceed the number of interstate wars. This trend is disturbing for three reasons. First, civil wars tend to last almost twice as long as interstate wars (33 months versus 18.5).[1] Second, once they begin they are very difficult to resolve short of a decisive military victory.[2] And third, even if the two sides do sign a peace treaty, most of these cases are likely to experience renewed violence in the future.[3] In short, civil wars are long, bloody, and they resist settlement.

Much has been written about why civil wars begin and why they are so difficult to resolve.[4] This literature has tended to focus on the stated goals of the belligerents to determine why they would go to war rather than on more general environmental factors.[5] Factions fought because they wanted control of the government, territory, or revolutionary change, and they ended their war when these differences were resolved at the bargaining table or one side conquered the other. But internal wars are not always premeditated, deliberate efforts to overthrow an unwanted system of government, or the result of purely aggressive aims. As Jeffrey Frieden observed, "Wars might be due to bellicose aims of [groups], in which case explanation rests on assertions about their preferences," or "to a hostile and uncertain environment, in which case even the best of intentions would be overwhelmed by the setting."[6] In short, civil wars can also erupt inadvertently from the uncertainty and fear that arise when the domestic environment suddenly changes, leaving groups nervous and insecure about their future.

This book is an attempt to examine more closely how different settings on the ground might affect groups' decision to fight, to negotiate, or to remain at peace. We have chosen to concentrate on environmental factors for three reasons. First, it is an attempt to balance the current emphasis on aggressive aims with an emphasis on how different environments may shape these aims. This is not to say that changes in the underlying environment explain everything about civil wars. This would swing the pendulum too far in the other direction and leave individuals and leaders unaccountable for their behavior. Governments and rebel groups, individual leaders and factions are not mechanical puppets of their domestic setting. Ultimately it is their choice whether to pick up a gun or throw it away. But governments and rebels are also not completely free of the tugs and pulls of the situation in which they make these choices. Serbs, Croats, and Muslims clearly picked up guns and shot at each other in the early 1990s. In part, this can be explained by their desire for greater territorial control. But it can also be explained by the fear and vulnerability they felt as the Yugoslav federation began to disintegrate. In short, we believe it is right to pay careful attention to the underlying aims of the actors making the decisions, but we also believe that a comprehensive discussion of civil wars must consider how the strategic environment in which competing groups find themselves shapes their expectations of each other's future behavior and factors into their decisions to fight, negotiate, or surrender. The trick is to try to figure out what part of the decision to go to war or to reject a negotiated settlement is the result of purely aggressive or predatory aims and what part is the result of the strategic environment.

Our second motive for concentrating on environmental factors is to explain certain mysterious patterns in civil wars. Why, for example, do rebels and incumbent governments sometimes act in ways that appear to be self-defeating—rejecting settlements, returning to fruitless wars, fighting enormously costly battles? Is it really because they are "irrational," as people have argued? Or is it because their range of "rational" choices is limited by structural constraints? Hutus might pick up machetes and kill neighboring Tutsi because they hate each other. But they might also kill because they fear their own life would be at risk if they fail to act. Rebel leaders can be driven to reject election results not because they are sore losers but because they fear they will be imprisoned by the new administration if they do not. In short, security fears might play a far greater role in certain situations than policy makers or social scientists have thus far recognized. Our second goal, therefore, is to try to identify when and where these fears come into play.

A final reason behind our focus on the strategic environment is more practical. Policy makers are clearly interested in preventing and resolving civil wars and will continue to feel pressure to intervene as long as civil wars produce very visible and disturbing images of human suffering. But past interventions have had only mixed success. Peacekeepers sent to Mozambique, El Salvador, and Nicaragua deserve at least partial credit for the successful implementation of peace accords in those states. But other peacekeeping missions have not been so successful. The thousands of U.S. soldiers sent to Somalia are credited with saving the lives of hundreds of thousands of starving civilians but failed to end the violence and actually helped to legitimize pillaging warlords. The UN's most extensive and expensive mission to Cambodia also had only mixed success. With UN assistance, Cambodia held its first democratic elections and successfully implemented a cease-fire, but the UN vision of a multiparty democracy never materialized. And it is still unclear whether Bosnia's peace accord will hold after the massive peacekeeping mission leaves.

This record points to a bedeviling policy problem that we hope to address as our third goal. On the one hand, it is unlikely that the international community will be able to ignore civil wars since outside intervention appears to play a crucial role in the resolution of these conflicts (almost every peace treaty that did successfully end civil wars over the last fifty years succeeded with the help of outside peacekeepers).[7] On the other hand, both the United States and the international community seem unsure when to intervene in these conflicts, how to intervene in them, and which conflicts to target. We hope to identify at least those situations where outside intervention can do the greatest amount of good and can have the greatest chance for success. In short, if it is true that structured insecurities are at the heart of some civil wars, then these are the cases where belligerents should be most amenable to conciliation and where small changes in the environment

could really make a difference. Outsiders might have great difficulty changing the goals and principles of competing groups, but security dilemmas are
one problem they can solve.

Finally, we hope to expose the limitations of structural or environmental
arguments as well as their strengths. As the rest of the volume will make
clear, although uncertainty and fear do play a role in the outbreak and
persistence of civil wars, a complex variety of causes—predation, ideology,
and unresolvable conflicts of interest—are also involved in decisions to fight
or cooperate. Not only do we hope to learn under what conditions security
concerns are likely to factor into decisions to fight but we also hope to
explore when other factors more accurately explain violence.

Security Fears and Civil Wars

Authors in this volume look specifically at five fear-producing environments that can encourage groups to go to war even if they do not necessarily
have aggressive aims. They are situations when (1) the government breaks
down or collapses, (2) a minority group becomes geographically isolated
within a larger ethnic community, (3) the political balance of power shifts
from one group to another, (4) economic resources rapidly change hands,
or (5) groups are asked to demobilize partisan armies. Each of these represents a period of change—a change in the degree to which the government
can constrain and punish behavior, a change in the distribution of resources
among competing actors, or a change in the ability of groups to defend
themselves. These are situations where previously peaceful groups are likely
to become increasingly suspicious of each other and, for reasons discussed
in subsequent chapters, then choose to go to war.[8] Let me review each in
turn.

Fear-Producing Environments

1. Government Breakdown

The recent breakdown of the Soviet Union was followed by a wave of
violence in Azerbaijan, Georgia, Moldova, Chechnya, Tajikistan, and the
former Yugoslavia. Many observers attributed these conflicts to long-festering
ethnic hatreds that were suddenly free to erupt. But an increasing number
of scholars have argued that these wars were at least partially attributable to
the great sense of uneasiness that arose because of the changes occurring

within the Soviet Union between 1985 and 1989. This brings us to our first fear-producing environment. Groups have little to fear from each other when the central government can effectively enforce rules and arbitrate disputes. There are, however, times when the government's ability to rule and to promote order and stability fail, and it is at these times when security dilemmas are most likely to emerge.

Governments can break down for a variety of reasons such as the demise of a ruling empire (as happened in the states of Eastern and Central Europe), the withdrawal of colonial rule (as happened between 1957 and 1968 in Africa), or prolonged economic hardship (as happened in Somalia).

When central control dissolves, domestic groups face a world of uncertainty and unanswered questions. How will power be redistributed? Will other groups within the society respect the status quo or will they take advantage of the situation to enhance their position within society? Will they remain at peace or will they go to war?

Individuals and groups respond to this uncertainty in different ways: they might begin to identify more closely with other ethnic kindred, they may move from one part of the country or region to another seeking sanctuary, they may insist on minority rights or privileges, or they may stockpile weapons as a means to protect themselves. These precautions, however, are not without costs. Although each strategy might enhance the security of the acting group, they often have the unintended consequence of threatening and alarming already anxious neighboring groups. This encourages neighbors to enhance their own defenses, which in turn makes the original group less secure. A classic security dilemma often results. In short, citizens might wish to weather these periods of domestic upheaval without first resorting to war, but the fear engendered by such changes (or the prospect of great change) can produce dangerous security dilemmas that are often difficult to resolve. "There would have been no war in Bosnia and Herzegovina," writes Woodward, "if Yugoslavia had not first collapsed."[9]

2. Geographic Isolation or Vulnerability

Competing groups might also feel insecure if their geographical position within a country makes self-defense difficult. This can occur in two ways. First, sudden territorial changes can leave one ethnic group isolated and vulnerable in a country or region dominated by a rival group. When this happens the diaspora group can become an easy target for physical attacks or a target for discriminatory political, economic, or social practices. This,

Barry Posen has argued, is what ultimately induced the war in the former Yugoslavia by convincing Serbs living in the newly independent Croatia to seek aid and protection from the larger Serb population living outside the region.[10]

Chaim Kaufmann identifies a second source of geographically induced insecurity. He argues that dangerous security dilemmas can also be triggered if peace treaties leave former adversaries geographically *intermixed* in their original state. If adversaries cannot retreat behind defensible boundaries (preferably their own state), each group will feel vulnerable to renewed attack and take measures to protect themselves. According to this logic, the Czechs and Slovaks managed their "velvet divorce" precisely because the two groups were already physically separated, while the Sudanese at least temporarily settled their war in 1972 because their warring populations were naturally divided into northern and southern regions.[11] The success or failure of a settlement, therefore, has more to do with where groups are physically located (and their ability to defend themselves) than with underlying issues or aims that ignited the war.

3. Changing Political Balance of Power

Groups can also become increasingly fearful if the political balance of power threatens to shift from one group to another. This can result when a minority group with a disproportionately high birth rate threatens to overtake the majority in numbers, as occurred between Muslims and Christians in Lebanon in the 1970s. It can result from a large influx of immigrants, as happened in Israel when a large number of Russian Jews arrived between 1989 and 1991 and subsequently voted the Likud government out of office. It can result from a large migration of refugees, as occurred in eastern Zaire when hundreds of thousands of Hutu refugees from Rwanda helped trigger the 1998 war with Tutsis in that state. A shift in the political balance of power can also result from a purposive policy adjustment, such as a change in electoral rules or an extension of suffrage. The negotiated peace treaty to end the war in Rhodesia included an important provision granting voting rights to all black citizens. This promised to dramatically shift the political balance of power away from ruling whites and greatly increased the threat they perceived from the far larger black population.

When political power shifts, or promises to shift, previously privileged groups (like the Christians in Lebanon or white settlers in Africa) can feel threatened and can choose to go to war or resist settlement while their position remains strong in order to prevent any transfer of power from occur-ring. Although these changes do not necessarily threaten the *physical* se-curity of the group, they do threaten their livelihood or economic survival and as such could be a strong incentive to confront the potential rival. As Bruce Jones observes in his chapter on Rwanda, "Fear of loss of 'security' in the broadest sense—economic, political, positional—was part of the motivation for the oligarchy's strident opposition to negotiated change."[12] A fear of a change in political power, therefore, can also motivate groups to fight.

4. Redistribution of Resources

"Security" dilemmas in the broad sense can also be triggered when the distribution of economic resources threatens to shift due to a period of eco-nomic belt-tightening, state breakdown, or the reforms demanded by eco-nomic liberalization and political democratization. Woodward attributes high levels of anxiety between Bosnian Serbs, Croats, and Muslim at least partially to the "budgetary austerities of macroeconomic stabilization, debt repayment and economic reform in the 1980's." According to her, "The insecurities engendered by economic decline, particularly for the middle strata whose standards of living had risen consistently for almost thirty years" made them far more suspicious of their neighbors and more susceptible to inflammatory nationalistic rhetoric.[13]

Domestic groups can also become fearful when the material remnants of the old state become available for redistribution. When states break down, control over vital industries, arms depots, important supply stocks, and aban-doned instruments of state must be reallocated.[14] This reallocation, however, promises to benefit certain groups at the expense of others and could leave a less assertive group permanently disadvantaged. Groups must therefore strategically calculate whether to exploit this opportunity and grab as many resources as possible while they can or whether they should sit back and accept the status quo. Given the strong incentives to enhance one's position and avoid exploitation, groups are encouraged to act like predators even if they themselves have no desire to attack. This dynamic appears to have taken place in Yugoslavia, shortly after the fall of the Soviet Empire. There Croatia accelerated its own military preparations after Serbs (who controlled the Yugoslavian army) "began to impound all of the heavy weapons stored in Croatia . . . thus securing a vast military advantage over the nascent armed forces of the [Croatian] republic."[15]

Finally, authoritarian elites are likely to feel especially threatened by the reforms demanded by economic liberalization and political democratization since they will almost certainly lose their priviledged positions as a result. In these cases the old leaders have strong incentives to protect their economic interests by turning the population against reform-minded groups.

5. Forced or Voluntary Disarmament

Perhaps the most debilitating security dilemma, however, is likely to emerge *after* groups have signed peace treaties and are asked to demobilize. As I argue in chapter 2, civil war peace settlements force combatants through a particularly risky and dangerous implementation period during which they become increasingly unable to protect themselves from surprise attack and increasingly unable to enforce any subsequent terms. Civil war peace treaties in effect "create security dilemmas in the reverse. As groups begin to disarm, they create an increasingly tense situation. The fewer arms they have, the more vulnerable they feel. The more vulnerable they feel, the more sensitive they become to possible violations. And the more sensitive they become to violations, the less likely they are to fulfill their own side of the bargain."[16] Domestic groups, therefore, might reject peace treaties and renew fighting simply because they fear the possible *after-effects* of settlement, and this problem could explain why rebels are often reluctant to disarm, even after they have been offered generous peace terms.

But What Triggers Violence?

Each of these environmental factors offers a compelling reason why neighboring groups might become suspicious and even fearful of each other in times of great change. But they don't explain why these fears then translate into violence. As Rui de Figueiredo and Barry Weingast accurately observe, "Although most ethnic groups face a security dilemma, the spiral dynamic occurs only occasionally." For every case of internal violence that erupted after the breakdown of the Soviet Union there are numerous cases that remained peaceful. Given how many countries have experienced periods of government malfunction, a change in the political balance of power, or a transition from authoritarian rule, it is striking how many of these countries weathered such changes in relative peace.[17] David Laitin, therefore, is right to argue that

> while it cannot be denied that the security dilemma helps explain the high levels of vigilance and active efforts at material acquisition by clan leaders [in Somalia], it is much more difficult to sustain the claim that the security dilemma itself, or the actions impelled by consider- ations by leaders of that dilemma, explain the continued spiraling of clan warfare that got out of control . . . in 1991.[18]

What then accounts for the outbreak of war during times of great political, economic, and military change? A number of authors in this volume believe that the decision to go to war is based on a group's assessment of how malicious or benign a potential rival might be. If the Croats, for example, become convinced that the Serbs are predatory rather than security driven, then the Croats are likely to initiate a war before they are hurt. If, however, they believe the Serbs really are security driven, they are likely to take a more cooperative approach.

But how do groups obtain this information? Woodward, Jones, de Fi- gueiredo, and Weingast believe that the majority of citizens obtain this in- formation from elites who use and manipulate information for their own self-advancement.[19] By focusing on the image of stranded Serbs in Croatia, for example, Milosevic gained the support of Serbs previously uninterested in war. Likewise, "The oligarchy [in Rwanda] played on and played up the security fears of the broader population in the face of the military war, in order to mobilize support for their regime and undermine moderate, ne- gotiated political alternatives."[20] Unscrupulous or predatory leaders, there- fore, often have incentives to portray rivals as more malicious than they actually are.

But individual citizens can also obtain information about what type of opponent they face from other sources. Exogenous shocks such as the earth- quake that hit Managua in 1972 and the 1998 currency crisis in Indonesia can provide important (and more accurate) information about elements within a state and provide the impetus to act. In the case of Nicaragua, it was only after Somoza refused to use vast amounts of outside aid to rebuild the capital that Nicaragua's middle class finally began to mobilize political support against him. Similarly, President Suharto's unwillingness to observe the terms of the IMF package in the aftermath of his country's recent eco- nomic collapse sent a clear signal to Indonesians that their leader would not change his ways even in the face of disaster. It is not difficult to imagine, therefore, that other external shocks could provide important insights into what type of rival a domestic group faced.

The ensuing chapters offer far more in-depth explorations of each of these fear-inducing environments as they apply or do not apply to recent civil wars. As the reader will soon see, it is often difficult to distinguish between groups who are fighting for security-driven motives and those who are fighting for predatory reasons. Nonetheless, each of the authors attempts to identify when mutual security fears have spiraled into war and to offer specific recommendations on effective intervention strategies.

Organization of the Book

The book consists of three parts. In chapter 1 Jack Snyder and Robert Jervis assess whether the concept of the security dilemma really does provide analytical insight into the problem of civil wars and they detail what implications these security dilemmas might have for strategies of intervention. In chapter 2 I analyze the question why civil war adversaries might walk away from promising peace negotiations and discuss the debilitating problems of demobilization and democratization. Part 2 includes four separate case studies. In chapter 3 Susan Woodward applies the idea of the security dilemma to the case of Bosnia and argues that fear and insecurity did play a role in the outbreak of war in Bosnia. She warns, however, that the Dayton accords have not succeeded in reassuring nervous groups and thus continue to encourage Serbs, Croats, and Bosnian Muslims to take refuge in increasingly homogeneous enclaves. In chapter 4 Bruce Jones examines the events in Rwanda that preceded the 1994 genocide and concludes that the Arusha peace accord broke down because a group of elites skillfully manipulated the security fears of the larger population to ensure that their own power and wealth would not be diminished. In chapter 5 David Laitin argues that the security dilemma has only limited application to the 1991 war in Somalia. That war, he argues, "can better be explained by looking at the relative military power of incumbent governments and their ability to squelch or ward off challengers." In chapter 6 Michael Doyle examines the complex encounters that surrounded the signing of the Cambodian peace agreement and explores how peace might be successfully reconstructed in the postimplementation period.

The third part of the book is a duo of thematic chapters drawing on these cases as well as other empirical material. In chapter 7 Chaim Kaufmann examines the need for the physical separation of competing ethnic groups once they have descended into intense armed conflict. Finally, in chapter 8 Rui de Figueiredo and Barry Weingast consider why average citizens choose to support bloody wars despite the huge costs they themselves will have to pay, and analyze how opportunistic politicians are able to manipulate fear to obtain this support.

NOTES

1. This data is available through the University of Michigan's Correlates of War project.
2. This phenomenon has been documented by a number of authors. See George Modelski, "International Settlement of Internal War," in James Rosenau, ed., *International Aspects of Civil Strife* (Princeton: Princeton University Press, 1964); Paul Pillar, *Negotiating Peace: War Termination as a Bargaining Process* (Princeton: Princeton University Press, 1983); Stephen J. Stedman, *Peacemaking in Civil War: International Mediation in Zimbabwe, 1974–1980* (Boulder: Lynne Rienner, 1991); and Barbara F. Walter, "The Critical Barrier to Civil War Settlement," *International Organization*, vol. 51, no. 3 (Summer 1997).
3. See Roy Licklider, "The Consequences of Negotiated Settlements in Civil Wars, 1945–1993," *American Political Science Review*, vol. 89, no. 3 (September 1995).
4. For a sample see Donald L. Horowitz, *Ethnic Groups in Conflict* (Berkeley: University of California Press, 1985); Harry Eckstein, ed., *Internal War: Problems and Approaches* (New York: Free, 1964); James B. Rule, *Theories of Civil Violence* (Berkeley: University of California Press, 1988); Ted Robert Gurr and Barbara Harff, *Ethnic Conflict and World Politics* (Boulder: Westview, 1994); Stephen Van Evera, "Hypotheses on Nationalism and War," *International Security*, vol. 18, no. 4 (Spring 1994); Ted Robert Gurr, *Why Men Rebel* (Princeton: Princeton University Press, 1970); Saul Newman, "Does Modernization Breed Ethnic Conflict?" *World Politics*, vol. 43, no. 3 (April 1991); Michael E. Brown, ed., *Ethnic Conflict and International Security* (Princeton: Princeton University Press, 1993); Roy Licklider, ed., *Stopping the Killing: How Civil Wars End* (New York: New York University Press, 1993); and Francis M. Deng and I. William Zartman, eds., *Conflict Resolution in Africa* (Washington, D.C.: Brookings Institution, 1991).
5. Notable exceptions are David Lake and Donald Rothchild, eds., *The International Spread and Management of Ethnic Conflict* (Princeton: Princeton University Press, 1998); and Michael E. Brown, *The International Dimensions of Internal Conflict* (Cambridge: MIT Press, 1996), both of which mix domestic and structural factors.
6. Jeffrey A. Frieden, "Actors and Preferences in International Relations," in David Lake and Robert Powell, eds., *Strategic Choice and International Relations* (Princeton: Princeton University Press, 1998), p. 52.
7. See Walter, "The Critical Barrier."

8. There is clearly a difference in intensity between threats to one's physical well-being and one's livelihood or political position, and some people might argue that a threat to one's economic security cannot produce a debilitating "security dilemma." The editors have decided to include both a narrow and a broad definition of security threats in order to explore the effects of both.

9. See Susan Woodward, "Bosnia and Herzegovina: How Not to End Civil War," chapter 3, this volume.

10. See Barry Posen, "The Security Dilemma and Ethnic Conflict," *Survival* (Spring 1993).

11. The lengthy debate in Bosnia over the exact boundaries of the ethnically based Muslim, Serb, and Croat federation is an excellent recent example of this concern over geography and its role in future security.

12. See Bruce D. Jones's "Military Intervention in Rwanda's 'Two Wars': Partisanship and Indifference," chapter 4, this volume.

13. See Woodward, "Bosnia and Herzegovina," this volume.

14. Posen, "The Security Dilemma and Ethnic Conflict"; James Fearon, "Ethnic Conflict as a Commitment Problem," unpublished paper, University of Chicago, 1993; Barry Weingast, "Constructing Trust: The Political and Economic Roots of Ethnic and Regional Conflict," unpublished paper, Hoover Institute, 1994; and Jack Snyder, "Nationalism and the Crisis of the Post-Soviet State," *Survival* (Summer 1993); all offer some variation of this argument.

15. Posen, "The Security Dilemma and Ethnic Conflict," p. 114.

16. See Barbara F. Walter's "Designing Transitions from Civil War," chapter 2, this volume.

17. This point is also made by James Fearon, in "Rationalist Explanations for War," *International Organization* (1995).

18. David Laitin's "Somalia: Civil War and International Intervention," chapter 5, this volume.

19. James D. Fearon and David D. Laitin offer strong empirical evidence for a related claim that different ethnic groups are far more likely to cooperate peacefully with each other than they are to fight. See "Explaining Interethnic Cooperation" *American Political Science Review*, vol. 90, no. 4 (December 1996).

20. Related arguments have been made by Snyder, "Nationalism and the Crisis of the Post-Soviet State"; V. P. Gagnon, "Ethnic Nationalism and International Conflict: The Case of Serbia," *International Security*, vol. 19, no. 3 (Winter 1994/95); Brown, *The International Dimensions of Internal Conflict*, 1996; Stephen R. David, "Internal War: Causes and Cures," *World Politics* (July 1997); and Edward Mansfield and Jack Snyder, "Democratization and War," *International Security*, vol. 20, no. 1 (Summer 1995).

21. See Jones, "Military Intervention in Rwanda's 'Two Wars,' " chapter 4, this volume.

Part I

Civil War and Insecurity

1 *Civil War and the Security Dilemma*

Jack Snyder and Robert Jervis

Since the end of the cold war a series of costly civil wars, many of them ethnic conflicts, have dominated the international security agenda. The international community, often acting through the United Nations or regional organizations like NATO, has felt compelled to intervene with military forces in many of these conflicts, including the four cases that comprise the heart of this study: the former Yugoslavia, Somalia, Cambodia, and Rwanda. The mixed record of partial successes, failures, and in some cases counterproductive interventions suggests an urgent need to extract lessons from these experiences with a view toward developing a better conceptual framework to guide future policy choices.[1]

Seeking a tool to help assess these lessons, we examine whether the concept of the security dilemma, widely used to explain conflict between states in the anarchical international system, provides analytical insight into civil wars as well.[2] A security dilemma is a situation in which each party's efforts to increase its own security reduce the security of the others. This situation occurs when geographical, technological, or other strategic conditions render aggression the most advantageous form of self-defense. In normal domestic life this does not apply because as, Thomas Hobbes pointed out, the state provides a buffer between the individual and the dangers of anarchy. But, as Hobbes also noted, because individuals are more vulnerable than are states, the security dilemma is likely to be more severe in civil than in international anarchy. When state authority disintegrates, patterns more familiar in international than in domestic politics move to the fore.

A full understanding of the role of security fears in causing and perpet-uating civil war requires more than just a knowledge of the threatening, anarchical situation facing the combatants. Behavior under the security di-lemma is shaped not simply by the strategic situation but also by the partic-ipants' perceptions of that situation and their expectations of each others' likely behavior in that situation. Thus, interveners must confront not only the circumstances that constitute the security dilemma—namely, anarchy and offensive advantages—but also the ideas and social forces that produced the dilemma in the first place and that may reproduce it unless the inter-veners can neutralize them.

Another complicating factor is that, in virtually every case that the con-tributors to this volume examined, the security fears of the parties to civil conflict were intertwined with their predatory goals—that is, with exploita-tive desires that would not necessarily diminish if their security problems were solved. Moreover, it is often difficult to separate security-driven and predatory motivations, since long-term fears may drive security seekers to take every opportunity to exploit others in an effort to build up their reserve of strategic resources even when they face no immediate security threat. In their efforts to gain the upper hand against potential rivals, actors may share the view of Catherine the Great: "That which stops growing begins to rot." So the strategies of interveners must not only judge which motivation pre-dominates but be designed for the most common mixed situation in which both kinds are present. As most of the contributors to this volume stress, few contemporary civil conflicts are driven purely by security fears.

The Security Dilemma and Strategies of Intervention in Collapsed States

A number of the civil wars of the 1990s have followed in the wake of the collapse of the Soviet Empire, the unraveling of other Communist states, or the governmental breakdown of so-called failed states in the Third World. Some states, such as Yugoslavia, broke up along ethnic lines, whereas others, such as Somalia or Tajikistan, collapsed into a more general disorder, where clans, regions, patronage networks, or other groups that could command some guns contended for the control of economic resources and territory. These contemporary civil conflicts seem to replicate the well-known pattern of Hobbesian competition for security in the "state of nature," where no sovereign power protects fearful individuals from each other. In this anar-chical setting prudent self-help may require preventive attacks to hedge against possible threats, even in the limiting case where everyone seeks only security.[3]

Policy makers, members of the informed public, and scholars commonly focus on the ways in which domestic conflict, often between different ethnic groups, leads to breakdown of authority. But causation can run in the opposite direction. The breakdown of internal authority and legitimacy may generate conflict among groups because each now fears that others will move against it. In Tajikistan, for example, conflict among ethnic groups and other kinds of factions was a consequence of the breakdown of state institutions rather than a cause of it.[4] It is not only that a strong state may be needed to keep ethnic hostility in check but also that the absence of effective law enforcement tends to produce defensively motivated behavior that magnifies or even creates conflict and violence. Thus, it is not surprising that David Laitin and James Fearon find that violent ethnic conflict within states is rare;[5] it often requires the disintegration of the state to set in motion the forces that lead to widespread ethnic violence.

When asked about the difference between the peaceful transition in South Africa and the bloodshed in the former Yugoslavia, Nelson Mandela replied, "In countries where innocent people are dying, the leaders are following their blood rather than their brains."[6] This parallels Sigmund Freud's famous response to Einstein's question as to the causes of war: "The ideal condition of things would of course be a community of men who had subordinated their instinctual life to the dictatorship of reason."[7] Both these claims underestimate the extent to which violence can be the considered response to a situation that offers both danger and opportunity, especially when actors can be badly harmed if they are not able to protect themselves.

Three general types of prescription follow from the security dilemma diagnosis. The first is the one recommended by Hobbes: establish a sovereign authority capable of enforcing a hegemonic peace upon all the fearfully contending parties. As Richard Betts has argued so persuasively, the question that drives civil conflict is, "Who rules?" Consequently, one solution to the security dilemma is to answer that question quickly and decisively.[8]

The second solution is to devise a situation in which the parties can provide for their own security through strictly defensive measures. The security dilemma evaporates if the best defense is not a good offense but simply a good defense: if so, everyone can be secure simultaneously. This can be achieved by making the contending groups more compact geographically, by evening out imbalances of power and dramatic shifts in relative power, by deploying weapons that are most useful in positional defense and least useful in attack (assuming that these can be distinguished), and by providing reliable monitoring of the military preparations of the contending groups.[9] As we will discuss further below, however, the cost of such policies is to reinforce the divisions within a society. At its most extreme, this can lead to splitting a country into separate parts; in other cases, it can solidify ethnic divisions and loyalties, making a state figuratively if not literally a federation.

A third solution is for the contending parties to lock themselves into an institutional framework that guarantees their mutual self-restraint once they lay their weapons down. Surrendering all power to a sovereign authority is one form of this solution, but in many cases this is unpalatable, because the only candidates for the role of hegemon are the feared and hated partisans of one of the warring groups. Consequently, the groups have an incentive to devise institutional arrangements that commit themselves to mutual cooperation without risking exploitation by the other.

Such arrangements may be based on either of two principles: delegation to neutral authorities or balanced power sharing among the interested parties.[10] Pursuing a strategy of delegation, the contending groups may commit themselves to support the creation of powerful independent bodies that are neutral among the warring parties: e.g., a professionalized army, neutral courts, depoliticized police, and a technocratic economic bureaucracy. Thus, the strategy of delegation to neutrals is a more benign consensual variant of the Hobbesian solution, creating a sovereign power that stands above the parties. Alternatively, the groups may commit themselves to a power-sharing scheme in which the warring groups retain their organizational coherence and manage many of their affairs internally while agreeing to share legislative and bureaucratic power proportionally. In this scheme the groups retain the corporate ability to look out for their own interests yet institutionally commit themselves to a set of rules governing cooperation on matters that cannot be conveniently left to the separate parties. Power sharing has some characteristics of the defensive stalemate solution, in that the groups retain some of their capacity for self-help, but instead of physically separating the parties power sharing seeks to establish a stable balance based on reciprocity in a partially integrated polity.

Both of these institutional solutions present conundrums from the standpoint of the security dilemma. The delegation strategy must overcome the warring groups' fear that they could be exploited by their enemies as they disarm themselves during the transfer of security functions to a neutral authority. The groups will also fear that the new authority might not be neutral, benign, and successful. Thus the groups may fear both that the new institutions will be too powerful and that they will not be powerful enough.[11] In the latter case, they will not be able to protect the group against its rivals; in the former case, those who dominate the institutions may put their own interests ahead of the community good, enriching and entrenching themselves at the expense of a well-ordered society.

Furthermore, institutions do not bind by magic; they normally do so by creating a pattern of behavior around which expectations converge. Yet these new institutions with no track record of shaping expectations must overcome the warring parties' powerful situational incentives to hedge against the risks of delegation. Such hedging, which might take the form of retaining significant armed force at the group's disposal, is likely to destroy the delegation strategy or turn it into a wary variant of the power-sharing strategy.

Insofar as power sharing rests on the residual ability of the groups to act in their own self-defense, it is as likely to recreate the security dilemma as solve it. Power sharing reifies the contending groups and ensures that all political mobilization must take place within the framework of the rival segments. Moreover, since power sharing eschews the full partitioning of the polity in favor of continued political and economic integration, it perpetuates the mutual interdependencies and vulnerabilities that heighten the security dilemma.[12]

It is precisely for these reasons that civil wars are so rarely resolved by mutual agreement between the warring factions, unless powerful outsiders intervene to guarantee the settlement.[13] We will take up this question of prescriptions for interveners in the final section. But first we will take up two issues on which these prescriptions hinge in part: the relationship between predatory and security motives, and the perceptual and social dynamics that create or heighten the security dilemma.

The Interaction of Predatory and Security Motives

The purest type of security dilemma is a situation in which security is the overriding objective of all of the protagonists, yet attempts by one party to increase its security reduce the security of the others. At the opposite end of the spectrum some conflicts may be driven entirely by the desire of one or both parties to exploit or dominate the other for reasons that would not diminish even if security were not in jeopardy. In between are a variety of situations in which security and nonsecurity motives are both present.[14]

It is important to keep the concepts of the security dilemma and predation separate and to understand that elements of each are present in almost every specific situation, albeit in different ways and different proportions. In a pure security dilemma, even if all actors are not perfectly satisfied with the status quo (i.e., even if they would choose another outcome were there no costs and risks attached to doing so), all prefer a world of the status quo to one in which any actor can use force to seek change. In other words, all would prefer to end anarchy if effective security guarantees were possible. This is not the case when actors are predators. Here the desire to expand and the willingness to run risks to do so is great enough so that a freezing of the status quo would not be acceptable.

No individual case is ever entirely of one type or the other. Actors often feel they need to expand in order to be secure. Sometimes such beliefs are rationalizations for more purely predatory drives; at other times they are not, and it is extremely difficult for later analysts, let alone contemporary observers, to tell which is which. Furthermore, unless such observers can provide the actor with alternative means to security, they must treat the actor as a predator in this situation, irrespective of its "true" motives. Predators are hardly immune from security worries as well. In Rwanda, for example, extremists in the Hutu-dominated government were fearful not only that a Tutsi victory or power-sharing agreement would end their ability to exploit the state for economic gain but also that they would be powerless to fend off demands for accountability for their past genocidal crimes.[15]

We are mindful of the risk of concept stretching: we acknowledge that the added value of the security dilemma concept decreases as situations move away from the ideal type of purely security-driven behavior. Nonetheless, we contend that understanding the interaction between predatory and security motives is valuable for designing effective strategies of intervention.

Such mixed situations might be analyzed in a number of ways. It might be that predatory and security motives are both present and can be treated as equal and independent. If so, policies to mitigate conflict would have to deter the parties' predatory inclinations at the same time that they reassure their security fears. An example is Otto von Bismarck's defensive alliances with Russia and Austria, promising to fight alongside whichever one attacked the other.

However, reassuring fearful predators may be distasteful; it could be seen as rewarding vile behavior and encouraging it in others. Moreover, a settlement that holds predators harmless gives them a chance to start up the game of predation at the next opportunity, as soon as international interveners withdraw. Thus, when both predatory and security motives seem to be present it may make sense to try to dig deeper to understand the underlying roots of these aims. In some cases predatory motives may be the primary cause, and security fears derivative. Because aggression in an anarchical balance-of-power system provokes resistance and hostility, predators' security fears are likely to be especially acute.[16] Conversely, in some cases security fears may be primary and predatory behavior derivative. As we will argue below, the security dilemma often tends to turn even security-driven actors into predators, defined as actors who prefer exploiting others to cooperating with them, even when short-run security threats are small. Thus, the security dilemma gives rise to predators, and predation intensifies the security dilemma.[17]

In a very few cases the situation facing the contending parties in anarchy may resemble Rousseau's stag hunt in that each side would prefer mutual cooperation but is driven to defect solely by the fear that the other side has or will develop a different preference. Even in stag hunt, however, the curse of foresight may cause predatory motives to develop. As many realist scholars have noted about international politics, the actor's concern is often not that the other side is currently aggressive or that the current situation is threatening but that it may become so in the future as others change their capabilities and intentions. Thus, it is incorrect to argue that security concerns and the security dilemma would disappear if the actors could be certain of others' benign intentions. The fact that others or their successors can change, and cannot commit themselves not to, are at the heart of the security dilemma. In these circumstances unilateral gains from defection may lead to the accumulation of relative advantages that serve as a hedge against future defection by the opponent.[18] Consequently, even if none of the parties starts with predatory motives, the desire to protect one's future position under conditions of the security dilemma can transform a situation from stag hunt into a prisoners' dilemma, in which exploiting the other side is preferred to mutual cooperation.[19]

Even without this dynamic, prisoners' dilemma is more common than stag hunt, because there is almost always some underlying conflict of interest between the parties. Even if cooperation would make both parties better off, they are likely to have conflicting preferences over the division of those joint gains. Although fear and vulnerability are not the only forces at work, they may still be important in exacerbating conflicts and interacting with other disturbing factors. In many cases the reaching of an agreement is inhibited both by fears that the other side will cheat and by hopes to gain a better distribution of the values in dispute. On other occasions the security dilemma may make a situation or settlement particularly fragile while the immediate cause of its destruction can be any number of particular shocks and frictions.

Even the existence of a severe conflict of interest does not mean that the security dilemma is irrelevant. Predatory preferences and behavior at one stage of a conflict, which cannot be immediately explained by the security dilemma, may have been generated by security-related preferences and behavior at an earlier stage. Just as stag hunt easily degenerates into prisoners' dilemma in the absence of a sovereign authority, so too prisoner's dilemma can easily degenerate into the game of deadlock, in which conflict is preferred to mutual cooperation. Most obviously, this can be the case with spirals of conflict. To understand the dynamics at work, we have to ask *why* the actors prefer to defect and determine whether at least a part of the reason is the drive for security. In some cases people may prefer conflict and deadlock because they think it is the best or the only route to their security: offensive military technology or high subjective requirements for security may place mutual security beyond reach, at least unless there are significant changes in the situation, including outside intervention. In other cases actors may come to believe that the other is such a menace that they can be secure only if it is crippled, if not destroyed. Deadlock may result, for example, when one party sees a preventive advantage in fighting now rather than later. Thus the security dilemma, and actions and perceptions that flow from it, can transform a difficult and tense situation, but one with possibilities for cooperation, into one of complete conflict of interest and physical combat.

In a parallel manner the disintegration of state authority may not only create or awaken security fears but generate behavior that makes later situations much more intractable. In these circumstances group identities may become increasingly important not only intrinsically but because the security of individuals becomes implicated with the fates of the contending groups. Group identity can then be a consequence of conflict as much as a cause of it and can be fueled by security concerns. Before the start of the fighting in the former Yugoslavia, most Muslims and Serbs did not believe that their security was menaced because of their ethnicity. In fact, in the normal competition in Yugoslav political and social life these categories were not the most salient. But, as the conflict developed, personal security and personal well-being more broadly became defined in terms of the security and well-being of one's ethnic group. While this was partly a matter of psychological identification, everyone else's psychological identification made the identification an objective reality for any given person: individual Serbs, Croats, and Muslims were menaced by people of the other ethnic groups whether or not the person's own sense of self was defined by ethnicity. Others were doing the defining in a way that put it beyond any one person's control. As a nineteen year old said recently in Sarajevo, "I was sitting in my class-room the other day and the teacher handed out a form where we had to write down whether we were a Serb, Muslim, or a Croat. We were told that we would be segregated into different classrooms according to our ethnicity. It's not what any of us asked for."[20] The situation is even sharper in situations when the relevant group identity is readily observable by externals—e.g., skin color.

Thus, the security dilemma can give rise to predatory behavior, zero-sum conflicts of interest, and inimical, mutually exclusive identities. Conversely, predatory behavior intensifies the security dilemma. Hobbes understood this perfectly well: in his view the reason for generalized fear in the state of nature was not simply the reciprocal fear of surprise attack but also the knowledge that men had unlimited appetites that would drive them to aggression out of greed. If men are greedy, or if resource scarcity makes them predatory, this intensifies security concerns, because it increases the expectation that others will defect. Once this expectation becomes entrenched, the security dilemma can take on a life of its own, trapping both predators and prey in rivalries whose costs outweigh any possible gains from exploitation. For ex-ample, Germany was not a status quo state in the years before World War I; nonetheless, its aggressive policy in 1914 can be understood only in terms of the security dilemma provoked by its own earlier belligerence, not as the result of a simple calculation that the predatory benefits of conquest would be worth the costs and risks.[21] This is one way to understand the paradox of the predatory "tinpot dictators," described in this volume by David Laitin, who fight harder and harder for the control of ever diminishing state resources.

Several of the contributors to this study argue that predatory strategies can create, exacerbate, or take advantage of the security dilemma in yet another sense. That is, leaders often try to manipulate security concerns in order to solidify their positions and extract additional resources from society. To strengthen their hold on their followers, they may incite conflicts that make the latter more vulnerable and entice or force them to join in the enterprise of collective "self-defense." This is calculated to intensify group solidarity and the need for a continued role for the predatory leaders. Viewed from the standpoint of the leaders' motivations, this may be a purely pred-atory manipulation, not a security dilemma, but viewed from the standpoint of their followers, who are trapped in the conflict spiral unleashed by the leaders' actions or misrepresentations, the security dilemma may become very real indeed. This is a central theme of the contributions by Susan Woodward on the former Yugoslavia, Bruce Jones on Rwanda, and Rui de Figueiredo and Barry Weingast, who draw on both those cases.[22] In this sense, a security dilemma may be viewed as an outcome of social processes, not simply a strategic situation.

The Security Dilemma as a Social Situation

Even when we conceive of the security dilemma as a situation, it is a social situation with social and perceptual causes, not simply a fact of nature. Thus, the security dilemma is a cause of behavior, yet it is also an outcome to be explained. None of the elements that fuels the security dilemma—neither anarchy, nor offensive advantages, nor expectations that others will defect—can be taken for granted as unproblematic givens that follow unmediated from technology or geography. If interveners are to undo the security dilemma, they need to understand the social and perceptual factors that shape it.

Arguably, international anarchy might be taken for granted as a starting point for analysis on the grounds that, at least since the Treaty of Westphalia, states have not been subject to any overarching sovereign power.[23] The anarchy that prevails in collapsed states and empires, however, is much more problematic. In those latter cases the anarchy is not long-standing but is caused by whatever caused the collapse of the state. Barry Posen claims that the collapse of the Yugoslav state triggered security fears that led to the competitive mobilization of ethnic self-help groups; that is, anarchy caused an ethnic security dilemma. However, if it was ethnic nationalism that tore apart the Yugoslav state and thereby caused the situation of anarchy, then anarchy is an effect, not a cause, of ethnonationalism. Of course, once put in motion by nationalist ideas or politicians the security dilemma may have unfolded largely by its own logic, just as Posen describes it. As Chaim Kaufmann argues, once inimical identities are hardened as a result of intense ethnic rivalry, it may not matter whether the strategic competition between them was triggered by a "mere" social construction.[24]

If the fact of anarchy has often been taken for granted by students of the security dilemma, they have long understood the role of perception and ideology in strategists' calculations of offensive and defensive advantages. In both world wars—indeed throughout much of modern history—soldiers and political leaders misread the implications of prevailing military technologies, in part because of the inherent difficulty of guessing the consequences of untested innovations, but mainly because of organizational biases coloring such assessments.[25]

Similarly, estimates of the likelihood that the opponent will defect cannot be inferred simply from the logic of the strategic situation. Few anarchical settings are as uniquely compelling as a burning house, in which everyone behaves the same regardless of the social, cultural, or intellectual understandings that they bring to the situation.[26] Theoreticians of Realpolitik disagree about the relative merits of aggressive versus defensive strategies of self-help, about which circumstances require balancing alliances and which allow passing the buck to other balancers, and about whether the other group is largely driven by fear or whether the other is (or has become) so deeply hostile that a just reconciliation is simply impossible—and so do real world leaders. Which path is chosen depends on the actor's theories of how the balance of power operates, guesses about the advantages of attacking, and beliefs about the other's goals and strategies.[27] Thus, estimating the likelihood that an opponent will defect requires understanding how the opponent subjectively sizes up the situation as well as assessing the opponents' mix of motivations.

Such estimates are ripe for social and psychological misconstruction. On the cognitive psychological plane, it is well established that people tend to exaggerate the extent to which the actions of others are determined by their innate disposition, while underrating the role of situational constraints, including the observers' own behavior. This tendency operates with special strength when the other's behavior harms the actor. Furthermore, not only are people who expect others to defect in prisoners' dilemma driven to defect themselves, but the other's defection will be taken as evidence that cooperation is not possible. In conflictual relationships this fuels the security dilemma, since both sides are prone to see the other as innately predisposed to defect.[28]

On the cultural plane, ethnic groups often hold mythic views of the perfidy of out-group adversaries, which establish a biased baseline for judging the likelihood of defection. As Posen acknowledges, it is not only the anarchical situation but also elites' purposeful misconstrual of historical conflicts that convinces the ethnic rank and file that the opponent's defection is likely. To trigger a security-driven conflict, all that is required is that people believe that such assessments *might* be true, a point familiar in international politics that de Figueiredo and Weingast show applies to civil conflict as well. The rest can be accomplished by rational calculations about the high cost of

misplaced trust and by belligerent actions by one's own side that elicit responses consistent with worst-case assessments of the foe. Thus if actors have
reason to believe that the costs of being conciliatory will be very high if the
other side does not reciprocate, they may behave aggressively even though
they think that the other probably is benign. Here, too, psychology can
compound the problem; people are loath to see themselves moving against
their neighbors simply because there is only a chance that these people may
be a menace to them. When people adopt a hostile stance toward others
they are likely to convince themselves that these neighbors are proven aggressors, not just a hypothetical danger.[29] Furthermore, Posen notes, the
actions that trigger a group's fears may be undertaken not only by manipu-
lative leaders but also by uncontrolled extremist factions or thugs who seek
to profit from the turmoil they create.[30]

Insofar as the security dilemma is the outcome of a social process and
not simply a strategic situation, interventions to manage the security dilemma may require more than simply creating military defensive advantages
and monitoring troop deployments. They may also require attention to the
content of history textbooks, the introduction of professionalized media, the
policing of undisciplined mafia groups, and the creation of alternative incentives for elite groups who might otherwise be tempted to "play the security dilemma card."[31]

At the same time, it would be wrong to infer that the security dilemma
is just a figment of people's imaginations. People and nations know from
hard experience that the real balance of power and real vulnerability to
outsiders, not just imaginings about them, are crucial to their fate. Although
estimates of the strategic situation may be subjective and erroneous before
the fact, once the fighting starts there is an objective strategic reality that
asserts itself. The Schlieffen plan fails, and the trenches are dug; panzers
penetrate the impenetrable Ardennes, and Paris falls, no matter what myths
were believed beforehand. Social mythmaking is preoccupied with pur-
ported strategic facts not because they are all made up anyway but precisely
because everyone realizes how important the assessment of those strategic
facts is to everyone's choices and the resulting outcomes. People try to understand their real strategic situation, because they know their fates depend
on it, but under uncertainty their ability to analyze these social facts is
clouded by cognitive biases and by the manipulations of strategic ideologists
who have their own parochial agendas. From this perspective the job of
interveners in civil conflict is both to create a strategically stable situation
and also to create a social setting that is conducive to the accurate assessment
of that situation by the contending parties.

Implications for Strategies of Intervention

Intervention by the international community, if done astutely, can promote the resolution of civil wars by facilitating any of the three mechanisms for solving the security dilemma. Intervention can establish a hegemon by helping one side to win or by imposing direct rule by outsiders. Intervention can also end a conflict by balancing the power of the contending groups, by creating defensive military advantages, or by helping the parties to arrange for a strategically defensible partition of the territory in dispute. Indeed, irrespective of the technologies involved, outsiders can in effect create a great defensive advantage by promising to come to the aid of whichever side is attacked.[32] If both sides know that resuming the fighting, or even behaving provocatively, will call down the intervener's wrath, then each gains a significant measure of security that does not come at the other's expense. Finally, intervention can provide the capability to monitor and enforce new institutional arrangements during a transitional period until locals' expectations converge on the new pattern and vested interests in the new status quo emerge.

However, intervention can also undermine these potential solutions. Inept intervention can prolong wars by preventing one side from prevailing, by transferring offensive weaponry to the parties to the dispute, or by preventing locals from locking in a de facto partition. Interveners can also exacerbate conflict by pursuing internally inconsistent strategies. Just as one cannot back a hegemon and partition power at the same time, so too one cannot delegate power to neutral bodies yet also provide for power-sharing arrangements that give the contending groups the wherewithal to hamstring these new institutions. As Susan Woodward's contribution to this volume shows, the Dayton accords on Bosnia are riddled with precisely these kinds of internal contradictions, yielding predictably counterproductive results.[33]

Regardless which of these approaches is adopted, a focus on security concerns and the security dilemma can lead to a better understanding of the situation and to fruitful prescriptions for both participants and outsiders. Analysis can go astray if it is insufficiently attentive to these topics. For example, many discussions about the importance of free elections as a way of helping to solve civil conflict neglect the participants' fear that there will be no subsequent free elections after the first one or that the majority will win and dictate to the minority. As a result, holding elections often intensifies civil and ethnic conflicts.[34] Similarly, much of the stress on the importance of disarming the participants makes the same error as the 1950s literature on international disarmament, which failed to realize that a reduction in arms that makes the participant less secure will be part of the problem rather than the solution.[35] Of course the ultimate goal is for the participants to no longer fear each other, but arrangements that lead one side or the other to fear that they are about to be stripped of all protection are not likely to produce even temporary peace.

Using the framework of the security dilemma and the related prisoners' dilemma allows analysts, participants, and outsiders to tap into knowledge of how they can increase cooperation in a situation in which both sides prefer to defect while the other side cooperates, yet both sides also prefer mutual cooperation to mutual defection. Parties to the conflict as well as interveners can try to make offense distinguishable from defense, give advantages to the defender, decrease the benefits of exploiting the other on any single play, make the payoff for cooperation much better than bearing the costs of conflict, make the sucker's payoff less than disastrous, and develop contingent strategies, such as tit for tat.[36] An agreement that could benefit both sides in the long run can be undermined if it is the case — or if it is believed to be the case — that one side can gain a major advantage from breaking it at a particular point. Outsiders can often function effectively here as guarantors. Even when they cannot or will not impose a settlement, they may be able to provide the forces that can protect each side against the other's defection and symmetrically remove from each the temptation to defect. At least as important, they may be able to provide each with information about what the other is doing that can reduce unfounded fears.

However, adopting a security dilemma perspective offers no panacea for interveners. One obvious difficulty is that outsiders may lack the will or resources to transform the structure of the game so radically. In addition, interveners who want to defuse the security dilemma face hard choices in deciding how they will try to accomplish this. Some strategies are antithetical to others.

For example, attempts to stabilize an existing security dilemma are likely to work at cross purposes with attempts to "deconstruct" it. Reducing the vulnerabilities of the parties and creating defensive advantages means working with groups as they are, even reifying and further entrenching them. In contrast, trying to reverse the social construction of a security dilemma is likely to mean undercutting the identity myths, institutions, and leadership that hold a group together. Thus, attempts to deconstruct a group increase its vulnerability, threaten its leadership, and thus intensify the security dilemma, at least in the short run. This tradeoff between short-run stabilization and long-run transformation is a constant theme in our case studies: working with the Somali warring factions versus disarming them, partitioning Bosnia versus integrating it, sharing power with genocidal Rwandan extremists versus excluding them from power. At least in the short run the interests of peace and justice may be in conflict with one another; to guarantee the peace may be to maintain an unjust settlement. Kaufmann's chapter argues that once ethnic conflicts are intense the right answer is to stabilize the strategic situation by moving people and partitioning the state. This may reward predators, however, and move the conflict from the internal to the international level. Other authors favor strategies that transform the underlying social relationships that led to the security dilemma in the first place. But these are extremely difficult to carry out in the face of resistance by the local actors and may produce more rather than less bloodshed as the first result.

In the long run, then, reducing the security dilemma may lead to the maintenance of a situation that outsiders and many of the participants regard as only a second-best solution, if that. Throughout this chapter we have talked about armed "sides"; these should not exist in an undivided country and making arrangements posited on their existence may go a long way toward ensuring that they do not disappear. Providing security for identifiable groups is one thing that outside intervention, especially military intervention, can do, however. The knowledge and resources required, although not trivial, are often within reach. But it is far from clear that outsiders either know what to do to encourage a united country or would have the required abilities to do so.

Similar tradeoffs are likely to arise in choosing between deterring predators and reassuring fearful parties. If the international community intervenes with overwhelming force, no tradeoff arises. Predators lack the ability to fight back effectively; they are packed off to jail or to retirement villas in the south of France. If predators cannot be so easily overpowered, however, difficulties arise. Since predators are also fearful; they need to be simultaneously deterred from predation and reassured about their survival. If predators have a secure regional base, like the Khmer Rouge, they can simply be contained there. But often predators cannot survive unless they maintain a monopoly of exploitative state power, in which case offense and defense are indistinguishable. The Tutsi minority in Burundi, for example, counted for its survival on maintaining a dictatorship and a monopoly over military power. To them, democratization and proportional representation in the military ranks and officer corps, measures pressed on them by international donors, were indistinguishable from a death sentence, since they felt that maintaining their control was the only way to guarantee against victimization by the Hutu majority they had brutalized.[37] The conceptual apparatus of the security dilemma may not provide a neat answer to such conundrums, but it at least highlights the tradeoffs that have so often been ignored in interventions by the international community. Compromises and settlements that appear to outsiders to be feasible and even to contain a modicum of justice may be out of reach because of the participants' beliefs and construals of reality, no matter how unreasonable these may appear.

Tradeoffs are also involved in choosing among the three types of solution to the security dilemma: establishing hegemony, creating a defensive stalemate, and institutionalizing cooperation, either through delegation to neutrals or through power sharing. For example, one conceivable solution to Laitin's problem of incessant conflict among hard-pressed tinpot Somali warlords is to return to the cold war practice of elevating one of them through massive military and economic aid to the status of a secure leader.[38] Yet enthroning an asset-stripping faction risks perpetuating the underlying problem.

Likewise, creating stalemates and transferring populations would make policing a cease-fire easier, yet, even if it works, this solution reifies the warring groups and rewards those who have played the security dilemma card. Moreover, in many cases, it may be impossible to devise a lasting stalemate dividing a country whose political economy has been deeply integrated. Thus the problem of obtaining security or of reaching any agreement in a civil war may be greater than it is in wars between well-established sovereign states. Not only are states harder to kill than are most domestic factions but there can be more rapid change as each group's power rises and falls in the normal ebb and flow of domestic politics and social change. Freezing the status quo—or freezing any settlement—is not likely to be feasible, and, indeed, many strains are placed on the settlement as power relations change. Lebanon and Nigeria cannot even conduct a census for this reason. Furthermore, there are often only two main factions, which heightens the relative gains problem.

Consequently, institutionalized cooperation normally seems to be the most attractive solution, though problems and tradeoffs abound here as well. We have already discussed the dangers of institutional delegation to others who have different incentives, as well as the dangers of reifying contending groups through power sharing. In light of these problems, how can institutions succeed in binding parties to a formula for resolving their conflict and making their promises credible?

As de Figueiredo and Weingast show in their contribution to this volume, gauging the opponent's character type is often as crucial to assessing the likelihood of defection in an internal security dilemma as in an international one. Forming an institution that restrains oneself, especially when one has a temporary advantage, can be seen as an index to one's type. Moreover, adhering to an institution can lock in one's type by creating vested interests in perpetuating a profitable arrangement.[39] This is true, for example, of the process of European unification. Not only could observers reason that a Germany that was willing to join in a significant degree of integration would not be an aggressive type, but the process of integration reinforced German incentives to cooperate and thus locked in the benign German identity and interests as well. As a high German official said, explaining his country's support for an expanded NATO: "We wanted to bind Germany into a structure which practically obliges Germany to take the interests of its neighbors into consideration. We wanted to give our neighbors assurances that we won't do what we don't intend to do anyway."[40] Changes in institutions and changes in behavior can sometimes do even more, changing actors' definitions of their interests and consequently changing the actor's type, not just revealing it or locking it in. For example, decades of participation in the institutions of NATO and the European Community have contributed to redefining German identity. Germans who once might have wanted to re-gain the "lost territories" in the East or gain political and economic hege-mony over Western and Central Europe now may have different preferences because of a decreased identity with Germany, an increased identity with Europe as a whole, and an associated set of changes in values and means-ends beliefs about what will make Germany as a country and themselves as individuals prosperous.[41]

In principle, integrative institutions may be able to engender similar trans-formations in the wake of civil wars, especially if the strongest local actors use these institutions to reveal their type as restrained cooperators at the outset. For example, during the civil war in El Salvador in the 1980s the armed conflict between the Salvadoran ruling elite and the Marxist rebel movement coincided with a rivalry between two factions within the ruling elite, one a moderate group including figures like President Cristiani and another a hard-line group associated with the infamous military death squads, which murdered civilians who were viewed as cooperating with the rebels. During the course of the war the moderate group in the pro-govern-ment faction grew stronger vis-à-vis the hard-liners. In part, this was because of the high military costs of continuing the stalemated war. In part, it was also because the conservative coffee-growing oligarchy gradually realized that a failure to settle the conflict was undermining its financial interests. Not only could they not grow coffee in a war zone, but they came to see that, in the era of economic globalization, profits from other kinds of commercial and manufacturing enterprises would be even greater than the benefits of repression-based agriculture. To take advantage of these changing incentives, peace was a necessity. To bring this about, the moderate faction of the ruling elite enlisted the help of international institutions, especially the UN mission, to broker and oversee the implementation of a peace settlement that included the disarming of the militant groups on both ends of the political spectrum and the creation of a more neutral army and police force. Cooperating with these international institutions not only brought about cooperative arrangements but helped the moderates reveal their true type to the wary rebels in a convincing way, even as it helped them to eliminate the death squads and marginalize their extreme right-wing supporters.[42]

Interveners can provide incentives to undertake such initiatives as well as the resources to make them safe and effective. One drawback of intervention-induced cooperation, however, is that it reveals less about the local actors' true character. Thus local observers might conclude that the most favored tinpot would remain a power-sharing democrat only as long as the foreign aid kept flowing. If so, the tinpot could prove himself to be a cooperator only by taking irrevocable steps to lock in the commitment to cooperate, such as the full integration of the dominant faction's army into a professionalized force commanded by neutral officers or ones drawn from all factions. For actors who are unwilling to go this far, then, external intervention may decrease their ability to demonstrate that they will remain committed to peacefully sharing power once they are no longer compelled to do so.

Credibility is also a problem for external interveners, who, as Walter shows, will not be able to transform local actors' expectations if their commitment is seen to be limited in time or scope. Although intervening to some extent ties the actor's reputation to finishing the job, the most credible commitments perhaps can only be made by states who have a real interest at stake from the beginning. This was a major problem in the intervention in Rwanda, where the Hutu hard-liners were correct to calculate that no real enforcement would be forthcoming. Indeed, an intervener's lack of will in one case may undercut the credibility of a different intervening power in another case: Bruce Jones's account reveals that the Hutu extremists killed a contingent of Belgian UN peacekeepers at the start of the genocide because they inferred from the American retreat in Somalia that the Belgians would respond to such violence by withdrawing.

Credibility problems are exacerbated, moreover, when the intervener is not a unitary actor. For example, the Nigerian government may have had a strong interest in maintaining order in Liberia (in part to show that it was a true regional power), but it lacked the state strength to see that this policy was implemented by the armed forces on the scene, which too often concentrated on looting. In somewhat the same way, the U.S. military has successfully resisted what little pressure there was from the civilian authorities to interpret its mission in Bosnia not as guaranteeing the cease-fire but as enforcing the Dayton Accords. As significant as these problems are, the basic point remains that external intervention is likely to be cheaper—and hence more credible—when the security dilemma drives the conflict than when substantive disagreements do, because less has to be changed: each side "merely" has to come to believe that the other cannot cheat and threaten it. This may make intervention easier to sustain, because of the perception that it is not only impartial but moral in preventing unnecessary conflict.

In short, outside intervention can help overcome the security dilemma in many ways, from increasing transparency and timely warning by giving each side accurate information about what the other is doing, to providing for the safety of the participants at local "summit meetings," to overseeing local arms control (which could include giving weapons and training, especially of types that are particularly appropriate for defense), to threatening to cut off aid to any faction that resumed the fighting, to keeping large numbers of troops on the ground to "guarantee" that agreements will be kept (the quotation marks indicating the ambiguity of this term). Yet poorly designed interventions can inadvertently institutionalize the security dilemma, as Woodward argues it has in Bosnia, through a failure to understand tactical tradeoffs. The contributors to this volume do not all agree on what is the right mix of tactics to defuse the security dilemma in conditions of civil war, nor do they agree on the relative weight of the security dilemma in comparison with other ways of analyzing the factors that perpetuate conflict. Nonetheless, their sharp analyses and vivid case material go a long way toward laying out those tradeoffs and suggesting an array of strategies that interveners can use to manage them.

NOTES

1. Two valuable efforts along these lines are Michael E. Brown, ed., *The International Dimensions of Internal Conflict* (Cambridge: MIT Press, 1996), and Ariel Levite, Bruce Jentleson, and Larry Berman, eds., *Foreign Military Intervention* (New York: Columbia University Press, 1992).

2. Robert Jervis, "Cooperation Under the Security Dilemma," *World Politics*, vol. 30, no. 2 (January 1978), pp. 167–213; Barry Posen, "The Security Dilemma and Ethnic Conflict," *Survival*, vol. 35, no. 1 (Spring 1993), pp. 27–47; Barbara Walter, "The Critical Barrier to Civil War Settlement," *International Organization*, vol. 51, no. 3 (Summer 1997), pp. 335–364.

3. In addition to Posen and Walter, see Chaim Kaufmann, "Possible and Impossible Solutions to Ethnic Civil Wars," *International Security*, vol. 20, no. 4 (Spring 1996), pp. 136–175; James Fearon, "Ethnic War as a Commitment Problem," unpublished paper, University of Chicago, 1993; David Lake and Donald Rothchild, "Containing Fear: The Origins and Management of Ethnic Conflict," *International Security*, vol. 21, no. 2 (Fall 1996), pp. 41–75.

4. Barnett Rubin, "Russian Hegemony and State Breakdown in the Periphery," in Barnett Rubin and Jack Snyder, eds., *Organizing Post-Soviet Political Space* (London: Routledge, 1998).

5. James Fearon and David Laitin, "Explaining Interethnic Cooperation," *American Political Science Review*, vol. 90, no. 4 (December 1996), pp. 715–735. Also see Matthew Krain, "State-Sponsored Murder: The Onset and Severity of Genocides and Politicides," *Journal of Conflict Resolution*, vol. 41 (June 1997), pp. 331–360.

6. Quoted in Anthony Lewis, "Mandela the Pol," *New York Times Magazine*, March 23, 1997, p. 43.

7. James Strachey et al., eds. and trans., *The Standard Edition of the Complete Psychological Works of Sigmund Freud* (London: Hogarth Press, 1964), p. 213.

8. Richard Betts, "The Delusion of Impartial Intervention," *Foreign Affairs*, vol. 73, no. 6 (November/December 1994), pp. 20–33.

9. See Jervis, "Cooperation Under the Security Dilemma"; Posen, "The Security Dilemma and Ethnic Conflict"; and Kaufmann, "Possible and Impossible Solutions."

10. An excellent overview of such approaches is Timothy Sisk, *Power Sharing and International Mediation in Ethnic Conflicts* (Washington, D.C.: United States Institute of Peace, 1996). Concise statements of these two viewpoints are Donald Horowitz, "Making Moderation Pay: The Comparative Politics of Ethnic Conflict Management," pp. 451–476, and Arend Lijphart, "The Power-Sharing Approach," pp. 491–510, both in Joseph Montville, ed., *Conflict and Peacemaking in Multiethnic Societies* (New York: Lexington, 1991).

11. Avner Greif, "Self-Enforcing Political Systems and Economic Growth: Late

Medieval Genoa," in Robert H. Bates, ed., *Analytic Narratives* (Princeton: Princeton University Press), pp. 23–63.

12. On the dangers of economic interdependence, see Kenneth Waltz, *Theory of International Politics* (Reading, Mass.: Addison-Wesley, 1979), chapter 7.

13. Walter, "The Critical Barrier."

14. Charles Glaser, "The Security Dilemma Revisited," *World Politics*, vol. 50, no. 1 (October 1997), especially pp. 189–198.

15. Arguing the former is Bruce Jones, "Military Intervention in Rwanda's 'Two Wars': Partisanship and Indifference," this volume; for the latter view, see Jack Snyder and Karen Ballentine, "Nationalism and the Marketplace of Ideas," *International Security*, vol. 21, no. 2 (Fall 1996), pp. 5–40; citing African Rights, *Rwanda: Death, Despair and Defiance* (London: Africa Rights, September 1994), by Rakiya Omaar and Alex de Waal, pp. 30–34, 44; Alan J. Kuperman, "The Other Lesson of Rwanda: Mediators Sometimes Do More Damage Than Good," *SAIS Review*, vol. 16, no. 1 (Winter-Spring 1996), pp. 221–240.

16. Jack Snyder, *Myths of Empire* (Ithaca: Cornell University Press, 1991), pp. 11–12, 22.

17. On the problem of dealing with predatory "spoilers" of a potential settlement, see Stephen Stedman, "Spoiler Problems in Peace Processes," *International Security*, vol. 22, no. 2 (Fall 1997), pp. 5–53.

18. Robert Powell, "Absolute and Relative Gains in International Relations Theory," *American Political Science Review*, vol. 85 (December 1991), 1303–1320.

19. Jervis, "Cooperation Under the Security Dilemma."

20. Quoted in Chris Hedges, "In Bosnia's Schools, Three Ways Never to Learn from History," *New York Times*, November 11, 1997, p. 4.

21. Marc Trachtenberg's failure to take this distinction into account underlies his dispute with Van Evera over World War I as a conflict of interest, as "opposed to" a security dilemma. See Marc Trachtenberg, "The Meaning of Mobilization in 1914," *International Security*, vol. 15, no. 3 (Winter 1990–91), pp. 120–150.

22. See also V. P. Gagnon, "Ethnic Nationalism and International Conflict: The Case of Serbia," *International Security*, vol. 19, no. 3 (Winter 1994/95), pp. 130–166.

23. We put aside here the question of the factors that determine how states react to, modify, and even create this condition.

24. Kaufmann, "Possible and Impossible Solutions."

25. On the chronic misreading of the offense-defense balance, see Jervis, "Cooperation Under the Security Dilemma," and Jack Levy, "The Offensive/Defensive Balance of Military Technology," *International Studies Quarterly* (June 1984).

26. For the burning house analogy, see Arnold Wolfers, *Discord and Collaboration* (Baltimore: Johns Hopkins University Press, 1962), p. 13.

27. Thomas Christensen and Jack Snyder, "Chain Gangs and Passed Bucks," *International Organization*, vol. 44, no. 2 (Spring 1990), pp. 137–168; Randall

Schweller, "Bandwagoning for Profit," *International Security*, vol. 19, no. 1 (Summer 1994), pp. 72–107.

28. Lee Ross and Richard Nisbett, *The Person and the Situation: Perspectives of Social Psychology* (New York: McGraw-Hill, 1991).

29. The attribution processes involved are explicated in Harold Kelley and Anthony Stahelski, "Social Interaction Basis of Cooperators' and Competitors' Beliefs About Others," *Journal of Personality and Social Psychology*, vol. 16 (September 1970), pp. 66–91.

30. Posen, "The Security Dilemma and Ethnic Conflict," p. 33.

31. The latter is V. P. Gagnon's phrase from his comments on Susan Woodward's contribution to this volume, conference on International Intervention in Civil Wars, Columbia University, February 14, 1997; on the other points, see Stephen Van Evera, "Hypotheses on Nationalism and War," *International Security*, vol. 18, no. 4 (Spring 1994), pp. 5–39; and Snyder and Ballentine, "Nationalism and the Marketplace of Ideas."

32. Stephen Van Evera, "The Cult of the Offensive and the Origins of the First World War," *International Security*, vol. 9, no. 1 (Summer 1984), pp. 58–107, reprinted in Steven Miller, ed., *Military Strategy and the Origins of the First World War* (Princeton: Princeton University Press, 1985), especially pp. 96–101.

33. Susan Woodward, "Bosnia and Herzegovina: How Not to End Civil War," this volume.

34. Snyder and Ballentine, "Nationalism and the Marketplace of Ideas"; Crawford Young, *The Politics of Cultural Pluralism* (Madison: University of Wisconsin Press, 1976), p. 158; Mahmoud Mamdani, *Citizen and Subject: Contemporary Africa and the Legacy of Late Colonialism* (Princeton: Princeton University Press, 1996), p. 300.

35. Virginia Gamba's multivolume UNIDIR study pays insufficient attention to this problem.

36. Jervis, "Cooperation Under the Security Dilemma"; on the last point, Robert Axelrod, *Evolution of Cooperation* (New York: Basic, 1984). Many of the more specific ways of doings this are summarized in Kenneth Oye, ed., *Cooperation Under Anarchy* (Princeton: Princeton University Press, 1986).

37. Snyder and Ballentine, "Nationalism and the Marketplace of Ideas," pp. 33–34; Réné Lemarchand, *Burundi: Ethnocide as Discourse and Practice* (Cambridge: Cambridge University Press, 1994), pp. 129, 176, 185, 187.

38. Note that Laitin denies that warlords' short-run security motives were decisive in the Somali conflict, and thus is skeptical that the security dilemma applies to his case. However, in light of our analysis of the interrelationship between predatory and security motives, especially in long-run strategic competitions, it seems to us that the Hirshleifer "war of attrition" model employed by Laitin overlaps heavily with the security dilemma. In any case, the point argued here applies equally to both.

39. Anna Eliasson, research in progress, Columbia University.

40. Quoted in Jane Perlez, "Blunt Reasoning for Enlarging NATO: Curbs on Germany," *New York Times*, December 7, 1997, p. 18.

41. Thomas Risse, Daniela Engelmann-Martin, Hans-Joachim Knopf, Klaus Roscher, "To Euro or Not to Euro? The EMU and Identity Politics in the European Union," *European Journal of International Relations* (June 1999).

42. William Stanley, *The Protection Racket State: Elite Politics, Military Extortion, and Civil War in El Salvador* (Philadelphia: Temple University Press, 1996), pp. 218–255; David McCormick, "From Peacekeeping to Peacebuilding: Restructuring Military and Politics Institutions in El Salvador," in Michael Doyle, Ian Johnstone, and Robert Orr, eds., *Keeping the Peace: Multidimensional UN Operations in Cambodia and El Salvador* (Cambridge: Cambridge University Press, 1997), pp. 282–311.

2 Designing Transitions from Civil War

Barbara F. Walter

Why do some civil war negotiations succeed in ending conflict, while others fail? Between 1940 and 1990 combatants in seventeen of forty-one civil wars initiated formal negotiations designed to end the conflict.[1] In eight out of these seventeen cases (47 percent) the combatants signed and implemented successful peace settlements; in nine cases (53 percent) they returned to war.[2] The fact that combatants were almost equally likely to return to war as they were to sign and implement deals once they entered negotiations is striking for two reasons. It is striking that despite all the impediments to cooperation almost half of all peace negotiations did succeed in ending the war off the battlefield. But it is also striking that, despite all the costs of disagreement and the possibility of elimination *on* the battlefield, more than half of all combatants involved in negotiations were willing to return to war.

To date, most scholars and policy makers have assumed that negotiations fail because combatants have no interest in working together, they do not want to compromise on their goals and principles, or they cannot resolve underlying conflicts of interest. But a close examination of the failed negotiations reveals that in a majority of these cases combatants were able to resolve their underlying differences and agree on a compromise settlement. Communists and Nationalists in Greece held formal talks in 1945 and eventually signed the Varkiza Agreement. Rival factions in Laos met eight times between 1961 and 1972, ultimately signing an agreement in 1973. Uganda's government signed a peace accord and power sharing agreement with NRA guerrillas in December 1985. Four separate conferences of "National Reconciliation" were held between the government in Chad and the guerrillas, two of which ended in signed settlements: the Kano Agreement of March 1979 and the Reconciliation Accord of August 1979. Even Chinese Communists and Chinese Nationalists met three times between 1938 and 1949 and eventually agreed to a democratic coalition government and a fully integrated army. The truly puzzling question is not why civil war combatants are unable to agree on a compromise settlement but why they would continue to fight even after they had reached one. Why do they return to war?[3]

I argue that resolving the substantive issues over which a war was fought is not enough to convince civil war combatants to accept and implement peace settlements. For the war to end combatants must overcome the much higher hurdle of designing enforceable and credible guarantees on the terms of the agreement—something that is very difficult for the combatants to do without outside assistance. The biggest challenge facing civil war opponents at the negotiating table, therefore, is not how to resolve issues like land reform, or majority rule, or any of the underlying grievances that started the war. These are difficult issues to resolve, but not the most difficult. The most difficult issue is how to design a treaty that convinces each of them to shed their partisan armies and surrender conquered territory despite the fact that they will be made increasingly vulnerable and less able to enforce additional terms as a result. If groups are able to obtain third-party enforcement or verification for the treacherous demobilization period and to guarantee each other a significant share of power in a new government, then combatants will implement their settlements. If a third party does not step forward, they will reject this option and continue their war.

I begin by considering a number of current explanations of why negotiations might break down, all of which fall into two basic camps: those that claim combatants might not *want* to settle, and are only playing along for tactical reasons, and those that argue that combatants might like to settle but simply *cannot* reach mutually acceptable bargains. In section 2 I propose an alternative explanation that argues that civil war peace negotiations frequently fail because combatants cannot credibly commit to treaties that produce enormous uncertainty in the context of a highly dangerous implementation period. In the final section I discuss what implications this theory might have for policy makers interested in the problem of persistent or recurrent civil war.

Possible Explanations for the Breaksown of Negotiations

To date, no study has addressed the specific question of why civil war adversaries might walk away from negotiations and return to war. Still, there are a number of possible explanations circulating in the literature for why this might be so. In general, explanations can be divided into those that claim negotiations fail because combatants want to win the war and are simply playing for time and those that claim combatants might wish to reach a compromise but, for one reason or another, cannot strike a mutually acceptable deal.

Combatants Don't Want to Reach a Settlement

A compelling and popular school argues that civil war negotiations will fail if competing factions are not serious about making concessions. As Donald Horowitz has argued, "Not all leaders in ethnically divided states want to promote accommodation."[4] Domestic groups negotiate, but they negotiate for reasons unconnected to actually obtaining peace. Rebels and incumbent governments might negotiate to placate outside patrons who demand participation in a peace process or to satisfy citizens weary of war. Leaders may also use negotiations as a way to rest and resupply their armies or stall for time. "The Prime Minister is just playing for time," proclaimed Zimbabwe's rebel faction after bungled negotiations in 1974, "he wants the whole problem to drag on until he reaches his retirement age."[5] Finally, groups might also have strong incentives to feign interest in negotiations for reputational reasons. Leaders who are intent on absolute victory must cater to world opinion if they hope to obtain important foreign aid once established in power; being known as belligerent could reduce their final reward. In short, leaders have many strategic reasons to participate in talks and even sign settlements they have no intention of actually supporting.

Combatants Can't Agree on a Settlement

A second camp asserts that negotiations can also fail due to problems with reaching a settlement.[6] The negotiations listed in table 2.1 might have failed when one of four bargaining problems emerged: (1) combatants could not agree on how to divide the stakes, (2) both placed an equally high value on winning the war leaving little room for compromise, (3) each had strong incentives to withhold or misrepresent private information, or (4) they committed themselves to strong demands from which they could not back down. Failed negotiations, therefore, could be the result of an imperfect bargaining process where civil war combatants aggressively pursue individually rational bargaining strategies that backfire, leaving everyone worse off.

Indivisible Stakes

The first and most obvious reason negotiations might fail is because the rebels and the incumbent governments could not divide the stakes in a mutually agreeable way. As Paul Pillar has written, "If the stakes are chiefly indivisible, so that neither side can get most of what it wants without depriving the other of most of what it wants, negotiations are less apt to be successful. Stakes are usually less divisible in civil wars than in other types of war" and this makes settlement less likely.[7]

The Value of Winning the War

Negotiations might also fail if both the rebels and the government place an equally high value on winning the war, causing them to bargain overly aggressively. Sometimes this strategy works, producing a better deal for the more determined party. But if both sides simultaneously pursue this approach and hold out for equally exceptional offers, no overlapping bargaining range will emerge, and groups could find themselves fighting long after it was mutually rational to settle.[8]

Problems of Incomplete Information

A third bargaining problem can result if combatants withhold important private information about their own relative power, making it more difficult to locate a compromise solution.[9] Enemies in a civil war have many reasons to be less than truthful during negotiations. For one, they have incentives to prove that they are better supplied, more willing to return to war, and less willing to compromise than their opponent, since the longer a group can hold out, the more likely it can convince its enemy to capitulate. But misrepresenting one's strength—while individually rational—could have the unintended consequence of motivating groups to fight far longer than they would if this information were public.

Groups might also withhold important information from each other if this knowledge could later be used against them. Rebels, for example, might be reluctant to reveal their true strength because this would force them to bring guerrilla forces out of hiding, divulge secret weapons depots, or possibly disclose strategic weaknesses. This information might facilitate settlement but could also leave them vulnerable to attack. Given this choice, groups might prefer to jealously guard their secrets, even if this might generate a long, drawn-out, and seemingly irrational war.[10]

Irreversible Commitments

Finally, adversaries in a civil war might also return to undesirable wars because both sides have committed to very strong demands in order to enhance their bargaining leverage from which they subsequently cannot back down.[11] This can be done, for example, by stirring up popular nationalistic sentiment in favor of a given goal or by making a leader's tenure in office contingent on obtaining certain concessions from an enemy. This bargaining tactic would allow a leader to credibly announce that "I'd like to make a concession but my followers won't let me," but if both leaders follow this tactic, no settlement will result.

Questions Left Unanswered

On the face of it, each of these arguments seems quite plausible. There are certainly cases where combatants have no desire to negotiate and simply go through the motions because outside pressure, military considerations, curiosity, or reputational concerns encourage them to do so. And there are also cases where adversaries clearly cannot find an overlapping middle ground in which to draw a solution. But neither of these explanations gets to the heart of the puzzle at hand. Arguing that negotiations break down because groups are not serious about cooperating tells us little about the conditions under which groups will sign and implement settlements. Explanations that fall within the second camp, on the other hand, cannot explain why so many settlements fail even after mutually acceptable settlements have been reached. Clearly, many of the cases listed in table 2.1 were not permanently waylaid by any of the bargaining problems listed above. In short, arguments that view the problem of civil war resolution as a problem of insincerity or a problem of "bargaining" help explain why some domestic groups might walk away from the negotiating table but are far from complete explanations for negotiation failure. There are simply too many cases where negotiations broke down despite the existence of a signed settlement for these explanations to be fully satisfying.[12]

Credible Commitments and Treaty Enforcement

In what follows I argue that even if combatants want to cooperate, and even if they are able to resolve the ideological and power political issues that ignited the war, they will still return to war if credible, enforceable guarantees on the terms of the agreement cannot be arranged. Once the underlying issues are resolved, negotiations become a search for guarantees — guarantees that each of the combatants will be protected as they demobilize their partisan armies and guarantees that they will not be permanently excluded from a new government once they do so.

Resolving a civil war is never simply a matter of reaching a bargain and then instituting a cease-fire. To be successful, a civil war peace settlement must consolidate the previously warring factions into a single state, build a new government capable of accommodating their interests, and create a new national, nonpartisan military force.[13] This means that domestic adversaries who wish to settle their war off the battlefield must at some point demobilize, disengage, and disarm their separate militaries, and they must then surrender whatever remaining power they have to a single administration, not necessarily their own.

These requirements, however, create two tempting opportunities for post-treaty exploitation, and both sides know this. Once groups send their soldiers home, hand in their weapons, and surrender occupied regions, they become sitting ducks for attack, and once they surrender their assets to a single administration they make it easy for their opponent to set up a one-party state. This process of consolidation and the vulnerability it creates is quite different from cases where independent states negotiate an agreement and then continue to face each other as separate, self-sufficient entities.

The fact that competing groups must consolidate power at a time when they can neither defend themselves against attack nor rely on a central government to do this for them greatly complicates cooperation. In fact, by promoting demilitarization under what are essentially conditions of anarchy, civil war peace treaties promise to create security dilemmas in the reverse.[14] As groups begin to disarm, they create an increasingly tense situation. The fewer arms they have, the more vulnerable they feel. The more vulnerable they feel, the more sensitive they become to possible violations. And the more sensitive they become to violations, the less likely they are to fulfill their own side of the bargain. The ultimate challenge facing civil war opponents at the negotiating table, therefore, is not simply how to stop the fighting but how in fact to design a contract that convinces groups to shed individual defenses and submit to the rules of a new political game—at a time when no government or police force can either protect them or guarantee compliance.

Phase One: Demobilization and the Safe Consolidation of Forces

But how do you credibly commit to an implementation process you know will leave your enemy helpless? And how do you commit to a power sharing agreement when leaders will have every reason and opportunity to seize power and set up a one-party state? In theory, the danger of demobilization should be clear to both parties early in the negotiations, and this knowledge should enable them to design safeguards that neutralize its negative effects. A security dilemma that is so clearly predictable should also be manageable. Three safeguards in particular should enable groups to avoid creating a destabilizing security dilemma. First, groups could unilaterally enhance their defenses to make a surprise attack more difficult to launch. Second, they could design less risky consolidation plans that reduce the opportunity to cheat. Third, they could send costly signals that they have no hostile intentions and thus create an atmosphere of trust.

In practice, however, none of these strategies are available to adversaries emerging from violent civil wars. Unlike interstate opponents, civil war enemies cannot maintain or enhance their individual defenses once they sign a treaty and thus change incentives to cheat. This would leave the state with multiple competing armies and forsake one of the main objectives of a peace treaty. Groups could choose to hide weapons or withhold elite soldiers from assembly areas in order to shield themselves from attack. But these defensive measures could themselves set off an unwanted security dilemma. Factions might be able to circumvent this problem by installing sophisticated verification and monitoring equipment, giving them time to rearm in case of an attack. But even the best intelligence would not eliminate the risk of aggression, and as long as cheating can cause enormous suffering, as it can in civil wars, it is unlikely that groups will rely on early detection to ensure their safety.[15]

Civil war factions could employ a second strategy and design less dangerous implementation periods. If the government and the rebels fear a one-step advantage, they could disarm in a step-by-step or tit-for-tat fashion, sequencing military disengagement in a way that gave neither side a relative advantage. They could choose to demobilize at exactly the same time, at exactly the same rate, or recruit and retrain a new national military before existing partisan forces were disbanded. On the other hand, if one side enjoyed a preponderance of military power while their opponent enjoyed a preponderance of political support (like the Kuomintang and the Communists in China), they could use these opposing strengths to deter the breakdown of an agreement. Each of these strategies could reduce the possibility of a debilitating one-step advantage and encourage groups to execute a deal.

But designing a safe implementation period is not as easy as it appears. Although each of these strategies might make the actual implementation period less dangerous, two serious problems remain. First, monitoring an opponent's compliance with these terms would be extremely difficult since weapons are easy to buy and easy to hide. One could appear to disarm by handing over arms, sending soldiers home, and destroying heavy weaponry *and still* keep elite regiments on alert and supply lines open. Second, creative implementation strategies do not change the end result. In civil wars demobilization can be postponed, it can be implemented incrementally and in a reciprocal fashion, but it cannot be avoided. And as long as both sides know this, a crafty opponent need only wait until full disengagement to strike. In short, reciprocal implementation strategies only ensure that neither side gains an advantage while they demobilize. They cannot guarantee that arms, ammunition, and soldiers will not be held back for an offensive later on.

There is a third way groups may reassure one another that they will, in fact, follow through with their promises. If factions are serious about peace, they should be able to communicate these good intentions through costly and credible signals.[16] Yet signals that might convince an opponent to comply with an agreement (such as unilateral disarmament) either expose the sender to such danger that even peace-loving groups should shy away from using them or are too easy to mimic by more Machiavellian groups to have the desired effect of relaying peaceful intentions. "They can hide anything they want to from us," said an American police officer and mid-level supervisor for NATO in Bosnia. "We're out here filling in forms that say everything looks good, but most of these police are ready to go into combat in a quick minute."[17] Negotiating factions, therefore, are damned if they do and damned if they don't. If they agree to demobilize, they leave themselves dangerously open to annihilation without necessarily conveying any peaceful intentions, but if they refuse, they trigger the very security dilemma they hoped to avoid.

Ultimately, the most difficult problem with civil war resolution is that the warring parties cannot credibly commit to the safe consolidation of their forces; no matter what they try they will be unable to either enforce this phase themselves or structure it in a way that makes it self-enforcing. Civil war adversaries, therefore, will require a third party to help enforce at least this part of their treaties for them.[18] Third parties can verify compliance with the terms of demobilization and warn of a surprise attack, they can guarantee that soldiers will be protected as they demobilize, and they can become involved if one or both sides resumes the war. Third parties can thus ensure that the payoffs from cheating no longer exceed the payoffs from faithfully executing the settlement's terms. Once cheating becomes difficult and costly, promises to cooperate should gain credibility and cooperation should become more likely. The success of civil war settlements, therefore, not only hinges on the ability of combatants to reach mutually agreeable political deals but also on outsiders' willingness to verify or enforce the process of demobilization.

Phase Two: Credible Commitments to Power Sharing

As difficult as security issues are to solve, however, they do not address any of the important governance issues that ultimately determine whether a settlement lasts over time. Thus, even if an outside state were willing to verify or enforce demobilization, this would not guarantee that the settlement's political terms would be implemented after outsiders left.

Groups that want to end their civil war through negotiation must disassemble their separate and competing administrative centers and rebuild a new central government. But here again negotiating factions find themselves in a somewhat paradoxical position. On the one hand, both sides are likely to demand some form of power sharing as the price for peace; agreeing to demobilize must have some reward.[19] On the other hand, each faction knows that tolerating a partner in government will be costly, since their rival will almost certainly pursue very different if not competing policies. They thus have strong incentives to try to capture the government.[20] This, then, is the second dilemma factions face: how do they convince their rival that they won't usurp power once partisan armies are disbanded, once their leader is installed as president, and once the instruments of government are under their control?

An extensive literature since the *Federalist Papers* has sought ways to design domestic political institutions to ensure that minority and opposition groups would not be exploited by those in power. Most of this literature has identified the dangers involved with concentrating power in the hands of a single party or individual and has addressed this problem by suggesting ways to divide authority among different institutional structures. Although considerable debate still exists, most of these scholars agree that deeply divided societies can best be governed under four basic institutional features.[21] First, divided societies are more likely to be stable and free of conflict if power is decentralized in a federal system.[22] Second, divided societies are more likely to be stable if power is dispersed in a parliamentary rather than a presidential system. Parliamentary democracies tend to promote multiparty systems, encourage the formation of coalition governments, and promise that even small parties have a chance to gain positions of power.[23]

Third, states with highly polarized populations are also more likely to democratize successfully if individuals are elected based on the proportion of votes cast rather than a strict majority of votes that tends to promote a zero-sum game. "Simple majoritarian democracy contains special problems for ethnically divided societies. Minority ethnic groups expect to be permanently excluded from power through the ballot box and fear electoral contests when the principle of simple majority rule is operative."[24] Proportional representative systems, by contrast, tend to be more consensual, they try to limit, divide, and share power; most important, they avoid winner-take-all results and promise that most groups will not be denied the opportunity to participate in the government.[25]

Finally, many scholars also agree that checks and balances are needed to bind the governing party once elected. The United States, for example, chose to institute a bicameral instead of a unicameral legislature so that smaller states like Rhode Island would have greater individual power to check larger, more populous states like New York. In short, domestic political institutions serve the important role of setting up rules for individuals and parties to follow, for establishing procedures to punish those that don't, and for injecting an important degree of predictability and structure to the competitive process. These arrangements should greatly reduce the possibility for abuse and encourage even small minority groups to submit to elections.

Institution Building in Post-Civil War Societies

But transitions from civil war are different. Countries emerging from civil war suffer from deeper societal divisions, newer and more fragile institutions, and greater temptations toward abuse than almost any other type of state attempting to democratize, and three problems in particular stand out. First, government institutions will still be too weak in the immediate aftermath of a civil war to prevent a rapid grab of power and thus enforce what the opposition can no longer enforce themselves. Most of the countries listed in table 2.1 were not democracies prior to their conflict. They had no history of democratic rule and no established judiciary. Instead, the party that won the first election was expected to build these institutions based on the guidelines negotiated during peace talks. Once in power, however, this party could easily ignore these directives and create institutions that appeared democratic on the outside, only to serve their narrow interests on the inside. "They say the newspapers are free," articulated Halidou Ouedraogo, president of the Burkina Faso Movement for the Rights of Man, "but a minister can still put a journalist in jail. They say the courts are independent, but there are always pressures from behind the scenes. We still don't have real participation of the people at a grass-roots level."[26]

Second, even if truly democratic institutions were established, domestic groups could still not rely on them to be effective overnight. As Larry Diamond has observed, "Over time, citizens of a democracy become habituated to its norms and values, gradually internalizing them. The trick is for democracies to survive long enough — and function well enough — for this process to occur."[27] Civil war opponents, however, do not have this luxury since a malevolent opponent would likely act quickly to grab state control.

The third problem groups face is that post–civil war societies rarely enjoy a strong civic culture able to bolster fragile institutions and serve as a secondary control on misconduct. In fact, war-weary populations often prefer order and economic advancement to liberalization or democracy; in many cases residents simply want peace. "Look at Rwanda, Burundi, Zaire," said Dr. Aliou Boly, a young business manager in Ouagadougou. "If that's democratization, I'm not for it."[28] Faction leaders, therefore, cannot count on the general population (or even their partisan supporters) to reject efforts by one party to set up dictatorial control if the alternative would be renewed war.[29] Each of these conditions would make it fairly easy for someone to appoint themselves president for life, jail opposition leaders, and outlaw political parties and should make combatants extremely suspicious of the promise that competitive elections will actually usher in multiparty rule.

In short, it is easy to imagine why parties would willingly submit to elections in situations where they might benefit from winning in the future, where they will not be maltreated if they happen to lose, and where it would be costly to subvert the system.[30] Under these conditions they have every incentive to cooperate. But what if elections and institutions could promise none of these things? What if the losers of the first election could not count on another opportunity to regain power? What if no limits were set on what the winning party could do once elected? Most important, what if a loss in the first election could be permanent and perilous?[31] These are the conditions that characterize countries emerging from violent civil wars.

If it is true, therefore, that groups who have recently fought violent civil wars fear the possible repercussions of settlement, then simply the chance to compete in elections—whether these elections are based on majoritarian or proportional principles and are then backed up by presidential or parliamentary systems with federal or nonfederal arrangements—will not be enough. Each of these systems still promises that the loser will likely be permanently excluded from government. Institutions and elections in and of themselves might be effective over the long run, after rules and practices become routine. Or they might have greater success stabilizing a less volatile situation. But if suspending democracy is relatively easy—as it would be immediately after a civil war—then groups will need far more convincing promises that their opponent intends to abide by the rules of the new democratic game than a written constitution and an open election.

Successful civil war peace settlements, therefore, must take a different approach. In order to convince former civil war opponents to demobilize and to surrender power to a single central administration, successful settlements must make it difficult and costly for either side to establish a one-party state. This can be done in a number of ways. First, both the rebels and the incumbent party can be guaranteed an important and equal voice in the new government, and this can be done by pulling key positions in the new administration out of the democratic process for the groups assign themselves. This way, nervous factions eliminate competition for the most influential positions and make sure that these key posts are not left to the whim of elections.

Groups should be particularly concerned with executive power since a politically powerful and popular leader will have few real barriers on behavior, especially in the early faltering stages of a new government. The tendency of all people," writes Henry Lockwood:

> is to elevate a single person to the position of ruler. . . . Let a person be chosen to an office, with power conferred upon it equal to that of the Presidency of the United States, and it will make but little difference whether the law actually gives him the right to act in a particular direction or not. He determines policy. He acts. No argument that the law has been violated will avail. He is the chief officer of the nation. He stands alone. He is a separate power in himself. The lines with which we attempt to mark the limits of his power are shadowy and ill defined. . . . The sentiment of hero worship . . . will endorse him.[32]

There are numerous ways to divide executive power so that no party or individual gains complete control. Groups can choose a single but shared presidency as the Conservatives and Liberals did in Colombia. They can favor a powerful coalition cabinet composed of equal numbers of government and opposition leaders as the Christians and Muslims did in Lebanon in 1958. They can also decide that if one party wins the presidency, the other party or parties can assign all the cabinet positions.

But simply guaranteeing that leaders will have a say in a new government will not be enough. Post–civil war factions do not simply fear that they will have little voice in government, they also fear that their very existence will be eliminated or marginalized in the process. These factions, therefore, are also looking for a way to preserve the existence and well-being of their group even under the worst circumstances.

There are at least two additional ways to guarantee a group's existence. First, a peace treaty can ensure that all security forces within a state are fully integrated, making it difficult for one group to abuse a rival.[33] The Zimbabwean rebel's published statement of its "Essential Requirements for the Transition" illustrates just how important an issue this is:

> The Security Forces during the interim period must be an army composed of a combination of the Patriotic Front's and the Regime's armies, and a police force composed of a combination of the Patriotic Front's and the Regime's police forces, operating in both cases alongside a United Nations Peacekeeping Force and a United Nations Civilian Police Force to supervise the cease-fire and ensure peaceful integration. The foregoing structure is essential to ensure that the

process towards genuine majority rule and independence will be irreversible.[34]

But how does one divide military power and still retain some form of unity? Groups can decide to split the national army and internal security forces 50–50, as the Northern and Southern Sudanese agreed in 1972 and Renamo and Frelimo agreed in 1992. They can set up autonomous regions for groups to police themselves, as the contras and Sandinistas did in Nicaragua in 1990. They can mix officers from one party with enlisted soldiers from another.

In short, disaggregating the state into individual parts and distributing these parts among the former rivals reduces the risks and uncertainties of democratization in four important ways. First, domestic groups who are in control of key ministerial positions such as the ministry of justice or share control of the prime ministership have greater incentives to support a new democratic government and fewer incentives to work to overthrow it. Second, splitting the military makes it extremely difficult for potential dictators to oppress or overpower other groups. Third, guarantees also allow opponents to distinguish early in negotiations which groups are serious about sharing power and which are not. A group intent on setting up a one-party state would never agree to such a guaranteed division of power and influence.

A government based on mutual guarantees, however, is not without its drawbacks. Consociational power sharing solutions or pacts have been criticized for being undemocratic, for having no "grass roots backing," for being the "ultimate form of elite manipulation," for leaving political leaders unaccountable to their communities, for "freezing" group boundaries, and for excluding important parties and interests who were not major players in a war.[35] The shared government between Hun Sen and the Royalists in Cambodia, for example, was paralyzed by infighting between the two prime ministers during its six-year reign, ultimately falling victim to a coup in 1997. Pacts are inflexible and can be highly inefficient. But the fact that these regimes are likely to follow conflicting policy initiatives and have difficulty obtaining a policy consensus are two of the reasons adversaries might find them so attractive. In fact, one of the interesting and counterintuitive conclusions to draw from this chapter is that leaders who have recently fought a civil war might actually find this paralysis quite appealing, since it ensures that their opponent will be unable to pass policies detrimental to them. There is great comfort knowing that policies will NOT be made.

Nevertheless, the fact that guarantees can be inefficient, exclusionary, and inflexible means that this type of government will not be stable over time. Eventually, citizens will demand greater efficiency from their government and new parties will demand more open, competitive systems. If these systems do not evolve they will eventually topple. Does this mean that mutual guarantees should be avoided? Only if groups prefer to return to war. Domestic groups emerging from internal violence have no way to circumvent this early guaranteed system of power sharing. But it does mean that a regime that is good at ending a civil war is not necessarily the type of regime that will be good at governing a country over time. A second transition will almost certainly be needed toward a more liberal democracy as democratic preconditions are established. The ultimate challenge facing civil war rivals over the long term, therefore, is not how to establish a liberal open democracy but how to adroitly metamorphose the inflexible institutional structures that are necessary to convince them to sign a settlement in the highly tense postwar environment into more liberal, open institutions over time. This is the next big question that confronts scholars and policy makers.

Treaties That Bind: Mozambique's 1992 Peace Agreement

The recent negotiations in Mozambique illustrate how critical credible commitments become to the success or failure of a peace treaty. I have chosen Mozambique because it represents a particularly unlikely case for successful settlement and would, therefore, show how cooperation might be possible even under difficult circumstances. The war in Mozambique was long (the average duration of civil wars listed in table 2.1 was fifty-three months, this war lasted seventeen years), it was exceptionally bloody (an estimated nine hundred thousand Mozambicans died, more then 3 million were driven from their homes, and half the total population of 16 million faced starvation),[36] and it was ethnically based—fought between the Makonde in the North and the Shangana of the South. Nonetheless, on October 2, 1992, the Frelimo government and the Renamo rebels signed a peace treaty ending what had been called "one of the most brutal holocausts against ordinary human beings since World War II."[37]

Specific political and military guarantees ultimately determined whether or not Frelimo and Renamo signed and implemented the Rome Accord. As in many other civil wars, there was a long delay in negotiations between the time the main grievances were settled and a treaty was actually signed; most of the negotiations concentrated on ways to reassure the rebels that they would not be attacked during demobilization and that the Frelimo government was, in fact, serious about sharing control of the state. For the most part, talks were not dominated by give-and-take bargaining over ideological differences or positions. Instead, success hinged on three critical issues. Would Frelimo accept a significant UN role in the transition period? Was Frelimo serious about dismantling its one-party state and sharing power? And would both Frelimo and Renamo be able to protect themselves after the UN left? Once Frelimo accepted a large UN military presence and agreed to a system of dual political administration, their promise to seek peace became credible and signatures soon followed.

Current Explanations for Mozambique's Success

Close observers of the war in Mozambique argue that Renamo and Frelimo settled their war in 1992 for one of four reasons. First, a lengthy military stalemate made it clear to both sides that they could not win a decisive military victory. "This," according to a UN election observer in Mozambique, "effectively moved the conflict from a stalemate to a "hurting stalemate" and convinced the groups to settle.[38] Second, outside aid to both parties had been significantly reduced and this encouraged groups to settle. Once the cold war ended, support for ideological battle between a Marxist-leaning government and rebels disappeared, and so did the sponsors.[39] Third, a growing drought threatened mass starvation and made it increasingly difficult for either side to feed its soldiers and supporters.[40] And, finally, outside mediators and observers continuously pushed the rivals to resolve their differences. "The skilled and deeply committed people of Sant'Egidio (the mediators)," argued Chester Crocker, "shaped history through their initial intervention, and as time passed, their efforts created a critical mass of facts and momentum so that there was something for "track one" decision-makers to support."[41] By all accounts, Frelimo and Renamo would have continued their war had it not been for the concentration of so many debilitating factors.

A closer look at the war, however, reveals that each of these variables had been present at intervals throughout the war and all were present years before Frelimo and Renamo signed a treaty in 1992. As Ibrahim Msabaha points out, "A mutually hurting stalemate produced an impetus for negotiations at several points in the sixteen-year history of the conflict."[42] Only the final negotiations, however, succeeded. Another author admits that "the Government had known for many years that even with substantial assistance, a military solution was not possible."[43] It seemed unlikely, therefore, that the removal of aid suddenly convinced them to settle. And the drought, which many believed pushed both sides to the table, was not a new condition in 1992. In 1983, nine years before settlement, approximately one hundred thousand people starved to death, yet that disastrous year did not encourage a similar settlement.[44] Even mediation was not unique to this final set of peace talks, for a number of countries had tried to arbitrate since 1985.[45]

To be fair, one could argue that negotiations succeeded in 1992 because all these factors converged into one costly bundle. But this still leaves important questions unanswered. If a military stalemate, outside aid, a drought, and mediation convinced groups to settle, why did negotiations drag on for twenty-seven months? More important, why did these talks linger two years after Renamo's central demand of the war (a multiparty political system and elections) was met in 1990?[46] What was so special about 1992 that finally convinced groups to sign?

The convergence of so many costly conditions might have convinced Frelimo and Renamo to initiate negotiations, but they were not sufficient to produce a successful settlement. Instead, commitment problems seem to better explain why Frelimo and Renamo continued to negotiate long after crucial political concessions were made, why both were willing to return to a hopeless war even after this point, and why they did finally settle in October 1992. In fact, the twenty-seven months of negotiations reveal how much of the talks revolved around Renamo's attempt to extract "guarantees" from Frelimo that the cease-fire would be peaceful and that they would still have "the ability to hold the government to commitments" even after they disarmed.[47]

The Main Grievances Settled

Like other negotiations in Zimbabwe, Nicaragua, El Salvador, and Sudan, the underlying issues in Mozambique's war were resolved long before a settlement was signed. Since 1989 Renamo had insisted that their goal was "constitutional reform" and their demands were fairly simple. At least officially, the rebels wanted some form of multiparty democracy and to be recognized as a legitimate political party within this new system.[48] By December 1990 Frelimo adopted a new constitution that provided for multiparty elections and new political parties, and by January 1992 they agreed to a more specific power sharing formula based on proportional representation and a directly elected president.[49] Thus, by early 1992 the main grievances of the war appeared to be settled.

Seeking a Credible Commitment

The fact that these issues were resolved but negotiations dragged on for an additional ten months (almost a full two years after the initial concessions were made) meant that the bulk of the peace talks focused on other issues. A review of the successive rounds of negotiations (twenty in total) reveals two patterns. First, most of the negotiations concentrated on the issue of "guarantees" (as both Renamo and Frelimo called them). Second, the final accords were only implemented after the two leaders agreed to set up a unique "dual administration" and after UN peacekeeping troops arrived on the ground.

Renamo's security concerns arose immediately in the first round of negotiations in July 1990 when three topics were discussed. Should a mediator be present? Should a cease-fire begin before, or after, the government discussed specific political and military reforms? And would the UN monitor the transition period between the cease-fire and Mozambique's first elections? The government rejected mediation and insisted that Renamo agree to a cease-fire before any political issues were discussed. Renamo, on the other hand, wanted mediation, demanded an agreement on political reform before any discussion of a cease-fire, and insisted on extensive UN involvement in "monitoring and guaranteeing implementation."[50] Renamo favored an elaborate UN operation similar to what had been established in Cambodia between a cease-fire and elections. According to Cameron Hume, U.S. observer to the Rome peace talks, "The choice of this option reflected the depth of Renamo's skepticism that the Frelimo government, operating under a Frelimo constitution, could be trusted to conduct fair, multiparty elections."[51] Renamo's leader, Afonso Dhlakama, contended,

> What will happen 24 hours after a cease-fire is in place? How will Mozambicans live afterwards? Does it mean that once a cease-fire is signed, President Chissano will abolish communal villages? Will he then do away with the People's National Security Service which has been killing Mozambicans under the cover of darkness? Will he abolish all laws [passage indistinct]?[52]

Renamo's leaders did not trust that the government would actually write a democratic constitution and create a multiparty state once Renamo laid down their weapons, and they certainly didn't believe they could hold the government to these promises once negotiations concluded. Renamo wanted guarantees that Frelimo would open up the government, and they saw extensive UN involvement as the only way to obtain this result.

The government rejected mediation and insisted that Renamo agree to a cease-fire before any political issues were discussed. Negotiations made slow, halting progress through June 1991, by which time President Chissano of Frelimo finally agreed to all three Remano demands. The government would accept formal mediation during the talks, would discuss political issues before discussing a cease-fire, and would accept international monitoring of a cease-fire and elections. But Dhlakama pressed Chissano further. What specific role would outside monitors have? Would Frelimo's security service (SNAPS) be eliminated before Renamo began demobilization?[53] These questions revealed the depth of distrust between the two factions and the real concerns the rebels had for their safety. The government, however, refused to discuss either issue.

Negotiations then moved to the equally contentious item of who would administer the country during the transition. Renamo refused to accept any Frelimo role in conducting the elections, fearing the incumbents could easily manipulate the process. Chissano's government, however, refused to allow the United Nations to register parties or conduct the elections and refused to let Renamo share responsibility.[54] In August 1991, during the sixth round of negotiations, Renamo broke off talks, claiming it would be suicide for Renamo to go forward with a solution that could so easily be manipulated by their opponent.[55] When asked what went wrong, one of the mediators replied that "Renamo had a 'deep fear of falling into the trap of integration.'"[56]

Negotiations recommenced in November 1991, and by August 1992 Frelimo finally accepted outside enforcement of the transition period.[57] This, according to the credible commitment theory, was one of two crucial guarantees the settlement would require to succeed.

Renamo received the second crucial guarantee less than a month later when Chissano and Dhlakama reached a "gentleman's agreement" that offered the rebels both military and territorial guarantees for their safety. The two leaders agreed that Mozambique's new national army would consist of fifteen thousand Frelimo soldiers and fifteen thousand Renamo soldiers. In addition, the government could retain its security forces, but they would now be monitored by a mixed Frelimo/Renamo oversight commission. Most important, however, they also agreed that Renamo could remain in the regions it already occupied prior to elections, while government administrators would be "allowed to establish a presence throughout the country."[58] This meant that Renamo would not be forced to relinquish administrative control over home regions before elections. If Frelimo won at the polls but refused to set up a coalition government, Renamo could retain these regions until Frelimo fulfilled its promises. And if Frelimo continued to refuse, Renamo would not be harmed. As long as Renamo occupied these regions, Frelimo would not be able to dominate the country politically, and as long as Renamo controlled half the national army, Frelimo would not be able to take these regions by force. This, as it turns out, was the second crucial guarantee. Two weeks later, on October 4, 1992, President Chissano and President Dhlakama signed the Rome Accord ending their war.

What happened during implementation? As the credible commitment theory would have predicted, neither group began to demobilize until UN troops arrived, and neither side was disarmed by the time elections took place in October 1994. Full disarmament, however, was not necessary for elections to run peacefully. President Chissano won the presidential election, and his party won five of the country's ten provinces. Renamo won a majority in the remaining five provinces, two of which were Mozambique's most populous.

What happened after the election confirmed Renamo's fears. Once Chissano had won at the polls, he refused to form a coalition government with Renamo and refused to include Dhlakama in his cabinet despite strong public and international pressure to do so. This meant that Renamo, although represented in parliament, had little if any official influence in government. Renamo responded by refusing to relinquish authority in the five provinces it had won. As a result, a double administration became the norm.[59]

Renamo accepted Chissano's refusal to set up a coalition government and did not return to war because the Rome Accord had allowed Renamo to retain sufficient political power to challenge Frelimo in the next election, had set up a dual administration that protected them from political obsolescence, and had retained 15,000 Renamo soldiers to help guarantee their physical safety. As Miguel de Brito, a former professor of politics at Mozambique's Institute of International Relations observed, "The last thing Dhlakama will do right now is return to war. Renamo has a lot of strength in the rural areas and enough influence with the international community to make sure the 1999 elections are fair. If they play their cards right, they could do much better next time."[60]

In conclusion, the 1990 to 1992 negotiations in Rome are a story of Renamo's attempt to extract credible commitments from a government that seemed strongly opposed to power sharing. Each successive concession by Frelimo served to increasingly reassure Renamo that they could not be permanently eliminated and would be protected from abuse should the government choose to renege on the deal. Although the stalemate, the drought, and international pressure probably convinced Frelimo and Renamo to initiate negotiations, it was "commitments" that ultimately convinced the two rivals to sign, implement, and maintain a settlement. Most important, it was the willingness of the UN to intervene with significant force, to stay through elections, and to not insist on full disarmament that allowed for this success.

Other Cases

The Mozambique case illustrates how external security guarantees and internal political, military and territorial commitments convinced Frelimo and Renamo to end their war through a negotiated settlement rather than a decisive military fight. A brief review of other wars listed in table 2.1 reveals a similar pattern. Six out of the eight cases of successful settlement (75 percent) were underwritten by extensive outside security guarantees.[61] These include Lebanon's 1958 and 1976 agreements, the Dominican Republic's Act of Dominican Reconciliation, the Addis Ababa Agreement in Sudan (1972), the Lancaster House Agreement in Zimbabwe (1979), and the Tela Agreement in Nicaragua (1989). Peace settlements signed since 1990 continue to follow this pattern: recent agreements in El Salvador, Mozambique, Cambodia, and Bosnia all included arrangements for a contingent of peacekeeping forces and all brought peace.[62] On the other hand, none of the failed agreements enjoyed similar outside security guarantees. China, Greece, Laos, Nigeria, Nicaragua (1978–79), Uganda, and Chad all held serious negotiations, yet none enjoyed outside enforcement. All eventually failed. This seems to indicate that while political agreement was necessary for successful settlement it was not sufficient to produce peace without outside enforcement.

In addition, the successful settlements listed in table 2.1 included a variety of creative political, military, and territorial guarantees. The Conservatives and Liberals in Colombia, for example, agreed to a 50–50 split of all government positions (including patronage jobs) and rotated their time in the presidency. The 1970 political agreement in Yemen created a highly decentralized governing structure based on regional autonomy and integrated the rebel Royalists into every level of government with the incumbent Republicans. In Sudan a federation was created between the North and the South. Its new constitution guaranteed the continued existence of a southern regional government and gave the South enough tax revenue to survive without help from the wealthier North. More important, the accord was able to fashion a national army that preserved the armed strength of both factions.[63] The whites in the new state of Zimbabwe were guaranteed 20 percent of all the seats in the lower House of Parliament despite the fact that they represented only 3 percent of the population. As a minority, they were also allowed to retain private control of most of Zimbabwe's richest land and keep their dual citizenship with England. The Sandinistas and Contras in Nicaragua solved this problem by creating twenty-three self-governing development zones (20 percent of the country) that the Contras could occupy and police themselves. It also retained Thomas Ortega (Daniel Ortega's brother) as commander in chief of the army, even after his opponent won the presidency.

In contrast to these detailed arrangements, most of the failed settlements included only vague references to future political arrangements.[64] In China the new coalition government provided only for a "cabinet system" in which the executive branch was responsible to the legislative branch. The Greek Communists and Nationalists only agreed to hold "a plebiscite as soon as possible (in any case during 1945) to decide finally on the question of a regime."[65] Elections for a new constituent assembly to draft a new constitution would be held sometime thereafter. In Laos the three faction leaders created a coalition government in name only, as General Phoumi's incumbent position was not weakened.

Although this brief review offers no definitive evidence for or against the credible commitment theory of civil war resolution, it does present strong preliminary support for it. Before we can really know what role credible commitments play in civil war settlement, additional research will be required to test all the alternative hypotheses in an empirically rigorous manner. This will likely involve multivariate analysis of a large civil war dataset and more detailed assessments of a number of case histories. Nonetheless, as an exercise in theory building, this chapter offers useful insights into some unobservable dynamics that could hamper peace negotiations.

Possible Challenges

There are, however, a number of possible challenges to the logic of this theory. One is that outside enforcement has no independent effect on civil war settlement and is actually endogenous to the model. In other words, outside states only offer to guarantee those settlements that would have succeeded on their own and do not offer them in cases where success appears unlikely. This criticism is quite serious but can be rebutted in at least two ways. First, if enforcement is offered only in cases where negotiations press toward success, then treaties should succeed whether or not outside forces actually arrive on the ground. The cases, however, show that implementation did not proceed in the absence of peacekeepers, was delayed until peacekeepers arrived, broke down when peacekeepers did not show, and collapsed when peacekeepers decided to leave early. In other words, the arrival or departure of outside enforcement appears directly correlated to treaty execution. In Chad the factions successfully formed a government of national unity and began an "orderly withdrawal" of their troops from the capital. But when the neutral African peacekeeping force made up of soldiers from Guinea, Benin, and the Congo failed to arrive, no other terms were implemented.[66] In Uganda guerrilla and government leaders signed a peace accord in December 1985 and asked Kenya, Tanzania, the United Kingdom, and Canada to establish a peacekeeping force. The United Kingdom and Canada, however, declined to participate, and the terms were never implemented. The peace agreement designed to end the war in Laos signed in February 1973, on the other hand, specifically called for the "withdrawal of all foreign forces within sixty days." The cease-fire never fully took effect and fighting continued until the Pathet Lao decisively defeated the government. In short, the arrival and timing of outside intervention does appear to have a direct effect on whether or not treaties are implemented.

Second, if it is true that third parties only intervene in successful cases, then it must also be true that outsiders can ascertain which negotiations will succeed and which will fail. But what observable indicators would they use to determine this? Outside states could intervene in only those cases where groups have actually drafted or signed settlements (assuming that these are most likely to succeed). They could target only the longest, most deadly wars, assuming that combatants have the greatest incentive to settle these cases. They could intervene in only those wars with costly military stalemates. Each of these conditions should help them identify which cases might succeed. Yet intervention did not appear to vary with any of these other variables. Outsiders sent peacekeepers to enforce settlements in both short and long wars, wars with high casualty figures and those with low casualty figures, wars where leaders were highly distrusted, and wars where the underlying issues were both resolved and unresolved. In fact, in five of the thirteen cases in which combatants had signed peace settlements in hand, outsiders did not step in. This suggests that outsiders followed no pattern in the types of wars in which they intervened and did not know when a settlement was likely to succeed or fail.[67]

Finally, a number of scholars might also challenge the assumption that power sharing is the "best" solution for civil wars.[68] They might argue, for example, that territorial partition offers a more stable and permanent solution, since it would circumvent the debilitating problem of asset consolidation. In theory, this might be true. Partitioning a country into separate states would allow the competing factions to remain independent and make a peace treaty easier to enforce. History shows, however, that governments rarely allow sections of their territory to be lopped off in order to avoid or shorten civil wars. This is confirmed when one looks at the successful cases, all of which were based on power sharing rather than partition. In short, partition might facilitate long-term peace and it might more effectively prevent renewed civil war, but it is a solution that rebels rarely seem to obtain through negotiations with their government once war has broken out.

This chapter was a study on how to write an enforceable contract under conditions of extreme risk—a condition conspicuously present in the aftermath of a civil war. It argued that negotiating an end to civil wars is tricky. The problem is often not that rival leaders have no desire to compromise or cannot locate a mutually acceptable middle ground, as the conventional view asserts. A large number of civil war adversaries actually do solve the underlying grievances driving their war. The more difficult problem is that even when all the other obstacles to resolution are resolved, civil war adversaries will still confront a unique set of commitment problems that stem from the need to integrate two or more separate organizations into a single state. For settlements to succeed, therefore, each faction must convince its opponent beyond a doubt that they will faithfully disengage their military forces and then honestly share power—something that requires a complex set of external and internal guarantees. The more secure and self-confident groups are for the safe consolidation of military forces, and for the opening of the political process, the more likely they are to sign and implement peace treaties.

This study offers at least four suggestions to policy makers interested in resolving civil wars. First, even the most promising negotiations will require outside enforcement if they are to succeed. Adversaries will generally push ahead with a peace plan when a third party has the political will to verify or enforce demobilization. If a third party fails to step forward, or in some way reveals a lack of resolve, the combatants may become reluctant to proceed and even signed settlements collapse. This does not mean that outsiders must send massive peacekeeping troops to coerce compliance from the participants. It does mean however, that its commitment must be convincing. If factions are uncertain whether peacekeepers will arrive, if they do not believe that peacekeepers can effectively verify compliance or protect them as they report to assembly areas, or if they are not convinced that peacekeepers will stay until demobilization is complete, then their role as a reassuring device will be undercut and it seems highly unlikely that factions will proceed with implementation.

Second, excessive reliance on the promise of free and fair elections as a means to introduce democracy to states emerging from civil war appears to be self-defeating. If groups who have recently fought each other fear that the victor of the first post-war election will set up an authoritarian state, outlaw the opposition, and possibly imprison them, it is likely that they will refuse to participate in negotiations and instead will choose to continue the war. Outsiders, therefore, should refrain from pushing for a "quick and easy" democratization process and understand that they cannot simultaneously end a civil war and set up a fully liberal democracy without some sort of democratic transition in between.

Third, because combatants are likely to become highly fearful and insecure as they demobilize, they can gain an added sense of safety if they are not forced to disarm fully, especially not before the political terms of an agreement have been fulfilled. Allowing groups to retain at least some arms in the open should help to reassure groups and act as an important deterrent against attempts by one group to establish dictatorial rule. Outsiders can allow groups to retain a measure of self-help by not demanding full disarmament before elections and by offering groups important "escape hatches" such as territorial autonomy, open borders, or generous asylum provisions.

Finally the civil war cases analyzed in this chapter suggest that at least one final lesson can be drawn from past experiences. When attempting to resolve civil wars, enforcement does matter. But it only matters in the short term. If outside states expect these settlements to last over time, they must consider how the institutional parameters of any new government shape groups' expectations about their future security and factor into decisions to fight or cooperate. Military force might be crucial for demobilization, but institutional design matters far more in the long run.

TABLE 2.1.   Civil Wars Ending Between 1940–1990 in Which Peace
Negotiations Were Initiated

Civil War[a]	Negotiations[b]	Signed Settlement[c]	Outcome[d]
Cases in which no settlement was reached or signed:			
Vietnam (1960–75)	Yes	No	Decisive Victory
Nigeria (1967–70)	Yes	No	Decisive Victory
Jordan (1970)	Yes	No	Decisive Victory
Nicaragua (1978–79)	Yes	No	Decisive Victory
Cases in which a settlement was reached or signed but not implemented:			
China (1946–49)	Yes	Yes	Decisive Victory
Greece (1944–49)	Yes	Yes	Decisive Victory
Laos (1960–75)	Yes	Yes	Decisive Victory
Uganda (1981–87)	Yes	Yes	Decisive Victory
Chad (1979–87)	Yes	Yes	Decisive Victory
Cases in which a settlement was signed and implemented:			
Colombia (1948–58)[69]	Yes	Yes	Settlement Succeeded
Lebanon (1958)	Yes	Yes	Settlement Succeeded
Yemen (1962–70)[70]	Yes	Yes	Settlement Succeeded
Sudan (1963–72)	Yes	Yes	Settlement Succeeded
Dominican Republic (1965)	Yes	Yes	Settlement Succeeded
Rhodesia (1972–79)	Yes	Yes	Settlement Succeeded
Lebanon (1975–76)	Yes	Yes	Settlement Succeeded
Nicaragua (1981–89)	Yes	Yes	Settlement Succeeded

[a] Conflicts were classified as civil wars based on the coding criteria proposed by J. David Singer and Melvin Small's Correlates of War project.

[b] See note 1, this chapter.

[c] If the combatants signed an agreement that attempted to address each other's war aims, that conflict was coded as having led to a "signed settlement." Settlements that only included terms for a cease-fire, the withdrawal of foreign troops, or amnesty for combatants were not considered "settlements," since they did not attempt to deal with the difficult issues that had ignited the war. These agreements could better be described as temporary measures to halt fighting, allow foreign states to exit gracefully, or present a coup de grâce to losing parties. In this way I distinguished those settlements that aimed to resolve the underlying conflict from those that did not.

[d] The outcome was coded as a "decisive victory" if one side could convince its opponent(s) to cease fighting without their demanding any major concessions in return. Although it is fairly common for even decisive military victories to end with some form of "negotiated" agreement, it is important to distinguish between treaties negotiated by groups who could continue military resistance and those treaties imposed after one side had already won the war. Wars were coded as ending in "successful settlement," therefore, only when three criteria were met. First, a treaty had to be jointly drafted by all combatants through give-and-take bargaining. Second, the agreement had to keep the opposition intact as a bargaining entity. Third, it had to end the war for at least five years. If a formal peace treaty was signed but broke down within this time period, it was considered a failed attempt, and the outcome in these cases was coded on the basis of the eventual military results.

NOTES

This chapter was first published as an article in *International Security*, vol. 24, no. 1 (Summer 1999). I wish to thank James Fearon, Henk Goemans, Peter Gourevitch, Robert Jervis, David Laitin, David Lake, John McMillan, Jack Snyder, Richard Tucker, Barry Weingast, Christopher Woodruff, the participants of the 1998 Olin Institute for Strategic Studies' seminar series, and especially Zoltan Hajnal for very helpful comments on earlier drafts.

1. Civil wars were coded as having experienced "negotiations" if factions held face-to-face talks and issues relevant to resolving the war were discussed. These qualifications eliminated scheduled talks that never took place, meetings where no substantive issues were deliberated, and talks that excluded key participants. An attempt was also made to apply a "good faith" proviso and exclude those meetings where one or both participants were obviously unwilling to yield on important issues. Although sometimes difficult to determine, certain actions did signal whether or not faction leaders honestly wished to cooperate. Their readiness to accept supervision, make public announcements of important concessions, discuss the details of a transfer of power, and participate in lengthy negotiations all generated costs to the groups involved and indicated more than a tactical interest in appearing cooperative. To say that a civil war experienced "negotiations," however, does not imply that groups would not willingly defect if they could benefit from cheating. "Negotiations" simply indicate that they were willing to consider an alternative to war.

2. See table 2.1 for the list of cases.

3. Throughout this chapter I treat both the government and the rebel faction as if leaders on both sides represent a homogeneous group with unitary interests. In reality, the interests of a group are often diverse and transitive and leaders frequently preside over fragile coalitions whose own internal politics dictate behavior. Nonetheless, this assumption is justified since I argue that *even if* leaders are fortunate enough to preside over a group in complete agreement on behavior, they will still encounter difficult commitment problems. For an article that specifically addresses how the internal politics of a group can affect decisions to negotiate or fight, see Barbara F. Walter and Andrew Kydd, "Extremists, Uncertainty, and Commitments to Peace," unpublished paper, September 1998.

4. Donald Horowitz, *Ethnic Groups in Conflict* (Berkeley: University of California Press, 1985), p. 564. See also Stephen John Stedman, "Spoiler Problems in Peace Processes," *International Security*, vol. 22, no. 2 (Fall 1997), pp.5 –53.

5. Goswin Baumhoegger, *The Struggle for Independence: Documents on the Recent Development of Zimbabwe, 1975–1980*, vol. 2 (Hamburg: Institute of African Studies, Africa Documentation Center, 1984), p. 7.

6. Much exciting research is being done in the area of strategic barriers to successful negotiation in international relations. See especially James Fearon, "Ra-

tionalist Explanations for War," *International Organization*, vol. 49, no. 3 (Summer 1995), pp. 379–414; and David Lake, *Entangling Relations: American Foreign Policy in Its Century* (Princeton: Princeton University Press, 1998).

7. Paul Pillar, *Negotiating Peace: War Termination as a Bargaining Process* (Princeton: Princeton University Press, 1983), p. 24. For similar arguments see Fred Ikle, *Every War Must End* (New York: Columbia University Press, 1971), p. 95; George Modelski, "International Settlement of Internal War," in James Rosenau, ed., *International Aspects of Civil Strife* (Princeton: Princeton University Press, 1964); and R. Harrison Wagner, "The Causes of Peace," in Roy Licklider, ed., *Stopping the Killing: How Civil Wars End* (New York: New York University Press, 1993). For a particularly interesting recent argument see James D. Fearon, "Bargaining, Enforcement, and International Cooperation," *International Organization*, vol. 52, no. 2, pp. 269–305.

8. See Fearon, "Bargaining, Enforcement, and International Cooperation."

9. See especially Roger B. Myerson and Mark A. Satterthwaite, "Efficient Mechanisms for Bilateral Trading," *Journal of Economic Theory*, vol. 29, no. 2 (April 1983), pp. 265–281; James D. Morrow, "Signaling Difficulties with Linkage in Crisis Bargaining," *International Studies Quarterly*, vol. 36, no. 2 (June 1992), pp. 153–172; and Fearon, "Rationalist Explanations for War."

10. Ironically, even if groups were willing to divulge this information, the fact that they have incentives to misrepresent these facts, and both side realize this, would make even accurate information suspect.

11. This is similar to the bargaining strategies Thomas Schelling discusses in *Arms and Influence* (New Haven: Yale University Press, 1966), chapter 2, "The Art of Commitment," pp. 35–92. See also Vince Crawford and Hans Haller, "A Theory of Disagreement in Bargaining," *Econometrica* (May 1982). My thanks to John McMillan for pointing this out.

12. One could argue that empty promises are easy to make since they will never be carried out. But public promises are not without cost. Ignoring or violating an agreement could easily negate many of the benefits a party had hoped to gain by appearing cooperative.

13. Civil war adversaries could choose to partition their country into two or more independent states and thus circumvent this problem of consolidation. As I discuss later in this chapter, however, governments rarely agree to negotiate a separation of territory, leaving power sharing as the only negotiable alternative.

14. For pathbreaking earlier discussions of the security dilemma see Robert Jervis, "Cooperation Under the Security Dilemma," *World Politics*, vol. 30, no. 2 (Winter 1978), pp. 167–214; and Barry Posen, "The Security Dilemma and Ethnic Conflict," in Michael E. Brown, ed., *Ethnic Conflict and International Security* (Princeton: Princeton University Press, 1993).

15. Barry Weingast offers an excellent analysis of the problem of extreme vulner-

ability in "Constructing Trust: The Political and Economic Roots of Ethnic and Regional Conflict," unpublished paper, Hoover Institution, 1994.

16. For a well-developed discussion on the use of such signals see Andy Kydd, "Game Theory and the Spiral Model," *World Politics*, vol. 49, no. 3 (April 1997), pp. 371–400.

17. Mike O'Connor, "Bosnia's Military Threat: Rival Police," *New York Times*, January 12, 1997, p. A6.

18. This hypothesis was presented and tested in an earlier article, which found that outside security guarantees in the form of active peacekeeping forces were a necessary condition for the successful implementation of peace treaties. For an in-depth discussion and analysis of this variable see Barbara F. Walter, "The Crucial Barrier to Civil War Settlement," *International Organization*, vol. 51, no. 3 (Summer 1997), pp. 335–364.

19. I use Timothy Sisk's definition of power sharing to mean any political system that "fosters governing coalitions inclusive of most, if not all, major mobilized ethnic groups in society." See Timothy Sisk, *Power Sharing and International Mediation in Ethnic Conflict* (Washington, D.C.: United States Institute of Peace, 1996), p. 4.

20. See Robert Dahl, *Polyarchy: Participation and Opposition* (New Haven: Yale University Press, 1971), p. 15.

21. For a good cross-section of these debates see Larry Diamond and Marc F. Plattner, *The Global Resurgence of Democracy* (Baltimore: Johns Hopkins University Press, 1993).

22. There is an extensive literature supporting this view. See James Madison, "Federalist no. 10," *The Federalist Papers* (New York: Penguin, 1961); Arend Lijphart, *Democracy in Plural Societies* (New Haven: Yale University Press, 1977); Horowitz, *Ethnic Groups in Conflict*; David Lake and Donald Rothchild, "Containing Fear: The Origins and Management of Ethnic Conflict," *International Security*, vol. 21, no. 2 (Fall 1996); and Alicia Levine, "Political Accommodation and the Prevention of Secessionist Violence," in Michael E. Brown, ed., *The International Dimensions of Internal Conflict* (Cambridge: MIT Press, 1996), pp. 311–340.

23. See especially Juan Linz, "The Perils of Presidentialism," and "The Virtues of Parliamentarism," in Diamond and Plattner, *The Global Resurgence of Democracy*; and Sisk, *Power Sharing and International Mediation in Ethnic Conflict*, p. 53–54. For a dissenting view see Donald Horowitz, "Comparing Democratic Systems," in Diamond and Plattner, *The Global Resurgence of Democracy*.

24. Sisk, *Power Sharing and International Mediation in Ethnic Conflict*, p. ix. For additional criticisms of majoritarianism, see Lijphart, *Democracy in Plural Societies*, pp. 25–28 and 114–118; Horowitz, *Ethnic Groups in Conflict*, pp. 629–630; and Levine, "Political Accommodation and the Prevention of Secessionist Violence," p. 333–334.

25. See especially Dahl, *Polyarchy: Participation and Opposition*, p. 115.
26. John Darnton, "Africa Tries Democracy, Finding Hope and Peril," *New York Times*, June 21, 1994, p. A6.
27. Larry Diamond, "Three Paradoxes of Democracy," in Diamond and Plattner, *The Global Resurgence of Democracy*, p. 104.
28. Darnton, "Africa Tries Democracy," p. A1.
29. This, of course, assumes that the ruling party does not enact oppressive policies. If one-party rule becomes too tyrannical, war might once again become the more attractive alternative.
30. According to Adam Przeworski, these are the conditions that make elections so attractive to competing groups as they transition from authoritarian rule. See Przeworski, *Democracy and the Market: Political and Economic Reforms in Eastern Europe and Latin America* (Cambridge: Cambridge University Press, 1991).
31. For a more comprehensive discussion of the destabilizing effects of political liberalization in war-shattered states, see Roland Paris, "Peacebuilding and the Limits of Liberal Internationalism," *International Security*, vol. 22, no. 2 (Fall 1997), p. 56.
32. Henry C. Lockwood, *The Abolition of the Presidency*, pp. 191–192, cited in Edward S. Corwin, *The President: Office and Powers, 1787–1984* (New York: New York University Press, 1984).
33. For an excellent discussion of the importance of an integrated security force see Sisk, *Power Sharing and International Mediation in Ethnic Conflict*, p. 57.
34. Baumhoegger, *The Struggle for Independence*, vol. 6, p. 1129.
35. For criticisms see Sisk, *Power Sharing and International Mediation in Ethnic Conflict*, pp. 38–39; Brian Barry, "Review Article: Political Accommodation and Consociational Democracy," *British Journal of Political Science*, vol. 5 (October 1975), pp. 477–505; and Horowitz, *Ethnic Groups in Conflict*, p. 586.
36. William Finnegan, *A Complicated War: The Harrowing of Mozambique* (Berkeley: University of California Press, 1992), p. 4.
37. Deputy Assistant Secretary of State for Africa Roy Stacy, speaking at a donor's conference in Maputo, quoted in Thomas Ohlson, "Strategic Confrontation Versus Economic Survival in Southern Africa," in Francis M. Deng and I. William Zartman, eds., *Conflict Resolution in Africa* (Washington, D.C.: Brookings Institution, 1991).
38. Robert B. Lloyd, "Mozambique: The Terror of War, the Tensions of Peace," *Current History*, vol. 94 (April 1995), p. 153. For the theoretical underpinnings of this argument, see I. William Zartman, *Ripe for Resolution: Conflict and Intervention in Africa* (New York: Oxford University Press, 1985).
39. Eric Berman, *Managing Arms in Peace Processes: Mozambique* (Geneva: UN Institute for Disarmament Research, 1996), pp. 19–20.
40. See Thomas Ohlson and Stephen John Stedman, with Robert Davies, *The New Is Not Yet Born: Conflict Resolution in Southern Africa* (Washington, D.C.:

Brookings Institution, 1994), pp. 113–116. See also Chris Alden and Mark Simpson, "Mozambique: A Delicate Peace," *Journal of Modern African Studies*, vol. 31, no. 1 (March 1993), p. 126.

41. Foreword in Berman, *Managing Arms in Peace Processes*, pp. xi–xii.

42. Ibrahim Msabaha, "Negotiating an End to Mozambique's Murderous Rebellion," in I. William Zartman, ed., *Elusive Peace: Negotiating an End to Civil Wars* (Washington, D.C.: Brookings Institution, 1995), p. 210.

43. Berman, *Managing Arms in Peace Processes*, p. 21.

44. Cameron Hume, *Ending Mozambique's War: The Role of Mediation and Good Offices* (Washington, D.C.: U.S. Institute of Peace, 1994), p. 10.

45. Allen Isaacman, "Mozambique: Tugging at the Chains of Dependency," in Gerald J. Bender, James S. Coleman, and Richard Sklar, eds., *African Crisis Areas and U.S. Foreign Policy* (Berkeley: University of California Press, 1985); Helen Kitchen, *Angola, Mozambique, and the West* (New York: Praeger, 1987); and Msabaha, "Negotiating an End to Mozambique's Murderous Rebellion."

46. See Finnegan, *A Complicated War*, pp. 246–247.

47. Quotes taken from Hume, *Ending Mozambique's War*, p. 34.

48. Ibid., p. 59.

49. Ibid., p. 86.

50. Ibid., p. 60.

51. Ibid., p. 59.

52. Voice of Renamo: "Dhlakama says Frelimo Army launching attacks to stop him leaving for summit." August 4, 1992, Lexis/Nexis, Section: part 4, The Middle East, Africa, and Latin America; Mozambique Peace Talks; ME/1450/B/1.

53. Hume, *Ending Mozambique's War*, p. 62.

54. Ibid., p. 66.

55. Ibid., p. 67.

56. As quoted in ibid., p. 67.

57. Donald Rothchild has argued that one of the reasons Dhlaklama was willing to agree to the plan was because of side payments by British business. For an interesting analysis of this issue, see Donald Rothchild, *Managing Ethnic Conflict in Africa: Pressures and Incentives for Cooperation* (Washington, D.C.: Brookings Institution, 1997).

58. Hume, *Ending Mozambique's War*, p. 133.

59. Maria Cremilda Massingue, "Mozambique Opposition Renamo is Two-Edged Sword, Scholar Says," March 9, 1996. Lexis/Nexis, Section: International News.

60. John Fleming, "Mozambique Rebel Now Works Inside the System," *Christian Science Monitor*, November 19, 1996, p. 6.

61. For a more rigorous empirical examination of these cases as well as the full set of civil wars between 1940 and 1990, see Walter, "The Critical Barrier to Civil War Settlement."

62. Only two civil wars reached successful settlement without an outside guarantee (Colombia in 1958 and Yemen in 1970), yet these were also the only two cases where the opposing parties could not launch surprise attacks on each other. Both wars were fought by relatively uncommitted armies whose loyalties could be procured by the highest bidder and thus did not represent an immediate threat to either opponent. Thus, it appears as if Colombia and Yemen were exceptions that prove the rule.

63. See Dunstan M. Wai, *The African-Arab Conflict in the Sudan* (New York and London: Africana, 1981) p. 171.

64. The settlements in Chad and Uganda both included specific political guarantees. In neither of these cases, however, was an outside state willing to enforce the final agreement.

65. From the Varkiza Agreement as outlined in *Keesing's Contemporary Archives*, October 13–20, 1945, p. 7486.

66. *Keesing's Contemporary Archives*, February 1980, p. 30067.

67. Outside states, however, have been more willing to intervene to help resolve civil wars through negotiation since the end of the cold war and less willing to push for a complete military victory. This fact helps explain the higher rate of successful settlement in civil wars since 1990—a time when outsiders have been both more willing to encourage negotiations and more willing to send peacekeepers.

68. See especially John J. Mearsheimer, "The Only Exit From Bosnia," *New York Times*, October 7, 1997, p. A21; John J. Mearsheimer and Robert A. Pape, "The Answer: A Three-Way Partition Plan for Bosnia and How the U.S. Can Enforce It," *New Republic*, June 14, 1993; and Chaim Kaufmann, "Possible and Impossible Solutions to Ethnic Conflict," *International Security*, vol. 20, no. 4 (Spring 1996), pp. 136–175.

Part II

Case Studies

3   *Bosnia and Herzegovina: How Not to End Civil War*

Susan L. Woodward

> The United Nations can only help parties to conflict to make peace if they cooperate in the process. If parties are determined to fight, it is impossible for the United Nations to stop them.
>
> Thorwald Stoltenberg, United Nations Co-Chairman of the
> International Conference on the Former Yugoslavia

> If the parties don't want peace, we can't bring it to them.
>
> General John Shalikashvili, Chairman,
> Joint Chiefs of Staff, United States Armed Forces

On December 20, 1995, a NATO-led, sixty thousand–strong intervention force from thirty-four countries, including all sixteen NATO allies, entered the former Yugoslav republic of Bosnia and Herzegovina to assist in implementing a "general framework agreement for peace" negotiated the previous month under American auspices. Designed to end a brutal civil war lasting three and one half years between three former coalition parties and their foreign supporters over the fate of the republic and the three parties' claims to the right of self-determination when Yugoslavia dissolved, the framework was the eighth consecutive plan proposed by third-party negotiations to end the Bosnian war.[1] Although the talks producing this agreement were the result of whirlwind shuttle diplomacy by American diplomats in the Bosnian capital, Sarajevo, but also in the neighboring states supporting two of the three parties, Belgrade (Serbia) and Zagreb (Croatia), and then in proximity talks between those three parties (one of the Bosnian three and the two external patrons of the other two), and the framework was widely seen to be little more than a cease-fire, its premise was that it would only work if the agreement represented the mutual interest of the three Bosnian parties to cooperate in building a new state and peace. What distinguished this plan from the other eight, and led to high hopes for its success, was the willingness for the first time of the United States to contribute ground troops to an international force helping to implement these "Dayton accords."

The Implementation Force (IFOR) was deployed on a twelve-month mandate, from December 20, 1995, to December 20, 1996. Convinced that peace was not yet self-sustaining, NATO powers then sent a second deployment, a Stabilization Force (SFOR) of thirty-five thousand for another eighteen months. But that too appeared insufficient time by the fall of 1997, when military and civilian assessments were nearly unanimous that war would resume in Bosnia if the soldiers pulled out in June 1998, and NATO and American leaders decided that a third deployment would be necessary. It is therefore too soon to judge the role of third-party intervention in helping to bring a definitive end to the Bosnian war.

What the Bosnian case does suggest, thus far, is that the framework of the security dilemma is useful, in understanding both the deterioration in relations that led to war and the difficulties in translating a cease-fire agreement into a lasting peace. It also suggests, however, that the willingness of outsiders to send in troops to help break the security dilemma by reestablishing a secure environment is not sufficient if the negotiated agreement itself does not address the security fears of the population and the structural conditions that can create a security dilemma. If the outsiders who assist in ending the parties' civil war do not understand the security dilemma, or are unwilling to see it operating in the particular case, they can even intensify the security dilemma and prolong the perceptions of vulnerability that inhibit cooperation.[2] In part this lack of understanding can result from a misunderstanding of the difference between interstate and internal wars. Although useful analytically, the framework of the security dilemma cannot be transferred directly without refinements—the Bosnian case demonstrates—from its origins in an interstate context to the circumstances defining internal wars.

The Bosnian War

There would have been no war in Bosnia and Herzegovina if Yugoslavia had not first collapsed. Four years before the talks at Dayton, between June and December 1991, two of the of six republics in the Socialist Federal Republic of Yugoslavia, Slovenia and Croatia, declared their independence, and left the people of Bosnia and Herzegovina without a country. While politicians and citizens in the rest of the country had to adjust to this situation created by the secessions—would they try to create a smaller Yugoslavia, go their separate ways as four more independent states, or redraw borders in the remaining territory to create states more in line with national identities?—Western powers were also taking decisions, for example, that Slovenia and Croatia would be granted international recognition on the basis of the right to national self-determination but that the internal borders of the federal republics were henceforth the legitimate *international* borders of independent states. While this sounds simple enough, the problem with Bosnia and Herzegovina is that it was constituted in the Yugoslav system as the home of not one but three constitutionally recognized nations—Croats, Muslims, and Serbs.[3] Moreover, the Bosnian identity on which a new state would be based had been created by and for the post–World War II Yugoslav system: as a buffer to those in Croatia and in Serbia who claimed Bosnia as part of their national patrimony and as a federal unit to create, on the basis of size, a balance of power among the six units, as the beneficiary of the socialist leadership's commitment to national equality, and as the geographic center and physical repository—the "Dinaric Fortress"—of the country's independent national defense strategy. Could a common Bosnian identity, despite its venerable pre-Yugoslav origins, survive the collapse and delegitimation of that system when nationalist parties were winning in the north?

In January 1990 the ruling Yugoslav communist party—holding an extraordinary congress to address the political crisis—simply collapsed when its republican leaders could not agree and the Slovene delegation walked out. Multiparty elections for republican-level governments were held in each of the six republics, beginning in April in Slovenia and Croatia. The Bosnian electorate had less than one year, between the declarations in July of the intent to pursue independence and their elections in November, to reorient political identity and allegiance away from Titoism and Yugoslav socialism. Although the federal prime minister's reform party drew the largest votes of any republic and the renamed, former communist party held its own well, the majority of the electorate voted their individual national identities in

MAP 3.1. The Socialist Federal Republic of Yugoslavia
Source: Brookings Institution Press.

what was largely *defensive* positioning: "If my neighbors vote for a national party to which I don't belong, I had better vote mine." Political parties representing them as Muslims, Serbs, or Croats formed the parliamentary majority, and the largest of each formed a tripartite governing coalition, similar to the power-sharing formula of federal Yugoslavia, and proceeded to parcel out ministries, benefits, and jobs to their supporters proportionately.[4] Municipal and village governments, by contrast, tended toward majority rule by the party representing the largest national group locally.

But when it came to deciding the political fate of the republic itself and how to guarantee the former rights of each to self-determination when the umbrella that provided them mutual guarantees—the state of Yugoslavia— was disintegrating, no agreement could be reached. The dispute escalated rapidly, under the time pressure of external events. From tripartite collaboration in ruling Bosnia, politicians moved to bargaining over mutually incompatible preferences, accompanied by defensive mobilization for war and efforts to freeze out the opposition parties and civic groups fighting to prevent nationalist division and war, and then—when Alija Izetbegović, the chairman of the seven-person presidency and president of the SDA, declared Bosnian independence on March 4, 1992—to a three-sided civil war.

The choices facing the republic's politicians in 1991 were three: (1) to remain part of a new reduced Yugoslavia along with Serbia, Montenegro, and Macedonia, (2) to become an independent multinational state, or (3) to imitate the dissolution along national lines begun by Slovenia and Croatia. In the third choice Bosnian Croats and Bosnian Serbs would "secede" from Bosnia and Herzegovina and join up with co-nationals in neighboring Serbia and Croatia, changing the internal borders of federal Yugoslavia to accommodate a concept of nation-states, and Bosnian Muslims would in turn create their own nation-state in the territory that remained or in common with other Slavic-speaking Muslims in the former country.[5]

The first option was favored by Germany, which had pushed the European Community (EC) momentum toward recognizing Slovenia and Croatia, but Alija Izetbegović, representing both Bosnian Muslims and the Bosnian republic, rejected this option as early as November 1990.[6] The second option appealed to EC foreign ministers, in their attempt to dissolve Yugoslavia into its component federal republics so as not to change existing (internal) borders. To facilitate this choice, the EC began negotiations with the leaders of the three coalition partners on the internal political arrangements of an independent Bosnia and required them to hold a referendum of voters on independence. But the leaders of the Muslim and Croat parties had already violated the legal obligation of the Bosnian constitution that such decisions be taken by consensus the previous October when they declared, over Serb objections, Bosnian sovereignty, and again on December 21, 1991, when Izetbegović requested recognition of the EC, without consultations. Although Bosnian Serb leaders entered into the EC-sponsored negotiations, by all accounts sincerely, they viewed the decision to hold the referendum on February 28–March 1, 1992, before the negotiations had scarcely started, as another step deciding Bosnian fate without them. Serb voters overwhelmingly boycotted the referendum, but Izetbegović took the resounding yes vote from Muslims and Croats as sufficient to declare independence, on March 4, and the United States pressured its allies to recognize Bosnian independence immediately. When the EC (now using the term *European Union* [EU]) conceded, on April 6, long before their negotiators had reached an agreement, the second option ended, and a war for the third option began.

There were two difficulties in following the Slovene and Croatian path of nation states. The population of Bosnia was thoroughly intermixed, not segregated nationally in separate areas sufficient to the secession of two and a rump Bosnia, and on May 20 the international community gave international law standing to the second option, independence, by declaring the Republic of Bosnia and Herzegovina a sovereign member state of the United Nations according to its borders in federal Yugoslavia.

A voluntary choice of national identity on a census form and even an independent secret vote for a political party do not make a nation. To prepare Bosnians for separate statehood, individuals had to be separated from their mixed identities, mixed environments, rituals of intercommunal coexistence, and nonethnic political preferences and social interactions. The choice of violence and nationalist propaganda was to force people by fear and circumstance to separate psychologically and then physically into national groupings and then to persuade them that they were safe only in political independence from each other. There would have been no reason for violence if distinct cultural borders and territorial enclaves already existed or if individuals and families had moved voluntarily. The political conflict over national goals within Bosnia-Herzegovina thus became a war for territory and to lay the conditions for statehood: for two party-armies, a war against the international decision, and for the third, to get concrete international support behind its decision.

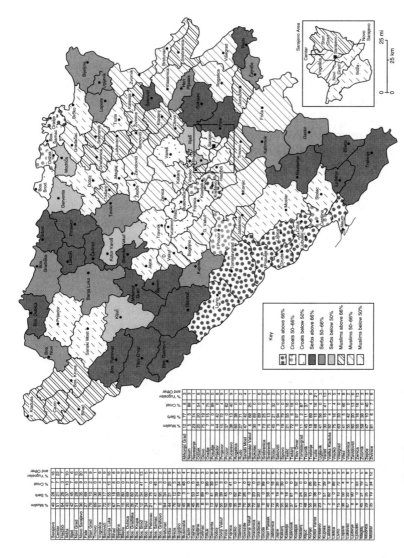

MAP 3.2. The Ethnonational Composition of Bosnia and Herzegovina, 1991
Source: Brookings Institution Press.

The Security Dilemma and Causes of War

Two explanations for the Bosnian war competed for attention in the myriad efforts by outsiders to stop the war. One was a thesis of ancient ethnic hatreds repressed by the communist regime. The death in 1980 of long-ruling dictator Josip Broz Tito, and the collapse in 1989–90 of communist regimes in the east were said to have removed the lid of repression and restraints of the cold war.[7] One version cited a historical conflict between Serbs and Croats that had led to war in Croatia in 1991 and also motivated the presidents of the republics of Croatia and Serbia to plan to divide Bosnia between them, with Muslims trapped in between. Another version saw these hatreds as internal to Bosnia, arguing that its three peoples had never been at peace except when an external force kept them from civil war.

The second explanation for war was predatory leaders who used nationalism and war to deflect attention from needed economic and political reforms that threatened their basis of power and political position.[8] Although there were several candidates for this explanation, all focused on the president of Serbia, Slobodan Milošević, because it was Serbs in Croatia (though fewer than one-third of them) and Serbs in Bosnia (though Croats as well) who took up arms against the peaceful secession of Croatia and Bosnia-Herzegovina from Yugoslavia. But when Milošević is said to have planned the two wars by inciting the Serbs to rebel and sending them aid in order to fulfill a nineteenth-century dream of Serb nationalists to create a Greater Serbia by expanding the borders of the Serbian federal republic, the argument becomes confused—melding, on the one hand, with this first thesis of historical conflicts, and on the other hand, with a nationalist argument attributing expansionism to Serbs *as a people*.[9]

The factual evidence for both these hypotheses is slim. While the collapse of Yugoslavia was an extremely complex process, its *dynamic*, and thus an analysis of its causes, can actually be captured usefully by the concept of a security dilemma and its spiraling behavior. Although the Yugoslav federal government continued to function up to the end in the second half of 1991, its authority and especially its enforcement power had declined so much during the 1980s (under the attack of republican politicians unwilling to compromise their autonomy and economic power for a common reform of the federal government, the budgetary strictures and financial-system reform requirements of an IMF debt-repayment program to stabilize the currency and create a market economy, and quarrels over political reforms that would provide the legal basis for a such an economy and a postsocialist democratic government) that the context of its dissolution could be said to resemble the conditions of anarchy in which a security dilemma in international relations is said to occur. Politicians in each republic jockeyed for republican (state) gains in the contest over economic and political reform and justified their fight in terms of "national" interests and rights, and they increasingly rejected or ignored federal authority in their republics such that the situation became increasingly anarchic. Federal politicians had no enforcement power if the republican leaders did not themselves consent. These leaders did not represent independent states seeking security, but in seeking to satisfy the interests of their republic and their own power by using the argument of national rights—and in the case of Slovenia and Croatia, building up separate armies to defend a fight for independence—they approximated the behavior associated by realists with the international system where information failures (and deliberate distortion), declining trust and credibility, and escalating armament (by individuals, localities, paramilitaries, and eventually separate armies) make cooperation on a mutually agreed outcome ever more difficult to achieve.

The structural condition associated with generating a security dilemma was reinforced by several particularities of the domestic Yugoslav (and subsequently Bosnian) scenes. First, the prewar Yugoslav system emphasized *rights* more than interests. But these rights were guaranteed by the overarching institutions of the federal government, in which each group could feel safe in its rights without denying rights to others. When the system's political contract of national equality and individual welfare could no longer be supported financially or normatively under the budgetary austerities of macroeconomic stabilization, debt repayment, and economic reform in the 1980s, then political nationalism began to take an exclusionary form. Individuals and politicians first claimed social and economic rights for their national group against others, as they faced worsening unemployment, frozen wages, and declining welfare funds, and then escalated those claims to political rights over capital assets and territory in moves toward exclusive states' rights for the republics, in the name of their majority nation instead of equality and, eventually, independence. The apparently zero-sum character of the economic and constitutional conflicts made it even more difficult to arrive at cooperative solutions when the overarching institutions began to succumb to the republics' increasing refusal to recognize federal authority whenever they saw it to be against their own interests.

Second, while the politicians' claims for states' rights were made in terms of the constitutionally guaranteed right to *national* self-determination, settlement patterns did not conform. These claims made the many people in each republic who were not of the majority national group feel vulnerable, in some cases as a result of real discrimination by public authorities. The lack of congruence between national identity and republican borders raised doubts about the stability of borders and created uncertainty for all those who lived in mixed communities, such as border areas in Croatia and much of central and eastern Bosnia, about fundamental rights of citizenship and political loyalty. This was particularly strong where people who did not belong to the majority nation in a republic held a local majority and could thus contemplate and demand autonomy or even a change of borders where they concentrated territorially. Most important, all national groups in Yugoslavia were numerically minorities. Nationalist calls for majority rule for *their* national group, in the context of a federal government increasingly unable to enforce legal protections of national equality, translated directly into fears of becoming a minority after four decades of entitlement to equal treatment and governmental protection.

Nowhere was this more acute than in Bosnia and Herzegovina, where Muslims formed a plurality (43.7 percent in 1991, up from 39.5 percent in 1981); Serbs had been a plurality of 42.8 percent in 1961 but had declined in proportion by 1991 to one-third (31.4 percent, but about 40 percent, if one adds the many Serbs who identified as "Yugoslavs" in 1991 and had to choose an ethnic identity when Yugoslavia ended), and Croats were only 17.3 percent. But within the context of Yugoslavia, Muslims were a small minority (a countrywide total of 10 percent in 1991). Rhetorical support from Croatia and Serbia to Bosnian Croats and Bosnian Serbs was enough to make Muslims feel a truly vulnerable minority, whereas Muslim politicians' insistence on an integral and independent Bosnia, in which Croats and Serbs would become a minority, made the latter two groups feel truly vulnerable.

Third, the resources held by each group were different, which enhanced each group's perceptions of being a minority at risk. Unlike the oft-cited, and misunderstood, nonviolent breakup of Czechoslovakia, in which the Czechs held dominant economic wealth, political power, and international support, in Yugoslavia the resources of economic wealth, political power, armaments, and international patrons were spread unequally among regions and groups and with insufficient cumulative impact to make one group clearly stronger or weaker. People also tended to perceive the resources of others—such as economic power over government policy, international patrons, demographic increase, or government jobs in the police or army—as more threatening (in the language of the security dilemma, more "offensively capable") than their own.

Fourth, despite the realist's argument that the international system is anarchic, the cold war was an international regime with norms, rules, and legitimate authorities that directly shaped the identity, interests, and power of Yugoslavia and imposed constraints that had a stabilizing result. When that international regime began to collapse, between 1985 and 1989, Yugoslavia found itself in a truly anarchic situation with all the uncertainty about its existence, its identity, and its access to finance, trading partners, and military alliances possible. When the republics stopped accepting the federal government as final arbiter in domestic competition for rights and privileges, the efforts of the international community to provide a substitute arbiter through mediation, beginning in June-July 1991 with the EC and the Conference on Security and Cooperation in Europe (CSCE), did nothing to reduce that external uncertainty or to facilitate communication that could vitiate the perception of zero-sum choices and defensive positioning between Slovenia, Croatia, Serbia, and the federal authorities (especially the army).

Finally, one might also add, although this effect is difficult to calculate, that the insecurities engendered by economic decline, particularly for the middle strata whose standards of living had risen consistently for almost thirty years, might have been exacerbated by a social organization that emphasized individualized rather than collective means of improving one's prospects and living standards, by a culture of distrust, grown in the soil of peasant society, a *longue durée* of externally imposed uncertainty, and arbitrary rule, and by localized systems of information (radio, TV, newspapers, and journals revolved within republics and regions, in contrast to political networks, which spanned the country).

It is in this structural context that the role of politicians becomes critical, not because they were attempting to gain or hold onto power, as all politicians do, but because of the arguments they chose to legitimize that power and their claims in the constitutional and economic conflicts of the 1980s. The politicians' rhetoric of national rights and loyalties centered on *survival*, arguing that the fate of the individual depended on the fate of the group, that the relevant group was the nation because it held rights to sovereignty, and that the role of the group for the individual and of the politician for the group was *protection*. Politicians in the wealthier republics began with the argument that their nation was being exploited economically by others, through the system of taxes and transfers underlying social equality and regional development, and that individuals' rights and well-being were best protected by national leaders.[10] Those whose population was declining numerically aroused fears about the loss of cultural identity through assimilation of a larger group. Political rhetoric claiming national groups to be *endangered* (*ugrožen*) by *other* national groups or leaders gave permission to individual acts of discrimination and harassment that governments, in the fever of political transition and first-time democratic election and campaigning, were particularly careless about prosecuting. Eventually politicians even resorted to warnings about the danger of *genocide* against their people — to mobilize supporters and loyalty through the political capital of revived memories of World War II and to invoke the collective obligation to solidarity of all who identified with that nation throughout the country.[11]

The months leading to war in Bosnia and Herzegovina were filled with threats and counterthreats by the leaders of the three nationalist parties ruling the republic, each maneuvering toward a political outcome from the perspective of national sovereignty. As Bougarel writes, the "conflict resulted less from a unilateral act of aggression than from a spiral of verbal, institutional, and physical violence."[12] The success of such rhetoric depends on credibility, however, and this was a result not of personal or group antagonisms in Bosnia but of the growing political uncertainty about the fate of the country after July 1990, when the governments elected in Slovenia and Croatia announced their intentions to pursue independence and when Serbian leaders including President Milošević responded by calling for new borders to include all Serbs in a Serbian state. In mid-1990 the Bosnian population "pronounced itself 74 per cent in favour of a ban on nationally or confessionally based parties," but "six months later, vote[d] in the same proportion for precisely such parties."[13]

The spiral had begun, according to Bougarel, with this breakdown of the political conception of Bosnian society, which was rapidly followed, according to a "deep logic of Bosnian society, reminiscent of the sociological theories of the 'prisoner's dilemma' and the 'self-fulfilling prophecy,'" by a breakdown in the "everyday conception of community relations."

> The practice of *komšiluk* (the culture of good neighborliness) . . . represents not so much abstract tolerance or social interaction, as a permanent guarantee of the pacific nature of relations between the communities, and thus of the security of each of them. If political developments place a question-mark over this pacific nature, each community will seek to ensure its security through communitarian

mobilisation and isolation, tending in this way to reinforce the general feeling of insecurity and precipitate breakdown in the codes of *komšiluk*.[14]

Leaders of the nationalist parties actually collaborated to persuade voters that their security depended on voting their national identity (or making a choice in the many cases of mixed identity) and even to vote for another nation's party rather than to give their vote to a non-nationalist party. The turning point cited by most Bosnian citizens, however, comes much later, at the moment when guns appeared in the hands of neighbors, shooting was heard in the village or armed thugs in various uniforms knocked down the door, or snipers and mortars took deadly aim at urban crowds of civilians. Seeking protection for their physical selves where they could, some fled, as families or as whole villages; others looked to neighbors, finding aid unpredictably and independent of ethnic loyalties; others armed or joined militias or armies. As social anthropologist Tone Bringa shows in her award-winning video documentary, *We Are All Neighbors*, the cohesion of *komšiluk* in a mixed Muslim-Croat village northwest of Sarajevo lasted long into the war. There the disappearance of neighborliness and the reluctant flight of its Muslim inhabitants occur practically overnight when an artillery gun of the HVO (Bosnian Croat army) simply appears on the hill overlooking the village. Moreover, for almost a year before the war began, petty arms dealers were having a field day in the growing sense of insecurity. A Bosnian journalist writes:

In downtown Sarajevo, in front of the Grand Hotel Europa, petty thieves and smugglers offered pistols, small-caliber sniper rifles, Kalashnikovs, and bazookas. The dealing went on freely, as though potatoes and not guns were being traded. In the more conservative heartland the strategy was the following. In a village populated by a Serb majority the arms dealer would gather a group of better-off men, and would warn them he had information that the Muslims of a neighboring village were preparing to attack. He would then offer arms for self-defense. The story would spread rapidly through the village. Not knowing what to believe, people would come to check out the sale. Seeing others buy, they would buy themselves. It seemed imprudent not to. Often, all arms would be gone in a day. The dealer would then move on to the neighboring, predominantly Muslim village, telling the same story, this time about the Serbs preparing the attack. Many people were borrowing money or selling livestock to buy a gun.[15]

The day before European recognition of Bosnian independence, the Bosnian presidency received a report estimating 600,000 armed persons in a republic of 4.4 million, in addition to the official stockpiles, armaments factories, and military installations of Yugoslavia's system of all-national defense.[16]

Thus, those who argue that there was no security dilemma in the run up to violence in Croatia and in Bosnia because this is a structural argument that ignores agency and thus denies leaders' culpability for *manufacturing* fears and defensiveness miss the point of the security dilemma: that it is perceptions that matter, and that it is a relational dynamic between two or more actors that leads to violence.[17] For example, to understand the fears and defensive positioning that led Bosnian Serb leaders to abandon political negotiations and shift to war in April 1992 does not excuse them from the consequences of that decision. But the context of that preemptive strike, based on warnings and fears fully broadcast in advance, includes (1) President Izetbegović's defection the previous October and December from the constitutional obligation that all three nations reach consensus; (2) the decision of the United States to reenter the conflict in support of President Izetbegović's request for immediate recognition and of the EU decision to ignore Bosnian constitutionality and the explicit warnings of the EU's Arbitration Commission when most Serbs boycotted the referendum; and (3) the March exodus of the Yugoslav federal army from Croatia, where they had been protecting Serbs in border areas (and by implication in Bosnia), to be replaced by United Nations peacekeepers monitoring a cease-fire agreement. Actions provoke reactions, particularly when each side is thinking defensively, is perceived by others to be acting aggressively, and there is no external authority or arbiter to reverse the spiral.

As for the explanation of ancient ethnic hatreds, the context of the Yugoslav conflict, as it moved from Slovenia to Croatia to Bosnia-Herzegovina and drew in outside powers such as Germany, appeared to many to imitate World War II. Those who first perceived themselves at risk as minorities in nationalizing states—Serbs in Croatia and in northern Bosnia, as well as many officers in the Yugoslav army from these regions—had memories of genocidal victimization at the hands of fascists in Croatia and Bosnia during that war, which contributed powerfully to the credibility of politicians and arms dealers who told them they were at risk again. As de Figueiredo and

Weingast argue, hate-mongering or fear-inciting leaders must have material to work with. In 1990–91 this included the rhetoric of nationalist politicians and actual acts of discrimination that helped confirm the groups' worst fears.

By not understanding this dynamic interaction between leaders and be-tween leaders and followers in causing the wars in Croatia and Bosnia, out-siders missed many opportunities to prevent war and even helped to exac-erbate the conflict and prolong the Bosnian war.[18] The same understanding applies to the effort to bringing the Bosnian war to an end, when both manufactured and justified fears for physical safety, loss of identity, and lack of protection in the future were no longer a matter of political rhetoric and historical memory but immediate experience.

Critical to an evaluation of third-party efforts to end the Bosnian war was the belief of the chief external negotiators of the Dayton framework for peace that the Bosnian war was *not* caused, even in part, by a security dilemma. Although interpretations varied substantially among different commanders of the international military force sent to implement the military aspects of the accords, the American principals did little to hide their conviction that the war was caused by Serbian aggression under direction from the president of Serbia, Slobodan Milošević, aimed at carving up Bosnia to create a Greater Serbia and carried out by Bosnian Serbs. At the same time, they rejected the argument of ancient ethnic hatreds, seeing a common interest among the vast majority of Bosnians in ending the war and a legacy of multiethnic coexistence and cooperation that could resume once predatory leaders were removed from the scene.

As the epigraphs to this chapter reveal, however, such an international undertaking may even have to assume the possibility of cooperation among former warring peoples. The question is whether the settlement and the actions of these outsiders to assist its implementation are designed to remove the obstacles to cooperation or are based on the wrong assumption and make those obstacles worse instead.

The Settlement and the Security Dilemma

The Dayton accords—negotiated in Ohio by the presidents of Bosnia, Croatia, and Serbia and signed by them at Paris on December 14 along with representatives of the United States, Britain, France, and the European Un-ion—committed them all to the second option of 1991, which had been adopted in spring 1992 by the international community: the "sovereignty, territorial integrity, and political independence" of Bosnia and Herzegovina.

At the same time, the accords built on two cease-fire agreements, both also a result of American diplomatic initiative, which effectively recognized the political intentions and military power of the three parties who had gone to war. The first, signed in Washington in March 1994, aimed to stop the war between Bosnian Muslims and Bosnian Croats by creating a federation of two equal parties and a military alliance directed against the Serbs—restoring, in other words, the parliamentary alliance of October-December 1991 and the military alliance of June 1992. The second cease-fire covered the entire country, agreed upon in two installments by representatives of Croatia, Yugoslavia, and Bosnia between September 14 and October 5, and effective October 10, 1995, and only after a NATO bombing campaign and a joint Croatian- and Bosnian-army (primarily Muslims) ground campaign in August and September had pushed Serb forces from 35 percent of the land they then held. The November political agreement obliged the three party-armies to translate their cease-fires into peace and to work together to create a single state. No borders could be changed, and no secession permitted.

The result of the war, however, had been the division of Bosnian territory and its population into three separately governed and nearly ethnically pure areas. More than half the population had become refugees in neighboring Yugoslavia and Croatia or farther afield (the large majority were in Germany, many others in Sweden, Switzerland, and Austria). The half remaining in Bosnia were in areas controlled by their national majority—an uneasy coexistence between original inhabitants and persons expelled from other parts of the republic or from neighboring Croatia, squatting in abandoned homes or in holding centers run by international humanitarian agencies, who had little in common except their declared national identity and being alive.

The Dayton framework addressed this contradiction between goal and reality by combining elements of each party's objectives. In compensation to the two parties whose war aims were denied, the country would be divided, as the cease-fire agreements set, between two substantially self-governing entities—a Bosnian Muslim–Bosnian Croat Federation and a Serb Republic. They would be linked into one state with a weak central government and power-sharing arrangements between the three national groups. At the same time, the negotiators took a stand against the forced resettlement of the population and insisted, in a policy aimed at reversing the "ethnic cleansing" of the war, that all persons have the right to return to their prewar homes.

Eleven annexes to the general framework set out the tasks and obligations of the parties and the commitment of the international community to assist in abolishing military confrontation lines and restoring countrywide freedom of movement, establishing common political and economic institutions, facilitating a restoration of the prewar multiethnic settlement pattern, and cooperating with an international tribunal (set up at The Hague in October 1993) to judge culpability for war crimes.

Behind the accords lie a number of heroic assumptions that are compatible with the logic of the security dilemma and its role in civil war termination: (1) that the signatures on the accord were sincere, representing a binding agreement among the parties to cooperate and accept the peace agreement as their own; (2) that the Bosnian population (both soldiers and civilians of all three national communities) were largely unwilling participants in the war, victims of their leaders' extremist nationalism and fear-mongering; (3) that the indictment of leaders held responsible for the population displacements (called ethnic cleansing) as war criminals and their removal from Bosnia to be tried in The Hague would eliminate the primary obstacles to elite-level cooperation in building a postwar state and to mass reintegration; and (4) that a twelve-month foreign military presence replacing the warring armies with a "secure environment" would free citizens from their security fears and vulnerabilities to return to former neighborhoods, reestablish old friendships, and rediscover mutual interests in peace and commerce. The design of the accords also directly addressed the structural conditions that can give rise to a security dilemma and to individuals' fears at three levels: military demobilization, territorial sovereignty, and an authoritative government.

Military Demobilization

The first task—laid out in a carefully crafted, detailed annex (1-A) on the military aspects of the peace settlement—was to separate armies and begin their demobilization. The United Nations Security Council agreed to authorize, and NATO to organize and command, a multinational military implementation force (IFOR) to assist in this task, thus providing the reassurance needed in the vulnerable period between cease-fire and peace. Heavily armed, with robust rules of engagement, IFOR was deployed throughout the country, with particular attention to the interentity boundary line between the federation and Serb republic that had become the final military confrontation line. It was to supervise the withdrawal of armed forces behind a four mile zone of separation, the cantonment of all heavy weapons, and the demobilization of more than half those under arms. As confidence-

and security-building measures between former enemies, IFOR also convened and chaired joint local and countrywide military commissions in which army officers met frequently to share information, inspections, and future plans on military holdings, exercises, and movements.

NATO officials followed a strict timetable for the separation of forces and within six months had moved on to the task of consolidating the peace, by destroying unreported caches of weapons as soon as they were found, stopping unauthorized movement of tanks, artillery, and aircraft, and ordering police carrying more than the allowed number of sidearms, rifles, and ammunition to hand them over. They were also tasked to monitor compliance with an arms control agreement negotiated with the parties in Vienna in June 1996. After the initial twelve months, a second deployment about half the size of IFOR—a Stabilization Force (SFOR)—extended the international military presence an additional eighteen months to continue to provide the stabilizing "security environment" for the other tasks and actors in the peace process and for the continued cooperation in sharing information among officers of the three armies. At the end of that eighteen months yet another NATO mandate to prolong the SFOR presence was agreed upon, one that replaced the previous time limits with six-monthly reviews assessing progress toward a "sustainable peace."

Territorial Sovereignty

The theory of the security dilemma assumes that borders are given and a government exists. Neither were true for Bosnia. In addition to these classic peacekeeping tasks of military separation, demobilization, and confidence building, which security dilemma theorists consider the core of civil war termination, peace would not emerge if the uncertainty regarding the sanctity of Bosnia's borders and that resulting from the absence of a functioning government were not also substantially reduced. These two additional layers of security, in fact, are related in cases of ethnonationalist conflict. Clearly, as Fen Hampson argues from his comparative study, "the success of a peace settlement is inextricably tied to the interests of neighboring regional powers and their overall commitment to the peace process. Where such a commitment is lacking, the risk of failure is higher."[19] In addition to neighbors' respect for a country's borders, however, studies of ethnic tolerance within a country demonstrate a direct relation between individuals' perceptions that their country's borders are secure or threatened and their levels of ethnic tolerance or intolerance toward groups of the same ethnicity as neighbors who are potential threats.[20] The success of the United Nations military deployment to the northern and western borders of Macedonia in preventing its descent into war along with Bosnia in 1992–97, although attributed to its role as a trip wire against Serbian aggression from the north, was clearly its contribution to internal stability at a time when the republic's independence had not yet been recognized internationally and was actively challenged by neighboring Greece. According to Macedonian officials, the greatest effect of the border deployment was to calm domestic tensions that might well have spiraled into interethnic violence.

It is not necessary to argue that the Bosnian war was an act of aggression from Serbia or Croatia aimed at carving up Bosnia to create a greater Serbia or a greater Croatia in order to see that their military and supply support to Bosnian co-nationals fighting for national self-determination (whether as territorial autonomy in Bosnia or secession to join Serbia and Croatia) was sufficient to evoke a defensive response from Bosnian Muslims. At the same time, the preemptive recognition of Bosnian independence by the EU and the United States exacerbated the fears of Bosnian Serbs and Bosnian Croats about what it would mean to be subordinate to a Bosnian Muslim majority in an independent Bosnia. Bosnian Muslim leaders responded that their only means of survival as a nation after the breakup of Yugoslavia was their own state. The wartime destruction of their physical and cultural presence (through population expulsions, rape, or murder, razing of mosques, burning of libraries and cultural monuments, and so forth) in areas claimed by Bosnian Serbs and Bosnian Croats, considered by many to be a genocide, certainly gave credibility to this claim.

To break the spiral of these mutual perceptions of threat and very real danger, the Dayton negotiators insisted that the presidents of Croatia and Serbia be party to the talks and cosignators on the agreement, committing them to Bosnian sovereignty within its prewar borders. Of the three Bosnian parties, they invited only the Bosnian Muslim leader, President Izetbegović to represent the undivided sovereignty of Bosnia and to sign for all its citizens. Although some parts of the accord were also submitted to the Bosnian Croat leader, Krešimir Zubak, he signed as president of the Bosnian Muslim–Bosnian Croat Federation, and the proximity talks would not begin until the Bosnian Serbs had signed over their authority to negotiate and commit to the president of Serbia. International commitment came in the signatures of the presidents of the United States, United Kingdom, and France, and the head of the European Union.

In addition to this personal commitment to Bosnian borders, the accords contained provisions for arms control between the three states — Bosnia, Croatia, and Yugoslavia (Serbia and Montenegro).[21] This second military annex,

1-B, on "regional stabilization," prescribed negotiations on regional confi-
dence- and security-building measures, a subregional arms control regime
of military balance of equipment and forces, calculated in proportion to
population on the ratio 5:2:2 for Yugoslavia: Croatia: Bosnia, and a regional
arms control agreement under the auspices and force-reduction principles
of the Organization of Security and Cooperation in Europe (OSCE). The
OSCE also accepted responsibility for subsequent supervision and monitoring of the negotiated limits. All military forces of foreign origin in Bosnia at
the time of the peace agreement (not only those from neighboring states but
especially "advisors, freedom fighters, trainers, volunteers, and personnel"
from Islamic states and groups assisting Bosnian Muslims) were required to
leave, with their equipment, within thirty days of the signing at Paris.

Nonetheless, NATO commanders refused the request of the Bosnian
Muslim leadership (made repeatedly since six months before the war began)
to deploy forces on the external borders against foreign threats. Priority remained on ending the internal hostilities and preventing their resumption
at potential hotspots within the country. The task of the military deployment
was to assist the Bosnian parties in restoring cooperation, ignoring the role
that certainty about the border plays in internal conflict and uncertainty.

Authoritative Government

The third structural condition inducing uncertainty that needed remedy
was the absence of a common government, economic system, and institutions to enforce, sanction, and monitor individual rights. The Dayton accords actually contain a constitution aimed at reassuring members of all
three communities that they would not be endangered minorities and could
safely shift from fighting to political activity. The right of national self-
determination is institutionalized by power-sharing arrangements for all government offices the three communities held in common, substantial devo-
lution of power and jurisdiction (including defense) away from the central
government to the two entities—the Federation and Republika Srpska, a
federation further subdivided into ten cantons (three Croat-majority, five
Muslim-majority, and two "mixed" in which Croats and Muslims share
power), and a political system based on representation and rights according
to national identity and ethnic subdivisions. The presidency is a committee
of three, one for each of the three nations, with a rotating chair. The upper
house of the State parliament has five Bosniacs, five Croats, and five Serbs;
although the lower house does not specify national qualifications, its mem-

bership is elected proportionally "within their respective entity," meaning one-third from each of the three nations. International administrators even went further, in making appointments to official commissions for the transitional period, by reaching for "a Bosniac, a Croat, and a Serb" to make decisions on elections, human rights, displaced persons and refugees, national monuments, transportation, and public corporations. Citizens can choose their residence freely and vote accordingly, but they can only be elected to the presidency and upper house in the territory identified with "their" national identity. Even voting rules and decision-making procedures were written into the constitution to guard against what was apparently seen as the greatest danger to citizens—the possible tyranny of one national group over another.[22] For example, the parliament can only take decisions by qualified majority. Any one of its three constituent nations can choose to define an issue in its vital interests, block proceedings by abstention, and return to its provincial assembly for a vote, followed by a vote in parliament requiring a majority of each nation (and two-thirds if the decision at issue was made by the presidency) and tallied by entity (and by nation within the federal entity). Citizenship is held within the entity, although the Bosnian government adopted an overall law on citizenship and can also issue papers, and special relations can be established between the Bosniac–Bosnian Croat Federation and neighboring Croatia, to reassure Bosnian Croats, and between the Republika Srpska and neighboring Yugoslavia, to reassure Bosnian Serbs.[23]

It was particularly important to the American contingent in the international operation that a postwar government be elected as soon as possible. They saw a functioning government as taking over the provision of internal security once the separation of forces had taken place, and so the Dayton accords required elections within ten months. Although widely criticized by human rights groups, commentators, and even by the secretary general of the organization responsible for organizing the entire election process and supervising the elections, the OSCE, who said it was too soon to guarantee conditions for free and fair elections, the American heading the OSCE mission in Bosnia insisted they be held on September 14, 1996, for all-Bosnian, entity-level, and cantonal (in the federation) presidents and legislatures. Only at the last minute did he decide that conditions were too insecure to proceed with municipal elections. The international officials coordinating implementation of the nonmilitary aspects of the peace agreement (the Office of the High Representative [OHR]) also compiled a "quick-start package" (QSP) listing all of the offices, committees, agencies, and commissions that would have to be created and filled by the newly elected governments as well as drafts of all major legislation necessary to establish common institutions, such as a central bank, a common currency, and harmonized customs and tax laws. After almost two months' delay negotiating innumerable compromises to get the three presidents to meet together (such as the terms by which Bosnian Serb President Krajišnik would swear loyalty to a Bosnian state and where to meet), the QSP became a matter of daily pressure on the parties to execute and legislate.

Measures to reassure the population and reduce uncertainty about their future also included economic reconstruction, an International Police Task Force (IPTF) to monitor and reform local police, and human rights monitoring. Critical in the minds of the outsiders assisting the peace process in Bosnia was the belief that economic incentives can bring parties to cooperate and that economic revival is the primary confidence-building measure of the process. A massive World Bank- and EU-led program of economic reconstruction and a shift among bilateral donors from humanitarian aid to reconstruction assistance were based on the view that economic activity can wean leaders from war, replace war profits with commercial profit, shift the balance of power to businesses interested in peace, and bring individuals from all sides of the war back into contact through markets and trade. Particularly in the first year after war, economic reconstruction was seen as providing a "peace dividend" to ordinary Bosnians and jobs for demobilized soldiers so that the population would not be as easily mobilizable for renewed war if leaders so chose. The freedom of movement necessary to restoring commerce and contact, and particularly the efforts by individuals to cross former front lines and return to homes located in areas governed by another national group, were to be given overall protection by the presence of international troops, if not specific personal protection.[24] International organizations ranging from nongovernmental organizations such as Human Rights Watch to international organizations tasked with helping to implement provisions of the accords, such as the OSCE, OHR, and IPTF, were present to provide publicity and transparency against those who might violate individuals' rights. The fact that they did not have enforcement power, however, was to present numerous ongoing problems.[25] The accords mandated a Commission of Human Rights for all Bosnia, and an ombudsman for each entity, to act as a check on government officials by giving publicity to violations of individual rights and initiating a process of judicial protection.

But most important in the mind of the Dayton negotiators was to break the link between leaders they saw as inciting nationalist hostility and the vulnerable mass of the population. They thus gave priority to the obligation on all parties to the accords to cooperate fully with the International Criminal Tribunal for the Former Yugoslavia in delivering to The Hague and trial all those leaders indicted as war criminals. When this did not happen immediately they went further, threatening to withhold economic aid from any Bosnian community that did not cooperate with the work of the tribunal. All persons indicted for such crimes were not allowed to run for office or play any other public role and were liable to arrest and extradition by the international troops. In implementing the agreement, the international authorities also sought to isolate these leaders further and to create independent television and radio stations and employ monitors of the mass media to reduce the distortion and hostility toward other groups that still characterized the media in each of the three communities; by summer-fall 1997 they were actively taking control of TV transmitters in the Serb Republic and imposing rules on mass media in both Serb and Croat areas. Beyond using the tribunal as a transitional mechanism before local courts and judges were up and running, the program to downsize and train the civilian police forces included a vetting process to prevent indicted war criminals from becoming members of the postwar police. In addition, an American organization, the United States Institute of Peace, lobbied among Bosnian groups and leaders for a Bosnian Truth and Reconciliation Commission, patterned after the South African experience, which looked set to be adopted and embraced by public opinion in late 1998.

A Closer Look at the Settlement

History has taught us that not a single honest man of ours can be unarmed; every single one will have a rifle to defend himself.

President Izetbegović, speaking at an election rally in Goražde, May 4, 1996, in his first public appearance after signing the Dayton accords[26]

Conditions in Bosnia after the first thirty-two months of peace implementation raise serious doubts about the Dayton negotiators' assumptions. Twelve months' deployment under IFOR proved insufficient to reassure the interveners that war would not resume, as did the subsequent eighteen months' deployment of SFOR. Public opinion in Bosnia shared this concern, ranging from 68 percent of Bosnian Muslims to 82 percent of Bosnian Croats in January 1997 that fighting would start again in a few years.[27] The behavior of neighboring states, particularly Croatia, continued to keep alive the external threat that Bosnia would eventually be partitioned by its neighbors, while the election campaign rhetoric of the three ruling parties continued to emphasize insecurity and protection, aiming to persuade citizens that their future safety depended on separation and defense through majority control by their own nation.[28] The SDA slogan in 1996 said it best: "A vote for the SDA is a vote for survival of the Muslim nation."

Voters rewarded this rhetoric by voting overwhelmingly for the three nationalist parties in the September 1996 elections.[29] In public opinion surveys in January 1997 94 percent of Bosnian Serb respondents believed that the Serb Republic should become part of Serbia (66 percent felt so strongly), and 79 percent of Bosnian Croats felt that Herzegovina should be part of Croatia (55 percent strongly); 91 percent of Bosnian Serbs and 84 percent of Bosnian Croats thought it "better for us to be independent than to remain part of Bosnia." In contrast to 98 percent of Bosnian Muslims who supported a single state for Bosnia and Herzegovina, and who based this support "in part on a sense of self-preservation,"[30] 94 percent Bosnian Serbs and 62 percent Bosnian Croats opposed a single state.[31] Many were also voting with their feet. In the first year after Dayton more than 80,000 Bosnians left their homes to move from an area where they were in the minority to one where they were with people of their own national group. Two years after the accord fewer than 30,000 of the 380,000 persons who had returned to their prewar homes did so if their home was in an area controlled by another group.[32] Bosnia was therefore becoming *less* multiethnic after Dayton, not more. The most striking figures were the exodus of Bosnian Croats, whose numbers in Bosnia had dwindled by November 1997 from a prewar population of 755,895 (17 percent) to fewer than 400,000 (9 percent) and, by some official reports in Croatia, to only 220,000 (5 percent).[33] Efforts by international organizations to facilitate return were obstructed by local authorities and citizens' groups on all sides who prevented people of other national groups from returning home to communities where they would dilute the absolute control of one national group or might become a Trojan Horse of renewed hostilities. The primary violators of human rights were the civilian police, and politicians in the federation harshly criticized the ombudsmen's reports of human rights violations as being disloyal to their nation.

If peace in Bosnia depends on overcoming fear and the obstacles to cooperation across the divisions of war, the experience of the first twenty-four months was not encouraging. To listen to international officials in the peace operation on the ground, the greatest threat to the Dayton accords was fear, "even if in some cases this is paranoia."[34] Like the Cambodian settlement, as analyzed by Michael Doyle, the Dayton accords had not altered the ambitions or goals of the three political leaderships and their political parties, reduced the insecurity felt by citizens about their future, or shifted power and responsibility to persons with different interests and goals.[35] The accords established a cease-fire in which the war continued by other means, and none had renounced the resort to violence to achieve those goals.[36]

Why should this be the case with a massive international presence in support of peace? Two explanations gained early prominence. One was that the Dayton accords represented a *process* that needed time—at least five years before one should assess success or failure. The other was that peace was a matter of *political will* and that as long as indicted war criminals, Radovan Karadžić and Ratko Mladić (the Bosnian Serb political and military wartime leaders), were allowed to run free, and IFOR commanders refused to arrest them, peace would not be possible. Although neither explanation is currently disprovable, a closer look at the peace agreement suggests a third explanation.[37] The ambiguities, uncertainties, and contradictions in the peace agreement and the overriding uncertainty about the future it induced, far from helping to remove obstacles to peace and cooperation, created the conditions for a serious security dilemma *after* the war. Even if most of the leaders who had no intention of cooperating and still wanted to defect from Bosnia or from Dayton were removed from the scene, the agreement encouraged mobilization along national lines and defensive perceptions and behavior.

Continuing Uncertainty About the Political Future

First, the Dayton accords did not reduce the uncertainty over the political future of Bosnians and Bosnia. The negotiators' attempt to stop the war with a package of minimally acceptable conditions from each of the warring parties for a cease-fire, so as not to have to impose a solution by military defeat or foreign occupation, did nothing to change the terms of the political conflict. In fact, it recreated the political alignments of the period immediately preceding the outbreak of war. The Bosnian Muslim–Bosnian Croat federation (the first of the cease-fires embedded in the Dayton framework) simply reproduced the parliamentary alliance on sovereignty between the SDA and HDZ of October 8, 1991, which led the Serbs to leave the parliament and set up autonomous areas. Just as international recognition in May 1992 led the Bosnian Croats to defect to their preferred position of separate statehood, so the September 1995 cease-fire with the Serbs, which the Dayton accords confirmed, together with the strategic shifts favoring Croats in the run up to the accords, ended any incentive for Croats to cooperate with Bosnian Muslims if it required compromise with the HDZ's definition of national rights. Similarly, the success in gaining American ground presence in support of Bosnian independence, combined with the dwindling numbers of Croats in Bosnia, reduced any incentive the Bosnian Muslims had to share power equally with Bosnian Croats. And the universal condemnation of the Serbs as responsible for the war, reinforced by the insistence that they not be allowed to negotiate on their own behalf at Dayton, that sanctions remain on the Bosnian Serbs until they prove fully cooperative with all the terms of the Dayton accords, and that the primary obstacle to implementation was Serb obstruction, left Bosnian Serb leaders even more determined to hold onto and strengthen the separate sovereignty of Republika Srpska.

At the same time, the Dayton framework leaves each of the three parties feeling insecure in their gains. The Bosnian Muslims won their independent state, but they control less than one-third of the territory, including almost none of the external borders. The Dayton constitution (Annex 4 of the accords) declares that this state continues "the legal existence under international law as a state" of the former republic of Bosnia and Herzegovina, but it also obliged the Bosniacs to give up their power base in the offices and powers of the former republican government, to merge with Bosnian Croats in the federation entity, to accept a weak common government, and to share power with the two parties who oppose a single state. The Bosnian Serbs gained their own republic, but its existence was under daily challenge — from Bosniac leaders who denounced its legitimacy the moment Dayton was signed, and from the internationally supported right of return to prewar communities and the electoral rules allowing absentee balloting in the interim that formed part of a Bosniac political campaign (including orchestrated Muslim returns to strategically located villages and towns that began in July 1996) to "liberate" the territory of the Serb Republic.[38] Control over the town of Brčko, which sits on the narrow corridor linking the two halves of the Serb republic and is thus seen by Bosnian Serbs as strategically essential to their survival, was assigned by Dayton negotiators, at the successful insistence of President Izetbegović, to international arbitration. The decision in February 1996 was to place the town and surrounding area under special administration headed by an American official, begin a plan of full restoration of multiethnic local administration and returns, and delay final decision until March 1997.[39] And, for the first two years of the Dayton imple-

mentation, conditions for economic aid left the Serb Republic with less than
3 percent of the total—in the first year, until a new government was elected
and fully operating, because international donors and the high representative
insisted that there could only be one representative of the Bosnian state, with
its seat and occupant in Sarajevo, and that Serb leaders would have to sign
contracts with the Muslim prime minister Muratović (whom they did not
recognize as legitimate) before a new postwar government was elected to be
eligible for any aid, and, in the second year, until Serbs agreed to their terms
for one central bank, one currency, and one system of communications and
transportation. Finally, the Bosnian Croats gained recognition of their right
to self-determination in the power-sharing arrangements and joint defense
of the federation, but they have been denied a separate republic within
Bosnia and were obliged to dismantle their wartime Croatian Republic of
Herzeg-Bosna (an order they managed to ignore despite their repeated promises to comply).

Third-party intervention during the war had combined a humanitarian
intervention to protect as many civilians as possible with measures, such as
economic sanctions on neighboring Serbia, an arms embargo, and a no-fly
zone, to lessen the lethal capacity of the armies and to facilitate ongoing
negotiations with the parties over constitutional principles and a map. Because the primary war tactic of all three parties was to control territory by
determining who lived there—displacing populations and creating ethnically pure areas under their control by terror, forced expulsion, voluntary
exchanges, or published lists of enemies and "war criminals"—the goal of
the negotiators was to foreshorten the war by an agreed division of territory
within one constitutional order. The result, however, was to place a premium
on gaining and holding territory as bargaining chips and to concede to the
logic of separation. Although a robust international military presence after
the peace agreement should have provided the environment for tentative
moves toward cooperation and reconciliation, the IFOR deployment to separate armies and monitor confrontation lines in fact provided an environment
for the parties to continue the consolidation of territorial control and defensive positioning without war.

Moreover, the map drawn at Dayton did not end the central focus on
territory. This was in part deliberate, because the accords identified territories
to be transferred from the control of one entity to the other at the end of
the war. But instead of encouraging the population to stay put, the international officials did little to stop the looting, firebombing and trashing of
homes and industries, and terrorizing people to leave that accompanied the

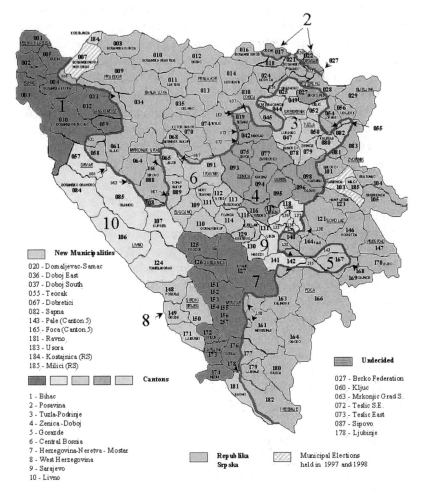

MAP 3.3. The Dayton Map: BiH Cantons and New Municipalities (According to the Federation Law passed February 1998)

Source: http://www-.osce.austria.eu.net/picsmap/cantonmap982.gif.

territorial transfers. Croat forces occupying the area of Mrkonjić Grad and Šipovo (the "Anvil") preceded its transfer back to Serbs by their near total destruction while United Nations soldiers, with no mandate to act in the interim between their mandate and the arrival of NATO forces, stood by. The greatest single exodus of the entire war occurred when five Serb-populated suburbs of Sarajevo were transferred to federation control, in February 1996. Although international military and civilian officials tried in vain to persuade local Serbs with a last-minute blitz of pamphlets and speeches that they would be safe, decidedly mixed messages coming from the Bosnian government (including delay until the last moment of the parliamentary vote on amnesty that was agreed upon at Dayton) and fear-inducing propaganda from Bosnian Serb official media had greater effect.[40] Only the violence was reduced by IFOR when it gave support for Serb buses to transport evacuees, while radicals from both Serb and Bosniac camps looted and burned. In a pattern that became more blatant over the year, the Bosniac leadership wanted no minorities in Sarajevo, and the Serb leadership had strategic interests in a wholesale Serb flight to populate areas in the Serb republic still considered insecure and vulnerable to assault, such as the strategic town of Brčko whose status remained undecided.

The Dayton map also designed a country of corridors and buffer zones that interrupt crucial lines of communication within each national territory. The purpose was to break up the contiguity of territory and prevent secession by the Serbs and Croats, but the effect was to create vulnerable enclaves of mixed population, such as Croats in central Bosnia, Serbs in the "anvil," and Muslims in the Bihać area and Goražde, who are neither welcome nor secure. It also drew borders difficult to defend and critical communication lines that each nation, thinking as a nation, does not control (such as the road between Trebinje and Pale for the Serb Republic and the road between Sarajevo and Una-Sana canton for Bosniacs).[41] The result was to strengthen the incentive of Bosnian parties to maintain troop deployments and raise police checkpoints around points of dispute or insecurity and to limit the freedom of movement so essential to contact and reducing information distortions and fears. Rather than creating a necessity to cooperate on mutual interest, the territorial vulnerabilities made each group more fearful of becoming hostage to another and thus motivated to increase the territory under their single national control.

The more the population transfers continued, with more people leaving homes than returned, and the more ethnically homogeneous the territories became, the more security within each territory seemed to matter. Bosnian Muslim leaders, in particular, revived their fears of being trapped in the interior without access to the sea (ironically, it was Serbia that had been preoccupied with having an access to the sea during the Yugoslav period and back into the nineteenth century)—a "miserable Gaza Strip," politicians began to say during 1998. This fear was intensified by political tensions between the two federation partners and the blatant refusal of the government of Croatia to abide by its commitment at Dayton on Bosnian access to a free port (a ninety-nine-year lease) at Ploče on the Dalmatian coast.[42] The unreliability of Croatia on this matter made Bosnian Muslim leaders even more sensitive about unimpeded access to an alternative route north through the Brčko area and the Sava River basin to central Europe, and it intensified their efforts to get international (and particularly American) support behind their claim for ultimate control over Brčko. This in turn led Bosnian Serbs to stay on a war footing in the area and to try actively, though unsuccessfully after SFOR agreed to use force in this one area to assist returnees, to prevent Bosnian Muslims from returning there.[43] At the same time, the Croatian government response to the dispute over Ploče was to revive active plans for a confederation between the Bosnian federation and Croatia, a relationship encouraged in the Washington Agreement, and permitted in the Dayton accords, that only revived fears among Bosnian Muslims that Croatia still intended to partition Bosnia in two.

Finally, the Dayton accord also allowed the parties to negotiate changes in the IEBL, in the context of the joint military commissions chaired by IFOR. The result was an ongoing exchange of hundreds of villages to make areas within political boundaries more ethnically pure. In towns within the federation that were still mixed Bosnian Croats began in the spring of 1996 to insist the populations be separated into different administrative units, creating divided communities along the model of Mostar. By mid-1997 they were having some success in central Bosnia. Far from tying up the loose ends of their wartime conflict over territory, each party was moving to consolidate territorial control to reduce the insecurity and defensive vulnerabilities created by the Dayton compromises and to consolidate power for the next phase. Each party took advantage of the cease-fire and the international military presence to harass and expel remaining minorities, to prevent the return of refugees and the internally displaced persons from another group, and to use the options for voter registration to increase the ethnic homogeneity of the locality and its government.

Military Balance

The aggressive posture in defense of national sovereignty by each of the three Bosnian parties facing uncertainty over the future was reinforced, moreover, by the contradictions in the military aspects of the peace settlement. Annex 1-A of the Dayton accords prescribed a classic peacekeeping approach to the interim between cease-fire and peace—the implementation of the program for military separation, weapons cantonment, and confidence-building through the exchange of information and frequent contact between officers on all three sides. The regional stabilization measures of Annex 1-B, which aimed to downsize forces and create a military balance between Croatia, Yugoslavia, and Bosnia, could also be seen as a way for outsiders to impose an arms control regime that would prevent rearmament and a new security dilemma between the three now independent states. But the one party *within* Bosnia with an incentive to rearm and to use the peace settlement as a period to prepare militarily to resume war for more territory if the political strategy did not "liberate" Republika Srpska—the Bosniac leadership (particularly the more radical wing, including the army and General Rasim Delić)—could perceive this annex as punitive, putting them at a distinct disadvantage in a regional force ratio of 1:12 if they should have to defend themselves alone against a combined Croatian-Serbian campaign (whether aimed at forcing a two-way partition or defending against new Bosniac military campaigns). At the same time, moreover, an American view of war termination held that a military balance *within* the country, between the two entities, was essential to detering new war and that Bosnian Serb military aggression remained the primary threat to Bosnia. Thus, in a semi-secret side deal negotiated at Dayton in order to win Izetbegović's agreement to the settlement as well as a vote from the United States Congress to deploy troops, the American negotiators added a program (called "arm and train" and later changed to "train and equip" so as to appear less threatening) of military assistance to the Bosnian Muslim–Bosnian Croat Federation.

The effect of the train and equip program, therefore, appeared to override the arms control arrangements. It reinforced the perceptions of vulnerability among Bosnian Serbs, encouraged them to cheat on arms control agreements and to maintain a military presence at weak points of their *internal* frontier,[44] making it more rather than less like an international border, and strengthened their view that protection lay in political and military relations with neighboring Serbia.[45] Croatian President Tudjman announced, upon signing the arms control agreement, that he had no intention of implementing it. The train and equip program also encouraged the militants in the Bosniac leadership to entertain the prospects of an eventual military victory to liberate territory from Bosnian Serbs, despite the near certainty, as assessed by outside military experts, that they could not win. Although the program required the federation to create a joint defense structure first, quarrels between Bosnian Croats and Bosniacs over every issue of integrating their armies into one, including military doctrine, led the American officials behind the program to concede to a transition, allowing command levels to unify over three years and army units to remain separate. At least on the rhetorical front, Bosnian Croats and their Croatian backers called the further arming of Bosnian Muslims a threat.

Perhaps most destabilizing of all the consequences of the train and equip program is its institutionalization of the results of the war and of a structure feeding a security dilemma by professionalizing and modernizing three armies for one state, one for each of the three national communities recognized constitutionally. This concept of security might in some cases be appropriate to interstate conflict, but it implied three states, not one, and, because all three retained unresolved grievances, there was little chance that the program would stay at equilibrium, at least in the minds of each leadership. The fact that the United States sought primary funding for the program from Islamic states (Turkey, Saudi Arabia, the Gulf states, in particular), that these states made clear their interest in channeling funds and equipment to Bosnian Muslims only, not to a program that included Bosnian Croats, and that arms began to arrive independently for the Bosniac army, such as from Egypt, all raised doubts about the future intentions of the Bosniac leadership and made it difficult for the other two sides to shift focus.[46]

Ethnic Power Sharing, Top-Down Implementation, and Impatience

"While the challenge of weapons is real, disarmament *per se* does not necessarily enhance security unless it is part of a broader political process that seeks to reconcile conflicting parties and enhance security," writes Mats Berdal.[47] As Barbara Walter writes, "Only when new political systems are established that promise to deter future aggression does the mutual trust needed for long-term cooperation emerge."[48] The power-sharing formulas of the Dayton constitution, while perhaps aimed at mutual trust, had the opposite result in the first years of its implementation.

One problem lay in the uncertainties mentioned above, that the Serbs and Croats saw their political rights as insecure, under constant challenge by the outsiders. Their defensive reaction, in turn, led to disillusionment about Dayton among Bosniacs and an increasingly defensive posture as well. Equally important was the contribution made by the Dayton accords to the process of creating political nations out of communal identities, a wartime goal of the nationalist leaders that still had a ways to go. The accords thus appeared to legalize the ongoing partition of the country rather than to soften social and political lines of division. This facilitated a form of elite-level interaction of a collusionist kind that had characterized the year before the war. Even during the war an entire network of cooperation among army commanders, arms traders, local authorities, and even some party leaders continued to operate, and with the cease-fire the three leaderships resumed their prewar habit of bargaining on a division-of-party-spoils over control of specific ministries and jurisdictions, the distribution of benefits going to each national territory and party, and—where division was not possible—multiplying co-presidencies. But the aim of this cooperation was to lock competitors out. The three ruling parties used the resources of the international operation—humanitarian, housing, and reconstruction aid, and assistance in demarcating territory, running elections, establishing governmental ministries, and resettling populations—to increase their advantages over opposition parties, to control state media, and to prevent the dispersion of power that is necessary to developing safeguards for individual rights. The opportunity for different interests and groups to emerge and gain expression appeared tiny. Rules for ethnic representation and voting encouraged caucusing by nation on most issues, discouraged voting on interests that crossed national lines, and hard-wired alliances, preventing the essential business of democracy and supporting an authoritarian approach to politics in which radicals had a natural advantage.

The system's similarity to the institutional structure and operation of 1980s Yugoslavia gave no assurance that the tensions and quarrels of the first postsettlement period would abate. They instead appeared to be becoming institutionalized in a political system vulnerable to constant stalemate, insufficient revenues, an inability to manage macroeconomic policy and trade, and the spiraling behavior that can revive a security dilemma. The strengthening of militarized units of police forces in response to the obligations of demobilization and arms control and the creation of separate intelligence services (most active was the Bosniacs' Agency for Information and Documentation, said to gather information and train against domestic "terrorists") did not foster trust between communities or make it easier for individuals within those communities to break down barriers to communication and gain more accurate assessments of events. Although the International Police Task Force mounted an impressive program of police reform and training, police continued to act as arms of insecure states rather than as community policing services providing law and order to protect individuals against the real threats to their security—violations of civil rights, banditry, looting, roaming criminal gangs, drunken armed soldiers running amok, crowds preventing return and burning down homes, and state terror.

Moreover, while the Dayton accords were based on the premise that individual Bosnians could cooperate as long as indicted war criminals— above all, wartime Bosnian Serb leaders—were no longer present, the accords also depended on the parties' cooperation and on working through governmental authorities who would be responsible for implementing agreements made. Thus, while many of those working for peace on the ground insisted that only a bottom-up, civil society, locally oriented, and reconciliatory approach would work to reintegrate the country, the officials followed a top-down approach. While loudly criticizing extreme nationalists as the obstacle to Dayton, the new administrators relied on leaders more or even took authority to a higher level by imposing *their* decisions on Bosnian leaders. This problem was exacerbated by the short deadlines imposed on the military deployment of American troops. If peace had to be achieved in twelve months, and then in eighteen months, it could not wait for the much slower process of rebuilding trust and social organization. This impatience to achieve the tasks of Dayton and leave quickly also led officials of the international operation (the Contact Group members and the Peace Implementation Council) to search for ever more noncoercive instruments to force leaders' compliance. Increasing use of economic aid as a political stick, punishing those who did not cooperate with the war crimes tribunal and the right of return to prewar homes by withholding economic assistance, and rewarding those who cooperated with Dayton implementation, however, did little to change leaders' behavior on issues they defined as vital.

The behavior of each party toward political demands from the Dayton officials can easily be explained by the particular nature of the political insecurities. The Bosnian Serb leaders in the first eighteen months seemed to put an exaggerated emphasis on being accorded both the reality and symbol of sovereignty within their republic, to the point of receiving no international assistance (1.3 percent). Bosnian Croats boycotted participation in the federation parliament until legislation redrawing administrative boundaries to divide the remaining mixed (Bosniac-Bosnian Croat) towns on the Mostar model would be considered and passed, and they insisted on separation or parity wherever they shared territory or offices with Bosniacs. The Bosniac leadership ignored the requirement that they dismantle the offices of the prewar republican government, which they controlled totally by 1993, not only after Dayton obliged them to shift to the joint federation offices but even after the September elections created the mandate for a new Dayton-constituted government. They also began to insist on majoritarian rules wherever they had a numerical majority, including rejection of extensive efforts by the deputy high representative, Michael Steiner, to create a special regime for Sarajevo as a model for the capital of a multiethnic Bosnia. The demands for parity from the Bosnian Croat leadership, they argued, had been far too cocky in relation to their numerical showing in the September 1996 elections.

After eighteen months of international assistance the delays in achieving Dayton goals, the demands of frustrated Bosnian Muslim leaders, and the threat that war would resume after troops departed fed growing impatience, particularly in Washington. With a new foreign policy team in place under Secretary of State Madeleine Albright and a new supreme allied commander of Europe, a shift in tactics began. They would be increasingly assertive, including the use of force by SFOR, to compel cooperation on indicted war criminals, on the return of refugees and displaced persons to their homes in minority areas (especially in some strategic areas such as around Brčko), and on creating common institutions, reforming the police, and stopping hostile propaganda on the airwaves, particularly in the case of Bosnian Serb leaders in Pale. TV transmitters were taken over by force, broadcasts jammed from the air, Serbs and Croats both required to broadcast messages and information from the international operation, some indicted war criminals were arrested, and force was even used to assist an alternative Bosnian-Serb leader in achieving power. The caution and impartiality of the military leadership in the first year of Dayton implementation were thrown overboard.

In abandoning impartiality, however, they also disturbed the delicate balance of the Dayton accords, leading Serbs and Croats to view American action as even more pro-Bosniac than they had thought and to think even more in terms of protecting their own national interests. Predictably, this had a spiraling effect on Bosniac behavior, which also began to think increasingly about Muslim interests—even the possibility of a Muslim state and a partitioned Bosnia. Even the international authorities were trapped in the spiral. Having succeeded, at least in the short run, in finding more cooperative leaders in the Republika Srpska, they began to see intransigence on the part of Croats and Bosniacs and moved to tighten criteria and threaten sanctions if they too did not cooperate.

The Bosnian case suggests that the dynamic and behavior associated with the security dilemma can occur within states and lead to civil war. Even clearer is the role of the security dilemma in the obstacles to reestablishing a sustainable peace that lie in fears for survival and defensive positioning on all sides. In addition to the focus on the military spirals of interstate conflict, however, the first stages of implementing the Dayton accords in Bosnia suggest that the political settlement to end civil-warlike conflicts must itself take into account the existence of a security dilemma. If the parties are ready to re-create one political space and to cooperate, but need outsiders' help in overcoming fears and defensive positioning that can lead others to respond in kind, then a military deployment for some time can make a crucial difference, as in Mozambique or El Salvador. But when the parties do not wish to cooperate in one political space, then even recognition of a security dilemma may not be enough, if the application of the concept treats the parties as strategic actors with sovereign responsibilities—if, in other words, they are treated like states in a realist's international order. The structural conditions that can create a security dilemma must be removed; they must also not be re-created. Ending a civil war requires more than a military drawdown and balance, more accurate information and transparency, and time. It requires either methods to get individuals to *un*separate psychologically from exclusionary groups and feel safe independently of national communities (including the risks of political dissent within their own community), in order to entertain other possible forms of social interaction, or it requires a genuine recognition that for quite some time they will feel safe only behind those barriers and rights to self-governance and that new forms of governing such countries internally must be devised.

NOTES

The author is Senior Fellow, Foreign Policy Studies Program, Brookings Institution, Washington, D.C. The analysis and documentation for this chapter draws heavily on the author's *Balkan Tragedy: Chaos and Dissolution After the Cold War* (Washington, D.C.: Brookings Institution, 1995) and on *Implementing Peace in Bosnia and Herzegovina: A Post-Dayton Primer and Memorandum of Warning*, Brookings Discussion Papers: Foreign Policy Studies Program (Washington, D.C.: Brookings Institution, May 1996).

1. On the many plans proposed for Bosnia, see Paul C. Szasz, "The Quest for a Bosnian Constitution: Legal Aspects of Constitutional Proposals Relating to Bosnia," *Fordham International Law Journal*, vol. 19, no. 2 (December 1995), pp. 363–407.

2. Third-party negotiators can thus be treated as the statesman in Jervis's analysis of the security dilemma and the "failures of empathy": "The dilemma will operate much more strongly if statesmen do not understand it." See Robert Jervis, "Cooperation Under the Security Dilemma," *World Politics*, vol. 30, no. 2 (January 1978), p. 181.

3. Since August 1993 Bosnian Muslims officially call themselves Bosniacs, in part to create a state people of Bosnia that had a name more associated with the country and in part to signal to outsiders who were not familiar with the previous Yugoslav system that the three Bosnian peoples were equally constituent nations, not, as the labels sounded, two ethnic peoples and one religious grouping. In Bosnia Serbs and Croats were also largely identified with their religion (Eastern Orthodoxy and Roman Catholicism, respectively) and its historical, cultural, and communal aspects, while the term *Muslim* was a constitutionally recognized *political* identity and recognition of *national* rights. These terms had their origin in the role that religious membership played in defining political and economic rights and social status in the *millet* system of the Ottoman Empire that ruled Bosnia from 1463 to 1878 and in the political use made of these communal distinctions when that system ended under Austrian rule (first protectorate, then annexation) between 1878 and 1918. In this essay I stay with the older term, because perceptions have been defined by that historical legacy and especially the Yugoslav constitutional order, 1945–1991. Beginning in 1993, however, it would be more appropriate to use the term *Bosniac*, as they have chosen to do. A useful and accessible introduction to that history is in Robert J. Donia and John V. A. Fine Jr., *Bosnia and Hercegovina: A Tradition Betrayed* (New York: Columbia University Press, 1994). See also Attila Hoare, "The People's Liberation Movement in Bosnia and Hercegovina, 1941–45; What Did It Mean to Fight for a Multi-National State? *Nationalism and Ethnic Politics*, vol. 2, no. 3 (Autumn 1996), pp. 415–445.

4. The Croatian Democratic Union (the Bosnian acronym is HDZ-BiH), which was a branch of the party elected to rule neighboring Croatia under President Franjo Tudjman; the Serbian Democratic Party (SDS), which was only one of many parties seeking to represent Bosnian Serbs and was one branch of a party formed among Serbs in neighboring Croatia; and the Party of Democratic Action (SDA), which was the largest of the parties claiming to represent Bosnian Muslim interests and had also organized successfully among Muslims in neighboring Serbia.

5. Another possible outcome, discussed among the presidents of the six republics before the country's dissolution, was the partition of Bosnia between Croatia and Serbia. First proposed by Croatian President Tudjman in July 1990 in secret

talks he initiated with Serbian President Milošević on the basis of territory that Tudjman claimed to be the legitimate historical borders of Croatia as confirmed by the 1939 agreement on Croatian autonomy during the first Yugoslavia, this alternative appeared to Bosnians as a constant *threat* rather than a choice.

6. Recorded in the five-part BBC (Brian Lapping Associates) documentary, "The Death of Yugoslavia," and cited in the book written to accompany the documentary, Laura Silber and Alan Little, *Yugoslavia: Death of a Nation*, revised and updated (London: Penguin, 1997), where they quote his speech to the Bosnian parliament on February 27, 1991: "I would sacrifice peace for a sovereign Bosnia-Herzegovina, but for that peace in Bosnia-Herzegovina I would not sacrifice sovereignty" (p. 211). There were, however, other views among Bosnian Muslim politicians.

7. Perhaps the best known example of this argument is Robert D. Kaplan, *Balkan Ghosts: A Journey Through History* (New York: St. Martin's, 1993), but it became the stock and trade of most political and journalistic commentary on Bosnia during the war.

8. Political scientists tended to emphasize this thesis more. See V. P. Gagnon, "Ethnic Nationalism and International Conflict: The Case of Serbia," *International Security*, vol. 19, no. 3 (Winter 1994/1995), 130–166; Silber and Little, *Yugoslavia*; and Bogdan Denitch, *Ethnic Nationalism* (Minneapolis: University of Minnesota Press, 1994), among many others.

9. On this tendency to attribute behavior to innate dispositions, see chapter 1, this volume, by Snyder and Jervis, p. 15–37.

10. "The fear of being exploited . . . most strongly drives the security dilemma; one of the main reasons why international life is not more nasty, brutish, and short is that states are not as vulnerable as men are in a state of nature. People are easy to kill." Jervis, "Cooperation Under the Security Dilemma," p. 172. The competing arguments of ethnic hatred and Serbian expansionism make outsiders blind to Slovenia, which was 87.6 percent Slovene in 1991, but it was Slovene politicians who first talked about exploitation in national terms to criticize federal redistributive policies and who warned during the 1980s about the "threat" of "cultural extinction" and "linguistic contamination" from the many non-Slovenes from other parts of Yugoslavia working temporarily in the republic. See Susan L. Woodward, *Socialist Unemployment: The Political Economy of Yugoslavia, 1945–1990* (Princeton: Princeton University Press, 1995), pp. 364–365, 371. The perceptual shift of "nations at risk (*ugrožen*)," recorded in political rhetoric during the 1980s, was crucial in setting the stage throughout the country psychologically for an escalating security dilemma and then war. In Sarajevo, at dinner only a month before hostilities began, a Serb woman originally from Serbia who had lived in Bosnia much of her life said to me, as if in desperation against the nationalists and their claims of victimhood and vulnerability, "I don't consider myself in peril (*ugrožen*)!"

11. For example, Serb nationalists in Kosovo claimed that antagonism and pressure

to leave from the Albanian majority were acts of genocide; the threat felt by Serbs at the discriminatory speech in election campaigns of Croatian presidential candidate Franjo Tudjman was associated with memories of the actual genocide against them by the fascist regime in World War II; the Bosnian Party of Democratic Action and its leader Izetbegović called the formation of a federal, reformist party by federal prime minister Marković an act of genocide; and mutual accusations of genocide were tossed frequently between the Bosnian Serb and Bosnian Croat parties allied in the governing coalition. See also Bette Denich, "Dismembering Yugoslavia: Nationalist Ideologies and the Symbolic Revival of Genocide," *American Ethnologist*, vol. 21, no. 2 (1994), pp. 377–381.

12. Xavier Bougarel, *Bosnie: Anatomie d'un Conflit* (Paris: La Découverte, 1996), p. 11.

13. Xavier Bougarel, "Bosnia and Hercegovina—State and Communitarianism," in David A. Dyker and Ivan Vejvoda, eds., *Yugoslavia and After: A Study in Fragmentation, Despair, and Rebirth* (London: Longman, 1996), p. 99.

14. Ibid., pp. 98–99.

15. Ejub Štitkovac and Jasminka Udovički, "Bosnia and Hercegovina: The Second War," in Jasminka Udovički and James Ridgeway, eds., *Yugoslavia's Ethnic Nightmare: The Inside Story of Europe's Unfolding Ordeal* (New York: Lawrence Hill, 1995), pp. 175–76. They add, "The dealers' stories could not have been as effective without the shooting and killing that started in Mostar as early as the fall of 1991 and in Bosanski Brod in early spring 1992"—from the spread of the war in Croatia into strategic Bosnian towns.

16. "Croatian 'Pro-Fascist' Party Members in Bosnia," TANJUG, April 6, 1992, reported in FBIS, *East Europe*, April 7, 1992, p. 38.

17. For example, the comments on an earlier draft of this paper by V. P. Gagnon, cited in chapter 1 of this volume.

18. For an analysis of missed opportunities, see Susan L. Woodward, "Costly Disinterest: Missed Opportunities for Preventive Diplomacy in Croatia and Bosnia and Herzegovina, 1985–1991," in Bruce W. Jentleson, ed., *Opportunities Missed, Opportunities Seized: Preventive Diplomacy in the Post-Cold War World* (London: Rowman and Littlefield, 1999).

19. Fen Osler Hampson, *Nurturing Peace: Why Peace Settlements Succeed or Fail* (Washington: United States Institute of Peace, 1996), p. 217.

20. Mary McIntosh, Martha Abele MacIver, Daniel G. Abele, and David B. Nolle, "Minority Rights and Majority Rule: Ethnic Tolerance in Bulgaria and Romania," *Social Forces* (March 1995).

21. Political upheaval in Serbia in November 1996-March 1997 and the diagnosis of inoperable stomach cancer for Croatian president Tudjman in mid-1996 raised the legal question, without answering it, whether these signatures were official commitments and thus legally binding on future occupants of the presidencies of Serbia and Croatia.

22. The institutions that Weingast proposes to create the trust necessary to prevent

preemptive war, by "t[ying] the hands of a potential aggressor" (Barbara Walter, "Domestic Anarchy and Civil War," unpublished manuscript, p. 13), have been designed to tie the hands of all three parties and guarantee against "negative tyranny."

23. The provision for confederation between Croatia and the Bosnian Federation, a central part of the Washington Agreement of March 1994 to gain the support of President Tudjman, was altered by the Dayton accords, but not so clearly that it did not become a matter for dispute and frequent interpretive intervention on the part of the Office of the High Representative (under both Carl Bildt and his successor, Carlos Westendorp), which declared in 1998 (under constant pressure from Croatia to define and formalize this relationship) that the Dayton accords overrode the federation constitution of 1994 and that all special relationships had to be bilateral, state-to-state agreements. That is, relations with Croatia and with Yugoslavia had to be approved by the Bosnian state parliament and could not be arranged between an entity and a third country. The question remained a matter of disputed interpretation and negotiations into late 1998 when an agreement was signed between Croatia and the Federation, not the Bosnian state, as a result of American negotiations.

24. The experience of American officers and soldiers in Bosnia under IFOR in 1996, as told to this author, for example, persuaded them that Bosnians would not cross the interentity boundary line (zone of separation between the two entities) if IFOR were not there.

25. Under urging from Human Rights Watch, the OHR began to sanction, censure, and even demand the resignation of mayors who were persistently not in compliance with the Dayton accords on issues of refugee return and human rights. During 1998 a Multinational Special Unit of international *gendarmerie* was created, within the chain of command of the NATO military forces, to respond appropriately to circumstances requiring policing rather than military skills. Set to be deployed in early August 1998, its effectiveness in providing international enforcement of individual rights remains to be seen at this writing.

26. Reported by BBC World Service, on May 5, 1996; cited by Patrick Moore in *OMRI Special Report: Pursuing Balkan Peace*, vol. 1, no. 18, May 7, 1996.

27. Bosnian Serbs fell in between, at 72 percent (of which 44 percent were very concerned, as opposed to 33 percent of the Bosnian Croats and 24 percent of the Bosnian Muslims). In response to the question "How much confidence do you have that these accords will result in a lasting peace for us?" the combined percent saying a great deal or a fair amount of confidence was 51 percent among Bosnian Serbs, 32 percent among Bosnian Croats, and 78 percent among Bosnian Muslims. From intensive nationwide public opinion surveys and focus groups commissioned by USIA, summarized in *Public Opinion in Bosnia Hercegovina*, vol. 4: *One Year of Peace* (Washington, D.C.: European Branch, Office of Research and Media Reaction, United States Information Agency, February 1997), pp. 40–41.

28. In the USIA opinion surveys, "Since 1995, increasing majorities of Bosnian Serbs and Croats agree with the idea that 'people can feel completely safe only when they are the majority nationality in their country.' " The two groups believe *increasingly* that "every nation should have its own state" and that "it is better for our town to be composed of only one nationality group." Bosnian Muslims disagree with the second set of questions, but had begun to split on the first. Ibid., p. 158.

29. Ironically, given the general assumptions about Bosnian parties, the smallest percentage of votes—fewer than 70 percent—was cast for the nationalist Serb (SDS) leader, Krajišnik, in contest with an explicitly antinationalist competitor, Mladen Ivanić. The highest vote tally for opposition parties went to Serb parties, and second to Bosniac parties, while there is no political competition in Bosnian Croat areas (opposition Bosnian Croat parties function in Bosniac areas; in summer 1998, however, the first cracks occurred when a splinter from the Bosnian Croat ruling party, led by its former head, did create an independent party, the New Croatian Initiative). The municipal elections one year later, in September 1997, showed the same pattern, giving electoral victories to the three ruling parties in all but a handful of municipalities, such as Tuzla, Velika Kladuša, and Banja Luka. The next round of general elections, in September 1998, repeated the pattern a third time, although there was far greater spread among Serb parties in the Serb Republic and substantial improvement in the Federation by non-national Social Democrats.

30. *Public Opinion in Bosnia Hercegovina*, p. 35.

31. Ibid., pp. 43, 47, 48, 50, and 51.

32. Data are gathered by the United Nations High Commissioner for Refugees, but they are inevitably estimates leading different groups to cite different numbers but the same source. Thus, a public statement by Mrs. Ogata, UN high commissioner, on November 20, 1997, said 34,000 had returned to minority areas out of 400,000 total returns of refugees and internally displaced since Dayton, whereas the U.S. Committee for Refugees cites the return of 27,000 to minority areas out of a total of 391,500 returns as of October 31, 1997, and the International Crisis Group assessment on November 18, 1997, reported 22,500 returns to minority areas out of 381,000 (171,000 refugees and 210,000 displaced persons) returning home. "Bosnian Minorities: Strangers in Their Own Land," *Refugee Reports*, vol. 18, no. 10 (October 31, 1997), pp. 6–7; "Post-war Bosnian returns mainly to one's ethnic area: UNHCR," *Agence France-Presse*, November 20, 1997, sent on "C-afp@clari.net," and ICG Report, "A Review of the Dayton Peace Agreement's Implementation" (Sarajevo: International Crisis Group, November 18, 1997), p. 4.

33. "Special Relations Necessary to Stop Exodus of Croats from Bosnia," communiqué faxed from Permanent Mission of Croatia to the United Nations, New York, November 11, 1997.

34. By paranoia is meant fears that have no basis in reality, although they might well be provoked by political rhetoric or by other experiences that leave a traumatic trace. Discussions with, among others, the late Klaus von Heldorff in Brussels, in November 1996, after two years in the European Union Administration in Mostar and with Michael Steiner, deputy high representative for the Dayton implementation, in Sarajevo, in October 1996.

35. Michael W. Doyle, "War in Peace in Cambodia," unpublished manuscript, January 31, 1997.

36. This began to change in the summer of 1998, when some political and especially military leaders asserted publicly that the war was over.

37. During 1997 American policy toward the Dayton process changed to address both hypotheses: a commitment made by President Clinton in November 1997, followed later by a North Atlantic Council decision, to extend the mandate of the SFOR troops, including Americans, after June 1998, without deadline, until a "sustainable peace" was in evidence, and, beginning in May-June 1997, the decision to assist forcefully a shift in the center of power in Republika Srpska from hardline nationalists in Pale to politicians in Banja Luka more willing to cooperate with the international community, to use political conditionality of economic assistance more assertively to get leaders' cooperation with the Dayton accords, and, by late 1997, to use the office of the high representative to make decisions for politicians about fundamentals—such as common license plates, flag and coat of arms, common currency, citizenship laws—if they continued to delay. For the purposes of the argument presented here, this policy change only delays assessment of whether time, new leaders, or the terms of the settlement and international approaches is more likely to bring closure and end the war.

38. Bosnian prime minister during the first year after Dayton, Hasan Muratović, led the way in referring to the exodus of Serbs from areas in and around Sarajevo that had been handed to federation control by the Dayton accord (Vogošča, Ilijas, Ilidža, Hadžići, and Grbavica) as the "liberation of Sarajevo." The phrase came to be applied by Bosniac politicians, from President Izetbegović to former Prime Minister Haris Silajdžić, to the entire territory of the former republic, for example, as the theme of Izetbegović's first public appearance since Dayton, at an election rally in Goražde on May 4, 1996, and in discussing Bosniac voting and return in areas of the Republika Srpska.

39. When the decision was put off yet again into 1999, in part to give time for this multiethnic approach to local administration and more assertive international support for Bosniac and Croat returnees to make the question moot.

40. Annex 7, article 6.

41. Evidence for this sense of vulnerability grew along with discussions about the possibility that Bosnia was actually partitioned and should be recognized as such. See an early statement by the Balkan Institute in its report on the implementa-

tion of the Dayton accords, for example: "Either a two-way or three-way partition of Bosnia would result in a militarily indefensible state. The Accords' map leaves Sarajevo exposed to artillery attack from the Bosnian Serb Republic. It also leaves Goražde, a territorial 'giraffe's neck,' completely exposed." *Prospects for Peace in a Post-IFOR Bosnia* (part 3 of 3), September 13, 1996, sent by electronic mail from "BalkanInst@aol.com."

42. Explicit negotiations to settle this matter were going on, under separate American leadership, throughout the fall of 1997 without any change in Zagreb's position.

43. An example of the tensions over Brčko can be seen in the media campaign on both sides in the months leading up to the February arbitration decision. See, for example, "The B&H Media Fortnight in Review: 6–19 January," vol. 2, no. 7 (January 22, 1997), a fortnightly report by MEDIA PLAN and the Institute for War and Peace Reporting, as sent over electronic mail through "omripub@OMRI.CZ."

44. See Raymond Bonner, "Bosnian Serbs Said to Hide Big Supplies of Heavy Arms," *New York Times*, October 19, 1996, p. 6, although there was much unresolved debate among European allies (especially the British, French, Italian, and American intelligence services), until targets were met in October 1997, about which of the three sides was cheating most, since all were doing so.

45. All assessments of the Bosnian Serb army are that it is so weak, disorganized, and unable (still) to conduct offensive operations that it is no threat to the federation. Moreover, it has no territorial aspirations, only to protect what it has now. If, however, one accepts the argument, which has much validity for March 1992 in explaining the Bosnian Serb preemptive attack on Sarajevo at the start of the war, that violence is chosen when one group is growing progressively weaker or believes that the other is becoming increasingly hostile, and so decides that it is better to fight sooner rather than later, then, in spite of their lack of capacity, the consequence of the program for "military balance," Bosniac campaigns to push returns, and the Brčko arbitration could still be Serb military action.

46. Mats R. Berdal also emphasizes the destabilizing potential of this program and its approach to ending civil wars in *Disarmament and Demobilisation After Civil Wars: Arms, Soldiers and the Termination of Armed Conflicts*, Adelphi Paper no. 303 (London: Oxford University Press for the International Institute for Strategic Studies, 1996), pp. 30, 38, and passim. On views within Bosnia, see "Bosnia-Herzegovina: Article Says Bosniaks Preparing for War," printed in FBIS-EEU-97–267, September 24, 1997, and translated from *Slobodna Bosna*, September 21, 1997, pp. 19–21.

47. Berdal, *Disarmament and Demobilisation*, p. 38.

48. Walter, "Domestic Anarchy and Civil War," p. 9.

4 Military Intervention in Rwanda's Two Wars: Partisanship and Indifference

Bruce D. Jones

Abstract

Between 1990 and 1994 two wars were fought in Rwanda: a military war between the Rwandan state and a rebel army, facilitated by partisan interventions, and a political war between Rwanda's dominant oligarchy and its political opponents. The former culminated in the military defeat of the oligarchic regime, the latter in genocide. Rwanda's dominant oligarchy manipulated ethnic tensions and security fears in order to create space for a radical final solution. Political indifference on the part of Western states manifested itself in a weak peacekeeping mission that sought to secure a peaceful end to the military war but fell victim to the violent end of the political war. Security fears, real and constructed, were tools more than causes of war.

Introduction

Between 1990 and 1994 two wars were fought in Rwanda: a military war waged between the Rwandan state and a rebel army and a political war waged between the oligarchy that dominated Rwanda's state and its political opposition. The former culminated in the military defeat of the oligarchic regime, the latter in genocide.

Prior to 1990 Rwanda was politically and militarily dominated by a clan-based oligarchy loosely known as the *akazu*, or "little house," that surrounded then President Habyarimana. The dominant position the akazu had constructed over almost two decades was challenged when the Rwandese

Patriotic Front (RPF) invaded Rwanda in October 1990. That challenge was subsequently amplified by an internal political opposition, which used the space opened up by the war (and by international diplomatic pressure) to press their own claims to a share of power. Between 1991 and 1993 regional and international actors succeeded in channeling the military war into political negotiations. As these negotiations took shape, the akazu turned increasingly to violent means to defend their power. In April 1994 the oligarchy launched a sweeping, breathtakingly violent bid to defend its power against all opponents. In an extraordinary act of regime defense, the akazu simultaneously restarted the military war against the RPF, wiped out internal political opponents, and conducted a mass genocide against the Tutsi population of Rwanda (the RPF's presumed political base.) This regime defense only failed in July 1994 when the RPF defeated the oligarchy's military forces, thereby also halting the genocide in Rwanda.

The military war was accompanied by a plethora of military interventions. Partisan military interventions by interested states were a permissive cause of the military war, and at key moments actively contributed to its prolongation. A plethora of neutral interventions by regional security organizations were sent to Rwanda to oversee cease-fires but had little overall impact on the course of war. Most important, a UN peacekeeping mission was sent to Rwanda to secure a negotiated settlement to the military war. It failed utterly to do so and did nothing to prevent Rwanda's oligarchic rulers from launching their genocidal regime defense. The incoherence of military intervention in Rwanda and its overall failure to minimize violence could hardly have been more complete.

Security fears played an important part in the connection between Rwanda's two wars. Fear of loss of "security" in the broadest sense—economic, political, positional—was part of the motivation for the oligarchy's strident opposition to negotiated change. In many cases such "fears" were indistinguishable from greed and predatory motives. More narrowly defined security fears—of being held accountable for past abuses, of a later coup by the RPF—reinforced (though did not generate) opposition from the oligarchy to negotiated peace. Most important, the oligarchy played on and played up the security fears of the broader population in the face of the military war, in order to mobilize support for their regime and undermine moderate, negotiated political alternatives. In other words, predatory elites with broad security fears and predatory motives constructed a narrow security dilemma at the mass level, to support their hostile opposition to peace. Security fears were present in Rwanda, and were part of what caused the violent repudiation of negotiated peace, but even more important, security fears were tools of war in the hands of a predatory elite.

This argument is explored in three sections. The first traces developments in the military and political wars, culminating when the two fused during the genocidal months of the summer of 1994, the second explores the course, and the failure, of military intervention, and the third examines the role played by security fears, real and constructed.

Rwanda's Two Wars: Military and Political Developments, From Insurgency to Genocide

The Military War: The RPF Takes on the Rwandan State

The starting point for a brief account of the military war in Rwanda is the invasion by the Rwandese Patriotic Front (RPF) in October 1990. The RPF was a movement that had grown up among the Rwandese refugee community in southern Uganda—the so-called Banyarwanda, exiled from Rwanda during violent political clashes surrounding independence in 1959.[1] Many of the leaders of the RPF had earlier fought in Uganda alongside then rebel leader Yoweri Museveni, as part of his National Revolutionary Army (NRA). The support of the Banyarwanda was critical to Museveni's victory in 1985–86, a fact acknowledged and rewarded by the many key positions in Museveni's government given to Banyamulenge leaders and the large contingent of Banyarwanda soldiers in the Ugandan army.[2] It was roughly four thousand of these soldiers that comprised the advance force of the RPF when they deserted their posts in the Ugandan army to cross into Rwanda at Kagitumba, Rwanda's northernmost town.[3] (See section 2 for details on Uganda's support of the RPF.)

The RPF quickly fought their way along the Kagitumba Highway, and within a few days had captured Gabiro, not only an important northern town but also location of one of the homes of President Habyarimana. The RPF celebrated, looting Habyarimana's villa and guzzling his stocks of imported pink champagne while driving through the town on armed vehicles captured from FAR supply posts.[4] The RPF's invasion threw the Rwandan regime into turmoil; it turned to outside friends for help.

French and Zairian troops were rushed to Rwanda to back up the disorganized and disoriented Forces Armées Rwandaise (FAR).[5] (See section 2 for details of French and Zairian support for the FAR.) With this backing in Kigali, the FAR launched a response to the RPF. Good luck and good tactics produced an early reversal of the RPF's fortunes. The RPF's commander, Major-General Fred Rwigyema, had been killed—officially by a stray bullet—in the first days of war. The FAR managed to capitalize on this fact when they ambushed and killed the RPF's two deputy commanders as they traveled between Gabiro and Kagitumba.[6] Leaderless, the RPF folded back into the Ugandan bush.

Despite being pushed back into Uganda, the RPF were far from defeated, and shortly afterward launched a second incursion, this time into northwestern Rwanda. This incursion operated differently, however, reflecting the style and training of the RPF's new commander, Major Paul Kagame, recalled from a training assignment in the United States. Kagame was one of Museveni's earliest supporters, and later his deputy chief of military intelligence, and had learned well the lessons of Museveni's brilliant insurgency campaign during the NRA years. This second phase of invasion operated on classic guerrilla lines. Kagame led the RPF along the Uganda-Rwanda border to the northwestern highlands of the Virunga mountains. In Virunga Kagame provided the RPF with the necessary leadership to sustain the rigors of life in the high altitudes and cold weather of the Virunga mountains.[7] From this vantage point they launched a series of guerrilla attacks in northern Rwanda that succeeded, by mid-1991, in making the northern part of the country a region where the FAR could not travel except at high risk.[8]

In November 1991 the FAR launched a strong attack on the RPF's position in the Virungas. Consistent artillery shelling of the RPF's position failed to dislodge the RPF. When the attack failed, the momentum swung back to the RPF's favour. During the first months of 1992 the RPF consolidated its position in the north, creating a de facto RPF-held zone extending along almost the whole Uganda-Rwanda border, and extending at its widest point roughly 25 kilometers inland (a sizeable portion of a country that measures roughly 100 kilometres at its longest point.)

The November attack followed a short-lived cease-fire between the two armies, brokered by regional states and regional organisations (see section 2). A new cease-fire was negotiated in June 1992, as part of a process of launching political negotiation (see section 2.) That cease-fire was more or less observed for seven months, while negotiations got underway. When those negotiations got stuck in January 1993, however, war quickly resumed. On February 8, 1993, the RPF launched their largest offensive since October 1990.

The RPF offensive was a major success. Thousands of the FAR's troops fled in the face of the advancing enemy, many of them deserting the army altogether. Within two weeks, with the FAR scattering in front of them, the

RPF fought to within 23 kilometers of Kigali. RPF, French, and Tanzanian military intelligence sources agree that had the RPF chosen at this moment to press for Kigali they would almost certainly have achieved victory.[9] That they did not was in part due to the fact that France sent reinforcements to Kigali to prevent such an outcome, in part due to international diplomatic pressure on the RPF to leave open room for a negotiated solution, and in part due to their own tactical considerations, which suggested that a political solution that brought them to power-sharing arrangements was preferable to an outright military victory.

After the February offensive the RPF controlled close to a third of Rwandan territory, including the economically important northeast and the entire border with Uganda. However, as a condition of a return to negotiations, in March 1993 the RPF returned to their preoffensive lines, leaving a UN-patrolled Demilitarized Zone (DMZ) in the territory captured in the February offensive.

The negotiations eventually called for a small contingent of the RPF (roughly six hundred troops) to be stationed inside Kigali to secure RPF politicians during a transition to power-sharing arrangements. The RPF and Rwandan government also agreed to a Neutral International Force being deployed to secure the peace deal. This resulted in a UN peacekeeping force being sent to Rwanda in October 1993. This state of affairs held until April 1994.

On April 6, 1994, the akazu launched their genocidal bid to retain power in Rwanda (see the following section.) For forty-eight hours the political and military picture in Kigali was confused, as different battalions of the FAR attacked each other, the FAR attacked UN forces deployed in Kigali and the DMZ (see section 2), and the elite Presidential Guard, along with government militias, began constructing roadblocks across the city and executing both Rwandan opposition politicians and Kigali Tutsis. For twenty-four hours the RPF held their positions on the northern side of the DMZ, waiting to see how the situation would clarify and what the UN forces would do in response.[10] When it became clear that the UN would not respond effectively, Kagame ordered a third major RPF offensive.

As the military forces of the akazu continued their program of genocide, the RPF moved swiftly and strategically through Rwanda to halt them. A multipronged RPF attack engaged the FAR in Kigali, attacked FAR positions in the east and north, chased the FAR west across Rwanda. In June the RPF offensive was set back by a significant French intervention (see section 2), which blocked their advance in the southwest, to which large sections of the FAR retreated. Eventually the FAR either retreated into Zaire through French-held southwest Rwanda or were pushed out of northwestern Rwanda by the combined assault of the multipronged RPF offensive. By July 17, 1994, the RPF controlled the entire country, bringing an end to the civil war.

Political War: The Oligarchy Versus All-Comers

While the RPF engaged the FAR in the military war, a political war was also being waged. Through a combination of intimidation, assassination, and propaganda, the akazu succeeded in reorienting the politics of the civil war, obscuring its political elements while emphasizing its ethnic component. As negotiations and diplomacy weakened their position, the akazu turned increasingly to political violence to defend their power. This political struggle culminated in massive genocide, halted in Rwanda only when the akazu's military forces were defeated by the RPF. To understand the tactics of this political battle, and the akazu's success in manipulating fear as a tool of war, it is necessary to understand something of the nature of one of Rwanda's major cleavages, ethnicity.

Ethnicity as Ideology

Most journalistic accounts of the Rwandan regime under President Júvenal Habyarimana referred to it as a Hutu regime. This fails to capture the reality of pregenocide Rwandan politics. For while it was certainly true that the vast majority of those who held power in Rwanda before the genocide were Hutu, they were not just Hutu, but Hutu of particular clans—especially the Bushiru—from particular regions—especially Ruhengiri and Byumba. The Habyarimana regime was in fact a clan-based northern Hutu regime that was as discriminatory against Hutus from southern Rwanda as against Tutsis.[11]

After gaining power in a coup in 1963, the members of Habyarimana's regime consolidated both formal and informal control over the Rwandan state and through it the main channels of Rwanda's commercial, intellectual, and cultural life. In the arena of formal power the Bushiru Hutu dominated the Rwandan state through a political party, the Mouvement Republicain National pour le Developpement (MRND), that President Habyarimana declared to be the only legal party. The relationship between the MRND and the state was similar to that of the old Communist party of the Soviet Union (CPSU) to the Soviet government. Government became in effect a subset of the party, and security and success within the party were the sine qua non of political advance in Rwanda. Similar to the CPSU, the MRND ran what amounted to a system of *nomenklatura* through which key positions in the regional bureaucracy, the education sector, the army, the state enterprises, and the church were given to party members or supporters. One measure of success of the Bushiru in working this system is that by 1980, 80 percent of command positions in the armed forces were held by members of Habyarimana's clan.[12]

At the elite level the inner circles of power, state enterprise, army command, regional prefectures, and church leadership were dominated by Habyarimana's clan family—indeed, so closely knit was this circle that it earned the nickname of the "little house" (i.e., the little house around Habyarimana), or akazu. Senior members of the akazu controlled the state banks and led the major enterprises, which were financed with concesionary state loans and received virtually all government contracts. Tourism and coffee, Rwanda's two foreign currency–earning industries, were dominated by akazu members. Critically, the akazu dominated the army, not only through all the major command posts of the regular army, the FAR, but through total domination of the Presidential Guard, a praetorian guard that was Habyarimana's first line of defense and, as it proved, first line of attack.

The akazu was a classic oligarchy, defined in clan terms, and like all oligarchies the maintenance of their own power became the central concern of that power. Also like all oligarchies, the akazu sought to diminish the attention paid to their exclusive composition. If journalists and others believed that the Habyarimana was a Hutu regime, it is in large measure because the akazu promoted that myth.

Manipulation of Ethnicity, Manipulation of Fear, and the Construction of Genocide

In this they were aided by Rwandan history and the nature of Rwandan ethnicity, which was open to interpretation and manipulation. The categories Tutsi and Hutu were, historically, complex ones that contained elements of ethnicity, lineage, clan, and social status, elements that related in differing ways in various parts of the territory.[13] To enhance their capacity to rule Rwanda, the Belgians—Rwanda's colonial masters—introduced rigidities into these relations, essentially equating Tutsi identity with ruling status, giving Tutsis privileged access to the state and economic opportunities, and even going so far as to introduce now notorious identity cards that noted the bearer's ethnic category. Through this interaction with Belgian colonial structures Rwandans came for the first time to be identified principally on the basis of their ethnicity. Tutsi and Hutu relations were thus radically transformed—or reconstructed—through interaction with Belgian colonial power.

That Rwandan social relations were malleable in this fashion reflects the fact that they exhibit the characteristics of ethnicity as that term is understood by proponents of the constructivist school of ethnicity. Indeed, Rwanda was an important early case of this approach to understanding ethnicity not as a given set of physical and genetic characteristics (a primordialist approach) but as a social outcome, a construction based on a multiplicity of interacting factors, potentially incorporating class, lineage, status, and other social attributes.[14]

The constructed nature of Rwandan ethnicity has historically left it open to rearticulation/manipulation by political elites. Indeed, throughout modern Rwandan history, political elites have highlighted their ethnic identities to mobilize support for political competition. Such an approach brought Rwanda's first president, Gregoire Kayibanda, to power in 1959, as Kayibanda capitalized on Hutu hostility to the Belgium-Tutsi administration and rode a wave of anti-Tutsi violence to power.[15] As Lemarchand has argued, with reference to similar processes in Burundi, that wave of violence caused tens of thousands of Tutsi to flee Rwanda, taking refuge in neighboring states, particularly Uganda.[16] (It was from this population of Tutsi refugees that the ranks of the RPF would be drawn in the late 1980s.)

Habyarimana and the akazu had learned the lessons of Hutu-Tutsi opposition in the Kayibanda regime and used ethnic tension to strengthen their own rule. However, by the late 1980s the akazu's discriminatory domination of the Rwandan state started to come under fire from the international community, which began to exert diplomatic pressure for democratic reforms. This pressure took the form of Structural Adjustment Program conditionalities as well as agitation by Western governments over human rights problems. France was particularly active in seeking multiparty democracy. These pressures led Habyarimana to announce democratic reforms in early 1990, though these were quickly shelved at the onset of the RPF invasion. However, Rwandan dependence on foreign aid (especially after November 1990), and its resultant vulnerability to Western pressure, brought democratization back onto the agenda in 1991–1992, when analysis by Western diplomats suggested that democratization must run parallel to peace negotiations if a viable peace was to be found.[17]

By April 1992 international pressure resulted in the formation of a coalition government, bringing the Parti Liberal (PL), Parti Socialiste Democratique (PSD), Mouvement Democratique Rwandaise (MDR), and others into power-sharing arrangements with the ruling MRND.[18] The first substantive act of this coalition government was to agree to a process of political negotiations with the RPF. This internal political shift, along with pressure on the Habyarimana government from France, and pressure on the RPF from the United States (by way of Uganda), produced agreement in the summer of 1992 to launch what would become a sustained process of political negotiations, the Arusha process.

The akazu reacted to the emergence of a new, formal opposition by formalizing their own network, principally through the creation of a pseudo party, the Coalition pour la défense de la République (CDR). The CDR brought together akazu members from both formal and informal circles of power: MRND ministers, army chiefs, religious leaders, enterprise leaders, and the owners of a group of newly established media enterprises, including hate radio stations, joined the CDR in an effort to ebb the flow of power away from their oligarchic control.

Despite their best efforts, neither the MRND nor the CDR were able to contain the Arusha peace process.

The end point of the Arusha process was a deal that saw a radical transfer of power in Rwanda, at least on paper, from oligarchic domination of the state by the akazu to power sharing between the regime, opposition parties that had been created during the turbulent civil war years, and the RPF.[19] Elsewhere I have written a detailed argument about which elements of the Arusha settlement produced violent reactions among power holders in Kigali.[20] These can be summarized here. First, and critically, the ruling MRND party, along with their powerful ally, the CDR, were assigned to a weak minority position in both the Broad-Based Transitional Government and the Transitional National Assembly. Second, the RPF were given a powerful share in what was to become an integrated national army, composed of RPF and FAR troops in a 40–60 ratio, but commanded by a 50–50 split of RPF and FAR officers.[21]

To the akazu this was perceived as a complete loss of power. From having oligarchic control over the state, they were to move to a position of weak minority in the power structure of Rwanda and lose their capacity to ensure their position through the military. This settlement was met with outrage and hostility in Kigali. The akazu were not about to give up power without a fight. As the Arusha deal began to take shape, particularly in the spring of

1993, the CDR began to place in motion and whip up support for a radical alternative to Arusha, a "final solution" that was ultimately manifested as the genocide of 1994.

The groundwork for what would become the genocide had begun to be laid almost as soon as the RPF invaded in October 1990. The genocide was being planned by a core group of political extremists: a hard-line faction of the ruling MRND, of the extremist political grouping, the CDR, leaders of the Presidential Guard, some of the leaders of the FAR, some of the country's local administrators (most regional bourgmeistre and many local prefets), and some church leaders. The great majority of these *genocidaires*[22] were members of the akazu.[23]

At the inner core of the akazu there had never been any willingness to consider a negotiated settlement with the RPF, at least not one that would constitute a diminishment of the oligarchy's power. At the wider edges of the akazu, however, frustration with the tight rein held by the akazu leadership had led some of its junior members to support efforts of the opposition parties to open up the corridors of power. A few even took the radical step of joining the new opposition parties, an act of betrayal for which they would pay dearly. However, as the shape of the Arusha deal became clear, many of the outer members of the akazu rallied to the center, including some who had flirted with opposition groups. This led to chaos among the opposition parties, as repentant akazu and others formed so-called power factions within the opposition parties that rallied to the oligarchy's cause. Here control over the state banks and enterprise sector was particularly useful, for the akazu was able to bribe and otherwise induce many such "repentants" into joining the power factions.

With the signing of the Arusha Accords, what had been a radical plan of an inner core took on a wider salience and gathered momentum. During the period in which the UN and moderate forces first concluded the Arusha process, and attempted to implement the Arusha deal, the power factions disrupted the mechanics of the opposition parties and deliberately threw off the power-sharing math of the Arusha Accords. Meanwhile, the genocidaires organized, financed, and trained extremist militias, the Interahamwe and Impuzamugambi, and directed the spread of hate and fear propaganda, notably through the notorious Radio et Television Libre Mille Colines (RTLM).

The critical tool in setting the stage for the genocide was propaganda that cast the civil war in ethnic terms. In pamphlets, songs, speeches, "official" documents, and through the directed actions of the extremist militias, the akazu communicated a message of fear: that victory by the RPF would presage the enslavement of the Hutu, that these "foreign devils" sought only to reimpose their historical overlordship, that these "cockroaches" were returning to infest Hutu lands and to take those lands away from the Hutu to whom they rightfully belonged.[24] The Arusha Accords were painted as a betrayal: a few Hutus had been corrupted by the Tutsi devils and the Westerners and had sold out to the enemy. The RPF was just a Trojan Horse: once establishing a beachhead in Kigali, another, larger army in hiding in Uganda would descend on Rwanda and sweep away the Hutu power.[25] Politicians who negotiated with the RPF, or who even advocated political solutions to the war, were portrayed as traitors. So virulent were the attacks on the moderate option of dialogue that when one Western diplomat visited Kigali in late 1993 she described the situation as near to civil war—not with the RPF, but among the Kigali factions.

Like all good propaganda, the genocidaires' message had a kernel of truth. An important part of the RPF's agenda was to establish the right of Banyamulenge to return to Rwanda.[26] On what land would they be resettled was an open question, despite some efforts to address the issue during the Arusha process. Some RPF were motivated in part by the memory of their families' degradation at the hands of the Hutu during the 1959 uprisings. And the Tutsi did—in a certain sense—have a dominant position in preindependence Rwanda, enough to give the "history" of Tutsi enslavement of Hutus some credence. The genocidaires worked to stir the population's fears, but skillfully, mixing real memories and real issues into the potion of fear which they fed to the population.

Critically, Rwandan ethnicity was fluid enough to be open to this type of reinterpretation/manipulation. Despite the fact they were themselves an almost exclusively northern oligarchy, the genocidaires pounded home the message that all Hutu must stick together for fear of RPF retaliation. The genocidaires' message was that the RPF was going to take revenge on all Hutu, regardless of clan or region, so better to join forces now and defeat the RPF. In a manner that supports part of Kaufmann's argument in this volume, as the akazu raised the stakes around ethnicity, Rwandans were convinced that the RPF would see ethnicity in the same way, and to be Hutu was to fear the RPF. Thus, the genocidaires created widespread fear among the Rwandan population—not out of nothing, but through the skillful manipulation of an existing social cleavage, ethnicity.

The goal was to negate negotiated diminishment of the akazu's power, the strategy was to wipe out the presumed political base of the RPF, and the triggering—or launching—event was the assassination of President Haby-arimana. On the evening of April 6, 1994, Habyarimana's plane was shot down on its return from further negotiations in Tanzania. The evening of the assassination, road blocks were constructed across Kigali, and the killings began. The first victims were Hutu opposition politicians, human rights workers, journalists: anyone who had joined the internal opposition to akazu rule. The killings swiftly moved on to Kigali Tutsis, who were wiped out in tens of thousands. From Kigali, the killings spread systematically to the countryside. From central command in Kigali, orders were sent to local Ministry of Transportation representatives to provide trucks for purposes of "national security";[27] squads of militia members were sent to towns and villages across the country to round up Tutsis and to assist the FAR in their execution; and the genocide machine swept across the country.

Popular fear was an essential strategic resource for the akazu when they launched their genocidal solution in April 1994. Civilians were press-ganged into manning the roadblocks or adding their strength to an execution team and called on to name their Tutsi neighbors and even family members. Although some Hutus managed to resist, those that did quickly fell victim to the machine guns and machetes of the FAR and Interahamwe. Even during the height of the killings the masterminds of the genocide continued brilliantly to manipulate ethnicity and fear to create space for their program. For example, in one town in southwestern Rwanda the bourgmeistre, bishop, and local FAR commander executed a plan of subtle brutality. Having convinced local Tutsis that they would be protected from the chaos if they congregated in a local school (leaving their machetes and hoes at home), the local Hutu villagers were corraled into participating in the execution of the Tutsi. The villagers were ordered to stand on the ridges of the surrounding hills, wearing nothing but skirts of banana leaves. When the villagers were deployed on the hills, a FAR company attacked the school, using grenades, machine guns, and machetes to wipe out more than sixteen thousand Tutsi in an evening.[28] The villagers were ordered to kill any Tutsi who escaped from the school. The brilliance was in the banana leaves: banana leaf skirts were worn on some occasions in colonial Rwanda by Hutus serfs performing agricultural tasks for Tutsi feudal lords; thus they invoked a historical moment of Hutu indignity; moreover, they clearly distinguished the villagers from the targeted Tutsi. The plan implicated the entire village—roughly two thousand people—in their participation in the genocide. Having participated in it, under no matter how much coercive direction, Hutu villagers were thus even more afraid of opposing the genocide movement.[29]

As Lake and Rothchild establish, "By itself, ethnicity is not a cause of violent conflict."[30] Rather, they note, competition for scarce resources often provides the source of violence. This was so in Rwanda, but in a peculiar fashion, for in Rwanda most of the violence during the civil war and genocide was perpetrated not by the victims of state discrimination but the masters of the system. The scarce resource in question was power: control over the state and through it the vast bulk of Rwanda's economic resources. The genocide was a systematic effort by the akazu to retain their oligarchic control of the Rwandan state and its resources; in effect, an extraordinary example of political elites using ethnicity to mobilize political competition— in this case, of the bloodiest kind. In their planning of the genocide we see a second reverberation of the memory of earlier ethnic domination: like Hutu elites in 1959, the akazu used the fear of Tutsi domination as a tool to legitimate violence against Tutsis in Rwanda and the Tutsi-dominated RPF. Once again, the manipulation of social cleavages by elites in political competition would lead Rwanda to massive violence.

Military Interventions and War Termination in Rwanda: Innovation and Failure

Military interventions in Rwanda did not impede the akazu in the execution of their violent political war. This despite the fact that there were a plethora of such intervention in Rwanda. Indeed, even in the intervention-rich environment of the years immediately following the end of the cold war, Rwanda stands out for having been the site of an extraordinary number of military interventions in a brief timeframe: during four years of civil war and genocide, no less than nine discrete military interventions attempted to influence the dynamics of conflict, while six separate military missions responded to the humanitarian emergency that followed.[31] Rwanda was a laboratory for intervention experiments: the first deployment of OAU troops through the Conflict Resolution Mechanism, the first on-the-ground collaboration between an OAU and a UN force, and an innovative, though ultimately problematic, UN-mandated, French intervention force for humanitarian stabilization. However, the central fact about those interventions as a group is that none prevented the massive escalation of violence in Rwanda. Moreover, the partisan interventions that accompanied the war were a permissive cause of war, prolonged the life of the war, and in so doing left space open to the akazu to construct their genocidal response. A brief historical account of the sequence of military interventions in Rwanda precedes an analysis of the reasons for their incoherence and overall failure to prevent large-scale violence in Rwanda.

Innovation and Experimentation: A Brief Account of Interventions in Rwanda

The starting point for an account of intervention is the support given by the Ugandan regime under President Yoweri Museveni to the RPF. Museveni has repeatedly denied providing direct support to the RPF, but from the outset of the RPF war Western diplomats in the region suggested that Museveni was providing the RPF with political and logistical support. This belief was confirmed by CIA reports based on live intelligence, which found evidence that the Ugandan military was transporting arms from depots in Kigali to the border for RPF use, making Ugandan military hospitals accessible to RPF casualties, and keeping civilians clear from strategic crossings into Rwanda, which had previously been unguarded.[32]

Ugandan support for the rebels was immediately countered by direct military intervention by French and Zairian troops in support of Habyarimana's regime. Troops from the two countries were rushed to Kigali to evacuate nationals and backstop the FAR. The Zairian intervention was short-lived, as Habyarimana was quickly forced to ask the Zairian government to repeal its troops when their behavior in Kigali—raping, looting, etc—became a greater threat than source of security. Perhaps more important than their behavior was their ineffectiveness: the Forces Armées Zairois (FAZ) troops were roundly defeated by the RPF at Gabiro. This intervention was thus of limited impact.

The French intervention was more substantive. Several hundred French troops stayed on in Rwanda and played an important role in backstopping the FAR in Kigali, freeing them from defensive tasks such as guarding the airport, and thereby enhancing their capacity to engage the RPF in the north.[33] The legal basis for France's involvement was a 1975 defense training agreement between the two countries, and, formally, French troops were limited to training and advisory capacities. What is hotly debated among Rwanda observers is whether or not the French actually fought alongside the FAR in the October counteroffensive. A number of Western journalists report having witnessed French soldiers directing artillery fire in the north as well as French pilots in spotter planes, which were used to target that artillery. Paris denies active French involvement, and no analyst or observer has provided rigorous proof to substantiate the allegations. In any case, French intervention was sufficient to slow the early rapid advances of the RPF and enhanced the capacity of the FAR to stage a serious defense against the rebels.

Partisan interventions—Ugandan and French—were thus important facilitators of the Rwandan military war. Uganda was, following Brown's formulation, "an active contributor to military escalation,"[34] making possible the RPF's military bid for power (or power sharing.) France can not be seen to have contributed to an escalation of military activity, per se, as their intervention was in defense of a regime with whom they had a defense agreement and that came under attack by a rebel army. Nevertheless, the long-term impact of French intervention was to provide early backup to what would prove to be a very nasty regime.

As the RPF settled into a pattern of guerrilla warfare, a series of regional military missions were deployed to Rwanda to oversee developments. Indeed, Rwanda became a laboratory wherein subregional and regional interstate organizations tested their capacity to engage in conflict management. The results were largely negative: the experience of regional intervention in Rwanda would prove one of extremely limited impact.

Talks aimed at generating a cease-fire between the FAR and the RPF had begun shortly after the October invasion. A series of summits organized by the Communité Economique des Pays de Grands Lacs (CEPGL) and Tanzania produced a temporary cease-fire on March 21, 1991. At this time the RPF and the government of Rwanda agreed to a proposal for a monitoring force, named the Military Observer Group and designated by its French acronym, GOM, that was to be composed of fifteen officers each from Burundi, Uganda, Tanzania, and Zaire as well as five officers from the RPF.[35] The participation of Ugandan and Tanzanian troops was presumed to balance that of Zairians and Burundians and thus to ensure the forces' neutrality. However, the cease-fire did not last long enough for the force to be deployed. Ironically, one of the causes of the breakdown in the cease-fire was disputes over how the military force would be implemented in practice.

A second cease-fire was signed between the government of Rwanda and the RPF in September 1991. The G'bado-lite cease-fire arrangement called for a revised observer group, with a more balanced composition, under the auspices of a nascent conflict resolution mechanism at the Organization of African Unity (OAU) (the first time the mechanism had been used, and the first time the OAU had deployed forces in a civil conflict of a member state.) The lead of the force was given to Nigeria, with the senior Zairian consigned to the role of deputy commander. The force was comprised of Nigerian and Zairian troops, with RPF and FAR representation. In later negotiations the composition was further revised to bring in troops from Senegal and Zimbabwe and to remove the Zairian presence. This observer group did manage to deploy, though not before the FAR took advantage of delays to launch their November 1991 offensive in the Virungas.[36]

Finally, this mission was substantially modified in June of 1992, when international peace negotiations got underway. Renamed the Neutral Military Observer Group (NMOG), the composition was reworked to draw in more remote participants.[37] This mission did deploy and reported to an regional/international body known as the Joint Military–Political Commission (JPMC).[38] In theory, it should have had an important role in confidence building between the two parties; there is no evidence, however, to support this theory. Some reports of cease-fire violations and the like were raised by NMOG during the negotiation process, but were never substantiated by evidence and were for the most part dismissed as irrelevant. NMOG was at best ineffective, its performance hampered by its reliance on support from the FAR, which was able to control its movements and keep it clear of sensitive areas.

What is notable about these various regional observer missions is that they appear to have done nothing to contribute to the search for a negotiated end to the Rwandan civil war. Increasing frustration with the ineffectual regional interventions eventually led, after some important developments in the war and negotiations, to the deployment of international neutral missions in Rwanda.

The important developments in the war have already been discussed— especially the February 1993 RPF offensive, which radically transformed the lines of battle and the situation on the ground. This offensive also led, among other things, to an important extension of France's intervention in Rwanda. As the RPF raced toward Kigali, two waves of French reinforcements were sent to Kigali to firm up the FAR's defenses. Although French reinforcements were not the only—nor even perhaps the principal—reason for the RPF's decision to halt their offensive outside Kigali, the combination of events had an important long-term effect. Critically, France's reinforcements and the RPFs decision to halt their offensive may have sent the message to the akazu that France would be there to secure them if and when push came finally to shove with the RPF. This might have reassured the akazu and increased their willingness to engage in political negotiations; were they even remotely willing to consider a negotiated peace, the French card should have acted as a sort of unilateral security guarantee. In the event, given their a priori hostility to a negotiated settlement, it firmed their resolve to engage their radical genocidal alternative. France could not have predicted the outcome, but the principal impact of this partisan intervention was to provide support to the growing development of the genocide movement.

As mentioned above, following the events of February 1993 the RPF agreed to turn over the territory gained during their advance to a UN-sponsored DMZ. As part of the same negotiations, a UN military observer group was deployed to the Uganda-Rwanda border. This mission, UN Observer Mission to Uganda-Rwanda (UNOMUR), was to play a similar role to NMOG, and indeed cooperated with it on the ground—the first ever UN-OAU military collaboration on the ground. Although taken more seriously than NMOG by many of the players in Rwanda, the observer group was confined to a border, which had long since outlived its strategic significance and had only a small force—roughly eighty men—to patrol even that border (along 100 mountainous kilometers). In practice UNOMUR proved to be as insignificant as its regional predecessors.

Most important—from both an academic and policy perspective—a UN peacekeeping mission was sent to Rwanda in the fall of 1993, at the conclusion of the Arusha peace process.[39] With a view to containing some of the potential difficulties associated with implementing a peace deal, the Arusha Accords called for the deployment of a Neutral International Force (NIF) to be deployed during a transitional period.[40] After some initial consideration of the idea, the OAU pronounced itself unable to meet the requirements of the Arusha force.[41] The NIF thus fell in New York's lap, which approved a new force, the UN Assistance Mission in Rwanda (UNAMIR) (SC/RES/872/ 5 October 1993), despite resistance, particularly from the United States.[42]

The experience of UNAMIR was not a sanguine one. The signing of a peace agreement in August 1993 did nothing to halt the rapid deterioration of the political situation in Kigali in the fall of 1993 and spring of 1994— indeed, reaction to the Arusha Accords became the organizing theme of increasingly violent political war waged by the akazu.[43] As peacemakers attempted to put the Arusha structures in place, the akazu geared up the machinery for their radical alternative to the Arusha power-sharing plan: the mass genocide against the Tutsi population and a return to war against the RPF.

The deployment of UNAMIR in Rwanda did little or nothing to shore up the Arusha transitional process. For a start, the mission did not deploy according to the schedule laid out by Arusha. This was hardly the UN's fault,

as the Arusha timetable called for a totally unrealistic thirty-nine days between signing the deal and deploying the force.[44] Nevertheless, the perceived
tardiness confirmed preconceived notions that the force's commitment
would be weak. From the first moment of deployment, thus, UNAMIR was
seen to be a paper tiger, a perception it would never counter and would
ultimately prove.

In the face of violent opposition the UN's security presence proved as
naught. When the genocide plan was put in motion on April 6, 1994, with
the assassination of President Habyarimana, UNAMIR was among the early
successful targets. The targeting of UNAMIR had actually been revealed to
the UN, when an informant disclosed to the force commander details of the
genocide plan. The plan included killing ten Belgian peacekeepers to effect
the withdrawal of the UN force. The plan unfolded as foreseen: ten peacekeepers were taken hostage by the FAR and then killed and brutalized.[45]
The attack produced the intended result: Belgium announced the imminent
withdrawal of its UNAMIR contingent, crippling the peacekeeping mission.[46] Within ten days the UN decided to draw down its force to symbolic
levels (UN Security Council Resolution 912).[47] Apart from protecting a few
thousand civilians in Kigali, the UN effectively left Rwanda's genocide planners a clear field to put their killing machine in motion. Although UNAMIR
was eventually reinforced, new troops did not arrive in Rwanda until August,
well after the end of the genocide and civil war.

Finally, while the genocide was underway, France sent a unilateral but
UN-mandated intervention force to southwestern Rwanda, in Operation
Turquoise.[48] The stated purpose of the intervention was to halt the genocide
and facilitate humanitarian access to victims of the genocide and of displace-
ment. In fact, Operation Turquoise established a presence only in a part of
Rwanda where the genocide had already been largely completed, although
a few thousand lives were saved by the operation. Humanitarians did gain
access to displaced populations and victims in French-held territory, but then
they were also given rapid access in RPF-held territories, so this point is
neutral. Most perniciously, the intervention slowed the RPF advance, allowing the FAR to retreat as an intact force into eastern Zaire, where they were
later able to establish a new base for insurgency operations.[49] The connec-
tions between this outcome and the 1996 civil war in Zaire are direct.[50]
French intervention, then, did nothing to aid the process of war termination
or conflict resolution; rather, it served to recycle the war when it might
otherwise have been by and large concluded through a more decisive RPF
victory.

Explaining the Failure: Differing Politics
and Political Indifference

That the wide spectrum of military interventions in Rwanda did not prevent the disastrous result that occurred is self-evident; why, requires explanation. Two broad factors account for the failure: differing politics and political indifference. Differing politics led to intervention and counterintervention, which facilitated the process of war; political indifference undermined the potential contribution of the UN's peacekeeping intervention.

Three sets of interventions can be discerned in Rwanda: partisan interventions that supported one side versus the other, neutral observer missions by regional and international security organizations, and a peacekeeping intervention by the UN that sought to secure a negotiated peace agreement. Of these the first and last deserve substantive consideration. Not only is it the case that the observer missions in fact had very limited impact on the course of war in Rwanda, they also have less potential impact than either a partisan or peacekeeping intervention, being narrowly limited in mandate by nature. Given space considerations, then, attention will be paid only to the partisan and peacekeeping operations in Rwanda.

Political Difference: Partisan Interventions

Just as peacekeeping interventions aim to terminate wars, so too do partisan interventions, albeit in a very different fashion. The termination of war through the military or political defeat of an opposing party is the essential aim of those military interventions that support one party to a conflict. What Rwanda demonstrates is that when such interventions fail to achieve that objective, the consequences can be seriously, even disastrously, deleterious to the societies in which they occur.

At no point in Rwanda is it reasonable to argue that partisan military intervention contributed to the termination of the Rwandan war. Rather, partisan intervention by Uganda facilitated the onset of war in Rwanda, and intervention by France extended its life at key moments as well as—to put it in its worst light—creating an opportunity for the akazu to develop their genocidal strategy.

One of the key questions that opens up when considering intervention in Rwanda is the question of the divergent politics surrounding the various military interventions that took place there. In foreign policy terms this is a banal observation: different states have different interests, or different politics, and will act in differing ways as a result. This reality, however banal, is often neglected in discussions of the role of outside intervention. Divergent policy aims are often tackled as a "coordination" or "coherence" issue, limiting them to the level of technical policy administration.

It is of course possible to view partisan interventions as tools of conflict management, as distinct from instruments of foreign policy. Military intervention in support of one combatant or one "side," if it is successful, may well end wars more quickly than other forms of intervention, such as mediation or peacekeeping. There were two likely points where this might have held true in Rwanda: more substantial Ugandan backing to the RPF in October 1990 might well have led to a more rapid defeat of the FAR (witness the success of Ugandan and Rwandan backing to Laurent Kabila's forces in Zaire in 1996–97) and more substantial French intervention in October 1990 might have led to greater disarray in the RPF and an early collapse of their effort. The question of partisan intervention can also be put in reverse: Would the Rwandan civil war have started and lasted, absent partisan intervention? Arguably, without Ugandan backing in 1990, the RPF would not have been able to launch the war, let alone sustain it, especially when French intervention allowed the FAR to respond. Equally, without French backing in 1990, and more particularly in 1993, the FAR would likely have been defeated by the RPF far earlier than in fact was the case.

In each of these scenarios of partisan support—both positive and negative—the total number of deaths from fighting in Rwanda would have been hugely lower than actually resulted, as each scenario sees war coming to an end before the akazu had a chance to launch their genocidal response.

However, when partisan interventions are viewed this way, the question of divergent politics falls into sharp relief. First, at a basic level, the success of partisan intervention is likely to be in large measure determined by the absence of *counter*intervention. The nature of partisan intervention is such, however, that this is a condition more likely to be absent than present. Certainly, the foreign backers of the parties to Rwanda's military war responded in kind to each other's partisan support: for example, Uganda's support to the RPF at the outset of the war was quickly countered by French intervention. This was not an absence of coherence or coordination, or anything like it: rather, the military expression of wholly divergent politics and political interest in the region.

Moreover, the consequences of partisan intervention—when it does not produce a quick cessation of hostilities—can be far-reaching, as French actions in Rwanda demonstrate. As noted, French support for the FAR in 1993 created a space in which the akazu constructed their genocide machine;

Operation Turquoise opened up a new space in Zaire for the remnants of the genocide regime to reconstruct their authority and strategic capacity, directly contributing to the outbreak of war in Zaire in 1996.

Thus, in Rwanda, partisan intervention was not primarily a tool of conflict management, but a facilitator of and contributor to internal war.

Political Indifference: Failure of UNAMIR

Rwanda's military war was fueled and sustained by partisan interventions; neutral interventions did little to end it. Whereas the partisan interventions fueled rather than contained the war on the basis of differing politics, it was political indifference more than any other factor that weakened neutral intervention in Rwanda. Whether a more appropriate, more concerted peacekeeping intervention would have been able to prevent transformation of Rwanda's war from low-level civil fighting into massive genocide is unknowable, though several key figures believe it might well have.[51] What is certain is that the peacekeeping intervention that did occur in Rwanda was flawed from the outset and never made a substantive contribution to the process of war termination. Ironically, although sent to oversee the end to the military war, the peacekeeping intervention in Rwanda actually fell victim to the political war. Failure to understand Rwanda's political war in a dynamic fashion, and translate its developments into military contingencies, is the surface cause of the weakness of the peacekeeping effort. This failure reflects a deeper cause, political indifference on the part of the Western powers.

Most critically, the peacekeepers—or at least their political masters—by and large were persuaded by the version of reality put out by the genocidaires through their propaganda tools, seeing the Rwandan war in ethnic terms rather than in the more narrow political terms by which it was more accurately characterized. Blinded to the real politics of Rwanda's war, peacekeepers responded unhelpfully to developments in Rwanda, and weakened their own potential utility.

The blindness was partially willful. In the fall of 1993 the UN's Department of Peacekeeping Operations (DPKO) sent a mission to Rwanda to assess the potential opportunities and risks for an operation. The mission reported back that there were some serious risks to a peacekeeping operation in Rwanda and, on the basis of this assessment, argued that an optimal mission would comprise eight thousand troops; five thousand men was seen as the responsible minimum. The larger figure was never put to the Security Council: advance messages from the American delegation in particular made it clear that there would be no support for a large mission in Rwanda. Thus DPKO had eventually to recommend a mission designed in large measure in mind of what the traffic would bear—i.e., political considerations.[52] The Security Council eventually agreed to send twenty-five hundred troops to Rwanda, to grow to five thousand if certain conditions were met. The mandate was strictly Chapter 6, with rules of engagement that were solely reactive. The agreement was reached after laborious negotiations that reflected a general, and particularly an American, reluctance to spend large sums of money on peacekeeping operations.

Having agreed to send a small mission with a fairly weak mandate to Rwanda, the UN system then hobbled it by failing to supply it with adequate equipment or financing. Absurdly, the budget for UNAMIR was only agreed upon by the UN machinery on April 5: six months after the mission deployed and one day before the situation was radically altered by the launch of the genocide. At one stage UNAMIR had to borrow funds from UNICEF simply to stay operational. More dangerously, UNAMIR was never provided with two things that might have proved critically useful: an intelligence capacity and defensive equipment. In particular, though promised eight armored personnel carriers (APCSs), the mission only received two, only one of which functioned for more than a couple of weeks. Just before the outbreak of genocide, UNAMIR was often in the position of having to tow the second APC behind the one functioning machine—presenting a disastrously accurate symbol of weakness to the genocidaires.

Ultimately, UNAMIR was attacked by the forces of Rwanda's political war and withdrew in the face of that attack, doing little to respond either to the genocide or the renewal of civil war. Arguably, with a stronger force, a more robust mandate, proper financing, and the equipment it needed to defend itself, UNAMIR could have responded more proactively in the face of the genocidaires' attack. However, with respect to war termination, the real issue was not APCs or finances but indifferent political support for the mission, which manifested itself in the small size of the mission, in the weak mandate, in a minimal intelligence capacity, and in a lack of political will to back robust action or reaction by UNAMIR.

UNAMIR's decisive weakness was its lack of political sensitivity to the political war, to internal opposition to Arusha. Most important, UNAMIR was composed on the basis of the willful illusion it was being sent to Rwanda to secure a commonly agreed peace.[53] One of the consequences of this weak political footing on which UNAMIR was composed was that it was not provided with a substantial intelligence capacity. This limited the capacity of

UNAMIR to investigate the growing signals of opposition to the implementation of Arusha. The combination of political indifference and poor intelligence meant that the direction of the political war, and signals of impending violence, went unheeded, if not unheard, in New York.[54] As the signals grew louder, and civil violence in Kigali and throughout the country increased with each step toward implementation of Arusha, New York failed to respond. No proactive measures to block Arusha's opponents were taken; no contingency planning occurred; signals of impending violence were dampened by the overworked, understaffed bureaucracy and ignored by the preoccupied Security Council.[55] Thus, having been composed on the basis of weak political support, UNAMIR was denied the tools that might have helped generate stronger support for action when the violence of the political war overtook the peace process in the military war.

In the face of strong opposition the UN's security guarantee proved as naught. Apart from protecting a few thousand civilians in Kigali, the international community effectively left Rwanda's genocide planners a clear field to put their killing machine in motion. UNAMIR's failure was a political one, that of attempting to secure in a neutral fashion a mutually agreed peace, when in fact the mission required was one capable of enforcing a controversial one. What was needed in Rwanda was a peace enforcement mission, capable of posing a credible deterrent to those forces—the genocidaires—who stood in opposition to the Arusha process.

Security Fears as a Tool of War

One way of determining the appropriate role for intervention is to explore its purpose in relation to security concerns and fears that it may quell. The editors of this volume have been concerned in particular to explore the connection between intervention and situations characterized by security dilemmas and, more broadly, to explore the role of security fears and their relation to military intervention. In Rwanda the evidence suggests that security fears were not so much a cause of war but a tool of it, a tool skillfully wielded by the akazu.

Rwanda's military war between the FAR and the RPF was not a product of a security dilemma. The concept of the anarchy of a country in civil war does not apply to the outset of the military war, based as the combatants were in two separate countries. The decision of the RPF to invade Rwanda in 1990 stemmed from decisions based around changes in the internal political context of Uganda.[56] Security fears in no way motivated the RPF.

Indeed, quite the opposite: many RPF commanders left positions of considerable power, influence, authority, and security in the Ugandan administration to launch a bush war replete with real security risks. The RPF's first commander, Rwigyema, gave up a senior position in the Ugandan administration and, by October 2, was lying dead on a Rwandan hillside. Fears for physical security were clearly not a dominant part of the matrix of motivation for the RPF.

In the case of the political war, however, there is a strong argument to be made that security fears played a much more important role. That role was complex, however. While there is evidence that security fears played a role in the breakdown of the Arusha peace process at the elite level, the stronger evidence suggests two things: that security fears reinforced a pre-existing opposition to negotiated peace on the part of the inner core of Rwanda's dominant oligarchy and that security fears were manipulated by this inner core to widen their base of support and purposes of political mobilization toward the genocide. Security fears were a contributory cause of the political war, but, more important, they were a tool for waging it.

Looked at from a theoretical perspective, there would appear to be an argument for describing the breakdown of the Arusha peace process — i.e., the successful launching of the violent tactics of the political war — as deriving from a security dilemma. Opposition to the Arusha Accords, this argument would have it, stemmed from fears that once in a situation of power sharing, and having demobilized a large portion of the FAR, Rwanda's oligarchy would find itself in a vulnerable position, open to renewed attack from the RPF, which could not be trusted to stick to peaceful politics. Indeed, some evidence supports this theory: in mid-1993, during discussions on demilitarization, a rumor was floating around Kigali that the RPF actually had a much larger army than it was admitting, a section of which would wait in reserve in Uganda until demobilization had been completed and then walk in to take power for the RPF. This rumor was connected to provisions of the Arusha agreement that foresaw a 50–50 split in command post for FAR and RPF officers in a proposed new national army. The akazu feared that lack of dominance in the army would undermine their ability to ensure their political position in transitional power-sharing structures. There were also fears about the nature of accountability that would take shape under Arusha. For the leadership of the akazu in particular, many members of which had built up sizable fortunes through state favors and contracts, accountability presaged financial ruin. These fears were made all the more credible by events in neighboring Burundi, where in the fall of 1993 the

Tutsi-dominated army killed tens of thousands of Hutus after assassinating the recently elected Hutu president, Melchior Ndadaye. These fears were clearly part of what motivated the akazu's opposition to the Arusha peace, motivated the political war that culminated in genocide.

Nevertheless, we cannot argue that security fears were a cause of the political war, that the breakdown of Arusha was caused by a security dilemma. For while security fears *reinforced* opposition to a negotiated peace, they did not *generate* that opposition. Rather, the leadership of the akazu was a priori hostile to any form of negotiated transfer of power to the RPF. The basis of their hostility was the attendant loss of their power, power that had been built up systematically through clan ties, corruption, and discrimination into a dominant position within the Rwandan state. Any form of negotiated power sharing with the RPF necessarily entailed at least a degree of diminishment of their power; the actual form of power sharing negotiated through Arusha in fact seriously curtailed their position. The implementation of Arusha failed not because the two sides were unable to trust each other absent a security guarantee but because a powerful element on one side of the table was committed to hostile opposition to peace. As Barbara Walter had argued, "Where intentions are hostile, there can be no security dilemma."

As demonstrated in section 2, the akazu revealed their hostility to negotiations with the RPF almost from the outset of the military war. Even before serious political negotiations were underway, the core of the akazu was building the ideological and political groundwork for what would become the genocide movement. Critically, some of the credible security fears noted above were actually generated by the genocidaires. Rumors of an RPF Trojan Horse army were circulated by the genocidaires in an effort to mobilize support in their own ranks among those less fully committed to the genocide option. Equally, fears about retaliation and accountability stemmed in large measure from CDR and RTLM propaganda; there was nothing in the Arusha Accords to provide any basis for such accountability. This propaganda, and other energetic actions of the genocidaires, had the critical effect of bringing a wider political group into their malevolent circle.

In this realm there is an important relationship between the weakness of international military intervention and the role played by security fears. A credible peacekeeping operation during the implementation of Arusha might have made the genocide propaganda less credible, allayed security fears of the population at large and of outer members of the akazu. Here a strong security guarantee would have diminished the effect with which the akazu wielded fear as a tool for mobilization.

For the inner core of committed genocidaires, we can only talk of security fear as a motivation if we use a very wide definition that incorporates the fear of loss of wealth, loss of prestige, loss of positional authority and the wealth extracting capacity that comes with it. Such fears are indistinguishable from predatory motives. Rather than portraying the genocidaires as a group of elites motivated to return to war by fear for their physical security, they can far more convincingly be portrayed as predatory elites who chose to sacrifice not only peace but the lives of almost one million Rwandans rather than see their own power and wealth diminished. They were, to use Stephen Stedman's term, spoilers.[57]

Peace in Rwanda fell victim to these spoilers, to a group of elites a priori committed to opposing negotiated peace. The weakness of the peace process against these spoilers was partially a function of the weaknesses of Arusha itself, partially a function of the political indifference surrounding UNAMIR. These spoilers skillfully manipulated security fears to two ends. First, rumors of retribution and accountability were used to counteract any dissension within the ranks of the akazu. Second, more widespread propaganda to generate fear was used to create the necessary space for their genocidal operations. Through the artful manipulation of an existing social cleavage the genocidaires successfully created the space for a machine of political violence that engulfed Rwanda in genocide. With devastating effect they manipulated social cleavages in Rwandan society, stoked real fears and created others, for the predatory purpose of the radical defense of their own narrow interests. It was the success of the spoilers of the inner core of Rwanda's oligarchy, the akazu, in creating this violent political war that destroyed the Rwandan peace process.

Outside military interventions, focused and targeted on military developments, facilitated, then failed to contain and ultimately fell victim to the violence of the political war. That a series of military interventions by regional and international powers and organizations did so little to contain violence in Rwanda reflects both the divergent political aims of those actors as well as political indifference on the part of the Western powers, other than France. In the case of UNAMIR this political indifference manifested itself in the form of political insensitivity and a resultant confusion of purpose. Sent to oversee the implementation of a commonly agreed peace,

UNAMIR never engaged in the real task of conflict management in Rwanda: containing the forces of hostile opposition that sought to destroy the very peace UNAMIR was sent to secure.

NOTES

1. Catherine Watson, *Exile from Rwanda: Background to an Invasion*. (Washington, D.C.: U.S. Committee for Refugees, 1991).
2. An excellent account of the early years of the Banyamulenge is provided by Rachel Van de Meeren, "Three Decades in Exile: Rwandan Refugees, 1960–1990," *Journal of Refugee Studies*, vol. 9, no. 3 (1996).
3. Figure given by Dr. Tito Rutaremera, Kigali, June 1996.
4. Interview with Aidan Hartley, formerly *Reuters*' rebel correspondent, who accompanied the RPF for much of October, Nairobi, June 1996.
5. The French acronym FAR will be used for the Rwandese regime because the English—RGF, for Rwandese Government Forces—is confusingly similar to RPF.
6. Details of the ambush provided by Major Wilson Rutayisire, interview, Kigali, June 1996.
7. RPF soldiers, interviews, Virunga mountains, July 1996.
8. Author interviews, Dr. Tito Rutaremara, head of RPF delegation in the National Assembly; Col. Franck Mugambage, Director of Cabinet, President's Office; Col. Frank Rutasire, Human Rights Liaison Officer (and informally, head of internal security for the RPF); Maj. Rutayisire; Hon. Patrick Mazimhaka, formerly RPF delegate to the Arusha talks, currently Minister for Rehabilitation and Social Integration (MINIREISO); and Christine Umatomi, deputy at MINIREISO; all Kigali, Rwanda, July-August 1996. Hereafter, Kigali interviews; positions given as at time of interview.
9. Confidential interviews, Dar-es-Salaam, December 1993.
10. Vice President Paul Kagame, Chatham House, November 1994.
11. Catherine Newbury, "Rwanda—Recent Debates Over Governance and Rural Development," in Goran Hyden and Michael Bratton, eds., *Governance and Politics in Africa* (Boulder: Rienner, 1992).
12. *Africa Research Bulletin*, October 1–31, 1990, p. 9874.
13. See especially Catherine Newbury, *The Cohesion of Oppression: Clientship and Ethnicity in Rwanda, 1860–1960* (New York: Columbia University Press, 1988), chapters 1–3; and René Lemarchand, "Burundi in Comparative Perspective: Dimensions of Ethnic Strife," in Brendan O'Leary and John McGarry, eds., *The Politics of Ethnic Conflict Regulation* (London: Routledge, 1994).
14. On instrumentalist accounts of ethnicity, see Leroy Vail, ed., *The Creation of Tribalism in Southern Africa* (London: Currey, 1989).

15. Lemarchand, "Burundi in Comparative Perspective."

16. Watson, *Exile from Rwanda.*

17. Confidential interviews, June 1995.

18. For details see André Guichaoua, *Les crises politiques au Burundi et au Rwanda (1993–1994)* (Paris: Khartala, 1995).

19. René Lemarchand, "Managing Transition Anarchies: Rwanda, Burundi, and South Africa in Comparative Perspective," *Journal of Modern African Studies*, vol. 32, no. 4 (December 1994), pp. 581–601.

20. Howard Adelman, Astri Suhrke, with Bruce Jones, *Early Warning and Conflict Management*, study 2 of the Joint Evaluation of Emergency Assistance in Rwanda (London: Danida, 1996). See also Bruce Jones, *The Arusha Process*, background paper for the Joint Evaluation of Emergency Assistance in Rwanda (London: Danida, 1995).

21. Gérard Prunier, *The Rwanda Crisis: History of a Genocide* (New York: Columbia University Press, 1995).

22. The French term is used here in the absence of a helpful English equivalent.

23. Because the akazu was such a loose concept in pregenocide Rwanda, it is difficult to say with as much certainty that all akazu were genocidaires. The relationship between the two groups is rather similar to the relationship, in the Soviet system, between government officials and membership in the Communist Party—intertwined and overlapping, but not identical.

24. Joan Kakwenzire and Dixon Kamukama, "The Development and Consolidation of Extremist Forces in Rwanda: 1990—1994," unpublished paper, Department of History, Makerere University, Kampala.

25. For accounts of the role of propaganda, see in particular *Death, Despair, and Defiance*, rev. ed. (London: African Rights, 1995); and Prunier, *The Rwanda Crisis.*

26. RPF Statement, October 1990.

27. From a letter shown to the author by a former employee of the Ministry of Transportation, confidential interview, Washington, December 1995.

28. The official RPF figure for this massacre is 19,576. By the author's own rough count, conducted in June 1996, this figure overestimated the dead by circa 20 percent.

29. This story according to a Tutsi survivor interviewed at the scene of the mass grave.

30. David A. Lake and Donald Rothchild, "Ethnic Fears and Global Engagement: The International Spread and Management of Ethnic Conflict." Policy brief, Institute for Global Conflict and Cooperation, January 1996 (www.ciaonet.org).

31. A wide definition of intervention is used here, encompassing, for example, Ugandan indirect military support to the rebel opposition. On the importance of using a broad definition of intervention in the Rwanda context, see Bruce Jones, "'Intervention Without Borders': Humanitarian Intervention in Rwanda, 1990–

1994," *Millennium: Journal of International Studies*, vol. 21, no. 2 (Summer 1995).

32. Interview, Herman Cohen, former Under-Secretary of State for African Affairs in the U.S. Department of State, Washington, June 30, 1995, and confidential interview, Dar-es-Salaam, December 1993.

33. Prunier, *The Rwanda Crisis*.

34. Michael Brown, Introduction, in M. Brown, ed., *The International Dimensions of Internal Conflict* (Cambridge: MIT Press, 1996).

35. Article 3, Cease-fire Agreement Between the Government of the Republic of Rwanda and the Rwandese Patriotic Front. Government of Rwanda and the Rwandese Patriotic Front, N'Sele, Zaire, March 22, 1991.

36. Kigali interviews. The N'Sele Cease-fire Agreement Between the Government of the Rwandese Republic and the Rwandese Patriotic Front, as amended at Gbadolite, September 7, 1991.

37. NMOG was composed of ten Nigerian, ten Senegalese, ten Zimbabwean, and ten other African officers, plus five representatives each of the RPF and the government of Rwanda.

38. The N'Sele Cease-fire Agreement Between the Government of the Rwandese Republic and the Rwandese Patriotic Front, as amended at Gbadolite, September 16, 1991, and at Arusha, July 12, 1992, Government of Rwanda and the Rwandese Patriotic Front. Arusha, Tanzania—hereafter, "The Arusha Cease-fire"; and "Terms of Reference of the Neutral Military Observer Group" (JPMC/RWD/OAU/2(1)).

39. This section draws on interviews conducted in New York with senior officials of the Department of Peacekeeping Operations (DPKO), as well as with officals of the French, Belgian, American, British, Canadian, Norwegian, Rwandan, and Zairian Permanent Missions to the United Nations, New York, June 1995.

40. "The Arusha Peace Accords," Government of the Rwandese Republic and the Rwandese Patriotic Front, August 4, 1993.

41. Howard Adelman and Astri Suhrke, "Early Warning and Conflict Management," *Joint Evaluation*, chapters 3 and 4.

42. Interview, Tanzanian Foreign Ministry official, Dar-es-Salaam, December 1993.

43. Adelman and Suhrke, "Early Warning."

44. Declaration Adopted by the Regional Summit on the Occasion of the Signing of the Peace Agreement Between the Government of the Republic of Rwanda and the Rwandese Patriotic Front, Arusha, United Republic of Tanzania, August 4, 1993. Government of Rwanda and the Rwandese Patriotic Front (1993), Arusha, Tanzania, August 4.

45. For a detailed account of this incident, see George Koch, "The Cross," *Saturday Night* (September 1996), pp. 64–84.

46. Confidential interview with an official of the Belgian Permanent Mission to the United Nations, June 1995.

47. The decision to draw down was never fully implemented. Only 270 officials were supposed to remain in Rwanda; in fact, over 450 stayed. *Adelman and Suhrke, "Early Warning,"* chapters 5 and 6.
48. Government of France, Terms of Reference, Operation Turquoise, Paris, 1994.
49. Prunier, *The Rwanda Crisis.*
50. Bruce Jones, *Rwanda Report: The Role of NGOs in the Response to the Rwandan Emergency* (Ottawa: CARE Canada, forthcoming), appendix 5: "War and Politics in Goma, Revisited: The Eastern Zaire Debacle."
51. General Romeo Dallaire, former force commander of UNAMIR, has made this claim repeatedly, including as testimony to the International Criminal Tribunal in Rwanda; it was also the conclusion of a panel of military experts convened by the Carnegie Commission for the Prevention of Deadly Conflict. See Carnegie Commission, Final Report, New York, April 1998.
52. Interview, DPKO officials, New York, June 1995.
53. Adelman and Suhrke, "Early Warning."
54. Bruce Jones and Astri Suhrke, "Early Warning in Rwanda," report to the Carnegie Commission on Preventing Deadly Conflict, New York, June 1996.
55. This assessment based on interviews with staff of DPKO and Security Council member missions to the UN, June 1995, as well as on DPKO and Security Council documents; see Adelman and Suhrke, "Early Warning"; also Jones, "The Arusha Process."
56. For more details, see Bruce Jones, "Civil War, Peace Process, and Genocide in Rwanda," in Taisier Ali and Robert O. Matthews, eds., *Civil Wars in Africa: Their Roots and Their Resolution* (Kingston and Montreal: McGill-Queens University Press, 1999).
57. Stephen Stedman, "Spoiler Problems in Peace Processes," paper prepared for the National Research Council, SAIS, March 8, 1997.

5 Somalia: Civil War and International Intervention

David D. Laitin

Dagaal waa ka-dare (War is worse)

Somali proverb

Abstract

The sources of the spiraling civil war in Somalia after President Siyaad Barre was deposed in 1991 are not to be found in the specifics of the Somali lineage system (as many area specialists claim) nor in the more general security dilemma (as some international relations experts insist). Rather, the war can best be explained by the war of attrition set off by the declining resources made available to coup winners in Africa after the end of the cold war. Under conditions of a war of attrition, international pressures on new leaders to democratize may enhance rather than reduce the chances for civil war. A modest proposal is offered to reduce the spiraling and enhance the chances for democracy in Somali-like civil wars.

Somalia, situated on the Horn of Africa, borders on the Red Sea to the north of the former British Somaliland and on the Indian Ocean to the east of the former Italian colony and then trust territory of Somalia. The two territories united when they achieved independence in 1960. Unlike nearly all other African states that contended with vast cultural heterogeneity within their boundaries, thereby hampering nation-building projects, Somalia is religiously (in Islam) and linguistically (in Somali, a Cushitic language) homogeneous. Its leaders did not need to grapple with the problem of national definition; rather, they faced the problem of refusal by the Organization of African States and the United Nations to acknowledge Somalia's rights to rule over contiguous land in neighboring Kenya, Ethiopia, and Djibouti that were largely populated by Somalis. Inability to reclaim these unredeemed lands (along with mischievous interventions by the Soviet Union, large-scale corruption, and factional bickering by a multitude of acephalous clans and the parties that represented them) broke the backbone of the postcolonial democratic regime and fostered a military coup in 1969, led by Mohammed Siyaad Barre. After about eight years of relatively meritocratic assignment of jobs and successful economic reform, along with a state ideology of scientific socialism, Siyaad put his energies behind a war to reclaim the Somali lands in the Ogaadeen desert of eastern Ethiopia. Initially a stunning success, due in part to Ethiopia's near breakdown with the fall of the emperor Haile Selassie, the effort was eventually repulsed when the Soviets switched sides to lend support to the Marxist military government that came to power in Addis Ababa. Somalia's defeat in 1978 led to recriminations and counterrecriminations and eventually the reemergence of the clan conflict that Siyaad had originally attenuated. Siyaad began to use U.S. foreign military assistance—justified as protection of Somalia from Ethiopian predation but in reality funded to balance Soviet power in the Horn and to secure a base for America's Rapid Deployment Force—to give arms to his clan allies to help them gain advantage over rival claimants to water holes and grazing lands. By the late 1980s Siyaad's inner coalition of three clans (Marreexaan, Ogaadeen, and Dhulbahante, called MOD) were in full-scale war against the Isxaaqs of the former British colony in the northwest (organized into the Somali National Movement, the SNM), the Majeerteens in the northeast (organized as the Somali Salvation Democratic Front, the SSDF), and the Hawiyes to Mogadishu's immediate west and south (organized as the United Somali Congress, the USC).[1]

The USC army drove Siyaad out of the country in 1991 and a Hawiye businessmen (Ali Mahdi) was installed as president, with the encouragement of the Italian ambassador. The Isxaaq and the Majeerteen armies refused to accept Hawiye rule (proximity to the capital and old colonial ties to the Italians were not sufficient justification for non-Hawiyes) and continued to fight. The issue was especially complex for the SNM. The Isxaaqs fought Siyaad Barre with the greatest loss in personnel (and their major metropolis, Hargeisa, leveled) and were angry that their army did not get to Mogadishu (where Isxaaqs had major land holdings) before the armies of the UPC. They were thus reluctant to return to their homeland in the north, but eventually did, creating a rump state. Meanwhile, a military leader of the USC army, Mohammed Farah Aideed, from a different subclan than Ali Mahdi's, challenged Mahdi's right to the presidency. By late 1991 not only was there an interclan war for control over Somalia, but an intraclan war for control over Mogadishu. Throughout the south, and in Mogadishu especially, warlords (*warranleh*) claimed control over bands of well-armed youths, who with their armed Land Rovers (called "technicals") roamed the cities and roadways plundering, extorting, and killing. By late 1992, due to the civil war, the entire infrastructure of the country was ruined, mass killing, starvation, and disease afflicted much of the population, there was no central government that could negotiate on behalf of the state, and international relief workers were nearly as vulnerable to attack as the Somali population.

The Somali civil war has not only had devastating consequences for Somalis but has had awesome implications for the international gendarmerie that sought to contain it. Those interested in creating a world order in which the conflicts that have the potential of causing civil wars can be peacefully negotiated, and one in which international actors can successfully cauterize the violence of those civil wars that in fact take place, will need to address two questions concerning the Somali civil war. First, "How might civil wars of the Somali type be prevented?" To address this question I shall first examine the causes of the Somali war, as delineated by the area specialists who know the case well. I will then briefly address the suggestion by many international relations specialists, and endorsed by the editors of this volume, that a major part of the explanation for the war is in the security dilemma. Having rejected both the area and international relations' specialists pet theories, I shall then propose an alternative, one that focuses on the resource extraction problem faced by coup victors, which has the potential of degenerating into a war of attrition. Identifying the cause of the Somali civil war allows me to address the first question, on how such wars might be prevented.

Second, "What sort of intervention is feasible, efficient, humanitarian, consistent with local norms of justice, and consistent as well with the gendarmerie's interests if such a civil war does break out?" My strategy for addressing this question is first to provide a short narrative of the actions of the international gendarmerie in Somalia. Second, I shall catalogue a set of tactical considerations that might be called lessons of international intervention, which have implications for future interventions, ones that might be equally humanitarian in intent but more efficient in operation. Third, I shall address a few strategic lessons of the Somali intervention, which should be helpful in designing a grand strategy of humanitarian military intervention in civil wars.

How Might Civil Wars of the Somali Type Be Prevented?

Explanations Offered by Area Specialists

The standard "story line" by country experts focuses on such factors as (1) the acephalous nature of Somali clans linked together in a segmentary lineage system that has from time immemorial fostered interclan wars, with the 1991 civil war no different from how lineage politics has operated in times past but now in the glare of humanitarian agency and CNN spotlights; (2) the particular brutality, corruption, and increasingly narrow base of Siyaad's regime; (3) the vast stock of weapons made available to Siyaad under the Somali-Soviet Treaty of Friendship and Cooperation, added to with the United States' providing weapons to Siyaad throughout the 1980s in exchange for access to Berbera—a cog in the U.S. Rapid Deployment Force machine—and finally enriched by the delivery of Soviet weapons to Siyaad by President Mengistu of Ethiopia in 1989, after the two military leaders agreed to a peace plan. These international agreements heavily militarized Somalia, thereby giving unremitting power to warlords (*warranleh*) over mediators (*wadaads*); and (4) the ecological conditions of the late 1980s (breaking in 1991) in which rainfall was so sparse, at least in the Ogaadeen, as to bring greater competition in the bush for access to wells and grazing land.

The Segmentary Lineage System

Linking the spiraling conflict in the Somali civil war to the segmentary lineage system is unsatisfactory. It can be (and has been) used to explain values on the dependent variable of the opposite sign than the value now being explained. The argument is that since segmentary lineage systems are acephalous, they operate a lot like realist models of interstate relations. Once conflict begins at any level, lineage elders seek to make strategic alliances with neighboring lineages, using affinal ties if necessary, to balance the power aggregated by their new enemy. With exogamy there is potential for a wide array of alliances. In its international relations analogue this system of relations is coded as a balance of power system. Most theorizing in international relations on balance of power systems, and in anthropology on the nature of segmentary lineage systems, emphasizes the high likelihood of war but also the high probability that wars would be short, since with a large number of smaller actors it is much easier for sets of weaker actors to ally in balance against the powerful.[2]

This describes well segmentary lineage politics in the Somali lands. Examples of conflicts that flare up and are put down through strategic negotiations of clan leaders, often through the intervention of well-respected mediators, pervade the work of leading students of the Somali social structure such as I. M. Lewis and S. S. Samatar.[3] For example, on the brink of the chaos, and foreseeing its horrors, S. S. Samatar wrote:

> The instability, anarchy and murderous shiftings witnessed today in the Somali scene are inherently endemic, deeply embedded as they are in the very warp and woof of the Somali world, both as individuals and as corporate socio-political units. The splintering of the opposition movements to General Barre's rule into bewildering fragments . . . reflect[s] the schismatic nature of Somali society.[4]

But, post-1991, the value on the dependent variable was not "frequent outbreaks of violence quickly cauterized" but rather "a spiraling of violence in which all forms of mediation failed, and in which the *warranleh* thoroughly dominated the *wadaads*." Samatar and others recognized this to be the case and have suggested that the existence of a centralized state and army allowed both for the use of clans for purposes of making war upon each other and also for the collapse of clans in their ability to build up new coalitions to recalibrate the balance of power, thereby cooling down violent conflict.[5] This is indeed an interesting explanation. The explanatory variable, however, is no longer the segmentary lineage system but the modern state's manipulation of it.

Most Somali scholars, especially I. M. Lewis, continue to explain the outcomes of interclan relations post-1991 with the same variables they used to explain the outcomes pre-1991. On the coding of the Somali social structure Lewis may well be correct.[6] But if we accept Lewis's claim that there is no significant change on the value on the independent variable, it is scientifically unacceptable—without at least specifying the functional relationship between the independent and dependent variables—to accept this factor as an explanation for a changed value on the dependent variable. Rather, some new factor has come into play that undermines the cauterizing role of the segmentary lineage system. This is the factor that requires emphasis as the source of the catastrophe.

Other Local Explanations

Nearly all other local explanations are more compelling than the one focusing on the segmentary lineage system, because in all of them there is a changed value on the explanatory variable (moral worth of the regime in power, number of weapons pervading the society, ecological conditions on the range) that is plausibly linked to a vastly changed value on the dependent variable (the degree of societal violence). Despite the plausibility of these explanations, there is a compelling reason to hold under some suspicion causal theories that rely almost entirely on local conditions and factors. Such explanations give us virtually no purchase on the question of what type of civil war was fought in Somalia and what are general guidelines for reducing its likelihood. Accepting any of these explanations implies that we need special experts on every country who would be able to use their local knowledge to foresee devastating civil wars. The problem with this is not that it is costly. Rather, the problem is that the record of area experts (whether it be those who studied the Soviet Union, South Africa, or Somalia) in foreseeing catastrophe (or in the case of South Africa, in foreseeing that catastrophe would reach its full limits only within the townships) is not very impressive.[7] More important, by focusing principally on local conditions for a conflict that has already occurred, we get very little purchase on how to identify conditions in other places, where systematic third-party intervention could play a decisive role in dampening imminent civil war, with the possibility of unimaginable noncombatant suffering.

Explanations Offered by International Relations Experts

The Security Dilemma[8]

There are many places and times where the security dilemma might well have kicked in, in a way that nurtured the spiral of Somali violence. First, for all nomadic groups in a battle against unforgiving nature, every grazing area, every watering hole, is vital for survival. Increased measures by any clan to enhance security must therefore be seen by leaders of other clans as threatening their physical survival. The security dilemma can thus be seen as a permanent condition of life in the Somali bush. Second, as Siyaad seeded clan warfare through strategic distributions of weapons he received as foreign aid, he surely threatened the survival of enemy clans, who themselves were impelled to seek comparable arms to secure their future. Third, after the collapse of the Siyaad regime in 1991, all clans feared for their futures if an enemy clan captured the reins of state power. Surely they armed themselves in part because of the disastrous potential consequences for their security of not arming. Fourth, in the course of third-party intervention, when international mediators promoted disarmament, each party was reluctant to disarm out of fear that it would give strategic advantage to the others. This calculation is the security dilemma in reverse, but it holds equally.

While it cannot be denied that the security dilemma helps explain the high levels of vigilance and active efforts at material acquisition by clan leaders, it is much more difficult to sustain the claim that the security dilemma itself, or the actions impelled by considerations by leaders of that dilemma, explain the continued spiraling of clan warfare that got out of control following the capture of the presidential palace by forces loyal to Ali Mahdi in 1991. I shall analyze this period carefully in order to show why in general the security dilemma dynamic was not the principal motivator of the violent spiral.

The Hawiye-led army, being the closest to the capital, delivered the conclusive blow to President Siyaad's security forces and captured the presidential palace well before other clan-based armies reached Mogadishu. Ali Mahdi, with support from the Italian embassy, and quasi legitimacy from the anti-Siyaad Manifesto Group, was sworn in as president two days after Siyaad's flight. Early on in his administration Mahdi called for a conference of national unity and reconciliation for March 1991. Most of the other armies of the fragmented opposition to Siyaad refused to attend this meeting. This is not because their leaders felt insecure, or that they feared physical annihilation if the USC's government came to power. They refused because they felt that Ali Mahdi had no right to declare himself president, since it was they who had fought harder and suffered greater under Siyaad's rule, and that they would be legitimizing his illegal action by agreeing to sit at his conference table. Meanwhile, in the north the Isxaaq-led SNM convened its own conference in Berbera, which included two of the major non-Isxaaq clans (both of them—the Warsangeli and the Dhulbahante—are Daarood). One might ask why the Isxaaq could convene a northern conference but not Ali Mahdi an all-Somali conference. The answer is that leaders of Somali clans other than the Abgaal (Ali Mahdi's Hawiye subclan) felt that Ali Mahdi had no right to convene a conference. They also felt that he who controlled the presidential palace would have power of appointment of ministers and power to accumulate wealth—both of which were valued goods. In fact, the leading negotiators from the Daarood clans demanded that negotiations take place in a neutral city, not Mogadishu, in the heart of Hawiye country, a city in which many Daarood had been massacred. This neutral city, they argued, should become Somalia's new capital. But these leaders were making a political calculation not about their physical security during the conference or under a Hawiye-dominant regime but about their ability to control a future Somali state.

When the rivalry between two Hawiye clans (the Abgaal and the Habar Gidir) developed into full-scale war, there is no evidence that the war lords feared to make peace because the other side would engage in revenge. They refused to make peace because they both were after the same prize — control over the state apparatus, however emasculated it may have become. Aideed saw himself as the anointed leader of the USC and felt he earned the presidency because of his successful operation against Siyaad's army in Mogadishu. He had contempt for the Italians and Egyptians for supporting Siyaad to the bitter end and then shifting their support to a hotelier, Ali Mahdi, for whom Aideed had no respect.[9] Or, to put this in different terms, the war in Somalia was a fight over power. Clan membership was used by leaders as a means of recruitment. The question is not why they armed even if they wanted peace; the question is really why the leaders would have spent so much to gain so little.

In sum, the security dilemma is a fact of life in nomadic society. It explains why clans armed themselves against each other, especially as the Somali state began losing monopoly control over violence after the 1977–78 war in the Ogaadeen. Furthermore, as the authors of chapter 1 of this volume point out, the perpetrators of the civil war put innocent civilians into a security dilemma, compelling them to arm themselves against civilians of other clans. But the security dilemma gives us little purchase on why clan warfare spiraled in 1991 and why the combatants were unable to negotiate a peace.

Commitment Problems Under Conditions of Uncertainty

A new theoretical tradition in the study of civil wars, associated with the papers by international relations specialists Barry Posen and James Fearon, tells a story about civil wars that is somewhat distinct from the security dilemma. In their different ways both focus on the question of the breakdown of a central state and the resultant anarchy that has violent potential. Posen focuses on strategic uncertainty, or a perceived window of opportunity, leading to calculations that may overestimate the probability of victory against traditional enemies within the state or underestimate the costs of such a war. Fearon focuses on the problem experienced by a group that inherits a state apparatus in making credible commitments to those groups that once had state protection but now fear, under the new regime, that protection would be lost. Minority groups may find it rational to challenge the state at time t_0 when the new state is still very weak, rather than wait for t_1, when the state would be strong enough to expropriate wealth and destroy the political autonomy of all minorities. The key here is that for the new state leaders an announcement that they have no intention of such expropriation would be incredible. Barbara Walter shows how control over the state apparatus (especially the military) by one side, due to this commitment problem, undermines any chance for reconciliation without Leviathan-like third party intervention.[10]

While the focus on uncertainty and commitment is extremely useful to give a general framework for thinking about the consequences of state breakdown, the spiraling interclan conflict in Somalia after 1991 isn't easily fit into this model. For one, going back to segmentary lineage politics, there are no permanent enemies in Somali clan relations. All contenders should have reckoned that ruling coalitions in Somali society are always subject to renegotiation. Losing the presidential palace does not mean, therefore, permanent loss of access to state office. Nor does it imply the likelihood of facing severe security risks once the new rulers consolidate their positions. (In fact, Ali Mahdi brought a leading Isxaaq politician into his coalition very early on. Experts point out only *ex post* that he was not a legitimate spokesperson for Isxaaq interests. The Isxaaqs had no reason to fear they would be especially threatened by Hawiye rule, although some Isxaaq leaders feared that Ali Mahdi would ally with Isxaaq subclans that were outside SNM power structures, but this isn't an issue of commitment.) In the case of the major "players" in the civil war in the south, it would be a wild exaggeration to say that the Abgaal had a historic enmity with the Habar Gidir, making the Habar Gidir fear that if Ali Mahdi were to consolidate his power the Habar Gidir's future would be in grave danger. (There was a conflict between these subclans exacerbated by Italian rule, whose agents favored the Abgaal over the Habar Gidir. But to speak of this as a historic humiliation, creating a mutual desire for extermination, is wildly out of proportion).

Second, Fearon argues that the commitment problem may not be set by worries over physical security but rather by worries concerning future bargaining power in the state over the distribution of state resources. How could Mahdi, from this viewpoint, assure the Isxaaq leaders that they would not be shut off from the government gravy train once the Hawiyes got full control over the state apparatus? This is a cogent point and it will get attention in the context of the war of attrition model. My point here is that the inability of Ali Mahdi to make a commitment over future bargaining power was not

the issue that led to the failure of a Hawiye-Isxaaq or an intra-Hawiye compromise that would have averted a civil war.

Third, and here I'm challenging Posen's argument as it might be applied
to Somalia, there is no evidence that the post-1991 collapse was seen as a
window of opportunity for decisive control over the state, in which calculations about the ease of victory were systematically wrong due to the chaotic
situation. A variant of Posen's argument, however, one that focuses on parties
misreading the resolve of their enemies once civil war begins, will be developed in the course of my exposition of the war of attrition. My point is
this: solving Ali Mahdi's commitment problem in 1991, or providing better
cost estimates for victory to the SNM leadership or to Aideed, would not
have helped prevent the Somali civil war.

The War of Attrition

The Somali civil war is not precisely of the "type" that fits models developed by Posen and Fearon and relied upon by Walter as a modal problem
for the understanding of the prolongation of civil wars. Rather, it shares many
characteristics with the war of attrition model described in the literature in
evolutionary biology and industrial organization. What is sparking these wars
of attrition is the vast change in resource-extraction capacities of dictators.

Rulers of states are heavily constrained by the access they have to financial
resources. Some (tinpot dictators), with a short time horizon, will plunder
the society as quickly as possible, before they are deposed. Others (dynasts)
might protect private property and encourage investment, in the hope of
increasing long-term returns on the tax base.[11]

With this idea in mind, one way to characterize the postcolonial African
state is as a "lame Leviathan."[12] The lame Leviathan state has the capacity
to incarcerate its internal enemies, tax international agencies (by threatening
to disintegrate) but not its own population, and provide domestic order
through foreign-funded police surveillance. It also has the capacity to reward
its sycophants with relatively attractive employment. The huge budgets of
African states, in Larry Diamond's words, "dwarfed in wealth and power both
existing social institutions and various new fragments of modern organization."[13] A small tax base but huge rewards for supporters kept these regimes
alive, but not for too long. Anger and resentment of those not receiving
payoffs would build up. Because the life expectancy of such regimes is therefore short, leaders had little interest in developing conditions, such as the
rule of law, that would be encouraging to capital investment. Rather, without

a rule of law, rulers could confiscate profits and plunder the society for as long as they could maintain themselves in power, partly in order to fund a luxurious retirement after the coup d'état that throws them out of office.

The largest source of resource extraction for the rulers was the super-powers and the former colonial states. From 1965 (with the first military coup in independent Africa) through 1989, coups d'état generally involved a leader who claimed to have no "ethnic" affiliation and would rule the country as a nationalist. (This was the case with Siyaad's coup in 1969). Once in control, leaders would ally either with the United States or the Soviet Union and get provided with military weapons and police surveillance technology far greater than any other group in the society could procure. (It is significant that a United States-Soviet condominium existed, in which once an African leader chose a side in the cold war, the other side would stop subsidizing his enemies. The superpowers learned how to do this after the ugly collapse of Congo-Kinshasa, when both sides stuck with their man).[14]

From the superpower point of view, the key calculation was to give the new dictator sufficient weaponry to maintain order but not enough so that he could decimate all domestic rivals. If properly calibrated, the dictator would be optimally venal and would continue to redistribute resources to rival groups as insurance. From a domestic point of view, for a rival to chal-lenge a postcoup leader—once he took control over the radio station, pres-idential palace, and customhouse—would be foolhardy. The enormous rela-tive military and surveillance power (the "prize") garnered by the first entrant into the presidential palace after the incumbent was deposed gave that en-trant excellent bargaining power. Usually, a bandwagon followed, with syc-ophants from all tribal or clan groups seeking to curry favor with the new regime, to get their "fair" share. (After Siyaad's coup I do not think there was one group in the country that feared they would suffer from a Marre-exaan general taking power. All groups cooperated in the setting up of the early cabinets). Civil war was preempted in pre-1985 coups because of the enormous relative power in international resource extraction to which the first entrants into the presidential palace had access. Over time dictators who got too venal faced challenges from groups no longer receiving the distributions they felt they deserved. Coups were then plotted, and if a coup were successful, the new leader would choose a superpower and the game would begin anew.

With Gorbachev's rule in the Soviet Union the support system for the African tinpot changed enormously. With the end of the cold war there was no incentive for the United States or the Soviet Union to prop up lame

Leviathans. To be sure, there are areas of Africa that still command attention from the United States. The U.S. has a "special relationship" with Ethiopia and has helped mediate the conflict between the state and the Oromo-based guerrilla opposition. The Sudan, too, captures U.S. attention for fear of Islamic fundamentalism that could spread to Egypt. Michael Clough calls this two-track policy "cynical disengagement."[15] In any event, with the USSR defunct there is no bidding war between superpowers for the support of African dictators, and the size of the prize has therefore diminished substantially.[16]

Coincident with the end of the cold war the international arms markets opened up in Africa in a way that grain markets still have not done. The implication of the widespread availability of arms is that challengers to incumbents today have a more level playing field than they did in the cold war. While challengers cannot get superpower support, their resource extraction capabilities (for example, taxing their diaspora or people who share their religion) are not much lower than that of incumbents. The probability of a successful military challenge is consequently much higher post-1985 than it was during the cold war.

The result of these two changes is that after an African coup the relative military power of the first entrant into the presidential palace is not significantly greater than other hopefuls. While it is true that even during the cold war there were examples of state collapse (e.g., Chad, Uganda), after the end of the cold war the pas de deux of coup and countercoup, which had been relatively peaceful, has a far more incendiary possibility for blowing up into chaos and violence. Gurr's Minorities at Risk data confirm this point. Since 1985 twenty-two African minority groups have been engaged in guerrilla activity against their state (or higher levels of rebellion), while in other periods (1960–65, nine groups; 1965–70, eight groups; 1975–80, twelve groups; 1980–85, ten groups) rebellion was far less pervasive. As for communal conflicts, the data report twenty-two groups engaged in rioting or more incendiary activities in the 1990s, while in earlier decades (1960s, eleven; 1970s, six; 1980s, five) there were many fewer.[17] Under conditions of post–cold war government collapse, then, regional and tribal aspirants have a greater incentive to contest for state power than compromise with it. Because of the nature of the African state over the past generation, there is insufficient capital investment in the society for there to be a strong bourgeois interest in peace. Moreover, since capital investment had been so paltry, the potential gains in plunder and corruption for controlling the state apparatus are greater than those of living in a countryside without any eco-

nomic dynamism at all. In sum: post–cold war control over the state apparatus, even though it has declined in its ability to tax superpowers, remains
relatively remunerative as compared with other routes to wealth, and, after
the collapse of a government, there is no longer certainty that the incumbent
can garner sufficient military resources to stave off challenges to his rule.

This scenario has striking parallels to the "war of attrition" that was first
developed by Maynard Smith and is now well-documented in the industrial
organization and international relations literature.[18] The war of attrition
game in biology explains animals' fights for prey. Fighting is costly. The goal
is to get the other animal to give up. The winning animal keeps the prey;
the loser is left wishing it had not entered the fight. In industrial organization
this dynamic is seen with duopoly competition and marginal cost pricing.
If there is declining demand and constant fixed costs, profits move toward
the negative. Both firms, however, would stay in the market in the hope that
the other would leave, the winner garnering monopoly price profits. In order
to drop out, which would give zero profits from that date on, each firm's
expected present discounted value of profits from any date on must equal
zero for it to be indifferent. Under conditions of uncertainty (where firms
do not know each other's cost structure) there could well be extended periods
of mutual losses (the war of attrition), until one of the firms ceases produc-
tion. The horror of the war of attrition model is the equilibrium possibility
that each actor may pay more for the prize (in biology, the lost opportunities
of hunting for another prey) than the prize itself was worth.

In Somalia, after the cold war ended, the value of the state declined (as
Siyaad could no longer claim a large prize in aid for siding with one of the
superpowers). His ability to retain power (due to loss of military and surveillance matériel coming from the superpowers) declined as well. Yet, given
the economic poverty of the country, the state's control over the customhouse, the siphoning off of economic aid, and the rewards for approving
private contracts, control over the state remained relatively attractive to clan
groups, as compared to specializing only in the private economy. Thus, if
any contending group faced the following calculation

$$A \text{ iff } PrS - qS - C > 0$$

A = attack; iff = if and only if; Pr = probability of victory; S = value of the state; q =
expected share for each member of the governing coalition; C = costs of the war.

it would contend for power. Two of these values (Pr and C) were clearly
moving in the direction supporting "attack."

What about the value of S? If S is divisible, Fearon's commitment problem analysis helps explain the fighting, as both parties would be after the rewards of the state with the present war fought over future bargaining power over those resources.[19] But suppose running a state has fixed costs F (the minimal price of order, pomp, core support group, and necessary state services) plus variable costs V (rewards for a wide circle of support groups), and that q is a function only of V. Furthermore, in the post–cold war world, the taxing power of the African state plummets toward F. In this case both incumbents and challengers recognize that rulers can no longer provide benefits to members of a broad coalition, thereby making qS approach zero. In a sense, along with Fearon's analysis, incumbents here are unable to commit to future distributions to allied clans in a broad coalition. In another sense, the lowered value of S itself lowers qS (even if q remains constant) and explains why challengers see little value in becoming coalition members. And so, even with a declining S, the higher value of Pr and the lower value of C lead contenders to have a positive expected value for fighting.

But can the declining value of the prize (S) actually explain sustained warfare for its capture, especially as with apparently endless war it appears that S is falling below F? Shouldn't it be the case that if S cannot support a coalition large enough to suppress civil war any clan that fights for it would not be able to hold onto it? How can it be rational to fight? In an incomplete information type of model that I am here informally elaborating, and consistent with Posen's point about miscalculation on the probability of winning, war could only be sustained if players were unsure about each other's resolve. While I have no direct information on this point, it is probably the case that in the war of the many clans against Siyaad there was mutual underestimation about each other's resolve. In the war between the Abgaal and Habar Gidir Ali Mahdi long felt that he would ultimately get Western aid and support, yet such aid never came. Meanwhile, Aideed and his followers among the Habar Gidir felt that they were the real military force behind the overthrow of Siyaad and that ultimately the more urbanized Abgaals would cave in. These misestimates of resolve may well have sustained the civil war to a point at which the costs of fighting inexorably increased and became far higher than the expected returns of capturing the state.

The logic of the model suggests that Aideed and Ali Mahdi continued fighting not so much because they feared being decimated by the other if they lost (and here segmentary lineage theory is useful, as it suggests that there are no permanent enemies) but because each leader strategized, if the war was costing more for the opponents, that they would sue for peace first.

If both leaders think this way, the war continues. I think the war of attrition model might also help explain post–cold war events in Liberia, Sierra Leone, Congo (former Zaire), Congo, and Uganda. As France is tentatively withdrawing from the use of military personnel to prop up dictators in its former colonies, my analysis suggests we will be seeing Somali-like civil wars in former French African colonies as well.[20]

What Sort of Third-Party Intervention?

My second question concerns the logic of third-party intervention once civil war spirals out of control. The Somali civil war did indeed spiral out of control. Although it had elements of a traditional interclan war, as the warring factions defined themselves along segmentary cleavage lines, the ensuing devastation went far beyond the boundaries of an interclan war. Refugee centers in the bush, even those organized around religious shrines, became fair game for combatants. Farmers, who were outside the standard clan cleavage structure, and who weren't even participating in the war, faced murderous attacks by bands of warriors. Humanitarian relief groups were themselves in jeopardy. Although there is no evidence, as was the case in Rwanda, that the killing was part of a plan to exterminate members of enemy clans, the human degradation was unimaginable. How, then, did the international community respond?

Sadly, it took the UN more than a year after Siyaad fell from power before it brokered a cease-fire in February 1992 between Ali Mahdi and Mohammed Farah Aideed.[21] Six weeks later the Security Council established the United Nations Operation in Somalia (UNOSOM I) to monitor the cease-fire and to provide emergency humanitarian assistance. The secretary general appointed Mohamed Sahnoun, a well-respected Egyptian diplomat, as his special representative, and he was provided with a staff of fifty unarmed monitors. The UN promised in its Resolution 751 (April 1992) to send as well a five-hundred-man security force, but it was not until September when lightly armed Pakistani troops arrived. Ill-equipped for combat, they could not safely patrol outside their own barracks. Frustrated, Sahnoun resigned in October.[22]

The United States had been a reluctant participant. Despite the fact that the U.S. was responsible for supporting the Siyaad regime when it was distributing weapons throughout the country, Bush ordered General Colin Powell to airlift all Americans out of Somalia amidst the chaos of Siyaad's abdication and to wash U.S. hands clean. With the gulf war eating up official attention, the humanitarian crisis on Africa's Horn was of low priority. Later, the U.S. resisted the implementation of the security force envisioned in Resolution 751. However, with the breakdown of the UN-brokered cease-fire, and with the massive numbers of starving and diseased victims of the civil war gaining international attention, President Bush committed U.S. forces to airlift relief supplies to the civil war's victims. In this U.S.-support operation of UNOSOM I, called Provide Relief, more than twenty-eight thousand metric tons of relief supplies were delivered to Somalia. By November President Bush agreed to up the ante and offer U.S. troops to lead a UN military action to avert an even greater human tragedy. On December 3 the Security Council, combining language of Chapters 6 (on peacekeeping) and 7 (on peace enforcement) of the UN Charter, passed Resolution 794, creating the United Task Force (UNITAF), with a mandate to create a permanent UN peacekeeping operation to provide humanitarian assistance and to restore order to southern Somalia. From December 1992 through May 1993 UNITAF involved about thirty-eight thousand troops from twenty-one nations, including twenth-eight thousand Americans, whose parallel operation during the UNITAF period was called Operation Restore Hope. President Bush insisted that Restore Hope be seen merely as a humanitarian mission to save civilian lives and promised that the mission would be over in a few months' time. With this precommitment President Bush made clear that the U.S. had no intention of resolving the civil war or rebuilding the state. The only goal was to save the civilian population from self-inflicted extinction.

Bush appointed Robert Oakley, a former ambassador to Somalia, as head of Operation Restore Hope. In his postmortems Oakley presents an unconvincing strategic calculus (in which accommodating the warlords was a first step to seriously involving civil society in the reconstruction of the country).[23] In reality, his approach was quite simple. The warlords had the capacity to terrorize anyone who ventured into the countryside. Although anarchy in the bush made the success of humanitarian efforts precarious even with warlord acquiescence, they were the principal threats to the security of the refugee centers that humanitarian agencies sought to reach. Eliminating the warlords would be a major military and political undertaking, and, if that were the first step in a U.S. plan, nearly the entire population of the south would have been put in jeopardy. And such a strategy would have been counter to the presidential admonition that all U.S. troops be gone from Somalia within three months. Although he made several efforts to trim the warlords' sails, for example in the appointment of governors in the localities and in the appointment of women in all local councils, he necessarily became hostage to the order that the warlords could provide, as this order was the key to the humanitarian effort. The long-term consequence of such a strategy was to make legitimate governance of Somalia (or even illegitimate governance by a hegemonic warlord) virtually impossible. There are many critics of Oakley's decision due to these consequences.[24] Yet it is undeniable that the quick opening-up of the humanitarian aid route saved thousands of lives.[25]

The U.S.-UN agreement in setting up UNITAF had ambiguous language in regard to the retransfer of the operation to UN command. The problem that faced President Clinton, who inherited Bush's operation that had no endgame, was how to get out of Somalia. Clinton wanted to pass the hot potato back to the UN, even though he knew full well that the UN would not be able to bring peace to the country. In March 1993, with Security Council Resolution 814, crafted by President Clinton's foreign policy team, UNOSOM II was mandated. This was an ambitious resolution calling for the rebuilding of state institutions. Moreover, it was the first ever Chapter 7 resolution that was explicit about enforcement, including the disarming of Somali clans. Yet it was to go into operation with fewer committed troops than during the UNITAF period.

The U.S. mission under the UNOSOM II rubric was led by Admiral Jonathan Howe. Given pressure from Secretary General Boutros-Ghali, from the international lobby of humanitarian agencies, and from the realization that the Oakley strategy provided no easy exit, Howe became implicated in what critics of the Somali intervention call mission creep—the move from humanitarian intervention to nation building. To be sure, as Martin Ganzglass argues, if Oakley had paid more attention to the possibilities of recreating a decent set of local constabularies, the safety of the Somali population would have been substantially aided, at relatively low cost.[26] But due to Oakley's initial decision to accommodate the warlords, and with the full expectation on the part of all combatants that there would be no significant outside force in the country after May 1994, the warlords had an incentive to resist international attempts to construct a civil society.

In light of the incentive to warlords to outlast the international gendarmerie, UN troops were not logistically equipped to handle the new assignment. Aideed took advantage of this in June 1993 when some of his supporters ambushed and killed twenty-four Pakistani soldiers. In response, the UN authorized (through Security Council Resolution 837) U.S. Rangers to apprehend those responsible, but in October eighteen Americans were killed and seventy-five wounded in their manhunt for Aideed. President Clinton forthwith announced the phased withdrawal of American troops that would be completed by March 1994. Thus ended the role of the international gendarmerie in the Somali civil war. By the time it left there was a precarious division of Mogadishu between the forces of Aideed and Mahdi, with no governing institutions for the rest of the country, although former British Somaliland had announced its formal though unrecognized secession and the Majeerteen region was operating under informal institutions of quasi sovereignty.

This analysis raises big questions: (1) Are there tactical lessons about Somali-type invasions that should be incorporated into future international interventions? (2) Can the U.S. (or any set of democratic states) make the necessary commitment to a Third World civil war ("We will stay there as long as necessary") that would give assurance to combatants that they need not store up weapons for the moment that the U.S. leaves? (3) Should the U.S. pick a warlord and shower him with weapons, on the condition that he hold elections once peace is restored? (4) Should the U.S. ignore the suffering of noncombatants in the short term in order to avoid propping up warlords? (5) Can the U.S. articulate a strategy of humanitarian relief that has a humanitarian exit option? (6) Must humanitarian relief missions give up any hope for a democratic future? I shall try to address these questions, first by looking at some tactical issues of administration and then by examining some strategic issues of general policy.

A Catalogue of Tactical Lessons

Mission Creep

As implied in the narrative, what has become known as the bogey of mission creep—where the goals of the operation expand with the length of time the intervening army is present—was not the result of small and imperceptible expansion of concerns. What occurred was an abrupt change in goals under the Clinton administration, whose analysts revealed little understanding of the tactical decisions made in the field that had already undermined the possibility of success in UNOSOM II. The Clinton administration, through its drafting and supporting UN Resolution 814, changed the focus of policy from humanitarian relief to nation building.

The logic of Operation Restore Hope was seen quite early by Jennifer Parmelee, in her *Washington Post* article "Waltzing with Warlords" (June

25, 1993). "Time and again," she wrote, "I asked the powers that be—the U.N., the United States—'Aren't you giving these guys too much prominence?' The reply invariably came back: 'They're the players. We've got to play ball with them.' And so, the world waltzed with the warlords." To assure a safe arrival of troops, Oakley did all he could to stroke these warlords. In fact, shortly after U.S. forces arrived they discovered a major arms cache, but since it belonged to Aideed's principal financier Osman Atto (who was also renting quarters to the U.S. mission), Oakley ordered that it not be destroyed. The military agreed that Oakley's diplomacy was making it easier to move supplies, and that was all there was need to know.[27]

Upon the arrival of the Howe mission, the warlords were essential for all agreements. In his first peace conference in March 1993 in Addis Ababa, an agreement that called for a truce and elections within two years was signed, but only by the warlords. This was a harsh lesson to him that, in Rosegrant's words, "their elimination had to evolve." Later on, when Howe sought to hurry up the evolution by ordering one of his assistants not to meet with Aideed, Aideed interpreted this as a threat, and he took successful enemy action against the U.S.

It is in this context that UN Resolution 814, which was drafted largely by the U.S. Mission, must be understood. As the U.S. ambassador to the UN waxed, the proposed operation was "an unprecedented enterprise aimed at nothing less than the restoration of an entire country as a functioning member of the community of nations."[28] This resolution called for the secretary general "to assume responsibility for the consolidation, expansion, and maintenance of a secure environment throughout Somalia" and to seek financing for "the rehabilitation of the political institutions and economy of Somalia." The Clinton administration, in showing its support, contemplated that eight thousand logistical troops would remain, along with a one-thousand-man Quick Reaction Force. John Bolton pointed out that this was not "mission creep"—rather it was a new policy of "assertive multilateralism."[29] Bolton was half-right. The goals were of "assertive multilateralism," but the means (compared with UNITAF) were paltry.

Howe's defense has been thoroughly disingenuous. "If . . . the UN is to be the agent of the international community," he wrote, "contributing nations should totally endorse its policy."[30] He neglects to mention that it was the U.S. that both pushed the UN's hand in passing Resolution 814 and blinded itself to the political realities it had already created through its agency in Operation Restore Hope. Mission creep was not guilty. Rather, the new policy was. Tactically, this means that we need not necessarily worry about a structural problem endemic to such operations called "mission creep" as many postmortems have suggested. Rather, we should think about an endgame that will allow the international gendarmerie to leave after it has completed its humanitarian mission, without engendering the return of escalating violence.

The Role of the UN in Chapter 7 Interventions

In Somalia the UN showed itself unable to assume leadership of an international military engagement. It could not take the lead when member states entrusted it with leadership. The secretary general's special representative, Mohamed Sahnoun, was entrusted with the administration of Security Council Resolution 751, creating UNOSOM I. While working in Somalia, he learned that his superiors had allowed a Russian plane with UN markings to deliver shipments to Ali Mahdi, thus undermining the UN's impartiality. Later the UN announced a deployment of three thousand troops to Somalia while he was in delicate negotiations concerning the first five hundred. Exasperated with the UN's inability to articulate and sustain any policy, Sahnoun quit in October 1992. During UNOSOM II, when the UN again had command, the command situation hardly improved. After the failures of the U.S. Quick Reaction Force to ambush Aideed, the Italians openly defied the UN command by engaging in direct negotiations with Aideed's movement. There was no way the Italians could be policed or punished.

Furthermore, the UN's staffing remains an international embarrassment. During the negotiations between the U.S. and the UN over the establishment of UNITAF, for example, the secretary general did not develop a serious plan (as Resolution 794 called for) for transferring power to UNOSOM after UNITAF's withdrawal. When a U.S. interagency team went to New York to connect with the UNOSOM team, they were shocked that the secretary general had virtually no staff working on the problem. The best the UN team could do is drag its feet, in the expectation that if it did nothing the Americans would continue keeping guard. There was no command center in the UN committed to getting the operation done correctly. Under UNOSOM II no UN planners were sent on site before the arrival of the commander and deputy commander. With the UN command operating with twelve thousand fewer troops than authorized, and many of the troops under strong restrictions as to what kinds of activities they could legally engage in, there was no way Admiral Howe could develop a coherent tactical plan. Furthermore, Howe was authorized to have a staff of eight hundred, but it took months to reach one hundred, and he described the applicant pool as a bunch of "people that nobody else wants."[31] Stories of UN incompetence in the field are legion. Major General Lewis Mackenzie, a Canadian and former head of UN forces in Sarajevo, made this comment about UN managerial capacity: "A UN commander in the field should not get into trouble after 5 P.M. in New York, or Saturday and Sunday. There is no one to answer the phone."[32]

Are these failures inherent in UN operations or are they just examples of poor management that can be fixed? John Ruggie, in a subtle analysis of UN-sponsored military interventions, suggests that the enormous holes that the UN dug for itself were not necessary and that we should not give up hope, with a little fine-tuning, of a more effective international force under UN auspices.[33] The UN's record in Somalia was so egregious, however, that it is difficult to calculate the expected payoffs of reform. The issue goes beyond administrative reform, or the possibilities with a more efficient secretary general. As a consensual organization, oriented toward diplomacy, the UN is nearly compelled to reject decisive in-the-field military command. In light of this the best role for the UN is to vote for interventions, whether of Chapter 6 or 7 (or some hybrid, as was UNITAF), and then to subcontract the operation out to a state (usually the U.S.) capable of carrying it out. An equitable share-the-burdens taxation scheme for member states would of course be necessary, and this might be facilitated by the Secretariat. But the UN should not be involved in combat operations.[34]

The Role of Nongovernmental Organizations

NGOs have come under especially harsh criticism in the wake of recent international military operations. For example, drawing on his own experience as an aid worker and journalist in Somalia, Michael Maren examined the economic and humanitarian damage done in Somalia, ironically, by the very organizations that distributed free food and administered development projects in the name of famine relief. Maren estimates that approximately two-thirds of food shipments for refugees in the area of Somalia in which he worked were being stolen. Some of the stolen food was sold on the black market in order to purchase arms, which in turn escalated conflicts, often creating more refugees. Foreign aid destroyed what was left of local markets by flooding the country with cheap or free food, thus ruining the livelihood of many farmers. Others became "rich from food"; one Somali referred to his second wife as "CARE wife," because the overabundance of relief food he sold enabled him to marry again. Save the Children Foundation, Maren shows with devastatingly powerful documentation, which ran heartbreaking advertisements throughout the world on the starving children in Somalia, had hardly an operating soup kitchen working in the country.[35]

NGOs were placed in unmanageable situations with the fall of Siyaad's government in 1991. The diplomatic community had evacuated, and there was no one else but the NGOs to take responsibility for those innocent people who were victims of the civil war that was not of their making. Yet, these NGOs, in order to survive, had to buy protection from the warlords, and soon many of these organizations became hostage to the warlords. Employees of NGOs would turn on their own employers for large sums of cash, making the helpers helpless. This is why many of them urged international military intervention. Once the intervention began, some of the NGOs were more of a nuisance to the gendarmerie's operations—in being easy targets for the warlords—than a help to the people. To an important degree the NGOs subverted the strategic space of the international gendarmerie, not allowing it to threaten quick departure and forcing its officials to bargain with warlords in the game of kidnap. Nonetheless, I think Maren's charges are far too general and unrealistic. Not all NGOs were as embarrassingly unhelpful as Save the Children. Furthermore, it is unfair to charge those organizations that were providing food with creating disincentives for farmers to plant their own crops, when thousands were dying of starvation. NGOs operated in a terrible environment; many made imprudent decisions. But living with NGOs—largely because they demonstrate international concern—must be part of the territory for any intervening force.

Investing in Local Knowledge

Anna Simons proposes that the dissolution of Somalia was caused by "misunderstanding" based not on "lack of information but a surfeit of partial information."[36] While she refers to the period before the entrance of international military force, it is reasonable to hypothesize that tactical errors in the administration of the international effort were due to insufficient investment in knowledge of the mores and the culture of the society that was being invaded. In the postmortems on the international military operations the claim of ignorance about local conditions is often made. James Mayall argues that Colin Powell's ideas were based upon his success in Desert Storm, but his dictum of "employ maximum controlled violence" on patrol had implications for the distribution of wealth, matériel, and power to clans about which he was unaware and that made peacemaking all the more difficult.[37] As evidence, Mayall and Lewis point out that the UN headquarters in Mogadishu was staffed mainly by Habar Gidirs, and this gave Aideed a strategic advantage in preparing for police patrols, an advantage the Abgaals did not have.[38] Mayall and Lewis, and in a related fashion A. I. Samatar, make a deeper accusation. They argue that the outside forces misunderstood the Somali concept of clan (*tol*) and acted as if these clan groups were well-bounded and exclusive. In fact, if outsiders understood how fluid clan membership is, and how decentralized power within clans are, they would not have invested as much hope in the warlords as they did.[39] Said Samatar argued in vain to UN and U.S. authorities that more effort should have gone into arming poets with a broad audience—in the name of peace—rather than warlords in the name of security.[40] This would have shown a truer understanding of what motivates peace in the local context.

Two arguments can be used to weaken the impact of this powerful charge. First, as Lewis and Mayall note, Mohamed Sahnoun and Usmat Kittani of the UN got considerable support from the Horn of Africa Center in Uppsala, funded by the Nordic countries and NGOs. Although the centre's advisory group ignored voices that were opposed to vigorous UN action, it built its recommendations for UN action on a firm foundation of local input. Moreover, it had Ambassador Oakley's ear, whom the authors praise for his local knowledge. The group advocated a "bottom up" approach to "re-empower traditional community leaders." Oakley instead concentrated his efforts on the high-profile warlords, and, in Lewis and Mayall's judgment, gave them new and unwarranted legitimacy.[41] But it would be folly to argue that this was done out of ignorance. Rather, it was done because Oakley was under orders to get food quickly to the camps and not to reconstitute the society. The priorities of the Uppsala group were different from the American army, to be sure. But this isn't a question of local knowledge.

The second argument is strongly but inadvertently made by Maxamed Afrax, from whom I have appropriated the epigraph for this chapter. He writes, "Culture and literature were among the areas most profoundly affected by the military regime." Theft, lying, hypocrisy, rape became indicators of *ragannimo* (manhood). Many of those who stood against Siyaad were his former military officers who turned against him, who were themselves implicated in torture. The Somali masses could give them little support, as they say: "Hal boooli ahi nirig xalaal ah ma dhasho" (A stolen she-camel does not give birth to a rightful baby). Eventually the people bowed to those with guns rather than to those with reason, reflecting "the new destructive political culture."[42] This point raises an important question. If traditional Somali political culture is reflected in the epigraph to this chapter, and if current activities reflect a new political culture, how could deep knowledge of tradition have helped the United States weather the post-1991 storm? If Somali political culture is so "new," why should the international gendarmerie learn about what no longer exists?

The dilemma is nicely revealed by Afrax's very statement of the problem:

> The entire fabric of Somali society has been ravaged. The very existence of the whole nation has sunk in a deep dark sea of unimaginable human and material disaster. . . . The communal mind of the society seems to be in a coma. No collective responsible effort, voicing national concern or calling for saving the savable, has so far emerged. For a nation proverbially known for its deep-rooted traditions of reasoning and a history of national consciousness, this is an utterly puzzling development. . . . Any attempt to deal successfully with this problem *requires* [my emphasis] a better understanding of Somali culture and society.[43]

And one can only ask, If the situation was so puzzling to a genuine expert of Somali society, what promise is there in requiring those who intervene to develop a better understanding of it? If Siyaad's "outrageous manipulations of the traditional kin system" were so devastating to its integrity,[44] what profit is there for outsiders seeking peace to study its (former) operations?

This is no plea for ignorance of the local. Rather it is a plea that we do not put too much weight on the insensitivities of international forces to the local scene as an explanation for its failures. In fact, with a secretary general and a U.S. ambassador who had professional backgrounds working in Somalia, the international gendarmerie had about as much local knowledge as we could ever hope for.

Is There a Third-Party Strategy of Intervention?

Triage

Stephen Stedman argues with persuasiveness and sang froid that in regard to the issue of collapsed states the U.S. and UN policy should be sensitive to the logic of triage, that is, to "provide aid only to those countries that have a chance to achieve sustainable development. The present policy—responding to a few crises at the expense of the needs of the many—is," he argues, "both unethical and untenable. It is a policy doomed to produce more, not fewer, humanitarian disasters."[45] While this is a cogent recommendation that merits careful consideration, I do not believe that it can be easily implemented. There is an international audience for catastrophe, and one hundred thousand dying children in a refugee camp engages this audience (because it is specific) far more than the one million whose lives are threatened by potential cholera, say, in Nigeria (because the threat is diffuse, in that it is hard to picture these victims in a compelling and clear way). Suppose the cost were equal to remedy these two problems. Stedman would favor giving support for the one million. I would answer that the costs of getting support for the latter are gigantic; while it is possible to garner support for the former. While it would be wrong to set criteria for aid giving based solely upon who bleeds most in CNN footage, it would be callous to ignore immense suffering in humanitarian disasters because the expected returns of another investment would be higher. The specificity of catastrophe from human disasters makes intervention feasible. And, because it is feasible, it would be unconscionable to ignore. The international gendarmerie therefore needs a strategy for entering Somali-type conflicts, even though the expected humanitarian returns of helping sustain development in other countries might be higher.

Creating Safe Havens, and Nothing More

My preliminary answer to the question of whether there was a cheaper model out there, one that could save lives but not embroil the international gendarmerie into a losing street war, was to focus on the possibility of creating safe havens.[46] Suppose after Operation Restore Hope (in which the U.S. did a bit more to restore local constabularies and local authorities in areas that were not in the principal zones of combat) the United States committed itself only to the protection of relief routes and refugee camps. A frigate or battleship off of the Mogadishu and maybe the Kismaayo coasts, with a few airplanes for necessary sorties, might have been deployed in this strategy of protecting the port and the routes to the refugee centers. The threat of bombing if supply lines are attacked would be the deterrent for warlords to look for their plunder elsewhere. The U.S. would say that as long as the supply lines were open for relief, and as long as there were camp areas where refugees would be safe, the humanitarian problem was solved.

With this plan the U.S. could and should offer its "good offices" for negotiations between warring parties but not make the solution to the civil war
a major part of its agenda. The U.S. could also (in line with my argument
in response to the question of the causes of the spiraling violence in post–
cold war civil wars) promise that, if the warring parties could agree on a
solution, it would be willing to supply relatively large amounts of weapons
and surveillance equipment to the chosen leader. The principal argument
in support of this approach is that without the wherewithal to commit troops
as mediators for the long term, it is dishonest (and even immoral) to press
for wider nation-building goals.

The big problem with this approach is that the refugee camps would
become the object of terror, with guerrilla armies formed principally to
extract supplies from the camps to continue their warfare, which would not
be monitored by the outside army. The kind of surveillance needed to keep
the camps free from predators—while perhaps met in the case of Operation
Provide Comfort for the Kurds in northern Iraq—is extraordinarily expensive. The likelihood that safe havens would not become supply camps for
contending armies is quite low.

Promotion of Democracy, with High Risk

The implications of the war of attrition model are quite depressing. The
thrust in American foreign policy of pressing for democracy and human
rights as a precondition for U.S. aid may need to be questioned. If the key
to civil war is the expectation that newly installed incumbents are not going
to have world-class surveillance techniques in order to oppress challengers,
and U.S. policy helps further that expectation, it might well be (through
excellent intentions) encouraging civil war. Perhaps the U.S. should go back
into the game—in the name of preventing humanitarian catastrophes—of
propping up tinpot dictators?

I would reject this tack, largely because dancing with a single warlord
seals the international gendarmerie to his fate. It is supremely difficult to
compel one's dance partner to subject himself to real elections and to abide
by the results.

Rather than picking a warlord, it is worth speculating how the dynamics
discussed herein could, through the reduction in the worth of the prize
awarded to coup winners, enhance the probability of democracy. Suppose,
for example, that after a coup with an insignificant superpower prize the
probability of escalating violence by contenders to the palace is .7. Suppose

further, with the prospects of a big prize so low, a significant group of (the albeit small set of) businessmen in the country (and the diaspora involved in trade with their home country) agree not to fund a war of attrition. Instead, they agree to the rule of law and a democratic constitution (in which contests for power would be uncertain for all contenders) and the concomitant protection of property rights. For each businessman the expected return on investment would be higher than the expected return of his group getting in power multiplied by the contracts that would come his way by virtue of his group getting the reins of power. Such an agreement is hard to reach, as it involves a very difficult coordination problem for businessmen from different tribal backgrounds and a solution to a commitment problem that, if a member of its tribe won the election, the regime would not confiscate property from the others. Let us put the probability of reaching a satisfactory agreement at .3. Some might argue that reducing the prize for the capture of the palace would be worthwhile, even if the risks of civil war are high, because the post–cold war situation makes possible the foundation for a rule of law.[47]

The question then becomes, Is there a way with a minuscule prize to lower the probability of a spiraling civil war, without deterring (by making the prize too high) businessmen from allying qua businessman (and not with tribal fellows) in the name of protection of property rights and the rule of law? It may be possible to formulate such a strategy for the promotion of a rule of law, but first a clear distinction between "military" and "police" intervention needs to be made.

Decoupling Military and Police Operations

The logic of Walter's dissertation is clear in the case of international intervention amidst the Somali civil war.[48] The only way that President Bush could justify to the American public that the U.S. military should intervene was by saying that the intervention would be short in duration and limited in goals. But by announcing these aims publicly he was also informing the combatants that once the massive U.S. force left the scene they could continue their warfare as before. Whether the logic is of a security dilemma or of a war of attrition, as soon as a third-party enforcer leaves the scene the war will continue. Under such conditions it would be irrational for either party to disarm. In fact, all parties to the war cantoned their armaments during the period of UNITAF control, ready to bring them out in the open once the massive U.S. operation left the field. Here is the nub of the strategic dilemma: if the international gendarmerie cannot commit to a long-term mediating role, it is likely to fail in getting a successful negotiated settlement to a civil war.

But as has been demonstrated in Cyprus, whose lessons are beginning to be taught to strategic planners in the contemporary cases of Haiti and Bosnia, leaders in the West can and should distinguish short-term military intervention from longer-term policing of a stalemate. Once massive military power creates a situation of peace, and there is a modus vivendi between the warring parties, it is then possible to subcontract the policing to another force. Canada, Finland, and Pakistan have developed expertise in their armies to play such a role. There is every reason that the UN should become the forum where countries negotiate a system of taxation (of countries) to pay for the policing. It should be made clear to all that, as in Cyprus, there is no guarantee of a stable peace and that the police force may be deployed for many years to come. Under conditions of an internationally created cease-fire with the gendarmerie (police, not military) in for the long term, domestic forces—as with the example of businessmen in the previous section—may be able to overcome the commitment problem that held back an agreement to promote the rule of law. More likely, however, the payoffs of having an expensive international police force—providing a new source of rents to distribute—will be high enough to deter an internal solution. But the long-term costs of having such police forces (even if they become permanent) seem far lower than the alternative: continued civil war, mass starvation, and killing.

Whether or not the decoupling option works, the solution to the endgame that was reflected in UNOSOM II's strategy of nation building seems worse. Without the U.S. willing to become trustees of collapsed states, it ought not devise strategies of intervention in which de facto trusteeship is the only route to success.

Part 1 of this chapter reviewed explanations for the civil war in Somalia that spiraled in the wake of Mohammed Siyaad Barre's fall in 1991. The standard explanation of area specialists, focusing on Somalis' segmented lineage system, was found wanting because such systems work well in ameliorating violent conflict after it breaks out. What needed to be explained, then, was the failure of the segmentary lineage system to produce a powerful peace coalition. The security dilemma, the standard explanation of international relations experts, and emphasized in several of the analyses in this volume, was not fully satisfactory in explaining the Somali case either. There was little evidence that the principal aim of the clan armies was to protect their kin from the observed arming of other clans. Two other international relations approaches, one focusing on miscalculations of strength under conditions of anarchy and the other on the commitment problem, were found to have important insights for parts of the Somali puzzle but were not in themselves satisfactory causal theories. The essay then borrowed from evolutionary biology and industrial organization to propose that the spiraling of the civil war was due to the declining relative resources of African incumbents compared to challengers, which can, when a leader falls from power, set off a war of attrition among contenders.

Part 2 of this chapter examined the role of the international gendarmerie in response to the catastrophe in Somalia, in order to answer the question of how best to organize third-party intervention. The analysis questioned the appropriateness of UN direction of Chapter 7 missions, as the overarching diplomatic mission of the UN too easily subverts the decisive field actions that are necessary for Chapter 7 missions. Also questioned was the possibility for any gendarmerie of combining rapid humanitarian relief in civil wars (which requires compromises with illegitimate strongmen) with a program of national construction (which demands undermining the power of those strongmen).

An implication of the analyses in parts 1 and 2 might be for the international gendarmerie in response to contests for state power in Africa to choose a strongman and to shower him with prizes, thereby undermining the incentive for other contenders to fight, and undermining as well any hope of legitimate governance for the near future. The chapter suggests a less autocratic but perhaps riskier implication of the analysis. This would involve rapid Chapter 7–type action (subcontracted to a major power) to put down spiraling civil wars, followed by the introduction of an international police force that is committed to long-term monitoring. Under these conditions, with no big prizes for strongmen, diplomatic efforts should be used to encourage pacts cross-cutting clan or tribal groups that would promote the rule of law.

Humanitarian efforts in putting out the flames of civil war have foundered on the failure to design an endgame for international forces. The proposal herein is a modest suggestion in thinking long term about an endgame that would be as humanitarian as the original motivations for military action.

NOTES

The author acknowledges James Fearon, Rui Jose de Figueiredo, Jeffrey Herbst, Jodi Lee Nelson, Peter Schraeder, Said S. Samatar, Duncan Snidal, Barbara Walter, Barry Weingast, and John Western for their help in the research for and fine-tuning of this paper.

The epigraph is taken from Maxamed Afrax, "The Mirror of Culture: Somali Dissolution Seen Through Oral Expression," in Ahmed I. Samatar, ed., *The Somali Challenge: From Catastrophe to Renewal?* (Boulder: Rienner, 1994), p. 248. Readers may note the author but not the editor of the cited volume relies on Somali orthography in spelling his name and in reproducing the proverb above. In this chapter I shall use the Somali orthography to represent the names of clans and towns, except (as with Mogadishu) where there is a standard spelling in foreign media. Names of Somali authors are reproduced as in their publications, but, for the key actors in the narrative, I have used the common media spellings.

1. The Daarood, Isxaaq, and Hawiye are the largest of the clan-families of the Samaale branch of Somali society. The MOD alliance constituted three of the five major Daarood clans (the other two are the Warsangeli and the Majeerteen). Two Hawiye clans (the Abgaal and Habar Gidir) play an important role in this narrative. I shall not be discussing conflicts within so-called Somaliland (the rump republic of the former British colony), and therefore Isxaaq clan divisions are not relevant to this paper. The other branch of Somali society, the Sab, includes mostly agricultural clans that were victims of but not participants in the civil war.

2. Propositional claims in segmentary lineage theory are hard to come by. The locus classicus is E. E. Evans-Pritchard, *Kinship and Marriage Among the Nuer* (Oxford: Clarendon, 1951).

3. I. M. Lewis, *A Pastoral Democracy* (London: Oxford University Press, 1961), pp. 156–157, and chapter 8; Said S. Samatar, *Oral Poetry and Somali Nationalism* (Cambridge: Cambridge University Press, 1982).

4. Said S. Samatar, *Somalia: A Nation in Turmoil*, no. 4 (London: Minority Rights Group Report, 1991), p. 26.

5. Samatar, *Somalia*, pp. 13, 27. Also making this point is Marc Michaelson, "Somalia: The Painful Road to Reconciliation," *Africa Today*, 2d quarter (1993), pp. 53–73. Michaelson insists that state centralization due to the military rule of Siyaad overshadowed the constraints of the segmentary lineage system, weakening traditional modes of conflict resolution.

6. See I. M. Lewis, "Segmentary Nationalism and the Collapse of the Somali State," in his *Blood and Bone: The Call of Kinship in Somali Society* (Lawrenceville, N.J.: Red Sea, 1994), for a demonstration of the continued relevance and viability of the segmentary lineage system. Postmodern critics of Lewis, e.g.,

Abdalla Omar Mansur (1995) "The Nature of the Somali Clan System," in A. J. Ahmed, *The Invention of Somalia* (Lawrenceville, N.J.: Red Sea, 1995), pp. 117–134, have yet to provide compelling field evidence that shows a different principle of social organization than the one Lewis has described. For a critique of Lewis's reliance on segmentary lineage explanations that parallels the one presented here, see C. Besteman, "Violent Politics and the Politics of Violence—The Dissolution of the Somali Nation-State" *American Ethnologist*, vol. 23, no. 3 (1996), pp. 579, 592.

7. Two area experts wrote in 1987 that, "indeed, there are already signs that a nascent civil war, and a potentially catastrophic one, is brewing in Somalia." Although they ended their book with a statement of "cautious [but unwarranted] optimism," their analysis correctly foresaw the chaos that could ensue should Siyaad be deposed. A better understanding of such expert analysis by outside powers and the UN could have helped cauterize the violence in 1991. See David D. Laitin and Said S. Samatar, *Somalia: Nation in Search of a State* (Boulder: Westview, 1987), pp. 154, 161.

8. For a definition of the security dilemma, see Robert Jervis and Jack Snyder, chapter 1, this volume, and Robert Jervis, "Cooperation Under the Security Dilemma," *World Politics*, vol. 30, no. 2 (January 1978), p. 169.

9. This portrait of Aideed's motivations was painted by Robert Oakley, private communication.

10. Barry Posen "The Security Dilemma and Ethnic Conflict," *Survival*, vol. 35, no. 1 (Spring 1993), pp. 27–47; James Fearon, "Ethnic War as a Commitment Problem," paper presented to the Annual Meeting of the American Political Science Association, New York, 1994; James Fearon, "Commitment Problems and the Spread of Ethnic Conflict," in David A. Lake and Donald Rothchild, eds. *The International Spread of Ethnic Conflict* (Princeton: Princeton University Press, 1998); and Barbara F. Walter, "The Resolution of Civil Wars: Why Negotiations Fail," Ph.D. thesis, University of Chicago, 1994.

11. See Mancur Olson, "Capitalism, Socialism, and Dictatorship," unpublished manuscript; Douglass North, *Structure and Change in Economic History* (New York: Norton, 1981); and Charles Tilly, *Coercion, Capital, and European States* (Cambridge: Blackwell, 1990), for resource-based theories of the state. See also Ronald Wintrobe, "The Tinpot and the Totalitarian: An Economic Theory of Dictatorship," *American Political Science Review*, vol. 84, no. 3 (1990), pp. 849–872.

12. See Thomas Callaghy, "The State as a Lame Leviathan," in Zaki Ergas, ed., *The African State in Transition* (London: Macmillan, 1987), pp. 87–116.

13. Stephen Stedman, "Conflict and Conciliation in Sub-Saharan Africa," in Michael Brown, ed., *The International Dimensions of Internal Conflicts* (Cambridge: MIT Press, 1996).

14. After coups there are short-term increases on military expenditures, best interpreted as coming from the "prize" awarded by international powers to coup victors. See William Foltz, "The Militarization of Africa: Trends and Policy Problems," chapter 7 in William Foltz and Henry Bienen, eds., *Arms and the African* (New Haven: Yale University Press, 1985), p. 172.

15. Discussed in Peter Schraeder, "U.S. Intervention in the Horn of Africa Amidst the End of the Cold War," *Africa Today*, 2d quarter (1993), pp. 7–27.

16. But note Peter Schraeder, "From Berlin 1884 to 1989," *Journal of Modern African Studies*, vol. 33, no. 3 (December 1995), who documents that French aid to its former African colonies has in fact doubled in the post–cold war years. These prizes give incumbency advantages to dictators that may help to preserve the cold war stability in those African states lucky enough to receive such aid.

17. Ted Robert Gurr, dir., Minorities at Risk, phase 3 dataset. The half-decade rebellion scores had to reach a level of "4," and the decadal communal conflict score had to reach a level of "5" to be counted in my enumerations. See also Ted Robert Gurr, "Peoples Against States: Ethnopolitical Conflict and the Changing World System," *International Studies Quarterly*, vol. 38 (1994), pp. 347–377, where the author notes that Africa is the region with the greatest number of ethnopolitical conflicts to arise post-1987. Gurr denies that the collapse of the bloc system had anything to do with these conflicts, as "Africa [is] the region least affected by Cold War rivalries" (pp. 354). My interpretation here suggests an indirect effect on the level of ethnopolitical conflict in Africa due to the end of the cold war.

18. See John Maynard Smith, *Models in Ecology* (Cambridge: Cambridge University Press, 1974), for the first exposition of the model. In industrial organization the state of knowledge in the field is summarized in Jean Tirole, *The Theory of Industrial Organization* (Cambridge: MIT Press, 1989), pp. 311–314, 380–385. For possibilities for cooperative solutions under war of attritionlike circumstances, see Stergios Skaperdas, "Cooperation, Conflict, and Power in the Absence of Property Rights," *American Economic Review*, vol. 82, no. 4 (September 1992), pp. 720–739. For an analysis of bargaining in a war of attrition, see James D. Fearon, "Domestic Political Audiences and the Escalation of International Disputes," *American Political Science Review*, vol. 88, no. 3 (1994), pp. 577–592.

19. James Fearon, "Rationalist Explanations for War," *International Organization*, vol. 49, no. 3 (Summer 1995), pp. 379–414.

20. Schraeder, "From Berlin 1884 to 1989," shows how France has winked at African state subterfuges of democratic reform in order to help its francophone African clients survive. Yet, as can be seen with political and communal conflicts in Congo, Mali, and Niger in the late-1990s, French legionnaires are less involved in propping up militarily puppet governments.

21. The short vignette on the history of international intervention in the Somali civil war that follows is drawn from Terrence Lyons and Ahmed I. Samatar,

Somalia: State Collapse, Multilateral Intervention, and Strategies for Political Reconstruction (Washington, D.C.: Brookings Institution, 1995); and Kenneth Allard, *Somalia Operations: Lessons Learned* (Washington, D.C.: National Defense University Press, 1995).

22. Mohamed Sahnoun, *Somalia: The Missed Opportunities* (Washington: U.S. Institute of Peace Press, 1994).

23. John Hirsch and Robert Oakley, *Somalia and Operation Restore Hope* (Washington, D.C.: United States Institute of Peace Press, 1995).

24. Oakley's defense on this issue is presented in Hirsch and Oakley, *Somalia and Operation Restore Hope*, pp. 56–64, 70–71, 78, and 191. Most of the papers in Walter Clarke and Jeffrey Herbst, *Learning From Somalia* (Boulder: Westview, 1997), agree that Oakley sided too closely with the warlords.

25. A ballpark figure is hard to come by. Steven Hansch, Scott Lillibridge, Grace Egeland, Charles Teller, and Michael Toole, *Lives Lost, Lives Saved: Excess Mortality and the Impact of Health Interventions in the Somalia Emergency* (Washington, D.C.: Refugee Policy Group, November 1994), provides reasonable statistical evidence that UNITAF input saved between 10,000 and 25,000 lives. Supporters of American efforts have given wildly inflated figures. Chester Crocker, in his "Lessons of Somalia," *Foreign Affairs*, vol. 75, no. 3 (1995), p. 3, gives a figure (without any empirical support) of 250,000. Michael Mandelbaum, "Foreign Policy as Social World," *Foreign Affairs*, vol. 75, no. 1 (1996), p. 30, gives the figure of 500,000, again without any empirical justification. Meanwhile, detractors of the policy err in the other direction. Alex de Waal, *Times Literary Supplement*, December 29, 1995, asserts without statistical evidence that the rains of 1991 were the principal cause of the miracle that saved thousands. The overall cost of the operation for the U.S. from 1992–94 was $2.3 billion, as estimated by John G. Sommer, *Hope Restored? Humanitarian Aid in Somalia, 1990–1994* (Washington, D.C.: Refugee Policy Group, Center for Policy Analysis and Research on Refugee Issues, 1994). A summary of the successes of Restore Hope, one that is open about the failures as well, is that of Allard, *Somalia Operations*.

26. "The Restoration of the Somali Justice System," Clarke and Herbst, *Learning From Somalia*. Oakley argues that he did all that was possible to build up local constabularies in Hirsch and Oakley, *Somalia and Operation Restore Hope*, pp. 87–92.

27. Susan Rosegrant, "A 'Seamless' Transition: United States and United Nations Operations in Somalia—1992–1993," Case Program, John F. Kennedy School of Government, Harvard University, CO9–96–1324.0, part A, and CO9–96–1325.0, part B, Part A, 1996, p. 18. After Aideed's death in July 1996, his son assumed leadership of the Habar Gidir forces, but relations broke down with Atto, leaving Mogadishu with two Habar Gidir armies fighting each other and the Abgaals. See U.S. Department of State, "Somalia: Profile of Asylum Claims

and Country Conditions" (Washington, D.C.: Bureau of Democracy, Human Rights and Labor, December 1996).

28. Rosegrant, "A 'Seamless' Transition," part A, p. 33.

29. John Bolton, "Wrong Turn in Somalia," *Foreign Affairs* (January-February 1994), vol. 73, no. 1, pp. 62–63. As assistant secretary of state for international organizations in the Bush administration, Bolton has an interest in emphasizing the differences between the Bush and the Clinton policies.

30. Jonathan Howe, "The United States and United Nations in Somalia: The Limits of Involvement," *Washington Quarterly* (1995), vol. 18, no. 3, p. 54.

31. Rosegrant, "A 'Seamless' Transition," part B, pp. 1–2. To be sure, during UNO-SOM II, the secretary general's military adviser had a staff of only two officers. Two years later, with the Haiti operation underway, there were over one hundred experienced officers on this staff. Still, without the incentives and the capacity to make and administer decisions, the UN cannot effectively execute Chapter 7 missions. While Robert Oakley and Michael Dziedzic, "Sustaining Success in Haiti," *Strategic Forum* (June 1996), vol. 79, see success in the close partnership between the U.S. and the UN, I believe the key to the success of the UN operation there (UNMIH) is that it operated simultaneously with the U.S.-controlled effort (MNF).

32. Ramesh Thakur, "From Peacekeeping to Peace Enforcement: The U.N. Operation in Somalia," *Journal of Modern African Studies* (1994), vol. 32, no. 3, p. 393. This changed a bit in 1993, with a twenty-four-hour Situation Room phone in New York.

33. John Ruggie, "The United Nations and the Collective Use of Force: Wither— Or Whether?" *International Peacekeeping*, vol. 3, no. 4 (Autumn 1996), pp. 1–20.

34. In the case at hand the UN was crippled by the secretary general's lack of objectivity on the issue. First, he strongly believed that the UN should do something big in Africa, largely because he got his political support from delegates of that continent. Second, he had a long-term antipathy to Aideed, going back to his days as Egyptian foreign minister. The UN was seen as a partisan from the moment the secretary general got involved in the issue. Here I want to avoid the particularities of the UNOSOM operations in order to examine more general areas of failure by the UN.

35. Michael Maren, *The Road to Hell: The Ravaging Effects of Foreign Aid and International Charity* (New York: Free Press, 1997).

36. Anna Simons, *Networks of Dissolution* (Boulder: Westview, 1995).

37. James Mayall, "Introduction," in James Mayall, ed., *The New Interventionism, 1991–1994* (Cambridge: Cambridge University Press, 1996), p. 17.

38. Ioan Lewis and James Mayall, "Somalia," in Mayall, *The New Interventionism*, p. 121.

39. Lewis and Mayall, "Somalia," pp. 122–123; Ahmed I. Samatar, "The Curse of Allah: Civic Disembowelment and the Collapse of the State in Somalia," in

Ahmed I. Samatar, *The Somali Challenge: From Catastrophe to Renewal?* (Boulder: Rienner, 1994), pp. 109–111.

40. Said S. Samatar, personal communication; but note that Robert Gosende of the USIA, along with the head of the U.S. Liaison Office in Somalia (who had previous diplomatic experience in Somalia), got a lot of Somali poetry on Radio Station Rajo (Hope).

41. Lewis and Mayall, "Somalia," p. 113. Howe is another story. He had little sense of the society into which he was dropped, and the disastrous early days of his incumbency were not solely due to the total lack of staff support available to him.

42. Afrax, "The Mirror of Culture," pp. 248–249.

43. Ibid., pp. 233–234.

44. Ibid., p. 234.

45. Stedman, "Conflict and Conciliation." His is not a case of *ex ante* support and *ex post* critique. In a policy paper of 1992, "Somalia: The Case for Triage," Stedman foresaw many of the problems that did occur.

46. This was mooted by Fred Cuny, a famine consultant, and many of the U.S. civilian agencies favored this plan. The NSC rejected it as it would require expensive surveillance. See Ken Menkhaus, with Louis Ortmayer, "Key Decisions in the Somalia Intervention," Pew Case Studies in International Affairs, Case 464 (Washington, D.C.: Institute for the Study of Diplomacy Publications, School of Foreign Service, Georgetown University, 1995), p. 4.

47. This idea was presented to me by Leonard Wantchakon of Yale University. See Adam Przeworski, *Democracy and the Market* (Cambridge: Cambridge University Press, 1991), for the notion of democracy as a contest with uncertain outcomes. See Barry Weingast, "The Political Foundations of Democracy and the Rule of Law," *American Political Science Review* (1997), vol. 91, no. 2, pp. 245–263, for the coordination problem involved in the emergence of a rule of law.

48. Walter, "The Resolution of Civil Wars."

6   War and Peace in Cambodia

Michael W. Doyle

Between May 23 and 28, 1993, the citizens of Cambodia voted in a long awaited election run by the United Nations. For Cambodia, a land that has seen war, devastation, national massacre, and foreign invasion all in the last generation, the election was the culmination of years of peace talks as well as fifteen months of peacekeeping by the United Nations Transitional Authority in Cambodia (UNTAC). Yet the news from Cambodia over the preceding months seemed uniformly bleak—massacres of ethnic Vietnamese, attacks on UN soldiers and civilians, harassment of opposition political parties, and incidents of renewed fighting. Journalists had been drawn to the setbacks, and many had written off UNTAC as a failure. But once the election was successfully completed, an opposite pattern was set in the reporting. All the problems that plagued the conduct of the eighteen-month operation were swept aside by the glow of a successful week of elections.

In the years since the 1993 election Cambodia continued to confound any straightforward assessment. On the one hand, Southeast Asia was, at last, at peace. Cambodia again was a recognized sovereign state. King Sihanouk, who embodied Cambodia's traditional legitimacy, again reigned. The Khmer Rouge, who abandoned the peace process, were increasingly marginalized and collapsed in fall of 1996. A coalition government of Prince Ranariddh's and Hun Sen's parties, the two predominant factions, ruled. The peace, on the other hand, was very fragile. Cambodia's borders with

Vietnam and Thailand were not yet demarcated and were the subject of acrimonious accusations of bad faith. The human rights supposedly embedded in the agreement on "pluralist democracy" proved to be fragile barriers against corrupt and arbitrary government policy. The spread of economic reconstruction beyond the "casino capitalism" boom in the capital proved much more difficult than anticipated as corruption and violent strife undermined the order that investment, whether domestic or international, requires. And, in July 1997, Hun Sen's minority faction of the ruling coalition, which had been staging a rolling, silent coup against Prince Ranariddh's majority royalist faction, staged an actual coup and expelled the royalists.[1]

A year of international isolation and the cutoff of a large portion of foreign aid followed. An active combined diplomatic effort by the Association of Southeast Asian Nations (ASEAN), Japan, the European Union, the United Nations, and the United States brokered the return of the opposition parties—Prince Ranariddh's and Sam Rainsy's—and another national election in July 1998.[2] But the electoral campaign was again marred by violence and intimidation and, unlike the UNTAC election, overwhelming monopolization of the media by the CPP and widely credited accusations of vote count fraud, allegations that Hun Sen, the official winner, seemed unwilling and the international monitors unable to address. Another coalition between Hun Sen and Ranariddh followed. Cambodia had a sovereign state and it had an elected parliamentary government, but it was far from reconciled, stable, or productive. Cambodia was a country free from civil war but far from civil peace.

In light of the theoretical literature on civil wars, Cambodia's semipeace also appears exceptional to the current generalizations about the difficulty of resolving civil wars (1 and 2) and the means needed to resolve them (3 and 4):

1. Civil wars are much harder to resolve, we are told, than are international wars because enforcing agreed upon bargains is so much more difficult when one or both parties are required to disarm before the peace is complete. Both sides continue to suffer security dilemmas. International peace agreements, in contrast, allow both sides to preserve their defenses.[3]
2. Civil wars driven by ethnic conflict are even more difficult to settle than those characterized by ideological conflicts. Ethnic strife occurs between parties whose identities are transparent and fixed, while ideological adherence is opaque, and adherents can change their minds.

Ethnic conflicts thus engender powerful offensive, preemptive incentives to seize (and "cleanse") rival territory, because once "cleansed," and a community destroyed, territory is permanently lost. Ideologies, on the other hand, are less spatially dependent than ethnic communities; hearts and minds can be won and rewon. Ideological wars—such as Cambodia's four way conflict among Maoist and Leninist Communists, republican and monarchist oligarchs—should thus be much easier to resolve than ethnic wars.[4]

3. Because of the insecurities, resolving civil wars requires supranational enforcement in order to persuade the parties to abide by a peace agreement.[5] (The most promising solution to ethnic wars is partition.)

4. Unfortunately, enforcement is one thing the UN does not do well. United Nations peacekeeping doctrine differentiates operations that implement an agreed peace—UN Charter Chapter 6 peacekeeping—from operations that roll back aggression or enforce law and order—Chapter 7 peace enforcement. Peacekeeping, such as occurred in El Salvador or Cyprus, relies on principles of consent, impartiality, and the nonuse of force; peace enforcement, such as that attempted in Somalia, relies on compulsion, collective security, and, where needed, force.[6] The UN is capable of succeeding in the first if it sticks to the principles of consent and the nonuse of force. It fails in enforcement because it cannot effectively compel, "when there is no peace to keep."[7] Hence the UN will be ineffective in helping to resolve civil wars.

Even though the Cambodian case confirms aspects of the logic underlying each of these four generalization, the Cambodian "war in civil peace" is also an exception to all four. One case cannot disprove any generalization; and, indeed, the wider record of civil wars lends considerable support to those generalizations. Cambodia's exceptionalism also reveals in an oblique light what the generalizations mean: both what the average rule-making case misses or reflects and what the forces underlying the average case (presumably) override.

As I shall first illustrate, the Cambodian civil war was partially settled. Second, even more strikingly, the ideological Cambodian factions continued to harbor offensive intentions, not unlike the preemptive incentives of ethnic wars, and these were largely responsible for the warlike tension that continued into the resulting peace—as well as the coup that occurred in July 1997. Victory in a civil war/peace is a very profitable outcome. It is often one of winner take all, offering security of bureaucratic place and substantial and assured private income. Third, even though no external supranational enforcement guaranteed the interim security of the parties, peace was made and held between the two predominant factions (the Khmer Rouge later abandoned the peace). Fourth, the UN did succeed in bringing a partial peace to Cambodia, but only by innovating and (in one important instance) by exercising force. The negotiation of the Paris Peace Agreement of 1991 and consequent construction of the United Nations Transitional Authority (UNTAC) under Chapter 6 contributed essential legal capacities to the conduct of the operation but did little to establish a framework of continuing consent or, in the end, avoid the need for the UN to provide political entrepreneurship and exercise impartial, non-neutral enforcement. The peace became a continuation of war "by [to adapt Clausewitz] other means."

I

A Peace Made in Paris

The agreements on a comprehensive political settlement of the Cambodian conflict (signed at the second Paris Conference on October 23, 1991) were a revolutionary blueprint for a comprehensive settlement.[8] The unique quality of the Paris Agreement lies in the fact that settlement process concerned what the UN secretary general, Boutros Boutros-Ghali, refers to in An Agenda for Peace as "peace-building" in addition to peacemaking and peacekeeping.[9] The international community charged the UN—for the first time in its history—with the political and economic restructuring of a member of the UN as part of the building of peace in which the parties would then (it was planned) institutionalize their reconciliation. The roots of the conflict lay in the collapse of the legitimacy of the Cambodian state. The strategy of peace embodied in the Paris Agreement lay in the UN's stepping in to help rebuild the legitimacy of the state, after the parties had failed to achieve a reconciliation of their own.

The parties to the agreement created two institutions to implement the peace: the Supreme National Council (SNC) and the United Nations Transitional Authority in Cambodia (UNTAC).[10] The agreement defined a transitional period running from the entry into force of the agreement, October 23, 1991, to the time when an elected constituent assembly established a new sovereign government of Cambodia (September 1993). During that period the Supreme National Council, a committee composed of the four factions, was to "enshrine" the legal sovereignty of Cambodia and UNTAC, an authority established by the Security Council in February 1992, was to implement the agreed upon peace.[11]

The Paris Agreement granted extraordinary power to the UN during the transition period. UNTAC was required

- to monitor the cease-fire and the withdrawal of all foreign forces, and to supervise the cantonment and demobilization of military forces,
- to control and supervise crucial aspects of civil administration,[12]
- to organize and monitor the elections, as a first step to a "system of liberal democracy, on the basis of pluralism,"
- to foster an environment in which respect for human rights and fundamental freedoms is ensured,
- to coordinate with the United Nations High Commissioner for Refugees (UNHCR) the repatriation of more than 350,000 refugees living in camps on the Thai side of the border,
- to help plan and raise funds for the social and economic rehabilitation of Cambodia.

Although the UN had experience in some of these areas through past peacekeeping operations, it was the combination of these tasks that made UNTAC one of the largest UN peacekeeping operations, requiring over fifteen thousand troops and seven thousand civilian personnel and costing over an estimated $2.8 billion during the span of eighteen months, the calculated transition period.

The Paris Agreement provided UNTAC with broad legal authority to enforce its mandate. Indeed the agreement specifically gave the UN "all powers necessary to ensure the implementation of the Agreement." UN sensitivity to charges of colonialism may have hindered the UNTAC mission from interpreting the agreements aggressively. But the determinants of the success and failure of UNTAC lay elsewhere—in the fierce political contest among factions. The Paris Agreement was the opening salvo in a new phase of the Cambodian War, to be waged by other means.

Successes

Considering that the main antagonists in Cambodia—the Vietnamese-installed government and the radical Khmer Rouge—were pressured by their big power sponsors to sign the 1991 Paris Peace Accords and did not cooperate fully with the UN, UNTAC's accomplishments before and after the May elections were remarkable.[13]

First, although the country was temporarily subject to the UN's "transitional authority," it also enjoyed for perhaps the first time the prospect of true independence from the control of any foreign power. Having endured French and Japanese colonialism before 1954 and American, Chinese, and Vietnamese competition for influence thereafter, Cambodia experienced national self-determination (and Southeast Asia, regional self-determination). The United States supported the Lon Nol coup of 1970, the Chinese backstopped the Khmer Rouge, and the Vietnamese installed the Hun Sen regime in 1979 (finally withdrawing their military forces in 1989). Some disturbing foreign presences continued to complicate Cambodia's future. Thai generals in the west and Vietnamese interests in the east participated in the illegal export of Cambodia's logs and gems. Many thousand Vietnamese entered the country to take advantage of the economic boom created by the UNTAC presence. But as of October 1993, for better or worse, Cambodia was in the hands of the Cambodians. (This is what the UN "transition" was supposed to transition to.)

Second, the mere presence of UNTAC had an impact. Its arrival signaled the end of full-scale civil war. The country became mostly peaceful. Some provinces were very tense, but skirmishes were limited in duration and the pitched battles of 1990 and earlier ended. The UNTAC presence also opened up the political system, helping opposition parties to compete against the incumbent regime. They acquired offices, held meetings, and had access to the media. Harassment continued, but not enough to undermine the electoral process. The jails, once crammed with political prisoners, held a vastly reduced population of inmates, all of whom seem to have had some (sometimes trumped up) criminal charge laid against them. While UNTAC did not exercise the control over the Phnom Penh regime envisaged in the Paris Accords, it made a dent in the most blatant corruption.

Third, 360,000 refugees were peacefully repatriated from camps in Thailand, despite dire prognostications from experts a year earlier. The Repatriation Component of UNTAC (staffed by UNHCR) organized this massive undertaking with the cooperation and support of its Military Component, the Cambodian Red Cross, and other humanitarian and relief organizations.[14]

Fourth, UNTAC organized an election in a country with a shattered physical infrastructure. The UN has monitored and supervised many elections, but Cambodia's was the first election the UN directly organized, from the planning stages through the writing of an electoral law, to registration and the conduct of the poll. Hundreds of foreign volunteers in nearly every village registered voters and spread information. Voters walked considerable distances and braved threats to hold onto their registration cards. UNTAC persuaded the Supreme National Council to pass a comprehensive electoral law (over the initial opposition of the Supreme National Council). It began to educate Cambodians about human rights and elections, employing an imaginative range of techniques that included traveling acting troops performing skits, Khmer videos, public rallies organized by UNTAC, debates among candidates, and extensive radio coverage.[15] Nearly all eligible Cambodians—almost five million—registered to vote.

The May 1993 election rewarded their efforts and, most of all, affirmed the determination of the Cambodian people to have a voice in their future. Despite months of attempted intimidation by some of the parties, more than 90 percent of the registered electorate turned out to vote. The Khmer Rouge had vowed to stop the election altogether. SOC waged a pitched battle against its main rival, FUNCINPEC, which included assassinations of FUNCINPEC party officials. According to the Human Rights Component of UNTAC, more than two hundred died during the campaigning period between March 1 and May 14, and this included a major attack launched by about four hundred Khmer Rouge and three hundred hastily recruited youths on Siem Reap on May 3 and 4. Despite threats from the government that people's votes would not be secret, UNTAC ensured they would be and apparently convinced Cambodians of that. UNTAC's Military Component took the measures necessary to guarantee the security of the polling and counting process.

Failures

If we look at UNTAC's official initial mandate, we can see three major areas of failure. The first lies in control over civil administration, the second in the failure to achieve a cease-fire and then canton, demobilize, and disarm the military forces (70 percent) of the four factions.[16] The third followed from the first two: a failure to reform the institutions of state control and start what will be a lengthy process of economic rehabilitation.

First, the Paris Agreements specified that UNTAC would control five essential areas of administration and do so over each of the four factions. By controlling them—so it was anticipated—UNTAC would be able to ensure that the political environment was neutral; no faction (and especially the predominant faction of the State of Cambodia) would be able to employ sovereign resources to tilt the electoral contest in its favor.

UNTAC had the apparent authority to control the factions, including the right to insert its officials within the factional administrations and to remove factional officials who did not respond to its directive. Yet, in fact, what UNTAC was supposed to control, it did not. What UNTAC seemed to control—e.g., expenditures in the ministry of finance of SOC—on closer examination was a mere front for decisions taken elsewhere. Much of the SOC administration had collapsed, and effective control had slipped to provincial governors and generals, so that "controlling" ministries that themselves did not control their nominal areas of responsibility meant little. But, even in Phnom Penh, in the areas of policy making where a central administrative apparatus was still functioning, the SOC administered around UNTAC. The Cambodian People's Party (the political party of the state of Cambodia) thus enjoyed the service of officials on the public payroll and access to public assets, while obtaining revenue from sales of those assets.

Second, the failure to achieve a cease-fire (phase 1) and then canton, demobilize, and disarm 70 percent of the military forces of the four factions (phase 2) had an equally devastating effect on the successful operation of the original mandate. As initially planned, the May elections were supposed to take place in a secure—cantoned and disarmed—political environment in which the relative military weight of the factions would play little direct role in either the electoral campaign or the voter's choice. During the campaign armies tilted all the electoral contests. Indeed, SOC attempted to coerce the opposition and the voters. At the same time, an atmosphere of violence raised its "popularity," since it had the only military force capable of containing the Khmer Rouge.

The Khmer Rouge refused to canton in June 1992, saying that UNTAC had failed to control SOC (which was true, but neither had it controlled the Khmer Rouge in its much smaller zones) and that Vietnamese "forces" remained in Cambodia (Vietnamese military formations had withdrawn in 1989)[17]. When the Khmer Rouge refused to canton, SOC and other factions, which had partially cantoned almost 55,000 soldiers, refused to demobilize and disarm; then most of the cantoned soldiers went on agricultural leave.[18]

Third, as product of the previous two failures, very little rehabilitation (peace building) occurred during the eighteen-month operation. Cambodia's massive reconstruction needs were postponed until after a legitimate government had been formed.

UNTAC thus achieved many successes, but it also missed some significant opportunities to reform and assist the Cambodian state. UNTAC achieved significant successes in establishing a peace over most of the country and in restoring key features of Cambodian civil society. It helped the return of refugees, encouraged the formation of Cambodian NGOs, engaged in human rights education, and, most significantly, helped give Cambodian society a sense of participation in politics through the national election and thereby helped secure legitimacy for the state. But it failed to demobilize the armies or control the SOC civil service. In 1993 the coalition of the two lead factions, CPP and FUNCINPEC, making up the Royal Government of Cambodia (RGC) inherited the continuing war with the Khmer Rouge, still well armed and ready to fight. The RGC, furthermore, had to accommodate both the existing SOC (CPP) civil service and add to them the newly enrolled FUNCINPEC officials. The results were a bureaucratic stalemate in which the two parties blocked each other, thus eroding overall government ineffectiveness and increasing tension. Threats of coups and counter-coups have disturbed the politics of Cambodia since 1993.

II

Accounting for a Semi-war

This leads to the central question of how the Cambodian peace failed and what role UNTAC played in helping or hurting the peace process. I begin an answer by considering whether the parties experienced defensive security dilemmas that had to be solved. I will argue that they would have had security dilemmas, but that the peace was undermined more by a second factor: the parties held offensive preferences beyond their security interests.

Security Dilemmas

There is good reason to suspect that civil wars may be particularly difficult to settle because of the special significance that security dilemmas have in domestic conflicts. International conflicts can be settled and leave both parties fully armed, capable of guaranteeing their own security. Civil wars, by contrast, presume disarmament, and often before some new entity sufficiently effective and national in scope can guarantee the security of formerly warring factions. In these transitional circumstances there can arise a dilemma:defensive efforts to enhance individual factional security can make other parties less secure.[19] Parties fully preferring the peace settlement may doubt that other parties also supporting the peace settlement truly do so. Uncertainty alone may lead to defections—hidden arms caches, covert external alliances—which undermine peace. This is conventionally called (after an argument of J. J. Rousseau) a stag dilemma. Factional preferences are CC, DC, DD, CD. The faction truly prefers the peace agreement (CC), but rather than be caught as the only sucker (CD) abiding by the peace after another faction has defected (DC), will choose to defect (DC) if it (mistakenly) thinks that the other faction will defect. The result can, but should not be, DD. Another possibility is the prisoner's dilemma, in which the preference ordering is DC, CC, DD, CD. Even though both factions prefer peace (CC) to war (DD), each also prefers to exploit the peaceful cooperation of the other (DC) to a situation in which both cooperate (CC).

There are a number of standard solutions to these dilemmas. Traditional or "first generation" peacekeeping is a solution to stag dilemmas. The UN or other international force interposes itself among the factions and objectively certifies compliance, thus providing the transparency that all parties are indeed living up to the commitments they made (and indeed prefer, CC).[20] Prisoner's dilemmas are more problematic, requiring that preferences be altered (for example reducing the cardinal gap between the value of DC and CC, DD and CD). But here too standard solutions exist. Graduated disarmament is one. Step by step (division by division) disarmament serves to iterate the problem, allowing the parties to develop trust through repeated interactions while each is still secure and able to sanction defections.[21] Power sharing is another, as each faction retains the ability to veto the acquisition of sovereign power and the entire resources of the state by any other faction.[22] A peacekeeping force, even one that merely defends itself, assists this process by its very presence. The international legitimacy that it carries lowers the net value (by raising the costs of defection) for the parties by internationalizing what heretofore had been a settled domestic conflict.[23]

Pertinent as these insights may be to the average civil war, they do not account for what went wrong in Cambodia after the signing of the peace in October 1991. By this remark I do not wish to exonerate UNTAC from its failings. Indeed, one of the problems of current UN peace management is that even if factions have preferences equivalent to the cooperative structure of the stag dilemma, excessively slow deployment of peacekeeping operations can undermine the transparency function that peacekeeping is designed to achieve.[24] Some of the UN battalions, moreover, were incapable of defending themselves. And one, worse still, exacerbated the ambient level of communal violence by its misbehavior.

The deeper problem, however, is that only the weakest factions seemed to have the preference structures of the stag dilemma or the prisoners' dilemma. Of course, no one can either read minds (either of individuals or, a fortiori, of factions) or infer preferences from the outcome—an unstable mix of peace and war (CC and DD).[25] But related evidence does illuminate key aspects of the factions' preferences as well as the complex character of the conflict. I turn to the conflict first and then the preferences.

The Conflict

The challenge of peace lay in the complex multiple character of the Cambodian conflict. Following the devastating bombing Cambodia suffered during the Vietnam War and the holocaust of more than one million Cambodians inflicted by the Khmer Rouge, the Cambodian conflict entered a new stage in December 1978, when, responding to repeated Khmer Rouge provocations, Vietnam invaded Cambodia. The Vietnamese invasion and the installation of the Heng Samrin–Hun Sen regime in 1978–79 gave rise to a guerrilla movement of the three major resistance groups: Prince Sihanouk's party the National Union Front for an Independent, Neutral, Peaceful and Cooperative Cambodia (FUNCINPEC), Son Sann's, the Khmer People's National Liberation Front (KPNLF), and the Party of Democratic Kampuchea (PDK, or the Khmer Rouge). Each of the four factions, including the Heng Samrin–Hun Sen (later called State of Cambodia, SOC) regime itself, contested the claims of the other to legitimate authority over Cambodia. In 1982, at the urging of ASEAN and China, the three groups opposing the Hun Sen regime formed the Coalition Government of Democratic Kampuchea (CGDK), headed by Prince Norodom Sihanouk.

The complexities of the conflict were evident. Like the most severe of ethnic civil wars, and like the Holocaust, in the Cambodian conflict nearly every family lost a close member—father, mother, sons and daughters—in the slaughter that followed from the Khmer Rouge cultural revolution. But the Cambodian civil war also resembled an ordinary interstate war—an occupation by Vietnam to be "resolved" simply by a withdrawal. For the Hun Sen regime and its Vietnamese and Soviet backers the conflict was a counterinsurgency war waged against a genocidal opponent (the Khmer Rouge). For the CGDK and its ASEAN, UN, PRC, and U.S. supporters the conflict was a case of international aggression by Vietnam and the occupation of a sovereign country. Conflicting claims to authority between CGDK and the Hun Sen government thus created problems of recognition for the international community. While the UN recognized the CGDK as the legal government of Cambodia, the State of Cambodia controlled more than eighty percent of the country.

The Cambodian civil war also resembled the international proxy wars of the cold war. Each of the factions depended on a foreign patron, which waged war against the other patrons over Cambodian soil. The United States had backed the republican forces (now become KPNLF); Russia backed the SOC; China, the Khmer Rouge; the Europeans, the princely faction, FUN-CINPEC. To a significant extent the civil war was an international war; and the international war was "civil"—a war among ideologies to determine not just who but what "way of life" would govern Cambodia. The international community, which in the post–cold war period is promoted as the solution to the security dilemmas of civil wars, was here its cause.

The Cambodian factions began to demonstrate a willingness to discuss peace only in December 1987, when Prince Sihanouk and Hun Sen informally met in Paris. With Sihanouk's advancing age, Hun Sen's desire to obtain international recognition for his regime, and military exhaustion as spurs to action, regional actors, and particularly Indonesia's foreign minister, Ali Alatas, began to take the lead, organizing two Jakarta Informal Meetings in 1988 and 1989. After nine years of front-line opposition to the perceived Vietnamese threat, ASEAN states were now ready for the right kind of reconciliation. Thailand's booming economy and its search for markets and investments made Cambodia and Laos and even Vietnam look more like business opportunities and less like strategic threats. Vietnam, for its part, seems to have become eager to shed its Cambodian burden. Its ten years of occupation had imposed heavy costs, both financial and human.[26] The occupation had barred Vietnam's full access to the world market, extended a dangerous strategic confrontation with China, and inflicted an embarrassing level of dependence on the USSR. Together, these precluded Vietnam's normalization within Southeast Asia. Indonesia was eager to display its capacities for regional leadership by brokering a regional peace. For Indonesia, rivalry with China meant that Vietnam was an ally it wished to cultivate, provided it could do so within an ASEAN context. Indonesia's good offices succeeded in identifying the need for an international control mechanism to supervise the transition to a peace, but they could not reach an agreement on how it would operate.

Perceiving what it thought was an opportunity to break the deadlock that had emerged at the regional level and concerned that Vietnam's prospective (September 1989) withdrawal of its forces from Cambodia would harden Hun Sen and Vietnam against a comprehensive solution,[27] French foreign minister Roland Dumas joined with Ali Alatas to cosponsor a (the first) Paris Conference on Cambodia in July 1989. Progress was made in defining agreement on the withdrawal of foreign forces, neutralization, the return of refugees, and other matters, but again the crucial sticking point proved to be the interim control mechanism. Disappointing the expectations of the co-chairs, the Cambodian factions flatly rejected the proposal that national reconciliation be achieved through an interim quadripartite government.[28] With the withdrawal of Vietnamese forces and the failure of the peace process, war resumed in Cambodia. The CGDK tested Hun Sen's independent staying power and Hun Sen demonstrated that his regime, though losing some territory, could hold on to the vast bulk of Cambodia.

The waning of the cold war now began to make possible the active cooperative involvement of the three key global powers: Russia, China, and the United States. For Russia the existing conflict (together with Russia's support of Vietnam and Hun Sen) was a continuing bar to a rapprochement with China, and it enhanced the influence of both China and the U.S. in Southeast Asia. Russia, nonetheless, was not prepared to abandon Hun Sen. Throughout the negotiations it thus sought to maximize Hun Sen's room for maneuver by minimizing the control the UN placed over the SOC. For China, with the end of the cold war and China's determination to achieve rapid economic development, the KR began to appear an unwelcome burden. Seeking access to the world market, appreciating the emergence of a less threatening, indeed exhausted, Vietnam, and beginning to build a close relationship with Thailand, China was prepared to settle for a peace, provided that it permitted KR participation. Throughout the negotiations, as a way to open political space for the KR, it sought to increase the control over the SOC that the UN would exercise. For the United States the opportunity to encourage a market-oriented Southeast Asia free from the hegemony of either China or Vietnam and to take Cambodia off its foreign policy agenda was a double bonus. Secretary Baker, moreover, feared that if the fighting continued it would inevitably escalate, forcing the U.S. into the dilemma of supporting either a Vietnamese "surrogate" (the Hun Sen regime) or Khmer Rouge genocide. And perhaps, most important, if the war escalated, Southeast Asia would again become an American domestic problem, stirring up all the domestic dissension of the Vietnam War period. The U.S., therefore, sought a comprehensive solution that transcended both the genocidal KR and the Vietnamese surrogate. It was prepared to gamble that Sihanouk, if he had sufficient UN backing in a transitional regime, would find a way to establish a "pluralist democracy" presided over by himself.[29]

Working with drafts from Australian foreign minister Gareth Evans and the papers of the UN Secretariat, the Permanent Five members of the Security Council steadily crafted the outlines of a comprehensive peace featuring a strong controlling role for a United Nations Transitional Authority in Cambodia (UNTAC). By August 27, 1990, at their sixth meeting, the five announced that they had reached a consensus on a framework. They asked the copresidents of the Paris Conference (France and Indonesia) to convene an informal meeting of the four factions in Jakarta at which, on September 10, the four accepted the framework and announced the formation of the Supreme National Council, consisting of all four factions and embodying Cambodian sovereignty during the transition process. But that was just the beginning of an eleven-month negotiating process in which the Security Council actively persuaded the four factions to turn the framework into a workable peace agreement.

Preferences

Thus, although the Cambodian parties were willing to sign a peace treaty, it is far from clear that they were willing to abide by one. In part, as well-informed participants at the Paris negotiations speculate, the parties had no real option but to sign the treaty. Their international patrons had cut them off from unilateral support in return for ensuring that each of their clients had a role in the negotiated peace. Vietnam and the PRC, patrons respectively of the SOC and the Khmer Rouge, had normalized relations in 1991, ending a bitter rivalry that had provoked a war in 1978 and Vietnam's invasion of Cambodia in 1979. Another interpretation suggests that perhaps the parties did want the agreement—but only to the extent that they were able to exploit it. All were exhausted by war, falling apart internally, and so each may have sought Paris as the final nail in the coffin of their rivals. The KR may have wanted to use the provisions of civil control over the five areas in the Paris Agreements as the means to destroy the SOC. Functioning administration over almost the entire country was the great advantage that the disciplined bureaucracy of SOC possessed over the other factions. Observers argue that the KR probably judged that no centralized Leninist-style bureaucracy could sustain itself under a regime of effective even though partial outside control. (Significantly, perhaps, it had been the PRC, the Khmer Rouge's one-time patron, that had written these provisions of the Paris Agreement). The SOC, on the other hand, may have sought the cantonment and demobilization provisions of the Paris Agreement as the vehicle through which to destroy the Khmer Rouge's single most vital asset—its disciplined army of ten thousand or so soldiers. Consequently, the KR was determined not to disarm, but hoped that UNTAC would succeed in controlling and thus gutting the SOC's administrative apparatus. The SOC was prepared to cooperate in cantonment and disarmament in hopes that a disarmed KR would dissolve, but were determined to prevent any effective control of their administrative assets. FUNCINPEC and KPNLF—the two very lightly armed factions at the border—wanted peace—"Paris," perhaps principally in order to have the elections, and this because they had no other asset apart from their popularity with the mass of the Cambodian population.

The preferences thus appeared to be the following. For the KR and SOC: DC, DD, CC, CD, for FUNCINPEC: DC, CC, DD, CD, and for some of the minor parties (KPNLF and the very aptly named Buddhist Liberal Democrats): CC, CD, DC, DD.[30] Given the fact that both the KR and SOC signed the Paris Peace treaty and that FUNCINPEC was widely regarded as its most enthusiastic adherent, evidence of what their actual preferences might have been needs some additional elaboration.

I have explained how both the KR and SOC preferred to manipulate the peace to their own advantage: DC over CC. Let me suggest evidence for how they preferred war to the full peace agreement: DD to CC. First, let us examine SOC. Just after the signing of the Paris Peace, the Khmer Rouge sent representatives to Phnom Penh to sit on the Supreme National Council. On the way from the airport they were set upon by a large and well-organized crowd, who mobbed their vehicle and attempted to lynch them. They took refuge—after being severely beaten—in the Royal Palace. SOC later excused the outbreak as an outburst of spontaneous mass revulsion at the return of the KR to the capital. While the revulsion may well have been justified, more impartial observers noted that in Phnom Penh at this time nothing happened without the acquiescence of the SOC, which continued to rule Cambodia with a heavy hand. Second, confidential memoranda of the SOC disclosed that they had no intention of complying with the control provisions of the Paris Peace and that they were systematically attacking FUNCINPEC, the opposing party, which had no substantial military force with which to threaten SOC's security.[31] Similarly, with regard to the Khmer Rouge, one can note that whatever the legitimacy of their complaints concerning the failures of UNTAC control of SOC as a justification for their own failure to canton, they themselves refused all access (much less cooperation or control) with UNTAC during the peace process. The KR, moreover, openly acknowledged that their ultimate aims, far from being the implausible "liberal pluralist democracy" outlined in the Paris Agreements, were a reiteration of the *Angkha*—the utter ruralization and communalization of Cambodian society that they had attempted in 1975–78.[32] Last, even militarily weak FUNCIN-PEC expressed a temporary preference for exploitation (DC) over compliance (CC) with the peace when it organized with French assistance an effort to forestall the May 1993 elections for a constitutional convention with a preemptive referendum for a Sihanouk presidency.

One cannot eliminate the possibility that Paris (CC) represented a true reconciliation and an acceptance of peace through pluralist democracy by the four factions; it is just that it is very difficult to find evidence in their previous or later actions to support it.

Aggressive Incentives

As noted in the beginning, recent scholarship has offered plausible reasons for identifying ethnic conflicts—in opposition to ideological conflicts such as those in Cambodia—as particularly prone to create preemptive and preventive incentives for "cleansing" territory or monopolizing state sovereignty.[33]

But ideological conflicts can also generate preemptive aggressive incentives. The first factor at work is the economic value of monopoly control of the state in a developing economy, particularly one undergoing a transition from socialism to capitalism, as was Cambodia. The state in these circumstances owns the vast preponderance of productive assets—natural resources, urban property, the authority to license their use, and the practical capacity to alienate (sell) those assets outright. Unless there is an agreement to share control, first come is first serve. In Cambodia today (1996–98) there is a tacit sharing of what has come to be called "casino capitalism." Each of the two parties in the governing coalition (SOC's CPP and FUNCINPEC) profits from the alienation of public property and the license of regulated industries. (Two of the most profitable are actually the two main casinos, one Hun Sen [CPP] and the other FUNCINPEC.)[34] Current power sharing is an outcome of the vote in 1993, which required power sharing in order to form a governing majority, and of SOC's military blackmail after they failed to win the election. The parties had failed to agree on power sharing in the Paris Peace negotiations. There is no guarantee it will continue, and this creates continuing preemptive incentives and a widespread spirit of *enrichissez vous*.

The second factor is the extreme character of some ideologies. The KR concept of pure rural community—untainted by any voluntary division of labor or exchange—was and is incompatible with a open market economy

and pluralist society envisaged in the compromise peace the parties negotiated at Paris. Liberal pluralist democracy is distinctly alien corn in traditional Cambodia, but it was the only alternative to no agreement at all when
the parties proved incapable of forming a power-sharing arrangement. But
the KR could not openly operate in an environment in which their peasants
would be free to seek employment or to sell their crop where they wished.
Like the notorious ethnic entrepreneurs of the former Yugoslavia and
Rwanda, the KR, too, had to preemptively cleanse and autarkically isolate
its territory.

III

Accounting for a Semipeace

A semipeace was achieved, and settling civil conflicts requires, it is argued, coercive enforcement. But, corresponding to the third generalization,
did the UN overcome the barriers to settling civil wars by guaranteeing to
enforce the peace? In this section I argue that it did not and then conclude
by focusing on how the semipeace actually was made. According to the
fourth generalization, traditional peacekeeping does not work in these circumstances and the UN is incapable of effective peace enforcement. The
UN, I thus conclude, achieved the unexpected by employing a new form
of enhanced peacekeeping, one that relied both on traditional consent to
mobilize local forces and, in the end, on a discrete, impartial (but nonneutral) use of force.

Third-Party Enforcement

Average civil wars may require third-party enforcement, but that is not
what UNTAC was prepared to do. UNTAC seemed to have the legal authority under the Paris Agreement to enforce the mandate over the opposition of one or more of the factions. But it did not enjoy the political support
of the Permanent Five or the contributing countries to employ forcefully
the military capacity it did have. In January 1993 Gerard Porcell, chief of
the Civil Administration Component, saw this as a crucial failure of UNTAC
will. He explained: "We don't have the will to apply the peace accords. This
absence of firmness with the Khmer Rouge was a sort of signal for the other
parties who saw there the proof of UNTAC's weakness towards the group
that from the start eschewed all cooperation."[35]

UNTAC, it seems, did lack the will to enforce the mandate. A number of the countries contributing troops to the mission were unwilling to engage in enforcement and let their views be known to Mr. Akashi and General Sanderson.[36] Reasons for this constraint are, of course, speculative. Most countries, almost certainly, were (naturally) reluctant to suffer the casualties that a more intrusive role would have generated. They may also have preferred a coalition government in the future of Cambodia to one constructed after a more radical democratic transformation.

Some countries shared UNTAC's official assessment that enforcement would have backfired. UNTAC did not have the military capacity to enforce the mandate and still maintain the security of the international presence, both governmental and nongovernmental. UNTAC could have pushed through Khmer Rouge lines, beginning with the incident in the spring of 1992 at Pailin and the "bamboo pole" that barred the way of Special Representative Akashi and General Sanderson. (Though we should recall the mighty Vietnamese army was incapable of defeating the KR after more than ten years of warfare.) But UNTAC could not protect the thousands of civilians and representatives of nongovernmental organizations from KR reprisal.[37] These civilians, moreover, were essential to the success of UNTAC's political mission. (When the French deputy force commander, General Loridon, disputed UNTAC's policy, he was sent home.)

Enhanced Peacekeeping and Discrete Force

Thus, how can we account for UNTAC's semipeace when peacekeeping is widely recognized, including by Secretary General Boutros Ghali, to be ineffective in enforcement—where there is "no peace to keep"?[38]

Some of UNTAC's success can in large part be credited to unique role played by Prince, later King, Sihanouk in negotiating among the parties and in providing the traditional as well as charismatic focal point for national loyalties.[39] Equally important, the willingness of the parties to sign a comprehensive peace agreement established a crucial facilitating role for the United Nations in implementing an agreed peace. The very multidimensional character of the resulting UN mandate proved to be a key when the agreement (such as it was) between the parties dissolved. With Security Council–approved adjustments in the mandate, reconciliation and peace could have been achieved by disarmament, control, education, and then renegotiation. Reconciliation through national election was available if and when the other dimensions failed. Thus multidimensionality allowed for single failures yet overall success.[40]

Most important, UNTAC's guarantee of a secret ballot rescued the peace in Cambodia. Without UNTAC's direct role in the election, the UN probably would have had to declare defeat and retreat from Cambodia. The KR prevented the conduct of the election in the villages it controlled. The SOC was prepared to tolerate an election it could manipulate, expecting to win from it international legitimacy. But, recalling the SOC's record of violent intimidation, what sort of election would have been conducted if the UN were merely in the capacity of a monitoring force? The UN would have had to withdraw from Cambodia altogether, citing SOC's intimidation during the campaign, or to tolerate the additional manipulation likely had the SOC actually conducted the poll.[41]

The deeper sources of the international role in Cambodia's semisuccess are as complicated as the sources of failure, and both sources operated at the same time. Contrary to our fourth generalization, the Cambodia operation was nonenforcing (consent-based), yet relied on a discrete use of force. It exemplifies a UN record of success in similar multidimensional peace-keeping operations as diverse as those in Namibia (UNTAG) and El Salvador (ONUSAL).[42] The UN's role in helping settle those conflicts has been four-fold. It served as the *facilitator* of a peace treaty among the parties, as the *manager* of fragile agreements supervising transitional civilian authorities, as the *organizer* of a new basis for peace, implementing aspects of human rights, national democratic elections, and economic rehabilitation, and as the *director* of discrete acts of crucial enforcement.

Facilitating Agreement

The conflicts characteristic of ethnic and civil wars result from funda-mental differences of political ideology or national identity. The combatants have compounded initial competition with reciprocal acts of violence whose memory erodes a rational calculation of advantages and generates bitterness and desire for revenge. Each party, moreover, often judges that a victory for its side can be achieved if only it displays the requisite fortitude. Leaders rarely control their followers and, indeed, fear that peace will undermine their influence. The very identity of the factions is fluid, as changes in the balance of forces raises, lowers, and sometimes eliminates parties with an effective role in the dispute. Conflicts in these circumstances are rarely "ripe for resolution."[43]

Achieving the peace treaty will therefore often require a difficult and lengthy process characterized by heavy persuasion by outside actors. In Cambodia the process began in 1982 with contacts between the Secretary General's special representative, Raffeeudin Ahmed, and the Phnom Penh authorities. Ahmed succeeded in establishing an independent diplomatic identity as a Secretariat representative separate from the UN General Assembly's condemnation of the Phnom Penh and recognition of the rival Sihanoukist and Khmer Rouge forces on the Thai border. Although he explored the parameters of peace, Ahmed lacked the influence that achieving a negotiated agreement would require. Indonesia and Australia then attempted a regionwide approach in a series of informal meetings in Jakarta. They, too, though enhancing mutual understanding of each other's concerns, failed to produce an agreement. Only when the negotiations were pushed up to the global level, with the end of the cold war, were the needed carrots and sticks made available. In the Paris negotiations of 1989 and, finally, effectively, in 1991, the USSR and China let their respective clients in Phnom Penh and the Khmer Rouge know that ongoing levels of financial and military support would not be forthcoming if they resisted the terms of a peace treaty that their patrons found acceptable. The United States and France and then Japan conveyed similar messages, together with promises of substantial financial aid for economic development, to the Sihanouk faction.[44]

Peace treaties thus may themselves depend on prior sanctions, threats of sanctions, or loss of aid imposed by the international community. The construction of an agreed peace, however, is more than worth the effort. The process of negotiation among the contending factions can reveal the acceptable parameters of peace that are particular to the conflict. Peace negotiations can mobilize the support of local factions and of the international community in support of implementing the peace. And an agreed peace treaty can establish new entities committed to furthering peacekeeping and peace building.

The UN has developed a set of crucially important innovations that help manage the making of peace on a consensual basis. First among them is the diplomatic device that has come to be called the Friends of the Secretary General. This brings together multinational leverage for UN diplomacy to help make and manage peace. Composed of ad hoc, informal, multilateral diplomatic mechanisms that join together states in support of initiatives of the secretary general, it legitimates with the stamp of UN approval and supervision the pressures interested states can bring to bear to further the purposes of peace and the UN.

For Cambodia the "Core Group, or "Extended P5," played a "Friends" role in the negotiation and the management of the peace process. Composed of the Security Council Permanent Five—the US, France, USSR, China, and the UK—and extended to include Australia, Indonesia, Japan, and other concerned states, it took the lead in the construction of the Paris Agreements. It provided key support to UNTAC, both political and financial, and it helped organize ICORC aid (almost $1 billion), while providing special funds for various projects. But the Extended P5 lacked a fixed composition. It, of course, included the P5 but then included or excluded others on an ad hoc basis, depending on the issue and topic covered and the "message" the group wished to send. For example, Thailand was excluded from certain meetings in order to send a signal of concern about its lack of support for the restrictions imposed on the Khmer Rouge. In Cambodia, moreover, there was not a sovereign government to monitor or support. Much of the Extended P5's diplomacy was therefore directed at UNTAC itself, protecting, for example, the interests of national battalions. It also served as a back channel for Special Representative Akashi to communicate directly to the Security Council.[45]

Playing a crucial role in the secretary general's peacemaking and preventive diplomacy functions, these groupings serve four key functions. First, the limited influence of the secretary general can be leveraged, multiplied, and complemented by the friends. The UN's scarce attention and even scarcer resources can be supplemented by the diplomacy and the clout of powerful interested actors. The Security Council, now overwhelmed by the range of global crises, benefits from the focused attention of powerful member states with a special interest in the dispute.[46] The second value is legitimization. The very act of constituting themselves as a group, with the formal support of the secretary general, lends legitimacy to the diplomatic activities of interested states that they might not otherwise have.[47] It allows for constructive diplomacy when accusations of special and particular national interest could taint bilateral efforts. The third value is coordination. The Friends mechanism provides transparency among the interested external parties, assuring them that they are all working for the same purposes and, when they are doing so, allowing them to pursue a division of labor that enhances their joint effort. It ensures that diplomats are not working at cross-purposes because they regularly meet and inform each other of their activities and encourage each other to undertake special tasks. And fourth, the Friends mechanism provides a politically balanced approach to the resolution through negotiation of civil wars. It often turns out that one particular Friend can associate with one faction just as another associates with a second. In the Cambodian peace process China backstopped the Khmer Rouge, just as France did Prince Sihanouk and Russia (with Vietnam) did the State of Cambodia. The Friends open more flexible channels of communication than a single UN mediator can provide. They also advise and guide the UN intermediaries, although the process tends to work best when they support rather than move out in front of the UN.

Enhancing Fragile Agreements

Even consent-based peace agreements fall apart. In the circumstances faced by "failed states," or partisan violence, agreements tend to be fluid. In the new civil conflicts parties cannot force policy on their followers and often lack the capacity or will to maintain a difficult process of reconciliation leading to a reestablishment of national sovereignty.[48]

Some of the international community even help undermine the peace. UNTAC enjoyed extensive support from a number of countries, including Japan, Indonesia, France, Australia, Thailand, and Malaysia, as well as the patient acquiescence of Vietnam and China in a considerable loss of regional clout. They provided diplomatic leadership, crucial financial support, and many of the essential battalions. Without their support, and the participation of dozens of other UN members, the Paris Agreements could never have been implemented. At the same time, most observers agree that the unofficial support the Khmer Rouge received from various Thai generals on the western border undermined the peace accords. There, in violation of UN embargoes, logs and gems and ammunition flowed freely, filling the Khmer Rouge's coffers and bunkers, permitting them to disdain the carrots of economic aid and ward off the sticks of embargo that the UN had counted upon to encourage their cooperation with the peace plan.[49] On the eastern border a similar but much less extensive trade in logs allegedly occurred, and widespread (though unsubstantiated) rumors floated through Phnom Penh of continuing ties between the SOC's secret police and the Vietnamese intelligence service.

Peace treaties and their peacekeeping mandates thus tend to be affected by two sets of contradictory tensions. First, in order to get an agreement, diplomats assume all parties are in good faith; they cannot question the intentions of their diplomatic partners. But to implement a peacekeeping and peace-building operation, planners must assume the opposite—that the parties will not or cannot fulfill the agreement made. Moreover, diplomats who design the peace treaty tend to think in legal (authority, precedent), not strategic (power, incentives), categories. Treaties thus describe obligations; they tend to be unclear about incentives and capacities.

All these militate against clear and implementable mandates. Diplomats seek to incorporate in the treaty the most complete peace to which the parties will agree. UN officials seek to clarify the UN's obligations. Knowing that much of what was agreed to in the peace treaty will not be implementable in the field, the officials who write the secretary general's report (which outlines the implementation of the agreement) contract or expand the mandate of the peace operation.[50] Confused mandates are an inevitable result of this tension.

These tensions also explain how the ideal framework (both legal and political) of a treaty can dissolve in days or months, as the Cambodian peace agreements did, and how the provisions of peace accords become so general, ambiguous, or unworkable that many of the details have to be worked out in the implementation process. To be minimally effective under those circumstances, the UN must innovate. The UN thus needs a flexible political strategy to win and keep popular support and create (not just enjoy) the support of local forces of order. In a failed state, as was the case in a society subject to colonial rule, what is most often missing is modern organization.

Recent peacekeeping experience has suggested a second peacekeeping innovation: an ad hoc, semi-sovereign mechanism designed to address those new challenges by dynamically managing a peace process and mobilizing local cooperation. It has often been remarked that Chapter 6 presents the United Nations with too little authority and Chapter 7 offers too much, and that Chapter 6 is associated with too little use of force and Chapter 7 with too much.

The value of these ad hoc, semi-sovereign artificial bodies is that they provide a potentially powerful political means of encouraging and influencing the shape of consent. Indeed, these semi-sovereign artificial bodies can help contain the erosion of consent and even manufacture it where it is missing. Created by a peace treaty, they permit the temporary consensus of the parties to be formally incorporated in an institution with regular consultation and even, as in the Cambodian Supreme National Council, a semiautonomous sovereign will. These mechanisms have proved crucial in a number of recent UN missions. They can represent the once warring parties and act in the name of a preponderance of the "nation" without the continuous or complete consent of all the factions. They can both build political support and adjust—in a legitimate way, with the consent of the parties—the mandate in order to respond to unanticipated changes in local circumstances.

In the *Agreements on a Comprehensive Political Settlement of the Cambodian Conflict*[51] the parties agreed not only to the terms of a cease-fire and the disarming of the factions but also to the maintenance of law and order, the repatriation of refugees, the promotion of human rights and principles for a new constitution, the supervision and control of certain aspects of the administrative machinery by a UN body, and, most significantly, the organization, conduct, and monitoring of elections by the UN. The parties to the agreements created two institutions to implement the peace: the Supreme National Council and the United Nations Transitional Authority in Cambodia (UNTAC).[52] The agreements defined a transitional period running from the entry into force of the agreements, October 23 1991, to the time when an elected constituent assembly established a new sovereign government of Cambodia (that was anticipated to occur around the end of August 1993).[53] During that period the Supreme National Council, a committee composed of the four factions, was to "enshrine" the legal sovereignty of Cambodia and UNTAC, an authority established by the Security Council in February 1992, was to implement the agreed upon peace.

During the early stages of the peace negotiation process the Cambodian factions flatly rejected the proposal that national reconciliation be achieved through an interim quadripartite government. As an alternative to Cambodian power sharing, the establishment of UN administration required the creation of a legitimate sovereign entity to delegate the required authority to the UN. The Cambodian parties and the international community therefore devised the concept of the Supreme National Council, composed of representatives of the four main factions, to serve as the legitimate source of authority for Cambodia—the "unique legitimate body and source of authority in which throughout the transitional period the sovereignty, independence and unity of Cambodia are enshrined."

The actual status of the SNC as the legitimate sovereign authority of Cambodia during the transition period was problematic, both in design and practice. On the one hand, the SNC, in its capacity as a sovereign entity, has signed two international human rights conventions that will bind successor governments.[54] The agreements, moreover, authorized the SNC to act as an "advisory" body to UNTAC. UNTAC thus had to abide by a unanimous decision of the SNC, so long as it was in keeping with the objectives of the agreements. Whenever the SNC reached an impasse Prince Sihanouk had the authority to give advice to UNTAC. On the other hand, the special representative of the secretary general was the final arbiter of whether a decision of the council adhered to the intent and meaning of the Paris Agreements. The agreements also gave UNTAC and the special representative a wide discretion, where necessary, to act independently and to make major binding decisions, whenever the SNC reached a deadlock. In practice, much influence was exercised over SNC decision making by the permanent members of the UN Security Council and other interested states acting through their Phnom Penh support group of local diplomatic representatives accredited to the SNC (the Extended P5 Cambodian version of the Friends mechanism). The SNC was a part—indeed the symbolically vital Cambodian part—of the circle of authority in Cambodia; it lacked the resources or coherence it would have needed to have a decided effect.

The council offered a chance for these parties to consult together on a regular basis and endorse the peace process. It also lent special authority to Prince Sihanouk and empowered the United Nations, represented by Special Representative Yasushi Akashi. Artificially created, the SNC thus established a semisovereign legal personality designed to be responsive to the general interests of Cambodia (even when a complete consensus was lacking among all the factions) and to the authority of the United Nations special representative. Acting in the name of Cambodia—as a step in the implementation of the Paris Agreements—the SNC acceded to all the major human rights conventions (including the first and second Covenants on Human Rights) and it authorized the trade embargo against illegal exports of logs and gems. It was the forum that endorsed the protracted and sensitive negotiations over the franchise. It legitimated the enforcement of certain elements of the peace, absent the unanimous consent of the parties and without the necessity of a contentious debate at the Security Council. It could have exercised greater authority, perhaps even designing an acceptable scheme for rehabilitation, if Prince Sihanouk or Mr. Akashi had been both willing and able to lead it in that direction. The important point is that civil society participate in the decision-making process, at a minimum through formally recognized consultative channels.[55] Semi-sovereign artificial bodies offer the possibility of midcourse adjustments and "nationally" legitimated enforcement. They artificially but usefully enhance the process of consent in the direction of the promotion of peace while avoiding the dangers associated with attempts to implement a forced peace.

Organizing a Transformation

Multidimensional, second-generation peacekeeping pierces the shell of national autonomy by bringing international involvement to areas long thought to be the exclusive domain of domestic jurisdiction. If a peace-keeping operation is to leave behind a legitimate and independently viable political sovereign, it must help transform the political landscape by building a new basis for domestic peace.

The parties to these multidimensional peace agreements, in effect, consent to limitation of their sovereignty for the life of the UN-sponsored peace process. They do so because they need the help of the international community to achieve peace. But acceptance of UN involvement in implementing these agreements is less straightforward than, for example, consenting to observance of a cease-fire. Even when genuine consent is achieved, it is impossible to provide for every contingency in complex peace accords. Problems of interpretation arise, unforeseen gaps in the accords materialize, and circumstances change. The original consent can become open-ended and in part a gesture of faith that later problems can be worked out on a consensual basis.

Traditional strategies of conflict resolution, when successful, were designed to resolve a dispute between conflicting parties. Successful resolution could be measured by 1. the stated reconciliation of the parties, 2. the duration of the reconciliation, and 3. changes in the way parties behaved toward each other.[56] But successful contemporary peacebuilding changes not merely behavior but, more important, it transforms identities and institutional context. More than reforming play in an old game, it changes the game. This is the grand strategy General Sanderson invoked when he spoke of forging an alliance with the Cambodian people, bypassing the factions. Reginald Austin, electoral chief of UNTAC, probed the same issue when he asked what are the "true objectives [of UNTAC]: Is it a political operation seeking a solution to the immediate problem of an armed conflict by all means possible? Or does it have a wider objective: to implant democracy, change values and establish a new pattern of governance based on multi-partism and free and fair elections?"[57]

The UN's role, mandated by these complex agreements rather than Chapter 7, includes monitoring, substituting for, renovating, and in some cases helping to build the basic structures of the state. The UN is called in to demobilize and sometimes to restructure and reform once warring armies, to monitor or to organize national elections, to promote human rights, to supervise public security and help create a new civilian police force, to control civil administration in order to establish a transitional politically neutral environment, to begin the economic rehabilitation of devastated countries, and, as in the case of Cambodia, to address directly the values of the citizens, with a view to promoting democratic education.

Going beyond the monitoring of a cease-fire or the interposition of a force, UNTAC undertook a multidimensional set of responsibilities in human rights, civilian administration, election organization, refugee repatriation, and economic rehabilitation. The international community charged the UN—for the first time in its history—with the political and economic restructuring of a member of the UN, as part of the building of peace in which the parties would then (it was planned) institutionalize their reconciliation. The roots of the Cambodian conflict lay in the collapse of both the domestic and the international legitimacy of the Cambodian state. The multidimensional strategy of peace embodied in the Paris Agreements lay in the UN's stepping in to help rebuild the legitimacy of the state, after the parties had failed to achieve a reconciliation of their own.

The Paris Agreements granted extraordinary power to the UN during the transition period.[58] UNTAC was required to supervise a military stand-down, including verification of the withdrawal of Vietnamese troops and the cessation of external arms supply. It also undertook to supervise demining and to canton and disarm the forces of the four parties, which then would be followed by the demobilization of 70 percent of the factions' troops. But the true complexities of the security mission arose later, when the military component had to step in to provide security for and logistically support a faltering civilian effort to organize the national elections.[59]

UNTAC thus helped create new actors on the Cambodian political scene: the electors, a fledgling civil society, a free press, a continuing international and transnational presence. The Cambodian voters gave Prince Ranariddh institutional power and the Khmer Rouge was transformed from an internationally recognized claimant on Cambodian sovereignty to a domestic guerrilla insurgency. *The peace-building process, particularly the election, became the politically tolerable substitute for the inability of the factions to reconcile their conflicts and the unwillingness of the troop-contributing countries to exercise credible enforcement.*

Authentic and firm consent to a peace treaty, in the aftermath of severe civil strife such as that endured by Cambodia, is rare. The international negotiators of a peace treaty and the UN designers of a mandate should, therefore, first, attempt to design in as many bargaining advantages for the UN authority as the parties will tolerate. Even seemingly extraneous bargaining chips will become useful as the spirit of cooperation erodes under the pressure of misunderstandings and separating interests. The UN counted upon the financial needs of the Cambodian factions to ensure their cooperation and designed an extensive rehabilitation component to guarantee steady rewards for cooperative behavior.[60] But the Khmer Rouge's access to illicit trade eliminated this bargaining chip. And the suspicion of SOC's rivals prevented a full implementation of rehabilitation in the 80 percent of the country controlled by the SOC.

Second, the architects of the UN operation should also design into the mandate as much independent implementation as the parties will agree to in the peace treaty. In Cambodia the electoral component and refugee repatriation seem to have succeeded simply because they did not depend on the steady and continuous positive support of the four factions. Each had an independent sphere of authority and organizational capacity that allowed it to proceed against everything short of the active military opposition the factions. Civil administrative control and the cantonment of the factions failed because they relied on the continuous direct and positive cooperation of each of the factions. Each of the factions, at one time or another, had reason to expect that the balance of advantages was tilting against itself, and so refused to cooperate. A significant source of the success of the election was Radio UNTAC's ability to speak directly to the potential Cambodian voters, bypassing the propaganda of the four factions and invoking a new Cambodian actor, the voting citizen. But voters are only powerful for the five minutes it takes them to vote, if there is not an institutional mechanism to transfer democratic authority to bureaucratic practice. Now, lacking such a mechanism in Cambodia, the voters are vulnerable to the armies, police, and corruption that dominate after the votes were tallied.

In these circumstances the UN should try to create new institutions to make sure votes in UN-sponsored elections "count" more. The UN needs to leave behind a larger institutional legacy, drawing, for example, upon the existing personnel of domestic factions, adding to them a portion of authentic independents, and training a new army, a new civil service, a new police force, and a new judiciary. These are the institutions that can be decisive in ensuring that the voice of the people, as represented by their elected representatives, shape the future.

In the end these difficulties highlight the crucial importance of risk-spreading multidimensionality itself. The UN should design in as many routes to peace—institutional reform, elections, international monitoring, economic rehabilitation—as the parties will tolerate.

Directing the Discrete, Impartial, but Non-Neutral Use of Force

The UN must avoid the trade-offs between too much force and too little. The dangers of Chapter 7 enforcement operations, whether in Somalia or

Bosnia, leave many observers to think that it is extremely unlikely that troop-contributing countries will actually sign up for such operations. The risks are far more costly than the member states are willing to bear for humanitarian purposes. But when we look at Chapter 6 operations, we see that consent by parties easily dissolves under the difficult processes of peace.

UN operations in the midst of civil strife have often been rescued by the timely use of force by the United Nations, as were the operations in the Congo, when Katanga's secession was forcibly halted, and as was the operation in Namibia, when SWAPO's violation of the peace agreement was countered with the aid of South African forces.[61] But both nearly derailed the peace process by eroding local, regional, or global support. Given those options, locally legitimated, impartial enforcement can become both necessary and effective. It is important to stress that the UN use of force must have an impartial dimension.[62] In Cambodia, for example, UNTAC—operating in full accord with the Paris Agreements—appealed to *all* the factions to protect the election. The appeal was impartial and based upon the peace treaty to which all the parties had consented. (This is now called strategic, as opposed to tactical, consent in UN circles.) The result was distinctly not neutral among the parties as the armies (most effectively, SOC's army) that were cooperating with the peace plan pushed the Khmer Rouge back from the population centers. This subcontracted use of force permitted a safer vote with a larger—hence more legitimate—turnout in the last week of May 1993.[63]

Thus, contrary to the third generalization, what peace was achieved was achieved without the provision of credible overall enforcement by external parties, either by the UN or by individual states. Contrary to the strong version of the fourth generalization, the distinction between Chapter 6 and Chapter 7 operations emerged in Cambodia not as a simple "bright line" demarcating the safe and acceptable from the dangerous and illegitimate. Consent and force were neither completely avoided nor completely embraced. Consent needs, we are learning, to be enhanced if the UN is to help make a peace in the contentious environment of civil strife. And force has proved vital in certain stages of Chapter 6 peacekeeping, and so it was in Cambodia.

There is no magic formula to eliminate the formidable challenges of making, keeping, and building peace in the midst of protracted civil wars. Some crises will not find their solution. But today, as the United Nations is under attack in the United States and elsewhere, we should not neglect its authentic peace-managing potential. Employing strategies of enhanced consent, the United Nations played a constructive role in Cambodia. With luck and statesmanship the UN helped develop a semipeace that is much less thorough than the hopes outlined in the Paris Peace Agreements but much better (so far) than any Cambodia has known in its independent history. This was a peace achieved over (and around and under) a civil conflict whose human costs has rivaled the worst ethnic cleansings. It was accomplished through enhancing the process of pressured consent without a credible threat of force to solve factional security dilemmas, which persist in Cambodia today as they do in many developing countries. The Cambodian peace, based on an agreed upon treaty and operating under the consent rules of Chapter 6 and nonuse of force, was rescued, in the end, by a timely—non-neutral but clearly impartial—use of force. Much of what occurred was simply exceptional, a mixture of luck, statesmanship, and particular circumstances. But the UN and the international community is in much need of supplementing good luck if its present challenges in Bosnia and elsewhere are to be met. We will need to understand the Cambodian circumstances that statesmanship exploited.

NOTES

Director of the Center of International Studies and Professor of Politics and International Affairs, Princeton University. This paper draws on my *The UN in Cambodia: UNTAC's Civil Mandate* (Boulder: Rienner, 1995). I am grateful to Richard Betts, William Durch, Daniel Markey, Jack Snyder, Barbara Walter and a seminar at George Washington University for valuable suggestions for revision. These remarks also benefited from interviews with numerous diplomats, UNTAC and UN officials.

1. During these months Prince Ranariddh described himself as a puppet. See Seth Mydans, "Cambodia's Real Boss Rules from No. 2 Post," *New York Times*, March 25, 1996. I discuss Cambodia's experience with truncated peace building in "Peacebuilding in Cambodia," *IPA Policy Briefing Series* (New York: International Peace Academy, December 1996).

2. The 1997–98 crisis is examined by David Chandler, David Ashley, myself, and others in Frederick Brown and David Timberman, eds., *Cambodia and the International Community: The Quest for Peace, Development, and Democracy* (New York and Singapore: Asia Society and Institute of Southeast Asian Studies, 1998).

3. Barry Posen, "The Security Dilemma and Ethnic Conflict," in Michael Brown, ed., *Ethnic Conflict and International Security* (Princeton: Princeton University Press, 1993), pp. 103–124.

4. Chaim Kaufmann, "Possible and Impossible Solutions to Ethnic Civil Wars," *International Security*, vol. 20, no. 4 (Spring 1996), pp. 136–175.
5. Barbara F. Walter, "Critical Barriers to Civil War Settlements," *International Organization*, vol. 51, no. 3 (Summer 1997), pp. 335–364.
6. Adam Roberts, "The United Nations and International Security," *Survival*, vol. 35, no. 2 (Summer 1993), pp. 3–30; Shashi Tharoor, "Peace-Keeping: Principles, Problems, Prospects," *Strategic Research Department*, Research Report 92–93 (Newport: Naval War College, 1993).
7. These are the conclusions of Boutros Boutros-Ghali, "Supplement to the Agenda for Peace," in *An Agenda for Peace* (New York: UN, DPI, 1995). And for discussion of the issue see John Ruggie, "Wandering in the Void," *Foreign Affairs*, vol. 72, no. 5 (November/December 1993), pp. 26–31; and Richard Betts, "The Delusion of Impartial Intervention," *Foreign Affairs*, vol. 73, no. 6 (November/December 1994), pp. 20–33.
8. October 23, 1991—UN document A/46/608-S/23177; 31 I.L.M. 183 (1992).
9. *An Agenda for Peace*, at para. 55–60.
10. See Steven Ratner, "The Cambodia Settlement Agreements," *American Journal of International Law*, vol. 87 (1993).
11. For the UN to administer Cambodia temporarily it was apparent that a special arrangement was required to vest Cambodian national sovereignty during the transitional period. A legitimate sovereign entity had to delegate the required authority to the UN, since the UN is precluded by Article 78 from adopting a "trusteeship" role over a member state. The Cambodian parties and the international community therefore devised the concept of the Supreme National Council (SNC). For further discussion see below.
12. At the suggestion of China the areas specified for the strictest level of scrutiny and control over *each* of the four factions were defense, public security, finance, information, and foreign affairs.
13. For insightful accounts of Cambodia's recent tragic history see Elizabeth Becker, *When the War Was Over* (New York: Simon and Schuster, 1986); David Chandler, *The Tragedy of Cambodian History* (New Haven: Yale, 1991); Ben Kiernan, *The Pol Pot Regime* (New Haven: Yale University Press, 1996); and Nayan Chanda, *Brother Enemy* (New York: Harcourt Brace Jovanovich, 1986). For accounts of UNTAC see Steven Heder and Judy Ledgerwood, eds., *Propaganda, Politics, and Violence in Cambodia* (Armonk: Sharpe, 1996); Doyle, *The UN in Cambodia*, pp. 13–88; Stephen Marks, "Preventing Humanitarian Crisis Through Peacebuilding," *Medicine and Global Survival* (December 1994), pp. 208–219; United Nations, *The United Nations and Cambodia, 1991–1995* (New York: UN/DPI, 1995), the UN blue book on Cambodia—a comprehensive chronology and collection of documents; Human Rights Watch/Asia, *Cambodia at War in Cambodia* (New York: Human Rights Watch, 1995)—an account of current human rights abuses by all sides; Janet Heininger, *Peacekeeping in Tran-*

sition (New York: Twentieth-Century Fund, 1995); Steven Ratner, *The New UN Peacekeeping* (New York: St. Martin's, 1995); Trevor Findlay, *Cambodia: The Legacy and Lessons of UNTAC* (New York: Oxford, 1995); William Shawcross, *Cambodia's New Deal* (Washington, D.C.: USIP, 1994)—the best coverage of UNTAC's socioeconomic legacy; Dennis McNamara, "UN Human Rights Activities in Cambodia: An Evaluation," in Alice Henkin, ed., *Honoring Human Rights and Keeping the Peace* (Washington: Aspen Institute, 1995); Frederick Brown, ed., *Rebuilding Cambodia* (Washington: Johns Hopkins University Press, 1993).

14. UNHCR, *The State of the World's Refugees, 1993: The Challenge of Protection* (Harmondsworth: Penguin, 1993), especially pp. 104–105.

15. For UNTAC's role in the election, see Michael Maley, "Reflections on the Electoral Process in Cambodia," Hugh Smith, ed., *Peacekeeping: Challenges for the Future* (Canberra: Australian Defence Studies Centre, 1993). Mr. Salman Ahmed, assistant provincial electoral officer in Kompong Thom, estimated that more than half the adults he encountered on his many visits to towns and villages followed Radio UNTAC on a regular basis. Interview, August 23, 1993.

16. For a valuable discussion of these problems, see Jarat Chopra, John Mackinlay, and Larry Minear, *Report on the Cambodian Peace Process* (Oslo: NUPI, 1992).

17. Akashi's definition of "foreign forces" brilliantly parsed the ambiguities built into the Paris Accords, going beyond purely military forces to include those acting as part of a foreign-directed conspiracy. Unfortunately, it would take a major investigation in each case to determine that the alleged individual was in fact a member of such a conspiracy. No such investigation appears to have been conducted in the case of the three named forces. Although each of them had at one time been members of Vietnamese military units, they had apparently resigned, settled in Cambodia, and married Khmer women with whom they had children.

18. The head of UNTAC's Human Rights Component, Dennis McNamara, concluded: "The exercise of 'control' in order to secure and neutral political environment and end human rights abuses would have been a daunting task even if the peace process had gone exactly as planned, given the time-frame involved and the resources available to UNTAC. With the refusal of the Party of Democratic Kampuchea to demobilize its troops and continue to participate in the process (which led to all factions not demobilizing) and related resistance to close UNTAC supervision of the State of Cambodia's security apparatus, UNTAC through its control function was hard pressed to prevent mounting political crimes." Dennis McNamara and Thant Myint-U, "Human Rights in Cambodia: What It Means?" *Phnom Penh Post*, May 21-June 3, 1993, p. 13.

19. Robert Jervis, "Cooperation Under the Security Dilemma," *World Politics*, vol. 30 (January 1978), and Posen, "The Security Dilemma and Ethnic Conflict."

20. John Ruggie, "The United Nations Stuck in a Fog Between Peacekeeping and Peace Enforcement," *McNair Paper 25* (Washington: National Defense University, 1993), suggests these points concerning traditional peacekeeping.

21. The locus classicus for this argument is now Robert Axelrod, *The Evolution of Cooperation* (New York: Basic, 1984).

22. Arend Lijphart, "Consociational Democracy," *World Politics*, vol. 21, no. 2 (Jan. 1969); and recently developed in Timothy Sisk, *Power Sharing and International Mediation in Ethnic Conflicts* (Washington, D.C.: Carnegie Commission and USIP, 1996).

23. Indeed, to complicate the picture with another level, one of the values of a peacekeeping force is that it provides an excuse that a peacefully inclined head of state can use to explain to his or her more nationalist supporters why they are not pursuing a more militant option. Participants in the Middle East negotiations suggest that UNDOF is one of Assad's useful excuses for not taking back the Golan.

24. Lt. Gen. John Sanderson, force commander of UNTAC, has stressed the importance of timely impact, stating in March of 1993: "Delays in the implementation of conditions acceptable at one point in time can allow the situation to change. While conditions for all parties to a negotiation may be considered suitable at the time of their commitment, the longer the delay between signature and implementation, the more the margin for changes on the ground, which may in turn cause them to change their position." Late deployment loses the momentum derived from popular support, from the commitment of the parties, and from the psychological weight associated with a large operation moving rapidly toward an agreed goal.

25. If we examine indirect, long-run, hypothetical consequences we could infer that all aggressive preferences are at root defensive. Henry Kissinger is said once to have remarked that paranoids also have enemies; we can safely assume that aggressors do as well. (Indeed, they manufacture them.)

26. It is worth noting, for example, that Hanoi acknowledged sustaining sixty thousand casualties in Cambodia. For a valuable analysis of some of these developments see Mohammed Noordin Sopiee, "The Cambodian Conflict," *ISIS Research Note* (Kuala Lumpur, Malaysia: ISIS, 1989), pp. 1–27.

27. The view was that if Hun Sen survived the withdrawal of Vietnamese forces and held on to 80 or more percent of Cambodian territory, he would strengthen his claim that there was nothing to negotiate; Cambodia's conflicts would be a matter for domestic Cambodian jurisdiction.

28. The parties went as far as identifying five crucial ministries that should be subject to quadripartite control. But, in the end, Hun Sen refused to accept Sihanouk as the executive of the transition and refused to have the Khmer Rouge on the executive committee. Sihanouk refused to allow a condemnation of "genocide,"

sticking by his KR allies. See Tommy T. B. Koh, "The Paris Conference on Cambodia: A Multilateral Negotiation that 'Failed," *Negotiation Journal*, vol. 6, no. 1 (January 1990), pp. 81–87.

29. Peter Rodman, "Supping with Devils," *National Interest*, vol. 25 (Fall 1991), pp. 44–50. The U.S., nonetheless, suffered a number of instances of what came to be called "Snooky Shock," as the ever mercurial Sihanouk danced between the Khmer Rouge and the Hun Sen forces. The British and the French played a supportive role at this stage. The French seemed eager to establish a close relationship with a Phnom Penh regime as a way perhaps to further a spread of the francophone commonwealth. Britain seemed most concerned to limit the UN's ever increasing financial overextension.

30. I should disclose at this point that I could not resist contributing a very small amount of money to this party and attending one of its rallies in Siem Reap in March 1993.

31. UNTAC, *Report of the CIVADMIN Component* (UNTAC, 1993); for discussion, see Michael W. Doyle, *UN Peacekeeping in Cambodia: UNTAC's Civil Mandate* (Boulder: Rienner, 1995), pp. 40–45.

32. This was explained to me at some length by a senior KR representative in February 1993. The KR counted on pervasive CPP and FUNCINPEC corruption to alienate students, intellectuals, and the peasantry and bankruptcy to dissolve the state. Together those forces would hand over Cambodia to the KR, protected by its disciplined army in its border communes.

33. Cambodia's conflicts did harbor an ethnic dimension. The KR implausibly claimed that the SOC military forces harbored large numbers of Vietnamese troops (who left in 1989). It proceeded to target and massacre hapless Vietnamese immigrants wherever it could, successfully "cleansing" communities of boat people engaged in fishing on the Tonle Sap.

34. See the report by William Shawcross, "Tragedy in Cambodia," *New York Review of Books*, November 14, 1996, pp. 41–46.

35. Quoted in Ben Kiernan, "The Failures of the Paris Agreements on Cambodia, 1991–93," p. 14, in Dick Clark, dir., *The Challenge of Indochina: An Examination of the U.S. Role*, conference report of the Congressional Staff Conference, April 30-May 2, 1993 (Aspen Institute), vol. 8, no. 4, pp. 7–19.

36. The Australian Parliament passed a resolution forbidding the use of Australian troops in peace enforcement. Japan also was especially adamant that its engineers and police not be exposed to danger. When a Japanese volunteer was killed, Japan—over the protests of the UN—withdrew its police from the provinces.

37. Interview with Lt. General John Sanderson, Canberra, Australia, March 28, 1993.

38. *Supplement to An Agenda for Peace: Position Paper of the Secretary-General on the Occasion of the Fiftieth Anniversary of the United Nations*, A/50/60;S/1995/1, January 3, 1995, p. 4.

39. Falling in the category of geopolitical luck is that—unlike Mogadishu in Somalia—the national capital and communication center was not itself an arena for armed factional conflict. SOC controlled Phnom Penh.

40. My view on this point benefited from an interview with Miss Hisako Shimura, DPKO, October 2, 1993.

41. There are some exceptions. Where UNTAC had the bargaining chips firmly in its own hands, there too it was able to impose its will when it came into conflict with the parties. UNTAC controlled currency because it could control access to the technically crucial prerequisite, international printing. The Civil Administration Division, for example, appears to have successfully gained control over visas and passports (Foreign Affairs area), largely because passports gain their utility through international governmental recognition. The UN, as the universal intergovernmental organization, could rely on its members to enforce its decree against any Cambodian faction that defied its will. So the SOC accepted the SNC-endorsed passport to avoid having all its passports decertified. (Foreign Affairs did not, of course, have equivalent success in controlling Cambodia's borders or its border trade, for the simple reasons that these functions were important to the factions, and some of Cambodia's international neighbors obtained great advantages through their complicity with smuggling.) One surprising case of foreign affairs "out of control" was an aviation treaty negotiated and signed by SOC with Malaysia in defiance of the Paris Agreements, which had allocated sovereign rights to the SNC during the transitional period.

42. Before the UN became involved, during the cold war when action by the Security Council was stymied by the lack of consensus among the P5, the international community allowed Cambodia to suffer an autogenocide and El Salvador a brutal civil war. Indeed, the great powers were involved in supporting factions who inflicted some of the worst aspects of the violence the two countries suffered. We should keep this is mind when we consider the UN's difficulties in Somalia and Bosnia.

43. I. William Zartman and Saadia Touval, *International Mediation in Theory and Practice* (New York: Westview, 1985).

44. See, for sources, Michael W. Doyle, "Making a Peace," chapter 2 of Doyle, *The UN in Cambodia*.

45. Yasushi Akashi, "UNTAC in Cambodia: Lessons for UN Peace-keeping," Charles Rostow Annual Lecture (Washington, D.C.; SAIS, October 1993); and Doyle interviews in Phnom Penh, March 1993, and New York, November 1993.

46. Some members of the Security Council have begun to express a concern that excessive independence by the "Friends" will undermine the authority of the council.

47. For a good discussion of the UN's, and especially the secretary general's potential strength as a diplomatic legitimator, see Giandommenico Picco, "The U.N. and the Use of Force," *Foreign Affairs*, vol. 73, no. 5 (September/October 1994), pp.

14–18. The "Friends" mechanism seems to answer many of the objections to UN mediation expressed by Saadia Touval, "Why the UN Fails," *Foreign Affairs*, vol. 73, no. 5 (September/October 1994), pp. 44–57.

48. See Roy Licklider, "The Consequences of Negotiated Settlements," *American Political Science Review*, vol. 89, no. 3 (September 1995), pp. 681–687; William Durch, ed., *The Evolution of UN Peacekeeping* (New York: St. Martin's, 1993); Mats Berdal, *Whither UN Peacekeeping?* Adelphi Paper 281 (London: ISIS, 1993); and Thomas Weiss, "New Challenges for UN Military Operations," *Washington Quarterly*, vol. 16, no. 1 (Winter 1993).

49. See the account by Raoul Jennar, "Thailand's Double Standards Must Be Stopped," *Phnom Penh Post*, October 8–21, 1993, p. 8. Jennar alleges not only financial but also military cooperation between the generals and the Khmer Rouge, claiming that it has continued after the May elections.

50. I first heard a variation on this point from Edward Luck.

51. October 23, 1991—UN document A/46/608-S/23177; 31 I.L.M. 183 (1992).

52. See Steven Ratner, "The Cambodia Settlement Agreements," *American Journal of International Law*, vol. 87 (1993); and his "The United Nations' Role in Cambodia: A Model for Resolution of Internal Conflicts?" in Lori Damrosch, ed., *Enforcing Restraint* (New York: Council on Foreign Relations, 1993).

53. The new Cambodian government would be and was created when the Constituent Assembly elected, in conformity with the agreements approved, the new Cambodian Constitution and transformed itself into a legislative assembly.

54. The SNC signed instruments of accession to the International Convention on Civil and Political Rights and the International Convention on Economic, Social, and Cultural Rights on April 20, 1992.

55. For a model of this kind of process developed for the Bosnian peace process see Abram Chayes and Antonia Handler Chayes, "After the End: A Preliminary Appraisal of Problems of Keeping the Peace in Bosnia If and When It Comes," in Richard Ullman, ed., *The World and Yugoslavia's Wars* (New York: Council on Foreign Relations, 1996).

56. For a good account of traditional views of reconciliation see A. B. Fetherston, "Putting the Peace Back Into Peacekeeping," *International Peacekeeping*, vol. 1, no. 2 (Spring 1994), pp. 11, discussing a paper by Marc Ross.

57. Dr. Reginald Austin, *Report on the Electoral Component* (UNTAC, 1993).

58. See appendix 1 for the complete UNTAC Mandate, pp. 17–22, in *Agreements on a Comprehensive Political Settlement of the Cambodia Conflict* (New York: DPI, 1992)

59. For the first time, unlike UN operations in Namibia, Nicaragua, Haiti, and Angola, the entire organization and supervision of the elections was left to the UN. UNTAC's responsibilities included establishing electoral laws and procedures, invalidating existing laws that would not further the settlement, setting up the polling, responding to complaints, arranging for foreign observation, and

certifying the elections as free and fair. The creation of laws and procedures was a critical legislative function granted to UNTAC regarding elections. This authority to draft legislation was not a power provided to UNTAC in other areas of civil administration and signified an innovative and intrusive role for the UN in the internal affairs of a member state.

60. This link was drawn explicitly by Deputy Secretary Lawrence Eagleburger at the Conference on the Reconstruction of Cambodia, June 22, 1992, Tokyo, where he proposed that assistance to Cambodia be "through the SNC—to areas controlled by those Cambodian parties cooperating with UNTAC in implementing the peace accords—and only to those parties which are so cooperating." Press Release USUN-44–92, June 23, 1992. Disbursing the aid through the SNC, however, gave the Khmer Rouge a voice, as a member of the SNC, in the potential disbursement of the aid.

61. William Durch, "The UN Operation in the Congo," in William Durch, ed., *The Evolution of UN Peacekeeping* (New York: St. Martin's, 1993), chapter 19, pp. 315–352.

62. Richard Betts suggests that nonimpartial and nonneutral use of force is needed to solve civil wars in order to economize on the use of force. The most economical intervention thus assists the strongest party to achieve effective sovereignty or assists the party whose interests are closest to those of the intervenor. Otherwise the international actor finds itself caught in the middle, without the support of any of the factions. This makes considerable sense for unilateral interventions with national objectives. But using the UN in this manner will be precluded in most instances by the variety of national objectives that enter into the multilateral intervention. The PRC did not want to see the KR destroyed; the USSR did not want to destroy SOC; and France and the U.S. did not want to destroy FUNCINPEC. Each of the great powers is a permanent member of the Security Council and has veto on UN activity. Similar diversity applies with regard to the aims of troop contributing countries. The gamble is as noted above: an impartial intervention will elicit enough support from international actors and from the parties that multilateral assistance will be sufficient to establish a peace, especially when supplemented by impartial use of force as described in the paragraphs above.

63. Conversation with Lt. General John Sanderson, UNTAC force commander, at the Vienna Seminar, March 5, 1995. On May 28, 1993, I observed this in process around the small town of Stoung, which was surrounded by the Khmer Rouge. The Indonesian battalion established an inner perimeter around the town. The CPAF (SOC army) created an outer perimeter and trucked in voters from outlying villages.

Part III

Comparative Analyses

7 When All Else Fails: Evaluating Population Transfers and Partition as Solutions to Ethnic Conflict

Chaim D. Kaufmann

Until recently there has been a near consensus among policy makers and scholars that the objective of ethnic conflict management should be to support and preserve integrated multiethnic societies. In the last few years, however, the idea that separating warring populations may be the best solution to many of the most intense ethnic conflicts has been gaining ground. Events in Bosnia have supported this trend, as observers note that the more the warring groups have separated the more peaceful their relations have become, while proposals to thoroughly reintegrate them command less and less support.[1] In addition, a growing body of scholarship that focuses on the role of intergroup security dilemmas in ethnic conflicts argues that intermixed population settlement patterns can promote escalation of violence, implying that separation of warring groups may dampen conflict.[2]

Separating populations, however, remains deeply controversial. Even when carried out safely, population transfers inflict enormous suffering, including loss of homes and livelihoods and disruption of social, religious, and cultural ties. Thus they can be justified only if they save the lives of people who would otherwise be killed in ethnic violence. Critics argue that ethnic population transfers, and the partitions that often accompany them, generally do not reduce suffering and death but actually increase them.

The most important empirical evidence marshaled against demographic separation rests on the outcomes of four famous twentieth-century partitions — Ireland, India, Palestine, and Cyprus — all of which were accompanied by large-scale population transfers and by substantial violence.[3]

The question addressed in this paper is, If the logic of demographic separation is correct, why were the partitions and population transfers in these
four cases so violent? There are three possibilities: the violence in these cases
could be evidence that the theory is wrong, it could have resulted from
idiosyncratic factors that do not shed light on the causal logic of the theory,
or the violence could be due to the factors identified by the security dilemma–based theory, which would mean that violence in these cases (and
future cases) could probably be reduced if policy makers facing severe ethnic
conflicts were more willing to consider the option of separating hostile
populations.

To answer this question I investigate the records of these four cases and
find that the critics' claims are not justified. In all four cases, separation of
the warring groups did reduce subsequent violence. Continuing or resurgent
intergroup violence in limited regions within some of the cases has resulted
not from partition or from separation, but rather from the incompleteness
of separation of the hostile groups in those specific areas.

This article is divided into three sections. The first assesses the state of
the debate on demographic separation as a remedy for ethnic wars and
identifies the empirical questions that must be answered in order to advance
it. The second section investigates whether the net effects of the partitions
and population transfers in the Irish, Indian, Palestinian, and Cypriot cases
were to reduce loss of life or to increase it. The third section considers
whether partitions and population transfers create undemocratic states.

The State of the Debate

This section lays out the sides in the current debate and the requirements
for advancing our knowledge.

The Case for Separation

Whenever ethnic communities cannot rely on a strong and impartial
central state to prevent civil strife, all groups must mobilize for self-defense.
However, the material and rhetorical measures that groups use to mobilize
for defense also pose offensive threats to other groups, creating a security
dilemma in which no group can provide for its own security without threatening the security of others. The intensity of this security dilemma is in part
a function of demography: the more intermixed the pattern of settlement of
the hostile populations, the greater the opportunities for offense by either

side, and it becomes more difficult to design effective measures for community defense except by going on the offensive preemptively to "cleanse" mixed areas of members of the enemy group and create ethnically reliable, defensible enclaves.[4]

The same dynamic also prevents deescalation of ethnic wars until or unless the warring groups are substantially separated (or one side conquers or annihilates the other). Solutions that aim both to restore multiethnic civil politics and to avoid population transfers, such as institution building, power sharing, and identity reconstruction, cannot work during or after an ethnic civil war because they do not resolve the security dilemma created by mixed demography.[5] As long as both sides know that the best security strategy for each is to engage in offense and in ethnic cleansing, neither can entrust its security to hopes for the other's restraint.[6] The policy implication is that the international community should endorse separation as a remedy for at least some communal conflicts; otherwise the processes of war will separate the populations anyway, at much higher human cost.

The critical causal factor is separation of people into defensible enclaves, not partition of sovereignty.[7] Conversely, partition without separation only increases conflict, as in Croatia and Bosnia in 1991–92.

The Case Against Separation and Partition

Among most international organizations, Western leaders, and scholars *population transfers* and *partition* have long been dirty words. With rare exceptions, the United Nations has supported states against secession movements, and the UN High Commission for Refugees (UNHCR) prefers to bring "safety to people, not people to safety."[8] Opponents argue that ethnic partitions and population transfers have three main flaws: (1) rather than dampening violence, partitions and population transfers actually cause violence, (2) they generate new conflicts, often by transforming civil conflicts into international ones, and (3) partitions create rump states that are undemocratic and culturally narrow, perpetuating intercommunal hatred.[9]

The first two criticisms are the most serious, because they concern the central issue, whether demographic separation saves or costs human lives. The third is also important, because it suggests that refugees may find themselves in a polity more repressive than the one they left.[10]

The implication of the critics' logic is that most of those who become refugees in ethnic conflicts could have remained in their original homes in safety and reasonable economic, political, and cultural freedom if partition and population transfers were not externally imposed on them. Their bottom line is that working to reintegrate ethnic groups at war with each other is both more moral and, in the long run, more practical than acquiescing in partition.

This is wrong. The security dilemma generated by intermixed populations ensures that ethnic wars always separate the warring communities; this process cannot be stopped except by permanent military occupation, genocide, or not having the war in the first place. When ethnic conflicts turn violent they generate spontaneous refugee movements, for several reasons: people are afraid to stay in areas where ethnic fighting is ongoing or expected to begin or they are forced to leave by their neighbors, marauding gangs, or a conquering army. Thus the question in the midst of severe ethnic conflict is not whether the groups will be separated but how—with protection, transport, subsistence, and resettlement organized by outside powers or institutions, or at the mercy of their ethnic enemies and of bandits? Refusal or failure to organize necessary transfers does not protect people against becoming refugees but inflicts disaster on them when they do.

The critics' charge that partitions and population transfers create illiberal states is also misguided.[11] Although it is true that not all partition successor states are liberal democracies, the successor states created by the partitions studied in this paper have not proved to be less democratic than either their predecessors or neighbors. Even though several of the successor states have discriminatory laws, such discrimination is generally less intense than what the prepartition minorities would likely have faced under majority rule.

Requirements for Resolving the Debate

The maximum universe relevant to this debate would be all cases of border changes or population movements that altered the ethnic makeup of one or more states. In practice, this universe would be uncountably large, so for this study I define a more manageable set of the cases most relevant to the policy utility of demographic separation today: specifically, twentieth-century ethnic partitions and secessions that have led to the formation of new states, roughly twenty in all.[12] Table 7.1 summarizes this set.

Within this set there is a strong association between high violence and large population transfers; almost all the high-violence cases involve more substantial refugee movements than any of the low-violence cases. This outcome, however, is consistent with the arguments of both sides in the debate:

proponents of demographic separation contend that high violence causes population movements, while critics contend the reverse.

To resolve this debate over cause and effect, the most important cases that deserve detailed investigation are the high violence partitions. Because both sides in the debate are most concerned with the causes of extreme violence, the low violence cases cannot be decisive. We should also focus on partition rather than secession cases, since our purpose is to assess whether international intervention reduces or increases the costs of ethnic conflict. This paper studies four of the five cases that qualify—Ireland, India, Palestine, and Cyprus—which have the additional virtue of being the same cases most commonly cited by the critics.

TABLE 7.1.   Ethnic Secessions and Partitions, 1900–94[a]

Secessions	Partitions
Low Violence	
Baltic States 1918	Norway 1905
Finland 1918	Austria-Hungary 1918–19[b]
Soviet Union 1990–91	Ottoman Empire 1918–19[c]
Slovenia 1991	Singapore 1965
Macedonia 1992	Slovakia 1993
High Violence	
Algeria 1962	Poland 1918
Bangladesh 1971	Ireland 1921
Nagorno-Karabakh 1991*	India 1947
Iraqi Kurds 1991*	Palestine 1947
Northern Somalia 1991*	Cyprus 1974*
Croatia 1991	
Bosnia 1992	
Abkhazia 1992–93*	
Eritrea 1993	
Chechnya 1994*	

[a] Cases of decolonization in which the colony and its inhabitants had never been part of the metropolitan state are not included, because in most instances the remaining metropolitan population was small and generally viewed as foreigners, not as local ethnic groups that could potentially contest for power. Algeria is an exception, because it had been legally part of the French metropole and also contained an ethnic French population of more than one million that wanted both to remain where they were and remain French citizens.
[b] No large-scale ethnic violence within or among the successor states, although one successor state (Hungary) fought a war with an existing state (Romania) that gained territory in the partition.
[c] No wars among successor states, but Turkey fought a war with Greece in 1920–23.
* De facto, not internationally recognized.

Separation and Violence

This section examines the records of the partitions of Ireland, India, Palestine, and Cyprus to judge the validity of the claims (1) that separation and partition increase rather than reduce short-run violence and (2) that they also perpetuate or actually increase intergroup hatred and violence in the long run.[13]

Ireland

Although the partition of Ireland has been accompanied by violence, this violence was not caused by partition itself but can be attributed to the fact that the partition did not separate the antagonistic communities, particularly in the North. As a result, the demographically mixed North has suffered to decades of continuing violence, while the relatively monolithic South has enjoyed peace.

Did the Partition of Ireland Reduce Violence or Increase It?

Political violence in Ireland increased markedly in the decade after the British government agreed to Home Rule and to partition in 1914. There were four major episodes: (1) the Easter Rising of 1916, in which approximately 450 died;[14] (2) the Irish War of Independence from 1919 to 1921, which killed an estimated 1,500 people;[15] (3) the 1922–23 civil war within the Irish Republic, which cost as many as 4,000 more lives;[16] and (4) sectarian violence in Ulster between 1920 and 1922, which left another 428 dead.[17]

Opponents of partition and separation might see this record as evidence for their position, but this would be a mistake. The first two episodes were not sectarian conflicts at all and had nothing to do with partition; rather, they were fought over whether Ireland would receive only Home Rule within the United Kingdom or whether it would gain full independence. The opposing sides in both rounds were Irish nationalists against the British army and police, not Catholics versus Protestants.

The third and fourth episodes occurred because the 1921 partition did not separate the two communities, particularly in Ulster. Separation was not an issue in the South, because the twenty-six counties assigned to the Irish Free State contained a population that was less than 10 percent Protestant.[18] This minority was far too small and too thinly spread to constitute a possible political or military force. Thus there was no security dilemma, and Ireland has not experienced a problem of sectarian violence to this day.

The source of both the sectarian violence in Ulster and of the Irish Civil War was the mixed demography of Northern Ireland. The six counties that remained part of Britain included a 34 percent Catholic minority, creating a fairly intense security dilemma.[19] With extreme nationalists in the South calling for action to undermine the partition, many Ulster Protestants believed that preserving their political, economic, and possibly even physical security required suppressing any accretion of power by Catholics. This security dilemma was further exacerbated by the irregular and commingled settlement patterns of the two groups within Northern Ireland (see map 7.1); if Catholics and Protestants had been mostly separated in distinct regions, then Protestants would still have controlled the province government but would have had little reason to interfere in local rule of Catholic areas. The result in 1920–22 was a wave of both organized and private violence in which 428 people were killed, more than 8,000 Catholics were driven from their jobs and about 23,000 from their homes.[20]

Northern Ireland's intermixed demography also created a security dilemma for nationalists in the South, who saw the vulnerability of the Ulster Catholics as demanding action to rescue them. This security dilemma did not lead to international war (the Irish government recognized that undoing the partition by force was infeasible) but it did help cause a short civil war in the South. The Irish Republican Army, which was operating in the North, refused to accept government discipline and was defeated by government forces in a war lasting from June 1922 to August 1923.[21] One could argue that even if there had been virtually no Catholics residing in the North the IRA would have fought for the cause of a united Ireland, but the IRA leaders' appeal to their membership to die for mere land would have been much less compelling than a call to rescue fellow Catholics from pillage and murder. Similarly, it would have been harder to accuse the government of treason for abandoning people who were not there.[22]

Could the Partition of Ireland Have Been Avoided?

The partition of Ireland could have been avoided in only two ways, either of which would have had worse consequences.

First, Britain could have granted Home Rule (or independence) to a united Ireland and coerced the Ulster Unionists into submission. In fact, the British government tried to do this in 1914 but was stopped by the risk of

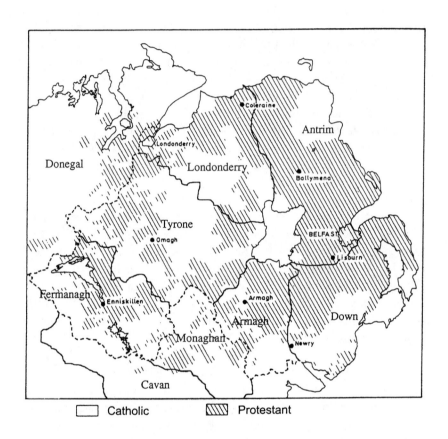

MAP 7.1. Religious Majorities in Ulster, 1914

civil war in Britain itself as well as by the evident willingness and capability of the Unionists to resist. Imposing Home Rule on Ulster was opposed by the Tory opposition in Commons, a majority of the House of Lords, King George V, and a great many army and navy officers.[23]

In addition, few if any doubted that the Ulster Protestants would fight.[24] On Ulster Day, September 18, 1912, 218,206 Ulstermen signed a "Solemn League and Covenant" pledging to resist Home Rule; 228,991 women signed a parallel document. This was most of the adult Protestants in the province.[25] Since 1912 they had been preparing a regional defense force, the Ulster Volunteer Force, which by 1914 had 85,000 to 90,000 members, and was fairly well organized and rapidly improving its equipment through purchase and smuggling.[26] It was said in London in spring 1914 that suppressing Ulster would require the entire British army and take twelve to eighteen months.[27]

The other possibility would have been to deny Irish independence indefinitely. This would have required suppressing all armed combinations and nationalist political cells throughout Ireland, a task that 40,000 British troops and 10,000 police could not carry out in 1919–21. The British would certainly have been forced to engage in brutal tactics against civilians, an alternative which the government in Britain rejected as too awful.[28]

Does Partition Increase Hatred and Generate New Conflicts?

In the seventy-five years since partition the Irish Free State has enjoyed virtually complete freedom from sectarian conflict. A united Ireland remains a rhetorical goal, but public support for action toward this end has faded over the years. The Irish government paid no political price for the 1985 Anglo-Irish agreement on Northern Ireland, even though the agreement contained no promises of eventual sovereignty.[29]

Northern Ireland, however, has never achieved peace between the two religious communities. Protestants still fear eventual Catholic rule (or union with Ireland); Catholics have been subjected to decades of discrimination, and repeated rounds of political violence have erupted.[30] The "Troubles" from 1969 to the present have claimed about thirty-four hundred dead.[31] The sources of the difference between these two histories are again demography and the security dilemma. The Protestant population of Ireland stood at about 8.5 percent in 1991, while the Catholic minority in the North had increased to 38 percent.[32]

Resolution of the conflict in Northern Ireland requires assuring the security of both communities, which in turn requires a credible joint guarantee by the only actors strong enough to provide it—the Irish and British governments. Very recently, prospects for peace have improved because the two governments finally seem prepared to provide whatever assurances are necessary. In April 1998 the Irish Dail formally amended the republic's constitutional claim on the North to require the consent of the province's population, and in May the Irish government condoned British Prime Minister Tony Blair's promises to Unionists that violent factions would be excluded from the new Northern Ireland assembly and that there would be no change in the status of Northern Ireland without the people's consent.[33]

What Should Have Been Done?

The partition of Ireland was unavoidable, but forcing 430,000 Catholics into Northern Ireland was not. Unfortunately, the Ulster Unionists commanded so much political support in Britain at the time that they were in effect allowed to set the boundaries of Northern Ireland. Seeking to incorporate as many Protestants as possible without endangering their majority in the province, they chose six of Ulster's nine counties, including two that contained more Catholics than Protestants.[34]

Ireland's best chance at lasting peace would have been to draw a partition line that separated the two groups as fully as possible, without regard to county lines or other prior boundaries.[35] Since no line could avoid leaving substantial minorities on each side, the British government should also have offered money to people willing to move as well as making clear that it could not protect those who insisted on staying behind. The result would have been a smaller but safer Northern Ireland.

India and Pakistan

The most frequently mentioned case in this debate is India. Critics of the 1947 partition blame it for causing more than fifteen million refugees and hundreds of thousands of deaths. This correlation, however, is spurious. The partition, the population transfers, and the violence were all caused by the irresolvable security dilemmas between the Muslim and Hindu communities of India, and especially between the Muslim and Sikh communities of Punjab Province, both of which were generated by the removal of the imperial power that had previously guaranteed the security of all groups. In short, independence from Britain, not partition, caused these tragedies.

Constructivist scholars of identity would charge the communalization of Indian politics, and therefore, ultimately, the violence, to manipulation of mass aspirations and fears by self-interested communal elites.[36] Whether or not we accept this model of mass political mobilization, however, the fact remains that the removal of British imperial power created real security dilemmas, which lent inherent credibility to political appeals based on community security.

Did Partition Cause the Violence?

The independence of India and Pakistan on August 15, 1947, not only divided the Indian subcontinent, it also involved the partition of two of colonial India's most populous provinces, Punjab in the northwest and Bengal in the east. Although intercommunal rioting had been on the rise in 1945 and 1946, independence and partition were expected to dampen the violence. Some population movements were expected, but they were not expected to be especially large, sudden, or dangerous. These expectations were met in Bengal, where more than 5,000 people were killed before independence but very few after, and where 3.5 million people moved across the new border with little loss of life.

Punjab accounted for most of the refugees and nearly all the deaths. From August to October 1947 the province was convulsed by an intense communal civil war involving some of the largest ethnic cleansing campaigns in history. Hundreds of thousands of people were killed in Punjab, and the war sparked large numbers of revenge killings elsewhere as well. More than ten million people from the Punjab and adjacent provinces had to flee for their lives.

By the late 1920s it was clear to all parties that India would achieve eventual independence. Given that British power was the ultimate guarantee of security for all communities in India, the prospect of its withdrawal activated potential intercommunal security dilemmas. Two such dilemmas were critical in determining the final outcome of the process: between Muslims and Hindus at the national level and between Sikhs and Muslims in Punjab.[37]

Muslims made up 22 percent of the population of India, compared with 68 percent Hindus,[38] meaning that under pure majoritarian rule the Muslims would be absolutely insecure in the event that the government should be captured by Hindu supremacists such as the Hindu Mahasabha movement. Although the largest Indian nationalist movement, the Congress Party, was formally committed to a secular India, in practice it never represented all Indian communities. Members of the Mahasabha and other Hindu nationalists such as B. S. Moonje were welcome in Congress, while members of Muslim parties were excluded as "communalist."[39]

Mohammad Ali Jinnah, leader of the Muslim League, demanded constitutional arrangements that would assure communal autonomy, especially: (1) guaranteed electoral majorities in the five provinces with Muslim-majority populations: Punjab, Bengal, Northwest Frontier Province (NWFP), Sind, and Baluchistan and (2) a weak federal system in which the central government would have little power over the provinces.[40] Muslim leaders further insisted that police functions should belong to the provinces and national defense to the British governor-general (i.e., that a Hindu-dominated central government should possess no tools of coercive force).[41] Agreement in principle on some of these points was reached at an All-Parties Conference in 1928, but the Congress leadership was forced to disavow the deal because of Hindu nationalist opposition.[42] In practice the Muslim demands might have exposed Hindu minorities in Punjab, Bengal, and Sind to Muslim domination.

The results of the 1937 elections intensified this security dilemma in three ways. First, electoral success persuaded Congress leaders that they could reach out directly to the Muslim masses, ignoring the Muslim political parties.[43] To survive, the Muslim League had to transform itself from an elite circle to a genuine mass party that could claim to represent most Indian Muslims. It succeeded, based on explicitly communal appeals such as the slogan "Islam in Danger," so the ultimate effect was to increase fear and mistrust between the two communities. Second, Muslims in the seven provinces ruled by Congress soon complained of abuses, including physical insecurity, because of government failure to restrict communal violence by Hindus, and these reports were widely circulated.[44] Third, Congress's aggressive political tactics led Muslim leaders to doubt whether British control over defense could last much beyond independence. A Congress-controlled government might contrive to reduce the governor-general to a figurehead as in Australia, then change the basis of recruiting of the army, and then be able to do anything at all.[45]

By 1940 Jinnah was convinced that nothing short of a separate Muslim state, "Pakistan," could provide security for the Muslim community. Further Hindu-Muslim negotiations proved fruitless, and in the face of increasing Muslim unity and evident determination, on June 3, 1947, Congress, the Muslim League, and Viceroy Earl Louis Mountbatten agreed to partition.[46]

It was further agreed that since both Punjab and Bengal contained only narrow Muslim majorities and large Hindu-majority regions, Muslim West Punjab and East Bengal would go to Pakistan, and predominantly Hindu East Punjab and West Bengal to India. Both states would gain independence on August 15, 1947, and the British-chaired Boundary Commissions would announce their decisions on August 17.[47]

Although the national-level Hindu-Muslim security dilemma necessitated the partition of India, it did not cause most of the tragedy that followed, except indirectly, by distracting the major players' attention from a second, even more severe, security dilemma between Muslims and Sikhs in the province of Punjab. Virtually all the Sikh population of nearly six million in 1941 was concentrated in Punjab. Although the provincial population overall was 56 percent Muslim, 27 percent Hindu, and just 13 percent Sikh, the Sikhs averaged considerably wealthier than the other communities and had exercised disproportionate power in provincial politics.[48] By the 1940s Sikhs and Muslims had not fought in several decades, but they had a long history of intercommunal hostility.[49] Sikhs also controlled a large fraction of the best land in Central Punjab and in the canal colonies in West Punjab (see map 7.2). Accordingly, Sikhs feared Muslim dominance even more than the Muslims feared Hindu rule; their wealth, political influence, religious freedom, and even physical security might all be at risk. From the Muslim point of view the Sikhs presented a special threat because their martial tradition meant that the whole male population had to be considered armed.[50]

The core Sikh concerns were driven by security and remained essentially unchanged from the 1920s onward. In several separate negotiations with different parties, Sikh demands varied considerably on issues such as representation in the Punjab legislature, the boundaries of Punjab, and representation in the central legislature, but they remained constant on the two points most central to their physical security: (1) creation of a political unit in which Sikhs would be, if not a majority, at least holders of the political balance between Muslims and Hindus (i.e., anything but a Muslim-majority Punjab) and (2) retention of their traditional overrepresentation in the army of whatever state they would be part of.[51]

To secure these goals Sikh leaders pursued every possible avenue of negotiation: first participation in all-India constitutional negotiations, then direct negotiations with Congress. After it became clear that partition could not be avoided, they tried direct negotiations with the Muslim League on Sikh status within Pakistan, an attempt to get the British to impose arrangements for Sikh security, a proposal for an independent Sikh state, and finally

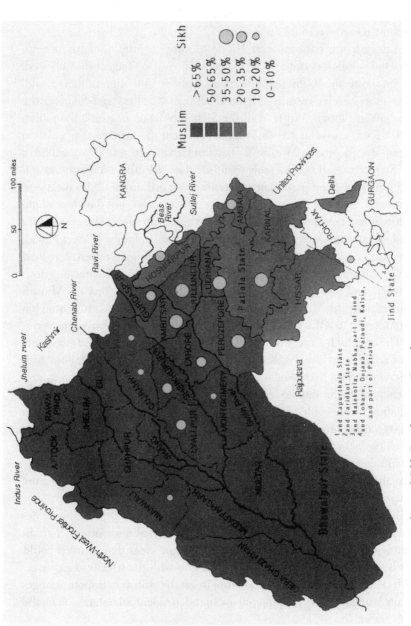

MAP 7.2. Muslim and Sikh Populations in Punjab, 1941

a proposal to partition Punjab along lines that would keep all Sikhs within India. All were rejected.[52]

By the summer of 1947 Sikh leaders were desperate. On March 2 the Punjab's coalition government of Congress, Sikhs, and the cross-communal Unionist Party collapsed in the face of a massive Muslim League civil disobedience campaign.[53] In February and March Muslims attacked Hindus and Sikhs in Lahore and Amritsar, the two main cities of central Punjab and the core of the region most likely to be disputed; more than three thousand were killed.[54] Possibly most threatening was Jinnah's proposal in December 1946 to Sikh leader Sardar Baldev Singh that the Muslims and Sikhs combine to seize all of Punjab, while still refusing to provide any guarantees of the status of Sikhs in Pakistan. This could only inflame both key Sikh fears: that Muslim rule would be oppressive and that the Muslims would not be satisfied with any initial territorial settlement.[55] Finally, it was clear that the June 3 partition agreement would, in all likelihood, leave nearly two million Sikhs stranded in Pakistan.

It appears that at this point Sikh leaders devised a four-point last resort plan to protect their national security unilaterally: (1) if the boundary award proved unsatisfactory, to contest as much as possible of the core Sikh areas in central Punjab and to resist possible Muslim attempts to contest any part of East Punjab, (2) to evacuate most Sikhs west of the line, (3) to eliminate the Muslim population east of the line, thus increasing the Sikh percentage in East Punjab after the war, and (4) later, to press the Indian government for redivision of East Punjab to create a true Sikh-majority province.

Although there is no written record of such a plan and its existence cannot be certainly established, there is suggestive evidence. As early as March 1947 the Sikh Panthic Party passed a resolution that it would fight Pakistan to the end.[56] Military mobilization began in April, and by June the Sikh Akali Fauj had eight thousand men and the British provincial governor was receiving intelligence reports of a plan for a terror campaign in East Punjab.[57] Several Sikh leaders, including Sardar Baldev Singh, the Sikh representative on the Boundary Commission, made clear that they would not respect an unfavorable award.[58] Fighting began well before the award was even announced; starting on July 30, Sikh forces attacked Muslim villages in the central region around Lahore and Amritsar that was disputed by both communities as well as Muslim communities throughout East Punjab.[59] By the end of August much of East Punjab had been cleared of its Muslim population.[60]

The main evidence that the Sikh evacuation from West Punjab was preplanned is that most departed before trouble broke out in their areas and most also demonstrated better preparation than Muslim refugees going the other way, succeeding in getting away with more of their property and fewer losses.[61] After the war Sikhs numbered roughly 30 percent of the Indian province of East Punjab and Hindus 70 percent. Sikhs then agitated for further division of Punjab to create a Sikh-majority state, which was accomplished in 1966.[62]

The war in Punjab also sparked additional ethnic cleansing in adjacent provinces. By September refugees bearing atrocity tales flooded Delhi and the United Provinces, leading to revenge massacres of Muslims, which in turn led to Muslim attacks on Hindus and Sikhs in West Pakistan cities such as Peshawar and Karachi. Both sides also attacked refugee convoys and trains passing through Punjab itself.[63] Altogether, hundreds of thousands of people were killed, and more than ten million refugees were exchanged between India and West Pakistan.[64]

An additional cause of loss of life in this war was the failure of the British, Indian, or Pakistani governments to take meaningful preparations to protect refugees in Punjab, in part because they all underestimated the scale and suddenness with which the war would escalate but also because the Indians and Pakistanis did not want to legitimate or encourage population movements.[65] The British-commanded Indian Boundary Force, which was supposed to control communal violence in Punjab, was, at fifty thousand men, far too small for the task, and many of its contingents proved unreliable for communal reasons. Transport and reception camps were not prepared. For weeks the Indian government also continued to send Muslim refugee trains directly through Punjab rather than around it.[66]

At no point did any side make energetic efforts to protect, feed, or shelter refugees in transit through Punjab. Many lives lost in Punjab would have been saved if refugees had not been directed *toward* the center of the Sikh uprising. Nearly all could have been saved had the British provided enough reliable troops to control the province or found allies who could. The lesson of Punjab is not that population movements must be costly but the more obvious point that refugees should not be forced to travel through a war zone.[67]

Although the war in Punjab accounted for the vast majority of all the deaths in communal conflict between 1945 and 1947, one other region of India is also especially important to this analysis. Unlike Punjab, the partition of Bengal markedly dampened the security dilemma in that province; it assured that the millions of Hindus in West Bengal would not have to live under Muslim rule, and, unlike Punjab, the division line did successfully separate districts populated mainly by each of the two communities. Most important, there was no third side with an overwhelming security motive to overturn the settlement. As a result, the announcement of independence and of the partition line lowered violence in Bengal by resolving both sides' security uncertainties. More than 5,000 were killed in the province in the year before independence, but very few afterward.[68] Between 1947 and 1951 3.5 million people moved between India and East Pakistan in orderly, planned transfers, without loss of life.

Did Partition Increase Hatred and Cause New Conflicts

The 1947–51 population exchanges resolved Hindu-Muslim security dilemmas throughout most of India and Pakistan, as very few Hindus remained in Pakistan, while the Muslims of India are too few, too thinly spread, and too far from any possible aid to even imagine resisting the Indian government, and they have not. Sporadic Hindu-Muslim violence still occurs in India, although at low levels compared with the fears of both sides in the 1920s–40s or the actuality of 1945–47.

The independence of India and Pakistan did generate one new conflict, over control of the former princely state of Jammu and Kashmir. This conflict occurred not because India was partitioned but because Kashmir, whose population was about two-thirds Muslim, was not. Drawing a partition line through Kashmir would have been easier than in Punjab or even Bengal, because most of the Hindu population of the state resided in the southernmost division, Jammu, adjacent to India, and the boundary between Jammu and the rest of the state is largely mountainous.[69]

Failure to divide Kashmir intensified Hindu-Muslim security dilemmas in three ways, generating a history of conflict that still continues. First, although communal relations in Kashmir had been better than in many other areas, and Maharaja Hari Singh initially attempted to remain independent, by October 1947 each community had reason to fear for its security. Both groups were aware that India and Pakistan each claimed Kashmir, both had heard about atrocities in Punjab, and some of the maharaja's troops began attacking the Muslim population.[70]

Second, Kashmir borders key economic centers of both countries and is thus strategically valuable. In October the maharaja invited in pro-Indian Sikh troops, and a few weeks later Muslim irregulars invaded from Pakistan. Both regular armies intervened. Battle deaths reached fifteen hundred before a truce was signed at the start of 1949.[71] India wound up in control of most of the state, but Pakistan invaded again in 1965, and there was more border fighting in 1971.

Third, under Indian rule Kashmiri politics have become increasingly communalized over time, threatening the security of all groups. From the early 1960s onward, increased political participation led to several cycles of Muslim autonomy demands and Indian government responses that actually reduced local authority. For example, from 1980 to 1982 the Kashmir government backed a proposal to allow 1947 refugees (i.e., Muslims) to return, sparking fears that Hindus and Sikhs now settled on refugees' former property would be dispossessed. When the 1983 election again returned the same government in a vote along communal lines, Indira Gandhi removed the state government and instituted repressive measures.[72] Since the late 1980s Kashmir has been fighting an ongoing Muslim insurgency, aided by Pakistan. More than 30,000 people have been killed, and virtually the whole Hindu population of the Valley of Kashmir (about 250,000) have fled their homes. It is uncertain how many Kashmiri Muslims support the insurgents, but nearly all have become profoundly alienated from Indian government rule.[73] Since May 1998 Kashmir has become the focus of Indian and Pakistani nuclear threats against each other.

The most important conflict within Pakistan since independence was the secession of Bengali-speaking East Pakistan (Bangladesh) from the mainly Urdu-speaking West in 1971 (which also caused the 1971 international war between Pakistan and India).[74] Possible explanations for this conflict include undemocratic institutions that allowed West Pakistan to dominate Pakistani politics, reaction against state repression, and ethnic and linguistic tensions, but it cannot be charged to the 1947 separation of Hindus and Muslims.

Finally, both Pakistan and India contain numerous additional ethnic minority groups, including Sikhs, Nagas, Tripuras, and others within India, and Baluchis, Pathans, and Mohajirs in Pakistan, that have agitated for greater autonomy or even rebelled.[75] Some of these disputes predate independence, and we have no way to determine whether any of them would have occurred in the context of a united India. There is one exception; the conflict that has emerged in recent years, mainly in the city of Karachi, between Mohajirs (refugees from India and their descendants) and the pre-1947 Sindhi community can be charged to the partition of India and resulting population exchanges and has, as of 1997, cost more than thirty-five hundred lives.[76]

What Should Have Been Done?

The problem with Indian independence was not partition but that partition did not go far enough. First, and most important, there was no provision for a Sikh homeland, either independent or as a province of India. Even though Sikhs were only 1.2 percent of the population of India, six million people as determined, organized, and armed as they were could not be ignored and still hope for peace. The hard part is that, because Sikhs were not an absolute majority in any district of Punjab, any homeland would have required planning for substantial population transfers and therefore substantial commitment of resources for refugee protection and resettlement.

Second, Kashmir should have been included in the general settlement, regardless of the maharaja's wishes. The result would likely have been a partition more favorable to Pakistan than the one achieved by war and would have avoided stranding a large community, both vulnerable and threatening, on the wrong side of the line.

Palestine and Israel

The War of Israeli Independence cost the lives of 6,000 Jews and probably more than 10,000 Arabs, and displaced well over a million people; about 750,000 Palestinian Arabs fled Israel, while over half a million Jews migrated from Arab countries to Israel.[77] As in Ireland and India, these costs were results of security dilemmas generated by independence, not partition.

Did Partition Reduce Violence or Increase It?

Neither; it had no effect. Very few people today would suggest that the partition of Palestine could have been avoided. From 1946 onward, the Jewish population mounted a revolt that British forces could not control, forcing their withdrawal. A unified independent Palestine was impossible because the Jews would not submit to rule by the Arab majority and the Arabs would not accept any arrangement that allowed political power for Jews or even continued Jewish immigration. Palestinian Arabs staged major riots in 1929 over these issues as well as a major rebellion from 1936 to 1939.

The departure of British power from Palestine, competing Arab and Jewish land claims, and the intermixed population settlement pattern created a security dilemma so intense that civil war was certain. The three main areas of Jewish settlement—eastern Galilee, the coastal strip from Haifa to Tel Aviv, and Jerusalem—all contained substantial Arab populations and, even more important, were separated from each other by all-Arab regions (see map 7.3). No partition plan that did not envisage substantial population

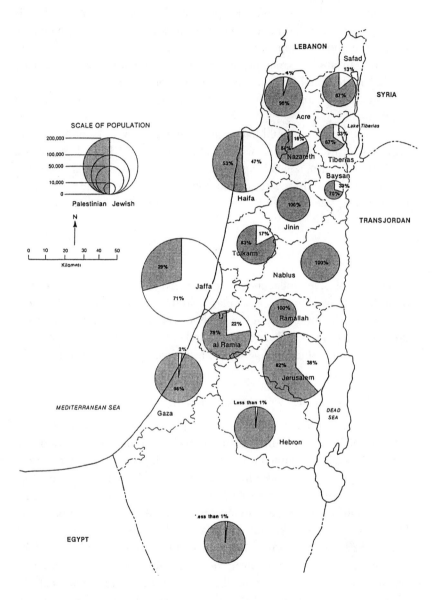

MAP 7.3. Palestine, 1946

transfers could have done anything to resolve this security dilemma, and the one voted by the United Nations in November 1947 did not.[78]

Faced with armed conflict internally, as well as external invasion, the Jewish state could survive only if it could (1) expand to link together its three main parts and (2) move out a large fraction of the Arabs from Jewish-controlled areas, especially from the most strategically critical locations. The pattern of ethnic cleansing during the war followed security dilemma logic. Israeli government leaders and military forces in some places encouraged Arab inhabitants to remain, in others harassed or frightened many into flight, and in yet others carried out forced expulsions, depending on strategic needs at each place and time.

Two polar opposite examples that took place just ten weeks and fifty miles apart illustrate this dynamic. In late April 1948 the Jews gained control of the city of Haifa, whose population was roughly evenly mixed. Almost immediately the entire Arab population, not just of Haifa but of all the coastal towns north to the Lebanese border, abandoned their homes and fled to Lebanon. The Israeli government was surprised and dismayed by this exodus, and Israeli politicians and soldiers tried to persuade the population to stay.[79]

In contrast, in early July Haganah troops surrounded the Arab towns of Lod (Lydda) and Ramle southeast of Tel Aviv and expelled their entire populations—sixty thousand in all—on forty-eight hours' notice, with only what property they could carry.[80]

What accounts for such different behavior is the difference in strategic need. The Mediterranean coast north of Haifa was an all-Arab region, with no Jews living in or beyond it who might need to be rescued. Lod and Ramle, however, sat astride the main Tel Aviv–Jerusalem road, at a time when the Jewish portion of Jerusalem was under siege and Israeli leaders were uncertain whether it could hold out. Resupply and reinforcement convoys had to travel through the streets of the two towns, and, routinely, had to fight their way through. Jerusalem could not be secured as long as these towns (and certain other villages further along the route) remained in Arab hands.[81]

The war ended in 1949 when the Israeli-Arab security dilemma was ameliorated, if not fully resolved, by nearly complete separation of the two communities. Israel secured a defensible territory that included the major Jewish settlements and the spaces between them. The remaining 156,000 Arabs made up no more than 15 percent of the new state's population and were disorganized and demoralized—and therefore were not perceived by Jewish Israelis as a significant threat.[82] Gaza, the West Bank, and the Old City of

Jerusalem came under control of the Egyptian and Jordanian armies; no Jews remained in these areas.

Did Partition Cause Increased Hatred and Generate New Conflicts?

Since independence Israel has not had significant internal intergroup violence but has fought four wars against neighboring states, in 1956, 1967, 1969–70, and 1973, has occupied parts of Lebanon twice, in 1978 and 1982–85, and since 1987 has faced organized resistance to its occupation of the West Bank and Gaza. Israel has been the target of continuing terrorism, and Israeli citizens have carried out terrorist attacks as well.

Partition played no role in causing the continuation of violence after 1949, which resulted simply from the presence of the Jewish state. Most Arabs remained unwilling to accept the permanence of a large Jewish presence in Palestine, while Israelis suspected the Arabs of genocidal aims. However, despite wars and terrorism, most civilians on both sides have been safe most of the time for nearly fifty years, which was not true before the population transfers. Over time many on both sides have abandoned the most extreme enemy images. Israel has signed peace treaties with two of its neighbors and enjoys calmer relations with most other Arab states than it once did.

The one new conflict generated since Israel's independence, the Palestinian *intifada*, which began in 1987, was caused in large part by Israel's policy of planting Jewish settlements in the West Bank and Gaza, in effect remixing populations that had been separated. Before the coming to power of the Likud party in 1977, most settlements were placed either just across the 1949–67 "Green Line" or as security outposts in remote areas. After 1977, however, the pace of construction accelerated, including placement of settlements deep in the midst of populated regions, most infamously the placement of four hundred Jews in the center of Hebron, a city of one hundred thousand Arabs. This generated a new security dilemma, both because the new settlements consumed more and more land and because provisions for their security required restricting freedom of movement among Arab towns.[83]

What Should Be Done?

Mutual security for Jews and Palestinians requires once again substantially separating the populations by removing those Jewish settlements furthest from Israel proper that cannot be maintained except by continuing military suppression of the Palestinians. This includes Hebron, the three settlements in Gaza, and dozens of others.

It is not necessary that all Jewish settlements be removed; many, which are sited directly across the Green Line from Israel proper and serve as suburbs to Jerusalem or to the coastal plain, could be incorporated into Israel without also including Arab population centers. Where populations are already separated it is easier to move borders than people.[84] Some might object to such a unilateral border adjustment on grounds of equity or law. It would, however, make both sides safer and might help them muster the political will to fully implement the 1993 Oslo peace agreement.

Cyprus

Critics of the 1974 de facto partition of Cyprus argue that, even though there have been virtually no casualties since then, the partition and population exchange have actually made the conflict worse, not better: "The division of Cyprus is little more than a long standoff that remains volatile and continues to require the presence of U.N. troops."[85]

In fact, however, the situation has remained remarkably stable since 1974. There have been only twelve deaths in ethnic strife on the island in twenty-four years.[86] This generation of calm compares starkly to the escalating ethnic violence on Cyprus from 1955 to 1974.

Did Partition Reduce Violence or Increase It?

Prior to 1960 Cyprus was under British rule; ethnically the population was approximately 80 percent Greek and 20 percent Turkish. In the 1950s the main Cypriot independence movement, EOKA, was a specifically Greek movement whose aim was union with metropolitan Greece (*enosis*). The Turkish community, fearing Greek domination, preferred continued colonial rule or, if independence could not be avoided, partition.[87]

The population settlement pattern on the island contributed to an intense security dilemma. Although most villages and "quarters" of major towns were populated exclusively by one group, Greek and Turkish settlements were spread throughout the island, with only a slight bias of Turkish concentration toward the north.[88]

As a result, from 1955 to 1974 Cyprus underwent four major rounds of civil war. First, starting in 1955, EOKA attacked British forces, Greek "collaborators" and communists, Turkish Cypriots serving in the British government and police, and, increasingly, the Turkish community at large; Turkish terrorist groups attacked Greek civilians. At least 509 people died before Britain granted independence in 1960.[89]

Second, although the new state's constitution incorporated power-sharing principles and prohibited enosis, Greek Cypriot leaders, including President Archbishop Makarios, continued to advocate Greek majority rule as well as enosis.[90] Governance was soon paralyzed by obstructive tactics of both sides, and in 1963 Greek Cypriots abrogated the constitution and established a new, all-Greek, government. In December 1963 civil war broke out again, and Greek forces soon controlled nearly the whole country, except for a few towns in the northern part of the island (see map 7.4). In August 1964 an offensive against the Turkish Cypriots' only remaining outlet to the sea was stopped by the Turkish air force. At least 550 died and 25,000 Turkish Cypriot refugees were resettled. From 1964 to 1968 most of the Turkish-held enclaves were under a de facto economic blockade.[91]

Third, after a military buildup by Greek Cypriot nationalists, including twelve thousand Greek army troops deployed on Cyprus as a deterrent to further Turkish interference, Greek Cypriot forces again attacked Turkish villages in April and in November 1967.[92] Turkey responded by threatening air strikes and troop landings. This time a U.S.- and UN-brokered deal led to withdrawal of the Greek army units, and in 1968 the movement restrictions on Turkish Cypriots were lifted. Deaths between 1964 and 1968 were probably about six hundred.[93] From 1968 to 1974 the sides conducted direct negotiations, but the Greek Cypriots would not give up the goal of enosis, and the Turks would not accept it.[94]

Finally, in 1971 a new Cypriot nationalist organization, EOKA B, which was supported by the military junta ruling in Athens, began terrorist attacks. On July 15, 1974, Makarios was overthrown in a bloody coup.[95] An unknown number of people, probably in the hundreds, were killed. Nicos Sampson, an ultrarightist infamous for heading massacres in 1963–64, was appointed president. A massive islandwide pogrom appeared imminent.[96]

Turkish forces then invaded Cyprus and overran 37 percent of the island, creating a Turkish-controlled zone in the north. Sampson's government collapsed, and Makarios resumed power. Approximately one thousand people, mostly Cypriot National Guard and Greek civilians, were killed in this operation, not many less than the death toll of the previous twenty years. The invasion, however, did save thousands who would likely have been murdered if men like Sampson had actually executed their program. Approximately two hundred thousand Greek refugees moved south of the line, and about

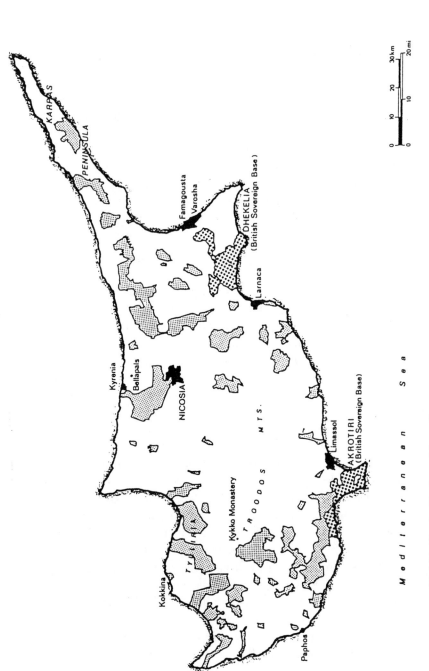

MAP 7.4. Turkish Cypriot Enclaves After 1967
Source: Pierre Oberling, *The Road to Bellepais: The Turkish Exodus to Northern Cyprus* (New York: Columbia University Press, 1982).

sixty thousand Turkish Cypriots moved north.[97] Even though the Turkish invasion was motivated in part by nationalist rather than humanitarian concerns, it saved lives; fortunately, we will never know just how many.

Did Partition Increase Hatred and Generate New Conflicts?

Greek Cypriots still have not accepted the partition of Cyprus, and no nation except Turkey recognizes the Turkish Republic of Northern Cyprus. Several rounds of negotiations have been held in which the Turks have offered to return some land or to reunite Cyprus as a loose federation, but these proposals have not been acceptable to the Greek side.

Despite the lack of reconciliation, the situation has remained calm as well as safe for a generation. Both sides know that the Turkish army garrison in the north could defeat any possible irredentist offensive, and neither side has shown any evidence of plans to try to disrupt the existing situation.

The Politics of Successor States

Critics of ethnic population transfers and partitions have overestimated the risks that these remedies pose to political development. There are two main issues: democratization and treatment of ethnic minorities.

The four partitions studied in this article have produced nine de jure or de facto successor states: the Republic of Ireland, Northern Ireland, India, Pakistan, Bangladesh, Israel, the Palestinian Authority, Cyprus, and the Turkish Republic of Northern Cyprus (TRNC). The degree to which the political institutions of these states qualify as democratic is most easily measured by the extent to which they hold periodic free elections that can alter the composition of the government and its policies, and whose results are not overturned by force, such as military coups.[98] Of the nine successor states, five (Ireland, Northern Ireland, India, Israel, and Cyprus) have political institutions that clearly meet democratic qualifications. Four (Pakistan, Bangladesh, the Palestinian Authority, and the TRNC) do not fully qualify, but even these states are not clearly less democratic than their prepartition predecessors, and all are at least as democratic as most of their neighbors.

Although Pakistan and Bangladesh have always had nominally democratic forms, each has been under military rule for slightly less than half the time since their respective dates of independence (Pakistan, from 1958–71 and 1977–88, and Bangladesh, from 1975–86). In comparison, British colonial rule in India had become, by the time of partition, largely democratic at the province level, though not at the national level and not in the princely states. Both Pakistan and Bangladesh have at least as strong democratic qualifications as any state in South, Southeast, Central Asia, or the Middle East except three: India and Israel (also partition successor states) and, arguably, Sri Lanka.

Although it did not emerge until after the 1993 Oslo Agreement, the Palestinian Authority can be considered a de facto successor state of the partition of the Palestine Mandate. While the authority has nominally democratic forms, it has not had a change of leadership and political expression is often suppressed. It does not, however, compare unfavorably with the British mandatory government, which had no representative institutions above the level of municipalities, or with other Arab states.[99] We could also ask whether the 1947 partition affected the political development of adjacent states that gained territory or absorbed refugees. There is little evidence that it did, as none of these states except Lebanon had democratic institutions either beforehand or afterward.[100]

The Turkish Republic of Northern Cyprus also has democratic forms but has never had a change of government. However, before partition in 1974, united, formally democratic Cyprus never had a change of government either and allowed no political role to the Turkish minority.[101] Compared with its neighbors around the Eastern Mediterranean, the democratic qualifications of the TRNC rank about average.

Even where there are democratic forms, we must also ask whether minorities are nevertheless effectively disenfranchised. Four of these nine successor states have significant minority populations. In the Republic of Ireland and in India minorities face no barriers to political participation, although the government of India has proscribed secessionist parties that threatened the territorial integrity of the state.

Arab citizens of Israel have faced significant repression, most severely in the first fifteen years after partition. While many formal discriminations have been lifted, until recently Arabs were barred from effective political influence by an informal understanding that parties dependent on Arab votes could not be part of a governing coalition.[102] In the last several years, however, this barrier has weakened. The Labor Party–led coalition that governed Israel from 1992 to 1996 depended on the support of two Arab parties, and Arab votes nearly decided the 1996 prime ministerial contest between Shimon Peres and Benjamin Netanyahu, in which Netanyahu led by 11 percent among Jewish voters but won the election by a margin of just 0.9 percent.[103]

In Northern Ireland Catholics faced few barriers to participation in national-level politics, but for five decades their influence on the province government and local bodies was reduced by gerrymandering, especially in the cities of Londonderry and Belfast as well as certain rural areas where Catholics were in the majority. In addition, a 1946 Representation of the People Bill disenfranchised certain categories of potential voters, disproportionately Catholics. These abuses were largely ended by the imposition of direct British rule in 1972.[104]

Although these restrictions on minority rights are serious, repression of ethnic minorities would likely have been worse in each case had partition and population transfers not occurred. Even if we imagine that it could have been possible in 1947 to construct a government of a united Palestine, which would have treated the Jewish minority more mildly than Arabs have fared in Israel, the Jewish community saw the prospect of Arab rule as so dangerous that it could have been imposed only by crushing their capacity to resist. Whatever tendencies toward tolerance such a government might have had initially would surely have been undermined by the violence and mutual security fears generated in the process of establishing control. The problem of the Protestants in a united Ireland would have been the same.[105]

Challenges for Separation and Partition

The analysis above suggests three lessons for management of ethnic civil wars. First, we need to identify the threshold of intergroup violence and mutual security threats beyond which we must resort to separation and partition, and we should set the threshold conservatively—no one wants to dissolve diverse societies, even deeply troubled ones, that have any hope of avoiding massive violence and attaining civil peace. The theory and evidence presented here can help us identify cases that are clearly over that threshold, but absent a fully developed theory of the causes of interethnic hostility in peacetime, we cannot know exactly where the true threshold may lie.

Even this limited knowledge, however, is of policy use. We should not fail to separate populations in cases that have already produced large-scale violence and intense security dilemmas, even if in some such cases we might later wish that we had acted sooner and in yet other cases we may not be able to decide whether to act.

Second, while the findings here do not suggest whether partitions of sovereignty should occur more frequently or less, they do imply that partition should never be done unless the national communities are already largely separate or will be separated at the same time. Partitions that do not unmix hostile populations actually increase violence, as in Northern Ireland, Kashmir, Palestine, and when Croatia and Bosnia seceded from Yugoslavia. Defensible boundaries are also essential; the UN partition plan for Palestine, which gave each side three disconnected patches, could only generate a bloody civil war.[106]

In all four cases discussed above, ethnic separation reduced violence. Where populations were largely separated to begin with, violence was much less intense than where they were tightly intermingled. When warring populations were separated, either by planned transfers or by ethnic cleansing, violence subsequently declined. Except in those regions where hostile communities remain mixed on the ground, all four cases have had less violence since partition than before, and all sides have lower expectations of future violence now than they did then.

Finally, the record of twentieth-century population transfers and partitions suggests major changes in how we treat refugees of ethnic wars. The international community should stop trying to prevent the movement of refugees away from threats of ethnic massacres and should instead support and safeguard their resettlement. The UNHCR's policy of bringing "safety to people, not people to safety" cannot be implemented in the midst of ethnic wars, and attempts to do so are likely to cost the lives of some of the people they are supposed to save. Concern that facilitation of refugee movements amounts to support for ethnic cleansing is misguided. Ethnic cleansing can only be stopped by an army on the ground strong enough to defeat the cleansers. Otherwise, making it harder for ethnic cleansers to expel their enemies only invites them to escalate to murder.

Similarly, the international community should stop pressing winners of ethnic wars to take back refugees from the other side and should stop pushing refugees to return when they fear for their lives if they do. After an ethnic war repatriating any substantial number of refugees back to territory controlled by the other group risks making control of that territory once again uncertain, re-creating the same security dilemma that helped escalate the conflict in the first place.[107]

NOTES

A version of this chapter was published in *International Security*, vol. 23, no. 2 (Fall 1998). The author's thanks are owed to Robert Art, Pauline Baker, John Mearsheimer, Robert Pape, Edward Rhodes, Jack Snyder, Monica Toft, Barbara Walter, Stephen Van Evera, and the members of the University of Chicago Program on

International Security and Policy for comments. Research for this article was supported in part by a grant from the United States Institute of Peace.

1. John J. Mearsheimer, "Shrink Bosnia to Save It," New York Times, March 31, 1993; Mearsheimer and Stephen W. Van Evera, "When Peace Means War," New Republic, December 18, 1995, pp. 16–21; Robert M. Hayden, "Schindler's Fate: Genocide, Ethnic Cleansing, and Population Transfers," Slavic Review, vol. 55, no. 4 (Winter 1996), pp. 740–742; Ivo H. Daalder, "Bosnia After SFOR: Options for Continued U.S. Engagement," Survival, vol. 39, no. 4 (Winter 1997–98), pp. 5–18; Robert A. Pape, "Partition: An Exit Strategy for Bosnia," Survival, vol. 39, no. 4 (Winter 1997–98), pp. 25–28; and Michael O'Hanlon, "Turning the Cease-fire Into Peace," Brookings Review, vol. 16, no. 1 (Winter 1998), pp. 41–44. In addition, some analysts who oppose partition of Bosnia admit that reintegration of the separated populations would be very difficult. See Charles G. Boyd, "Making Bosnia Work," Foreign Affairs, vol. 77, no. 1 (January/February 1998), pp. 42–55; Susan L. Woodward, "Avoiding Another Cyprus or Israel," Brookings Review, vol. 16, no. 1 (Winter 1998), pp. 41–44; and Jane M. O. Sharp, "Dayton Report Card," International Security, vol. 22, no. 3 (Winter 1997/98), p. 133. Flora Lewis, "Reassembling Yugoslavia," Foreign Policy, no. 98 (Spring 1995), argues that Bosnia could be reintegrated.

2. Barry R. Posen, "The Security Dilemma and Ethnic Conflict," in Michael E. Brown, ed., Ethnic Conflict and International Security (Princeton: Princeton University Press, 1993), pp. 103–124; Chaim D. Kaufmann, "Possible and Impossible Solutions to Ethnic Civil Wars," International Security, vol. 20, no. 4 (Spring 1996), pp. 136–175; Daniel L. Byman, "Divided They Stand: Lessons About Partition from Iraq and Lebanon," Security Studies, vol. 7, no. 1 (Autumn 1997), pp. 1–29. See also Myron S. Weiner, "Bad Neighbors, Bad Neighborhoods: An Inquiry Into the Causes of Refugee Flows," International Security, vol. 21, no. 1 (Summer 1996), pp. 37–38; and Clive J. Christie, "Partition, Separatism, and National Identity," Political Quarterly, vol. 63, no. 1 (January-March 1992), pp. 68–78. On why separation can resolve ethnic conflicts but not ideological civil wars, see Chaim D. Kaufmann, "Intervention in Ethnic and Ideological Civil Wars," Security Studies, vol. 6, no. 1 (Autumn 1996), pp. 62–103.

3. Radha Kumar, "The Troubled History of Partition," Foreign Affairs, vol. 76, no. 1 (January/February 1997), pp. 22–34.

4. Posen, "The Security Dilemma and Ethnic Conflict," pp. 108–111.

5. The processes of war, especially reports of real or imagined enemy atrocities, also harden ethnic identities and solidify hostility and mistrust, creating additional hard-to-counter threat perceptions even in excess of real threats, and this effect persists for a considerable time even after the end of large-scale fighting. Kaufmann, "Possible and Impossible Solutions," pp. 141–145, 150–151.

6. For additional types of proposed solutions for ethnic conflicts, see Donald L. Horowitz, "Making Moderation Pay," in Joseph V. Montville, ed., *Conflict and Peacemaking in Multiethnic Societies* (New York: Lexington, 1991), pp. 451–476; Arend J. Lijphart, "The Power-Sharing Approach," in ibid., pp. 491–510; Gidon Gottlieb, *Nation Against State* (New York: Council on Foreign Relations, 1993); I. William Zartman, "Putting Things Back Together," in I. William Zartman, ed. *Collapsed States: The Disintegration and Restoration of Legitimate Authority* (Boulder: Rienner, 1995), pp. 267–273. For an analysis that focuses on perceptual rather than structural aspects of intergroup security dilemmas, and recommends solutions based on institution and confidence building, see David A. Lake and Donald Rothchild, "Containing Fear: The Origins and Management of Ethnic Conflict," *International Security*, vol. 21, no. 1 (Fall 1996), pp. 41–75.

7. Although in principle final political arrangements could be based on either regional autonomy or separate sovereignty, in practice demographic separation is likely to be accompanied by partition, for three reasons. First, one side will often insist on partition. Second, whenever the international community intervenes to facilitate population transfers, it will need to specify partition lines, whether these are between what are to become autonomous provinces or between independent states. Third, because international law favors sovereign states, granting sovereignty will usually improve a group's ability to maintain its security.

8. UNHCR, "Working Document for the Humanitarian Issues Working Group of the International Conference on the former Yugoslavia" (New York: UNHCR, 1992). According to former UN Secretary General Boutros Boutros-Ghali: "The new danger which will appear in the world in the next ten years is more fragmentation. . . . We will not be able to achieve any kind of economic development, not to mention more disputes on boundaries." "UN Chief Fears World Could Split into 400 Mini-States," *Montreal Gazette*, September 21, 1992. On international practice toward secession movements, see Lee C. Buchheit, *Secession: The Legitimacy of Self-Determination* (New Haven: Yale University Press, 1978).

9. Robert Schaeffer, *Warpaths: The Politics of Partition* (New York: Hill and Wang, 1990); Amitai Etzioni, "The Evils of Self-Determination," *Foreign Policy*, no. 89 (Winter 1992–93), pp. 21–35; Gidon Gottlieb, "Nations Without States," *Foreign Affairs*, vol. 73, no. 3 (May/June 1994), pp. 100–112; Kumar, "The Troubled History of Partition."

10. Additional criticisms of partition and population transfers include claims that they damage prospects for future economic growth and that international support for one instance creates a "moral hazard" encouraging proliferation of secession movements. These issues are considered in Kaufmann, "Possible and Impossible Solutions," pp. 170–173.

11. The claims of both sides in this debate about effects on political development are best understood as "other things being equal," since political development is also affected by numerous nonethnic factors, such as economic development, income distribution, preexisting political institutions, etc.

12. I define partitions as separations jointly decided upon by the responsible powers: either agreed between the two sides (and not under pressure of imminent military victory by one side) or imposed on both sides by a stronger third party. Secessions are new states created by the unilateral action of a rebellious ethnic group.

We could study ethnic population transfers between states to see whether they reduce subsequent interstate violence. Indeed, the records of the two largest ethnic population transfers in twentieth-century Europe—the Greco-Bulgarian-Turkish population exchanges in the 1920s and the expulsion of ethnic Germans from Eastern Europe after World War II—suggest that they may. Each of these exchanges was preceded by a series of wars that cost many times more lives than the population transfers did, and each has been followed by interstate peace.

13. The following discussions pay special attention to the roles of the minority communities in each case, since it is usually minorities who are most concerned about their group's security and who press hardest for partition.

14. Alan J. Ward, *The Easter Rising* (Arlington Heights, Ill.: AHM, 1980), p. 13.

15. Hughes, *Ireland Divided*, p. 49; and Ward, *Easter Rising*, p. 126.

16. J. J. Lee, *Ireland, 1912–1985: Politics and Society* (Cambridge: Cambridge University Press, 1989), p. 69.

17. Patrick Buckland, *Ulster Unionism and the Origins of Northern Ireland* (Dublin: Gill and Macmillan, 1973), p. 176; and Charles Townshend, *The British Campaign in Ireland, 1919–1921* (London: Oxford University Press, 1975), p. 342.

18. 1911 Census, reported in Buckland, *Ulster Unionism*, pp. 179–180.

19. Ibid.

20. Buckland, *Ulster Unionism*, p. 176; D. G. Pringle, *One Island, Two Nations?* (Letchworth, U.K.: Research Studies, 1985), pp. 239–242; and Frank Gallagher, *The Indivisible Island* (London: Victor Gollancz, 1957), pp. 225–265.

21. J. Bowyer Bell, *The Secret Army, 1916–1970* (New York: John Day, 1971), pp. 29–66; and Dennis Kennedy, *The Widening Gulf: Northern Attitudes to the Independent Irish State, 1919–49* (Belfast: Blackstaff, 1988), pp. 72–77.

22. In the June 1922 election the most extreme nationalist party, De Valera's faction of Sinn Fein, gained only 36 seats versus 92 others, but even De Valera did not favor prompt action against Northern Ireland. The IRA was not united either; an emergency convention in June voted narrowly against rebellion. Bell, *The Secret Army*, pp. 30–34.

23. When in March 1914 the British government attempted to deploy troops to reinforce arms depots in Ulster, most of the officers who received the orders mutinied. War Minister J. E. B. Seely, Army Chief of Staff Sir Henry Wilson,

and Army Commander-in-Chief Sir John French sided with the mutineers, assuring them that force would not be used against Ulster. When ordered to withdraw this promise, Seely and French resigned, leading to a threat of mass res-
ignations by military officers. At this point there was a real risk of a complete
split in the British Army. Elizabeth A. Muenger, *The British Military Dilemma
in Ireland: Occupation Politics, 1886–1914* (Lawrence: University Press of Kan-
sas, 1991), pp. 168–172, 188–191; Hughes, *Ireland Divided*, pp. 34–36.

24. Buckland, *Ulster Unionism*, p. 64; Townshend, *Political Violence*, p. 343; and
    Gallagher, *The Indivisible Island*.
25. John F. Galliher and Jerry L. DeGregory, *Violence in Northern Ireland: Under-
    standing Protestant Perspectives* (New York: Holmes and Meier, 1985), p. 10.
    Despite class, rural-city, and other cleavages within the Ulster Protestant com-
    munity, Unionism commanded absolutely solid support. In 1910 all Protestant-
    majority districts in Ulster elected Unionist MPs. Buckland, *Ulster Unionism*,
    frontispiece, pp. 22–34, 179–180.
26. Townshend, *Political Violence*, pp. 252–255; and Muenger, *The British Military
    Dilemma*, pp. 177.
27. Hughes, *Ireland Divided*, p. 35.
28. Townshend, *British Campaign in Ireland*, pp. 189–192; and Sheila Lawlor,
    Britain and Ireland, 1914–1923 (Dublin: Gill and Macmillan, 1983), pp. 85–86.
29. In 1991 82 percent were prepared to postpone union if that would help bring
    about an internal settlement in the North. Market Research Bureau of Ireland,
    reported in Gemma Hussey, *Ireland Today* (London: Viking, 1993), pp. 186–
    188. In a 1996 poll only 38 percent in the Republic supported unification. Carl
    Homore, "Desire for Union Now a Need for Peace," *Houston Chronicle*, Sep-
    tember 22, 1996.
30. Richard W. Mansbach, ed., *Northern Ireland: Half a Century of Partition* (New
    York: Facts on File, 1973).
31. Joseph Ruane and Jennifer Todd, *The Dynamics of Conflict in Northern Ireland:
    Power, Conflict, and Emancipation* (Cambridge: Cambridge University Press,
    1996), p. 1.
32. *Ireland: Statistical Abstract, 1995*, pp. 55, 409.
33. "Dublin Parliament Poised for Peace Poll Go-Ahead, *Press Association*, April
    21, 1998; and Frank Millar, "Blair and Trimble Appeal to Undecided Union-
    ists," *Irish Times*, May 21, 1998.
34. Lawlor, *Britain and Ireland*, pp. 124–126; and D. W. Harkness, *Ireland in the
    Twentieth Century: Divided Island* (New York: St. Martin's, 1996), pp. 34–37.
35. A Boundary Commission operated from 1924 to 1925, but was limited to rec-
    ommending only very minor changes, which were in any case not implemented.
    Report of the Irish Boundary Commission, 1925 (Shannon: Irish University Press,
    1969). A better partition would have given the Unionists all of counties Antrim
    and Londonderry, much but not all of Down, Armagh, and Tyrone, and a few

small bits of Monaghan, Fermanagh, and Donegal. The large Catholic-majority region spanning Londonderry and Tyrone (see map 7.1) is mountainous and was thinly settled.

36. Paul R. Brass, *Language, Religion, and Politics in North India* (London: Cambridge University Press, 1974); Mushirul Hasan, *Nationalism and Communal Politics in India, 1916–1928* (Columbia, Mo.: South Asia, 1979); Gyanendra Pandey, *The Construction of Communalism in Colonial North India* (Delhi: Oxford University Press, 1990); and Milton Israel, *Communications and Power: Propaganda and the Press in the Indian Nationalist Struggle, 1920–1947* (Cambridge: Cambridge University Press, 1994).

37. The Hindu-Muslim security dilemma was most severe in the belt of North India where the percentage of Muslims ranged from 20 percent to 60 percent. In the South, where Muslim minorities were quite small, intergroup security dilemmas were weak and communal mobilization and violence remained low before, during, and after partition.

38. *Census of India, 1931*, vol. 1, part I (Delhi: Manager of Publications, 1933), p. 392.

39. H. V. Hodson, *The Great Divide: Britain-India-Pakistan* (Oxford: Oxford University Press, 1985), p. 59. Moonje argued that Hindus should negotiate with Muslims only from a position of strength and that Gandhi's philosophy of non-violence "will lead to destruction and extermination of the Hindus from the face of the world." Letter, March 16, 1922, cited in Mushirul Hasan, "Communalist and Revivalist Trends in Congress," in Mushirul Hasan, ed., *Communal and Pan-Islamic Trends in Colonial India* (Delhi: Manohar, 1985), p. 206. According to Jawarlhalal Nehru, many a congressman "was a communalist under his national cloak." Jawaharlal Nehru, *An Autobiography* (London, 1936), p. 136.

40. Jinnah also called for one-third of the seats in the central legislature and a 75 percent majority requirement for action by the legislature. Although Jinnah did not dominate Muslim politics until much later, a wider meeting of a number of Muslim groups in 1927 had agreed on a similar program, as had another such meeting in 1925. V. P. Menon, *The Transfer of Power in India* (Princeton: Princeton University Press, 1957), pp. 36–37; Uma Kaura, *Muslims and Indian Nationalism* (Columbia, Mo.: South Asia Books, 1977), pp. 29–30; and R. J. Moore, *The Crisis of Indian Unity, 1917–1940* (Oxford: Clarendon Press, 1974), pp. 24–25.

41. Aga Khan at the Second Round Table Conference, London, 1931, reported in Kaura, *Muslims and Indian Nationalism*, pp. 72–73.

42. Moore, *Crisis of Indian Unity*, pp. 101–104; Kaura, *Muslims and Indian Nationalism*, pp. 42–51; R. Coupland, *The Indian Problem: Report on the Constitutional Problem in India* (New York: Oxford University Press, 1944), vol. 2, p. 125; and Hasan, "Communalist and Revivalist Trends in Congress," p. 210.

43. Congress swept most of the country, gaining control of seven provinces. Subsequently, it took the position that it represented all Indian nationalists, so its

own Muslim members, not Jinnah or others, were the true arbiters of Muslim opinion and interests. Actually, however, it contested only 58 of 482 Muslim seats and won just 26, 19 of these in Northwest Frontier Province based on Pathan protest votes against Punjabi political dominance. Hodson, *The Great Divide*, pp. 66–72; *Return Showing the Results of the Elections of 1937*, Cmd. 5589, cited in Coupland, *Indian Problem*, pp. 15–16, 121–123.

44. Rajendra Prasad, *India Divided* (Bombay: Hind Kitabs, 1946), pp. 146–152; and Stanley Wolpert, *Jinnah of Pakistan* (New York: Oxford University Press, 1984), pp. 164–169.
45. Kaura, *Muslims and Indian Nationalism*, pp. 128–129.
46. In 1946 elections the Muslim League won all the Muslim seats in the central assembly. In the Punjab legislature the Muslim League won 79 of 86 Muslim seats, while the intercommunal Punjab Unionist Party declined from 99 seats in 1937 to 18, two of whom immediately defected to the Muslim League. E. W. R. Lumby, *The Transfer of Power in India, 1942–47* (London: George Allen and Unwin, 1954), pp. 69, 145–148.
47. Ibid., pp. 162–164.
48. *Census of India, 1931*, vol. 1, part 1, pp. 387, 392; *Census of India, 1941*. Prior to 1927 Sikhs were 24 percent of the electorate and held 18 percent of the seats in the provincial council. Sikhs also maintained special claims to Punjab on grounds that they provided a disproportionate share of the province's revenue, that it contained all their important religious sites, and that Sikhs had been the last rulers of the region before the British. Anup Chand Kapur, *The Punjab Crisis* (New Delhi: S. Chand, 1985), pp. 39, 43.
49. Sikhism was transformed from a purely religious movement to a distinct militant community in response to Muslim rule, and Sikhs fought 250 years of almost continuous war against Muslim princes from about 1600 until the British take-over in 1849. Sikh rulers of the Punjab were still remembered in the twentieth century for harsh repression of their Muslim subjects. Sikh troops also helped suppress Muslim rebels during the Sepoy Mutiny in 1857–58. Kapur, *The Punjab Crisis*, pp. 6–9; and Hodson, *The Great Divide*, pp. 18–20.
50. Sikh tradition requires males to carry a ceremonial dagger at all times and to take up arms when necessary to defend righteousness. Sikhs also comprised a greatly disproportionate fraction of the Indian army, 13 percent in 1930, compared to slightly more than 1 percent of the population. Kapur, *The Punjab Crisis*, p. 7, notes 9, 10, p. 20, note 47.
51. Kapur, *The Punjab Crisis*, pp. 51, 98, 111.
52. Kapur, *The Punjab Crisis*; Satya M. Rai, *Partition of the Punjab* (New York: Asia Publishing House, 1965), pp. 37–38; and Lumby, *The Transfer of Power in India*, pp. 185–186.
53. This agitation was sparked by a government attempt in January to disarm the Muslim National Guards. Ian Talbot, *Khizr Tiwana, the Punjab Unionist Party, and the Partition of India* (Surrey: Curzon, 1996), pp. 68, 148, 154–161.

54. This violence was partly sparked by Sikh leader Master Tara Singh's calls in the provincial assembly on March 4 for "Death to Pakistan" and "The pure shall rule; no resister will remain." Moon, *Divide and Quit*, p. 77. The police in Lahore and Amritsar, who were mostly Muslim, were not effective. Violence also spread to Muslim-majority areas in Western Punjab, in turn followed by attacks on Muslims in Southeastern Punjab. Ian Talbot, *Punjab and the Raj* (Riverdale, Md.: Riverdale, 1988), pp. 227–228; Rai, *Partition of the Punjab*, p. 83, note 25; and Anita Inder Singh, *The Origins of the Partition of India, 1936–1947* (Delhi: Oxford University Press, 1987), pp. 218–220.

55. Singh, *The Origins of Partition*, pp. 205–206; and Lumby, *The Transfer of Power in India*, p. 186. In June a last attempt to mediate between the Muslim League and the Sikh leadership by moderate Muslim League leader Nawab Mushtaq Achmad Gurmani was disavowed by Jinnah. Moon, *Divide and Quit*, pp. 82–87. According to Moon, Jinnah had frequently threatened the Sikhs that division of Punjab would not be in their interest, but had never encouraged them on their prospects in Pakistan. See also Kapur, *The Punjab Crisis*, pp. 94–95.

56. This was the only organized Sikh party, holding 22 of 33 Sikh seats in the Punjab assembly. Talbot, *Punjab and the Raj*, p. 227; Rai, *Partition of the Punjab*, p. 40; and Kapur, *The Punjab Crisis*, p. 50.

57. By June the Hindu RSSS had 58,000 men and the Muslim League National Guards 39,000. Talbot, *Punjab and the Raj*, pp. 232–233. At the end of March the superintendent of police in Delhi predicted that "once a line of division is drawn in the Punjab all Sikhs to the West of it and all Muslims to the east of it will have their _____ chopped off." Quoted in Moon, *Divide and Quit*, pp. 87–88. The previous governor of Punjab had begun predicting civil war as early as 1945. Wolpert, *Jinnah of Pakistan*, p. 249.

58. Talbot, *Punjab and the Raj*, p. 232; Hodson, *The Great Divide*, p. 338.

59. Although, in the end, this fighting did not affect the final partition line, it appears that Sikh forces did temporarily occupy some locations west of the partition line. Talbot, *Punjab and the Raj*, pp. 233–234; *The Sikhs in Action* (Lahore: Superintendent of Government Printing, 1948); and Moon, *Divide and Quit*, pp. 151–152.

60. Moon's judgment is that the Sikhs were deliberately making room for two million refugees from Pakistan. *Divide and Quit*, pp. 279–280.

61. Hodson, *The Great Divide*, p. 411; and Moon, *Divide and Quit*, pp. 122, 281.

62. Kapur, *The Punjab Crisis*, pp. 149–183. This did not end conflict over the scope of Sikh autonomy, which flared into violence again between 1980 and 1992.

63. In many areas police and officials of the "wrong" community fled, further reducing restraints on pogroms. Menon, *The Transfer of Power in India*, pp. 419–23; Hodson, *The Great Divide*, p. 406; and Lumby, *The Transfer of Power in India*, pp. 193–195.

64. The number of deaths is disputed. Hodson estimates two hundred thousand, Moon less than two hundred thousand. Lumby says "hundreds of thousands," an Indian High Court judge later estimated five hundred thousand, and the Pakistani government claimed more than five hundred thousand Muslims alone. Kumar says that more than a million died. Hodson, *The Great Divide*, p. 418; Moon, *Divide and Quit*, pp. 268–69, 293; Lumby, *The Transfer of Power in India*, p. 199; *Sikhs in Action*, foreword; Kumar, "The Troubled History of Partition," p. 26.

65. Congress agreed to "communal option" for officials but maintained that the general population throughout the country should stay where they were. Rai, *Partition of the Punjab*, pp. 73–75.

66. Hodson, *The Great Divide*, p. 412; Rai, *Partition of the Punjab*, p. 79; and Moon, *Divide and Quit*, pp. 278–279.

67. Barry Posen provides a formula that can be used to estimate the number of troops needed to protect a refugee movement, in this case roughly 250,000. Posen, "Military Responses to Refugee Flows," *International Security*, vol. 21, no. 1 (Summer 1996), p. 106, note 51.

68. Although accounts are incomplete, it appears that total deaths in intercommunal violence in India in 1946–47 not directly related to the Punjab civil war may have been about twenty thousand. Suranjan Das, *Communal Riots in Bengal, 1905–1947* (Delhi: Oxford University Press, 1993), pp. 167–205; Francis Tuker, *While Memory Serves* (London: Cassel, 1950), pp. 424–426; *Keesing's Contemporary Archives*, January 17–24, 1948, p. 9049; Menon, *The Transfer of Power in India*, pp. 294, 434–445; Lumby, *The Transfer of Power in India*, pp. 120–122.

69. Majid Husain, *Geography of Jammu and Kashmir State* (New Delhi: Rajesh, 1987), p. 54.

70. Sumit Ganguly, *The Origins of War in South Asia: Indo-Pakistani Conflicts Since 1947* (Boulder: Westview, 1994), pp. 34–35, 42.

71. Alastair Lamb, *Kashmir: A Disputed Legacy, 1846–1990* (Hertingfordbury, U.K.: 1991), pp. 131–136; and Ganguly, *The Origins of War in South Asia*, pp. 13–14.

72. The arrival in 1983 of Muslim refugees from a massacre in Assam and the assault in 1984 by Indian forces on the Sikh Golden temple in Amritsar did not help either. Sumit Ganguly, *Between War and Peace: Crisis in Kashmir*, pp. 76–90; and Lamb, *Kashmir*, pp. 327–330.

73. Ganguly, *Between War and Peace*, pp. 107–108, 133, 152–156; "India and Pakistan Plan Kashmir Talks," *New York Times*, June 24, 1997. In 1998, in the first free elections in the Kashmir in nearly two decades, the antiseparatist National Conference won 4 of 6 seats, while turnout was low because of a boycott called by Muslim separatists. Surinder Oberoi, "Three Die and Twelve Abducted during Kashmir Elections," *AAP Information Services*, March 1, 1998; and "Betrayal in Jammu and Kashmir," *Hindu*, April 5, 1998.

74. Ganguly, *The Origins of War in South Asia*, p. 58.

75. Myron Weiner, *Sons of the Soil: Migration and Ethnic Conflict in India* (Princeton: Princeton University Press, 1978).

76. *Reuters World Service*, January 28, 1995; and *Reuters North American Wire*, April 28, 1997.

77. Chaim D. Herzog, *The Arab-Israeli Wars* (New York: Random House, 1982), p. 108; Walid Khalidi, *All That Remains: The Palestinian Villages Occupied and Depopulated by Israel in 1948* (Washington, D.C.: Institute for Palestine Studies, 1982), p. 582; and Joseph P. Schechtman, *The Refugee in the World*, p. 262.

78. The plan divided Palestine into eight parts: three main Jewish and three main Arab enclaves, meeting at two points in such a way that none of the Jewish or Arab enclaves were contiguous. A seventh small Arab enclave (the city of Jaffa) was surrounded by Jewish territory and the eighth ("internationalized" Jerusalem) by Arab territory. T. G. Fraser, *Partition in Ireland, India, and Palestine* (New York: St. Martin's, 1984), pp. 177–183.

79. British District Police Reports, April 26 and 28, 1948, cited in Schechtman, *Refugee in the World*, p. 191.

80. Benny Morris, "Operation Dani and the Palestinian Exodus from Lydda and Ramle in 1948," *Middle East Journal*, vol. 40, no. 1 (Winter 1986), pp. 82–109.

81. Jewish terrorists not under government discipline carried out an even more brutal cleansing operation at the village of Deir Yassin, which also overlooks the Jersualem road.

82. Howard M. Sachar, *A History of Israel* (New York: Knopf, 1979), pp. 382, 395.

83. Ze'ev Schiff and Ehud Ya'ari, *Intifada: The Palestinian Uprising—Israel's Third Front* (New York: Simon and Schuster, 1989); and Geoffrey Aronson, *Creating Facts: Israel, Palestinians, and the West Bank* (Washington, D.C.: Institute for Palestine Studies, 1987).

84. Alexander B. Downes, "The Holy Land Divided? Theory and Practice for a Successful Partition of Palestine," unpublished manuscript, suggests that Jews now living in the West Bank exchange places with the Palestinians of Gaza. This seems to me excessive.

85. Kumar, "The Troubled History of Partition," p. 29. Kumar further claims that there was a war scare between Greece and Turkey over Cyprus as recently as August 1996, but this actually amounted to no more than some moderately warm rhetoric by Greek Prime Minister Costas Simitis, plus Turkish protests about attacks on three consulates. See Michele Kambas, "Greek PM Slams Turkey on Arrival in Cyprus," *Reuters European Community Report*, August 17, 1996.

86. Five in 1975, two between 1989 and 1993, and five in 1996. "List of Deaths on Green Line since 1974," *Agence France-Presse*, August 11, 1996; Patrick Baz, *Agence France Presse*, August 14, 1996; and Michele Kambas, *Reuters World Service*, October 15, 1996.

87. Nancy Cranshaw, *The Cyprus Revolt: An Account of the Struggle for Union with Greece* (London: George Allen and Unwin, 1978), pp. 42–50, 62–67, 71–75;

Christopher Hitchens, *Hostage to History: Cyprus from the Ottoman Empire to Kissinger* (New York: Farrar, Straus, and Giroux, 1989), pp. 42–46; Tozun Bahcheli, *Greek-Turkish Relations Since 1955* (Boulder: Westview, 1990), pp. 28–30.

88. Richard A. Patrick, *Political Geography and the Cyprus Conflict: 1963–1971* (Waterloo, Ontario: University of Waterloo, 1976), pp. 8–11.

89. British official figures, reported in Cranshaw, *The Cyprus Revolt*, p. 406.

90. Makarios was, however, prepared to be patient on the latter, since he did not want to provoke Turkish intervention. Cranshaw, *The Cyprus Revolt*, pp. 341–345, 366–367; P. N. Vanezis, *Makarios: Pragmatism Versus Idealism* (London: Abelard Schuman, 1974), pp. 123–133; and Stanley Mayes, *Makarios: A Biography* (New York: St. Martin's, 1981), pp. 159–166.

91. Patrick, *Political Geography and the Cyprus Conflict*, p. 46; and Cranshaw, *The Cyprus Revolt*, pp. 367–373. The presence of seven thousand UN peacekeepers during the latter part of the fighting had little effect.

92. Makarios's personal interest in enosis waned after the April 1967 military coup in Athens, but he felt unable to oppose the projects of Greek Cypriot nationalists, which commanded great popularity. In 1970 he barely survived a nationalist assassination attempt. Mayes, *Makarios*, pp. 183–186, 206–207.

93. Hitchens, *Hostage to History*, p. 65; Bahcheli, *Greek-Turkish Relations*, pp. 73–74, 173; and Patrick, *Political Geography and the Cyprus Conflict*, p. 119.

94. For details of the negotiations and internal politics of the sides, see Polyvios G. Polyviou, *Cyprus: Conflict and Negotiation, 1960–1980* (New York: Holmes and Meier, 1980), pp. 62–132; and Bahcheli, *Greek-Turkish Relations*, pp. 89, 167, 175–188.

95. Although EOKA B was an illegal organization, it enjoyed great popular support among Greek Cypriots, including much of the Cypriot National Guard. The funeral in January 1974 of its founder, General George Grivas, was attended by one-fifth of the entire Greek population. Polyviou, *Cyprus*, pp. 120–130; and Pierre Oberling, *The Road to Bellepais: The Turkish Cypriot Exodus to Northern Cyprus* (New York: Columbia University Press, 1982), pp. 149–150.

96. Sampson was elected to the Greek Cypriot House of Representatives in 1969 on the slogan "Death to the Turks!" Oberling, *The Road to Bellepais*, p. 160. According to Makarios, Sampson and the head of the Athens junta in 1974, General Ioannides, had come to see him back in 1964 and proposed: "Your Beatitude, here is my project. To attack the Turkish Cypriots suddenly, everywhere on the island, and eliminate them to the last one." Quoted in Orianna Fallaci, *Interview with History* (New York: Liveright, 1976), p. 318.

97. Cranshaw, *The Cyprus Revolt* p. 395; and Polyviou, *Cyprus*, p. 203.

98. Samuel P. Huntington, *The Third Wave: Democratization in the Late Twentieth Century* (Norman: University of Oklahoma Press, 1991), pp. 5–13.

99. A British plan in the 1920s to create a legislature was blocked by Arab opposition. Bernard Wasserstein, *The British in Palestine: The Mandatory Government and the Arab-Jewish Conflict, 1917–1929* (Cambridge, Mass.: Basil Blackwell, 1978).

100. The presence of refugees from Palestine had some impact on the civil war from 1975 onward, although the main cause of the war was tensions between the native Christian, Sunni, and Shiite populations. David Gilmour, *Lebanon, the Fractured Country* (New York: St. Martin's, 1984).

101. Since 1974 the (Greek) rump state of Cyprus has had several changes of government in free elections. Eric Solsten, *Cyprus: A Country Study* (Washington, D.C.: Government Printing Office, 1993).

102. Ian Lustick, *Arabs in the Jewish State: Israel's Control of a National Minority* (Austin: University of Texas Press, 1980).

103. "Rabin Meets Hadash, DAP Representatives; Shas Hints at Abstention Tomorrow," *Jerusalem Post*, November 9, 1993; "Netanyahu Wins Israeli Election," *Associated Press*, May 31, 1996.

104. Schaeffer, *Warpaths*, pp. 166–167.

105. Critics also charge that partition successor states discriminate against minorities through citizenship and language laws, for example Israel's Law of Return, which grants automatic citizenship to Jewish immigrants, and its 1950 Absentee Property Law, which bars the return of Arabs who left the country during the 1947–49 war. However, official languages, citizenship laws, or immigration practices that favor the majority are actually features of most nation-states, including such liberal democracies such as Norway, Denmark, Sweden, Germany, France, and Italy.

106. Existing administrative unit boundaries are often given excessive weight, as in Kashmir in 1947 and Ulster in 1921. See Steven R. Ratner, "Drawing a Better Line: *Uti Possidetis* and the Borders of New States," *American Journal of International Law*, vol. 90, no. 4 (October 1996), pp. 590–624.

107. The severity of this risk depends on the robustness of the winning side's territorial control. Nigeria could afford to reabsorb refugees of the Biafran War because the war's decisive outcome meant that there was little chance of a new revolt. The Republika Srpska, which is far more fragile, cannot. International demands that the Rwandan Patriotic Front (RPF) accept the return of more than two million Hutu refugees placed the RPF in an impossible position. Because the RPF represented less than 10 percent of the population, it could not claim legitimacy if it refused repatriation, but the return of large numbers of Hutus, including adherents of the former government, was bound to lead to a new round of civil war, and did. "Hutu Rebels Terrorize Three Nations; The Slaughter Continues," *International Herald Tribune*, January 29, 1998.

8 The Rationality of Fear: Political Opportunism and Ethnic Conflict

Rui J. P. de Figueiredo Jr. and Barry R. Weingast

The appeal to nation is made by politicians in terms of arguments about survival in which the fate of the individual depends on the fate of the group, and the role of the group and its leaders is protection. . . . Fear of becoming a minority is exactly what is motivating the people to fight.

Susan L. Woodward, "Intervention in Civil Wars:
Bosnia and Herzegovina"

Introduction

Students of violent ethnic conflict commonly attribute a prominent role to extremist, even genocidal, leaders who incite citizens into a violent frenzy. Many further argue that leaders do so as a means of remaining in power (Brown 1996; David 1997; Mansfield and Snyder 1995). Following a Rikerian line of "heresthetics," these arguments hold that leaders use violent conflict as a means of transforming politics from an issue on which they are likely to lose power into one on which they can retain power (Riker 1980).

What these accounts fail to explain, however, is why citizens participate in such megalomaniac visions. Without the support of their constituencies, leaders who attempt to initiate ethnic terror could not succeed. Our central question is, Why do citizens whose primary interest is in peace choose to support bloody ethnic wars?

Posen (1993) advances an important argument about the origins of ethnic conflict. The security dilemma, long a staple of international relations theory (e.g., Jervis 1978; Waltz 1979), suggests that many ethnic groups, like states, fear for their survival. The spiral dynamic (Jervis 1976), whereby mutual interaction sets off reciprocal fears that spiral into war, seems to describe many instances of ethnic violence. According to Posen, the collapse of the state creates conditions of anarchy and hence the security dilemma for groups. When combined with advantages for the attacker and primordial or historical hatreds and conflict, violence is likely to erupt.

Although Posen's argument represents a useful starting point, it does not constitute a full explanation of ethnic violence. First, the collapse of the state is often coincident with and the product of the move toward ethnic violence, not a process antecedent to ethnic violence (Lake and Rothchild 1996). Second, although most ethnic groups face a security dilemma, the spiral dynamic occurs only occasionally. As Fearon and Laitin (1996) demonstrate, journalists and scholars focusing on violent conflict greatly exaggerate its incidence (see also David 1997). Investigating two areas commonly cited as cauldrons of ethnic conflict, the former Soviet Union and Africa, Fearon and Laitin find that widespread conflict occurs in only a fraction of the potential cases.[1] Even in states that erupt into violence the security dilemma is present all along; yet violence—brutal and horrifying as it is—typically remains episodic, concentrated in relatively narrow time periods. Finally, as we focus on in this paper, the security dilemma is not sufficient in and of itself to explain the conditions under which hawkish leaders or subgroups succeed in garnering the support of an often reticent public audience that typically prefers peace to violence. The security dilemma and spiral dynamic alone cannot explain when and why ethnic conflict occurs. We attempt to supplement the existing discussion by exploring additional necessary conditions for ethnic conflict.

Understanding the ethnification of politics requires addressing two fundamental puzzles, one economic and one political (Weingast 1998). The *fundamental economic puzzle* of ethnification concerns its huge costs. Individuals and groups locked in these struggles forgo the enormous benefits of economic and social cooperation in favor of bitter violence and hardship. Why do citizens take actions leading to this negative-sum outcome? The *fundamental political puzzle* of ethnification concerns its timing. How do we explain the often sudden eruption of ethnic violence, especially when it follows a long period of peace? Addressing this puzzle requires three components: an explanation of the period of quiescence, the timing of violence, and why violence erupts so suddenly, often in full force in a very short period. Although the literature on ethnic politics is voluminous and provides considerable insight into the ethnification of politics, it fails to provide a satisfactory answer to either fundamental puzzle.

To build our explanation of ethnic violence we rely on game theory. The hallmark of rational choice theory for explaining macrosocial failure is its approach to social dilemmas of cooperation. In a variety of circumstances individually rational actions produce socially irrational outcomes (Axelrod 1984; Elster 1989; Hardin 1995; Taylor 1976). We draw on the tradition of social dilemmas to construct our argument.

In our approach three factors interact to produce ethnic violence: leaders with a tenuous hold on power, fear among the citizenry, and uncertainty about the true intentions of propagators of violence. Students of ethnic violence commonly cite the first two factors as important. Further, many have commented on how leaders can create self-fulfilling prophecies in order to confirm citizen's fears (Jervis 1976; Van Evera 1994). In this paper we build a model that incorporates all three effects. By explicating the mechanisms that allow some leaders to induce citizen fear, we demonstrate the critical role of the third factor of ambiguity in understanding the link between a leader's claims and the rising fear among citizens.

Leaders who face a high risk of losing power often pursue a strategy we call *gambling for resurrection*, an attempt to maintain power by inducing massive change in the environment that has only a small chance of succeeding.[2] For leaders who have failed in the normal course of politics, gambling for resurrection offers the hope of forestalling loss of power. This strategy may have large costs, but these costs are borne by the citizenry, not by the leader. And, if the strategy works, the leader remains in power.

A leader's attempt to gamble for resurrection does not automatically succeed, however. If it did, no leader would lose power. To succeed, gambling for resurrection must somehow engage the average citizen. But when and why does it work?

As many observers point out, the answer lies in fear: citizens are willing to support extreme ends when they fear for their lives, livelihoods, and families. Jervis (1978) notes, for example, that a state or polity's "subjective security demands"—and thus, presumably, its willingness to support less capable but more aggressive leaders—will increase as perceptions of an external threat increase. The literature on elite manipulation has suggested some reasons for this result. Gagnon (1995), for example, argues that appeals for support must entail messages laden by material and nonmaterial values.

Others have argued that monopoly control of the media is a primary force for fomenting nationalist fervor. While agreeing with this focus, we attempt to further enhance the point made by Snyder and Ballentine. As they point out, "[In Yugoslavia] . . . media monopoly merely gave elites in the republics the tools to sell nationalist myths. The motive and the opportunity were created by the Serbian elite's fear of democratization, by the plausibility of these myths to consumers in a segmented market and by the unevenness of journalistic standards" (1996:29). Indeed, one limitation of the existing literature is that it fails to explain cases in which—in Fearon and Laitin terms—such appeals fail, or are not attempted at all, despite conditions of monopoly or near monopoly control of the media.

Our approach provides a missing link in the explanation of how leaders engage average citizens who prefer peace over conflict and, in particular, how the plausibility of the threat can be enhanced if certain power and informational conditions exist. As Gagnon (1995:165) argues, the cause of war in Yugoslavia was "the provocation of violence by threatened elites." Serbian leader Slobodan Milosevic used Serbian citizens' fear of an aggressive Croatian regime to garner support for war with Croatia. But he could not do this on his own. Milosevic had to create sufficient causal ambiguity about why hostilities and violence occurred. In this sense we argue that the critical factor beyond Milosevic's direct control was that the Croatians' actions "confirmed" (in the Bayesian sense) Milosevic's claims about them.[3] Given the causal ambiguity about growing tensions, Croatia's actions increased the "average" Serbian citizen's subjective assessment that the Croatians were bent on violence against Serbs. Had the average citizen known for sure that Milosevic sought to incite the Croatians, the average citizen would not have reacted with the fear of bad consequences that moved them to support Milosevic.

To see how this works, consider the elements of our model of the outbreak of war between Serbia and Yugoslavia: Milosevic and the Croatians negotiate over the future of Yugoslavia, which may or may not result in a new pact. The pivotal Serbian constituency is uncertain about the nature of both the Croatians and Milosevic: Are the Croatians bent on violence against all Serbs, and is Milosevic sufficiently treacherous and corrupt to sabotage negotiations and initiate ethnic conflict as a means of remaining in power? Serbian citizens can only observe whether negotiations succeed or fail. If negotiations succeed, Serbians know that the Croatians are not bent on violence and Milosevic is not treacherous. Yet, if negotiations fail, pivotal constituents can never really know why. Perhaps it failed because aggressive Croatians sabotaged peace, or perhaps it failed because a treacherous Milosevic sabotaged it. Thus, the pivotal Serbian constituencies face a critical *causal ambiguity* as to why a new pact failed to preserve Yugoslavia.

We show how the absence of a negotiated pact combines with the ambiguity of why peace fails to increase the Serbian citizens' subjective likelihood that Milosevic's claims about the Croatians are true. The failure of a pact allows Serbians to rule out the best possible world—the combination of cooperative Croatians and a nontreacherous Milosevic. This failure raises the probability of the other possible scenarios, implying an increased probability that the Croatians are bent on violence.

In practice a series of interactions had the effect highlighted by the model. First, the Croatians and Milosevic failed to negotiate a peaceful settlement within the confines of Yugoslavia. Second, several actions by the Croatians "confirmed" Milosevic's claims: Croatia's assertion of independence, including its adoption of the symbols of the former Ustache regime (which murdered Serbs during World War II), calls by Croatia's leader for a "greater Croatia," and extremist Croatians' calls for annexing parts of Bosnia-Herzegovina and Serbia. For the Serbian constituents these events only ruled out the possibility that *both* Croatia and Milosevic were honestly pursuing peace.

In our model cold calculations based on fear induce the pivot to side with Milosevic. Further, a corrupt Milosevic can manipulate this fear in facing a cooperative opponent. Such manipulation require more than Milosevic's interest in retaining power. The Croatians must "confirm" (in the Bayesian sense) Milosevic's assertions. Without the ambiguity of why peace failed, Milosevic could not manipulate his constituents' fear.

Our model yields two further results. First, it predicts that if beliefs about the likelihood of victimization exceed a critical level, the average citizen will support ethnic violence to prevent such an outcome. Further, as the stakes of victimization rise relative to peace, the critical probability triggering support for ethnic violence can be much closer to 0 than to 1 (Weingast 1998). This implies that citizens may act on an idea—that Croatians are bent on violence against Serbs—even though they deem the idea unlikely. They act this way because the consequences of being wrong are so onerous.

Second, the model shows that violence was not inevitable in Yugoslavia. Had Milosevic's liberal, reform-minded opponents been in power, they would not have pursued ethnification; neither would Milosevic, had he been more secure about his political future. Indeed, had many of the institutions of the ancien Yugloslav regime remained in place throughout the early 1990s, conflict would have been less likely (Woodward 1995).

The logic of the Rwanda case also involved a set of leaders with a tenuous hold on power, who pursued a risky and gruesome strategy to retain power. In the August 1993 Arusha peace accords the Hutu leaders agreed to give up considerable power to the Tutsi insurgents, the Rwanda Patriot Front (RPF). But the accords were not immediately implemented, and this allowed the Hutus the opportunity to gamble for resurrection. Two features of the Rwandan genocide must also be explained: why Hutu leaders organized mass participation in the genocide and, especially, why they forced moderate Hutus to participate under threat of death. Our explanation of the Rwandan case is this. If they did nothing, Hutu leaders would lose power to the RPF. The latter stood to gain sufficient support among the Tutsi minority and moderate Hutus to survive. Genocide reduced the likelihood that an RPF regime could survive in three ways. First, genocide against the Tutsis directly eliminated a large portion of the most natural supporters of an RPF regime. Second, forcing the moderate Hutus to participate created the possibility that vengeful Tutsis might view them as culpable. Third, genocide meant that an RPF regime had no way to commit to *not* taking reprisals against the perpetrators. Forcing mass participation therefore meant that all of the post-violence citizenry were potential targets of reprisals. If moderate Hutus participated in the genocide, they would have cause to fear rather than support an RPF regime. Genocide, combined with fear of reprisals, would mean that an RPF regime had only a tenuous basis of political support and hence a low probability of surviving. Rwandan genocide undermined the RPF's future control over Rwanda, granting Hutu leaders a chance at returning to power. The costs were massive.

These cases portray ethnic violence as a form of gambling for resurrection by leaders, losing power, who care little about the larger consequences of their actions. Our accounts go beyond the assertion that fear drove the average citizen to behave as leaders desired; they reveal the mechanisms underlying why citizens did so. In this view ethnic conflict is a social dilemma. Each citizen, acting alone, cannot affect the outcome. Fear of extreme consequences beyond their control drive citizens to support violence to avoid becoming a victim. The choice faced by pivotal constituencies is not between war and peace. The problem is that a third alternative is worse than war: violent victimization. And, yet, this fear of victimization is not automatic, and a leader's appeal to such fears will not automatically succeed.

Our models demonstrate that generating sufficient support for ethnic conflict requires a particular interaction with the opponents, which can lie beyond the leader's direct control. In the Yugoslav case Milosevic's opponents had to act in a manner that increased the likelihood his views were correct. In the Rwandan case Hutu leaders depended on the inability of an RPF regime to commit not to take reprisals as a means of securing the Hutu leaders' position.

This chapter proceeds as follows. The next two sections study the eruption of violence in Yugoslavia. Section 2 sketches the substantive details, while section 3 analyzes the model. Section 4 provides a brief synopsis of the events in Rwanda and then in section 5 we analyze a model of the emergence of violence there. Our conclusions follow.

Ethnic Conflict in Yugoslavia: A Synopsis

A large number of factors underpin the ethnification of Yugoslavian politics in the late 1980s and early 1990s. The end of the cold war altered the area's geostrategic importance and hence the great powers' interests and inclinations (Woodward 1995). Western states appeared to act without deep appreciation of the potential for violence. Slobodan Milosevic was far more ruthless than his political competitors and bent on any means of retaining power (Gagnon 1995; Ignatieff 1993b; Silber and Little 1996). Finally, the region's episodic violence, with two civil wars earlier in this century, meant that each group had memories of victimization.

During the Tito era, and the immediate years following his death, domestic institutions helped create and maintain ethnic peace (Burg 1983; Djilas 1991; Woodward 1995). Specifically, institutions helped to decentralize policymaking in Yugoslavia, providing ethnic groups with some protection against one another. A balance was created among groups and regions in which none could predominate. Institutions requiring consensus among the major groups and regions granted each group a veto over national policy. Moreover, the practices and norms of the Yugoslav state limited the ability of nationalist politicians within any one group to exploit nationalist issues and group fears.

These institutions enhanced each group's and region's ability to prevent sudden victimization. Specifically, each region faced two threats, from other regions directly and from the possibility that one group might gain control of the national apparatus. Decentralization reduced these threats in two ways. By housing a large portion of resources independently in each region, decentralized control meant that regions had their own resources to resist direct attempts to usurp their autonomy. Similarly, by giving each region an effective veto over national policy, decentralized power meant that states could resist appropriation of federal power by any one group. Decentralization further implied that any new leader of Yugoslavia bent on violence would first have to dismantle the institutions of the ancien régime, a process that would allow the regions time and preparation to respond. These arrangements did not render ethnicity unimportant during the ancien régime (indeed, studies show that it was; see, e.g., Burg and Bernbaum 1989). Instead, their existence shows that ethnicity was not the dominant social and political concern. Decentralized power meant that the citizens of Yugoslavia were able to garner some of the gains from social cooperation.

During the 1980s, Woodward (1995, 1997) suggests, two factors helped erode the institutions providing group protection. First, international events revolving around the negotiations to reschedule Yugoslavia's international debts forced reform. International donor agencies, such as the International Monetary Fund and World Bank, required regulatory reform, drastic reductions in budgets (including redistributive payments), and greater central control over the economy. These had the unintended effect of reducing the resources provided to the regions and squelching the regionalized protections limiting the authority of—and hence risk from—the central state.

Second, Slovenia and Serbia, for very different reasons, sought to undermine these institutions to maximize their autonomy. Slovene leaders wanted less central control so they could break free of Yugoslavia and enter the European Community. Serbia wanted to control Yugoslavia without institutional restraints on its power.

In combination, these two factors undermined the institutional basis for political stability. They eliminated the restrictions inherent in the ancien régime, increasing the possibility that one region or the central state might take advantage of another. These fears were reinforced as Milosevic announced that Yugoslavia was no longer a pan-Southern Slavic state, but a Serbian state. Simultaneously, he began making outrageous claims about the Croatians. Finally, he took steps to gain control over the Yugoslav army and began strengthening it. Slovenia left as quickly as possible.

In response, at the same time they were trying to negotiate a settlement with Serbia, Croatian elites courted Western Europeans, especially the Germans, to seek recognition as a separate—and European—state, affording independence and hopefully protection from Serbia.

Although the Croatians' move toward independence seemed perfectly reasonable to many Westerners, within Serbia it came to be construed as confirming Milosevic's expectations. Moving toward independence is exactly what would be expected of an expansionary Croatia bent on violence. So too was Croatia's adoption of the symbols and currency of the previous Ustache regime (which victimized Serbs during World War II).[4] Further, under Tudjman, Croatia aggressively rewrote its constitution, explicitly stating that Croatia was a state of Croats, as opposed to one of Croatians (Denitch 1994).[5] Finally, Croatia's purging of Serbs from positions of local authority (e.g., magistrates and especially police) unleashed domestic violence of Serbs against Croats and vice versa (Glenny 1992:13–14; Ignatieff 1993b; Woodward 1995). None of these steps served to mollify the concerns of Serbs within Croatia.

Milosevic pushed his nationalist agenda within Serbia. His most virulent attacks occurred when his power seemed to be waning (Gagnon 1995). He used extreme measures in an attempt to suppress his political competition (Silber and Little 1996). Monopoly control over the media allowed him to press his extreme views relentlessly with the Serbian public, suppressing all access by his political opponents (Gagnon 1995; Thompson 1994).

Throughout the late 1980s and early 1990s Milosevic was one of the central innovators bringing nationalist politics back into the region (Silber and Little 1996; Thompson 1994; Woodward 1995). This began with the conflict of Serbs within the Southern Serbian (and virtually independent) province of Kosovo where Serbs were a small fraction relative to the majority of Albanians. Next came greater Serbian control over Kosovo and the northern province of Vojvodina. Then the conflict with Slovenia, and, finally, that with Croatia.

Throughout, Milosevic emphasized the historic Serbian myth of victimization, that "Serbians win the war but lose the peace." Many Serbs believed that Yugoslavia had been designed to limit Serbian power, and Milosevic played upon this belief.[6] Within Yugoslavia Serbian power had been divided. No other ethnic group was explicitly distributed into several regions (Woodward 1995). Nothing natural separated Serbs in Serbia from those elsewhere. Indeed, migration implied that many Serbians came from other provinces, including many prominent politicians.

Finally, it is important to suggest the nature of the reciprocal threats caused by the breakup of Yugoslavia. Consider first the perspective of Croatians. Croatians felt they now had a madman next door, gaining control over a largely Serbian army. Further, Milosevic was willing to employ this power for political ends, using violence to gain control over Kosovo, including ruthless suppression of the Albanian majority. How Milosevic would use this power in the future was of grave concern to Croatians.

The risks were also great from the perspective of the domestic Serbian audience. First, Serbia's borders were in large part arbitrary, and nationalist extremists on many sides laid claim to the territory of their respective opponents. This was especially true of Milosevic, with designs on territory in all directions, but also of Croatian extremists who advocated capture of territory throughout Yugoslavia, even Serbia, from as early as the 1960s (Gagnon 1995; Magas 1993; Silber and Little 1996).

Although Croatian violence directed at Croatian Serbs might be a limited program that would not spread elsewhere, Serbians could not be assured of this. Such violence contained the seeds of a much larger conflict. Tudjman's calls for a greater Croatia hardly suggested moderate or limited ambitions. According to Silber and Little (1996:86–87):

> Tudjman also made clear his total disregard for Bosnia-Herzegovina, calling the central Yugoslav republic a "national state of the Croatian nation." . . . [Extremist Croatians] openly advocated the annexation of Herzegovina, the Southern part of Bosnia-Herzegovina. Extremist ambitions to extend Croatian territory as far as Zemun, a town just north of the Serbian capital Belgrade, even entered the popular humor at the time. One joke said HDZ stood for *Hrvatska do Zemuna*, which means Croatia all the way to Zemun.

Thus, Croatia might use its mobilization to move into Bosnia-Herzegovina, granting it significant geostrategic advantages from which to force concessions from Serbia. Having moved into Bosnia-Herzegovina, Croatia might next form an alliance with disgruntled elements in Kosovo and Vojvodina, attempting to dominate Serbia from all directions. Macedonia, Yugoslavia's southern province, might also side with Croatia, using the opportunity to assert its independence and reduce the risk from Serbia. Croatia's immediate threat was to its domestic Serbs, but nothing limited Croatia's threat to its borders. Croatia's ambitions could have easily exploded into a wider conflict, one that might dominate Serbia. If Croatia undertook these steps, an unprepared Serbia could easily become more than a mythical victim.

From the perspective of ordinary Serbians, then, there was the combination of multiple threats and political chaos. Significant uncertainty prevailed about who wanted what and how grand the designs of Tudjman and Milosevic were. This uncertainty meant that the citizens had to decide what was most likely to endanger their security and threaten peace. The task for the Serbian population was to view the events and determine whether the failure of the peace process and the aggressive behavior of the Croatians represented a gambit by Milosevic, Tudjman, or both. Uncertainty therefore created an unfortunate dilemma for Serbians. The problem for the Serbians was that Milosevic represented, at that time, their best chance against an aggressive Croatia. But if Milosevic was trying intentionally to ruin the peace process, despite a conciliatory Croatia interested only in independence within its borders, then supporting Milosevic's blatantly aggressive actions risked losing an opportunity for a peace that most Serbians wanted.[7] Given Serbian institutions and Milosevic in power, Serbians could not simultaneously lower the risks of ethnic conflict and lower the risks of becoming a victim. Ultimately, as history unfolded, Milosevic retained support and, along with the Croatians, embarked on a long, drawn-out, and bloody struggle in Croatia and Bosnia-Herzegovina.

A Model of the Ethnification of Politics in Yugoslavia

Sustained peace in a society with ethnic, religious, or regional divisions requires mutual trust, tolerance, and reciprocity (Fearon and Laitin 1996; Weingast 1998). As Posen (1993) suggests, these phenomena disappear when a potential ethnic security dilemma undergoes a spiral dynamic. The central question of this section concerns the conditions under which a divided society will exhibit a spiral dynamic. To explore these questions we propose a model of prewar Yugoslav politics that examines the social dilemma underlying cooperation among groups in a divided society. Although the case is motivated particularly by the eruption of war between Croatia and Serbia, it serves to highlight the way in which political opportunists can use the structure of interaction and information to advance their own political objectives.

The Model

The sequence of decision making in the game proceeds as follows (figure 8.1). A nonstrategic player called "nature" (N) makes the first move and chooses Milosevic's (M) type: with probability p_1, it chooses M as treacherous (T); with probability $1-p_1$, M is not treacherous (NT). As we detail more formally later, the two types are distinguished by how they trade off their own retention of power against potential hardships borne by their constituents: a treacherous type cares only about retaining power, while a nontreacherous type prefers not to retain power if the cost is ethnic war.

The game's second move is also a choice by N. With probability p_2, Nature chooses the Croatian (C) type as aggressive (A); with probability 1-p_2, C is not aggressive or cooperative (NA). Again the two types are distinguished by their preferences: aggressive types prefer subjugation and, perhaps, even genocide of Serbs over cooperation; cooperative types prefer cooperation over subjugation.

The convention of a move by N does not literally mean that M and C's types are randomly chosen in a lottery just prior to the groups' interaction. M and C's types may be fixed well in advance by complex historical processes, and, indeed, after the fact, we can observe the true nature of leaders such as Milosevic. Instead a move by nature is a convenient means of representing the uncertainty that other actors experienced at the time about the preferences of M and C.

M makes the game's third move and must choose between participating in peace negotiations or sabotaging the peace process. Next, C must choose between participating in peace negotiations or sabotaging the peace process.[8] If both participate in peace negotiations, then a peace pact is reached. If either or both choose to sabotage the peace process, no pact is reached. Finally, in the last move the pivotal Serbian supporter[9] P must choose between supporting the incumbent M and supporting his reformist opponents.[10]

As we described earlier, during the Yugoslav crisis observers external to the negotiation process had only a limited view into the proceedings. Although outsiders could observe the outcomes of the negotiations—whether

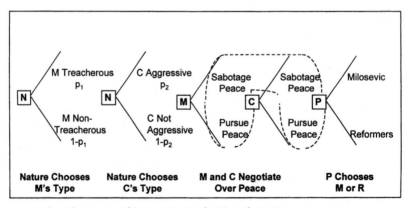

FIGURE 8.1. Sequence of Interaction in the Yugoslavia Game

a pact had been reached and what other actions the parties were taking—the *reason* for those outcomes was less clear (Magas 1993; Gagnon 1995; Ramet 1992).[11] To capture this lack of observability, the pivot's incomplete information is a critical aspect of the model. The game assumes that both M and C know one another's type and that this is common knowledge. Although M and C possess complete information when they make their decisions, the Serbian pivot P does not. P does not observe M's type, C's type, or whether either participates in or sabotages the peace process. P's only observation is that either a peace pact has been concluded or peace fails.[12]

The outcomes of the game are determined by N's choice of the leaders' types, whether a peace pact occurs, and P's choice of M or R. Depending on these factors, we make the following assumptions about the possible outcomes that may occur. We summarize each of these outcomes in figure 8.2.

If P chooses M when C is aggressive, Serbia is prepared for war, labeled W. If P chooses R in this case, Serbia is unprepared for war, leading to potential subjugation and genocide, labeled S.

Suppose, alternatively, that M is treacherous and C is not aggressive. If P chooses M, high ethnic tension results, with little chance for political and economic reform or prosperity, labeled HT. If P chooses R, on the other hand, ethnic tension exists but is lower than under M; choosing R also leads to some economic and political reform and hence some prosperity. This outcome is labeled TR.

Finally, suppose that M is not treacherous and C cooperative. If no pact is reached, and P chooses M, then Serbia and Croatia become independent, without war, but fail to cooperate, an outcome labeled I. If a pact is reached

M's Type	C's Type	Outcome of Negotiations	P's Choice	Outcomes
T	A	Either	M	Prepared war (W)
T	A	Either	R	Unprepared war (S)
NT	A	Either	M	Prepared war (W)
NT	A	Either	R	Unprepared war (S)
T	NA	Either	M	High ethnic tension (HT)
T	NA	Either	R	Low tension, some reform (TR)
NT	NA	Failure	M	Noncooperative independence (I)
NT	NA	Failure	R	Peace, cooperation, and reform (CR)
NT	NA	Success	M	Peace, ethnic cooperation (C)
NT	NA	Success	R	Peace, cooperation, and reform (CR)

FIGURE 8.2. Outcomes in the Yugoslavia Game

and P chooses M, the result is peace, some ethnic cooperation, but little economic and political reform or prosperity. This outcome is labeled C. If, alternatively, P chooses R whether or not a pact is reached, the result is peace, ethnic cooperation, economic and political reform, and hence potential prosperity, labeled CR.

Given these outcomes, we can specify the preferences of all of the players. To reflect our earlier narrative, we make a number of assumptions about the leaders' preferences. First, for both C and M of any type, all outcomes in which they disarm unilaterally are less preferred to all outcomes in which they do not. In other words, all types of elites will only negotiate for peace if the other side does so as well. Second, both types of C prefer reformers over Milosevic. Third, an aggressive C prefers outcomes in which they can maintain their military posture to any outcomes that require them to reduce it. The reason is that an aggressive C's primary objective is to ensure its hegemony over the Serbs in the Kraina, parts of Bosnia-Herzegovina, and even parts of Serbia. Reducing its military stance or political independence will only serve to hinder this objective. Fourth, a nonaggressive C prefers peace over both sides maintaining their militaristic postures. Fifth, a treacherous M prefers all outcomes in which he retains power over all outcomes in which he does not, but also outcomes in which Serbia does not disarm to those in which it does. Sixth, a nontreacherous M wants peace over all else, although, if peace is going to be achieved, he prefers to retain power. These assumptions rest on the idea that peaceful or militaristic behavior by either side was more than simply cheap talk. Militaristic moves, which occurred in practice, involved institutional changes that were observable and hard to reverse, such as constitutional revisions to enhance both confederalization or federalization, policies that ceded control of the military, disarmament, and eliminating nationalistic policies. Further, these commitments, such as disarmament and redistribution, would also alter the ability to conduct a war and thus would have been credible moves to tie the leaders' hands (Fearon 1997). Even though our model assumes for simplicity a single stage in which the players either commit to peace or not, the fact that such moves are made incrementally during the negotiations means they were actually verifiable. For example, disarmament would occur simultaneously in small steps; if one side did not take a step it had committed to, peace would fail. Thus, we assume that any such peace agreements would be enforceable. Because an unenforceable pact would soon fall apart, we simply code this as a failed pact.[13]

Finally, we specify the pivot's preferences. As noted earlier, the modal Serbian wanted peace and reform. Under a certain world P's preferences are straightforward. If C is aggressive, then P would support M. If C is cooperative, then P would support R. Given these basic preferences, we can order P's preferences over each of the possible outcomes. P's most preferred outcome is CR. P ranks C next, ethnic cooperation without reform under M. P ranks I next, since, in this case no cooperation is achieved but peace still obtains. Next is TR, low ethnic tension with some reform under R. Next is HT, high ethnic tension and no reform under M. The two worst outcomes involve violence. P ranks a prepared ethnic war under M's leadership second to last. P's worst outcome is an unprepared ethnic war under R's leadership, leading to ethnic subjugation and potential genocide. In sum, P ranks the alternatives as CR, C, I, TR, HT, W, and S.

Equilibrium Behavior

We determine an equilibrium for the game in a series of stages. The first stage concerns the interaction of M and C in the peace process. Based on M's and C's preferences, along with the elimination of weakly and iteratively dominated strategies (Morrow 1994), there is a unique set of equilibrium strategies for C and M, given the choices by N (see appendix for a more formal discussion of this result). Peace succeeds only in the case in which M is not treacherous and C is not aggressive. Figure 8.3 summarizes these realizations.

After observing the outcome of the peace process, P must choose between retaining the incumbent M and replacing M with the opposing reformers

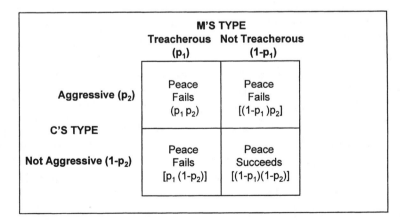

| | M'S TYPE | |
	Treacherous (p_1)	Not Treacherous ($1-p_1$)
Aggressive (p_2)	Peace Fails ($p_1 p_2$)	Peace Fails $[(1-p_1)p_2]$
C'S TYPE		
Not Aggressive ($1-p_2$)	Peace Fails $[p_1(1-p_2)]$	Peace Succeeds $[(1-p_1)(1-p_2)]$

FIGURE 8.3. Milosevic and Croatian Interaction the Peace Process

R. P's strategy choice depends on its beliefs about whether C is aggressive, and hence on whether M and C conclude a peace agreement.

Although P only observes whether the peace process has been successful, it can make inferences about the two unknown types. If P observes a peace agreement, then it can infer M and C's type with certainty. A peace pact implies an honest M and a cooperative C; only this combination of types results in a peace pact. All other combinations of types result in no pact.

A failed peace process also contains information for P. Failure implies that the combination of an honest M and cooperative C did *not* occur; P knows that at least one and possibly both of the elite representatives are corrupt, but it is not sure which. In other words, P is left with uncertainty about whose aggressiveness ruined the prospects for peace.

Technically, no pact allows P to revise its prior beliefs (according to Bayes's rule) about the probability p_2 that C is aggressive. Failure implies that only the type combinations represented by the upper two cells and the lower left cell of figure 8.3 could have occurred. The revised or *posterior* probability q that C is aggressive, contingent on observing C's rejection of the peace offer, is given by:

$$q = p_2 / (p_1 + p_2 - p_1 p_2) > p_2. \tag{1}$$

Because the denominator of expression (1) is less than 1, P's posterior belief that C is aggressive exceeds its prior belief, p_2. The failure of peace increases P's wariness of C.

Given these beliefs, it is possible to analyze the optimal behavior of P. As noted previously, if a peace pact is struck, P believes that C is not aggressive with probability 1. P's choice of M leads to outcome C, ethnic peace without reform, while choosing R leads to outcome CR, ethnic peace with reform. Because it prefers CR over C, P will choose R when peace occurs. This is an interesting result with respect to M's strategy, since it highlights the importance of the lengths to which leaders will go to ensure their power. A nontreacherous M knows that choosing peace when C is cooperative ensures his own replacement. However, he still signals that Croatia is not aggressive by negotiating a peace pact because the prospect of ethnic tension is even less appetizing to him.

When peace fails, P makes its choice under uncertainty. If it chooses M, depending on the state, two different outcomes can occur: with probability q, C is aggressive, resulting in a prepared war, W; with probability 1-q, C is not aggressive, leading to high ethnic tension and no reform, HT. This means that P's expected value of choosing M, given the failure of peace, is:

$$qW + (1-q)HT. \tag{2}$$

If instead P chooses R, C is aggressive with probability q, resulting in an unprepared war and subjugation S; C is cooperative with probability 1-q, resulting in low ethnic tension and some reform, TR. Thus, if P chooses R, its expected utility is:

$$qS + (1-q)TR. \tag{3}$$

Choosing M over R requires that the value of (2) exceeds that of (3) for P, or that

$$qW + (1-q)HT > qS + (1-q)TR \tag{4}$$

which can be rewritten:

$$q(W-S) > (1-q)(TR-HT).$$

Inequality (4) has a natural interpretation. W-S is P's value of the difference between prepared war and subjugation or victimization, given that C is actually aggressive. When W-S is multiplied by q, the posterior probability that C is aggressive, the left-hand side of (4) can be interpreted as the expected net benefits from "correctly" supporting M instead of R when C is aggressive. On the right-hand side the term (TR-HT) represents the difference between supporting R instead of M given that C is not aggressive. When (TR-HT) is multiplied by (1-q), the posterior probability that C is cooperative, the right-hand side can be interpreted as the expected net benefits to P from "correctly" supporting R when C is cooperative. Taken as a whole, the inequality says that, for the pivot's support of Milosevic to be rational, the expected benefits from supporting M over R when C is aggressive must exceed the expected benefits from supporting R over M when C is cooperative.

Implications

The model shows that the *ethnification of politics* need not be driven by a high probability that C is aggressive. Two separate factors drive ethnification when p_2 is low. First, the failure of peace *increases* P's posterior subjective belief that the Croats are aggressive. This allows a treacherous M to manipulate P even when C is not aggressive, for P can never really tell whether peace failed because of M's treachery or because C is aggressive. P rationally updates its beliefs even though it knows that the peace might have failed because of M's treachery rather than because C is aggressive.

To see how this updating works, consider a simple example. Suppose that the probability that M is treacherous is .5 and that C is aggressive is .1 (i.e., $p_1 = .5$ and $p_2 = .1$). The four states of the world, corresponding to the four cells in figure 8.3, occur with the following probabilities:

M treacherous/C aggressive:	0.05;
M not treacherous/C aggressive:	0.05;
M treacherous/C not aggressive:	0.45;
M not treacherous/C not aggressive:	0.45.

If C rejects M's offer, P rules out the state in which M is honest and C is peaceful. So P's posterior beliefs hold that C is aggressive with a probability of nearly 0.18, almost double its prior of 0.1.[14]

P's uncertainty about the source of the failure of peace is critical in increasing the posterior probability of aggression. If either M's or C's type were known by P, this updating would not occur. This is clear if P knows C's type—it would support M only if C is aggressive. If M's type (but not C's) were known, P would update its beliefs differently. When Milosevic is known to be honest, the failure of peace implies that C is aggressive with probability 1 (in figure 8.3, the only possibility is the upper right cell). If a peace agreement occurs, then, as before, P can infer that M is honest and C is cooperative. If M is known to be treacherous and peace fails, then P learns nothing about C, so its beliefs about C's type remained unchanged. This demonstrates that *it is the ambiguity of the rejection* that allows a treacherous M to manipulate P, even when C is cooperative.

The second factor driving the ethnification of politics when p_2 is low is the size of the stakes (Bates, de Figueiredo, and Weingast 1998; Weingast 1997). Even assuming that economic and political reform increases welfare, the increase is not likely to be high. In contrast, if an aggressive Croatian regime attacks an unprepared Serbia, Serbs stand to lose everything—their property, their families, their lives. The consequences of victimization are simply far larger then those of reform. Thus errors in guessing the leader's true intention are not weighed equally. Returning to inequality (4), the benefits of correctly choosing Milosevic as leader when the Croatians are aggressive (W-S) therefore swamp the costs from incorrectly supporting him when C is not aggressive (TR-HT).

The ethnification of politics depends on the pivot's assessment of the likelihood that C is aggressive. Inequality (4) can be rewritten so that P will choose M if $q \geq (TR-HT) / (W-S + TR-HT) = q^*$. Thus the model predicts that there exists a *critical probability* q^*. Whenever q exceeds q^*, P supports M over R and thus the ethnification of politics ensues. Further, when W-S greatly exceeds TR-HT, the denominator of the expression defining q^* greatly exceeds the numerator, implying that q^* will be quite low, closer to 0 than to 1.

The disparity in the stakes combines with the critical probability q^* to imply that P does not act like an objective historian; that is, P does not take action to defend itself from an aggressive C only when it believes that C is more likely to be aggressive than not (i.e, when $q > .5$). Instead the disparity of stakes implies that P *will rationally act on its fears about C's type even when q is quite low*. P is not a dispassionate outsider weighing the relative likelihood that C is aggressive. Instead, P must consider the expected values of its choices, weighing the probabilities by the relative magnitudes of the stakes.

Taken together, the two effects have the following implications. First, the disparity in stakes implies that fear can drive P into M's camp. The dire consequences of potential subjugation mean that, even if subjugation is relatively unlikely, pivotal Serbians will still side with M if $q>q^*$, who can better protect them.

Second, a treacherous M facing a cooperative C drives P to support him by sabotaging the peace process, thereby raising P's estimation that C is aggressive. The failure of peace makes M more attractive to P relative to R.

Third, it is not simply M's ruthlessness that drives P to support M. Nor is it brainwashing or the endless repetition of outrageous claims by an M who monopolizes the media. Lots of dictators use these techniques in an attempt to survive and nonetheless perish. So why did Milosevic succeed? Our model suggests why. M's manipulation succeeds only when C's visible actions support M's claims. The failure of peace rules out the possibility that both types are good, raising the probability that C is aggressive. The model shows that P's support for M requires that C's actions "confirm" M's claims in the Bayesian sense—that they increase P's estimation of the likelihood that M's claims about C are true.

Further, although the model involves a single stylized peace process, several rounds of interaction occurred among Milosevic, Serbia, and Croatia. Arguably, all had the effect revealed by the model, notably, Croatia's adoption of the Ustache symbols and its subsequent treatment of the Croatian Serbs. These events can be given a benign interpretation; that is, as consequences of reasonable decisions taken by a cooperative Croatia facing Milosevic. And yet, as the model suggests, because these events would *not* occur if M were honest and C cooperative, these events cause the Serbian pivot to revise upward its belief that C is aggressive. In sum, Serbian support for violence did not follow simply from Milosevic's motives, his ruthlessness with opponents, or his endless repetition of outrageous claims about the Croatians. Rather, the Croatians' visible actions interacted with these features to confirm (in the Bayesian sense) Milosevic's extreme claims, causing sufficient support for Milosevic to initiate the ethnification of politics.

Fourth, the model encompasses a real "spiral" dynamic, whereby C reacts to M and the Serbian pivot, P, reacts to C. Suppose that, in fact, M is treacherous and that Croatia is cooperative. Then C's observation of M's type at the start of the game causes it to be concerned about M and Serbia. Peace fails due to M's sabotage. The failure of peace, in turn, increases P's fears about C, causing P to support M, leading to higher ethnic tension. The interaction increases the fear of subjugation, leading to escalatory actions rather than ethnic peace. The individually rational pattern of interaction and growing mutual suspicion leads to the socially irrational outcome of ethnic war.[15]

The model goes beyond the metaphor of ethnic conflict as a security dilemma and a spiral dynamic. It shows precisely how the nature of the leader matters. Suppose that domestic Serbian politics differed, so that M was secure about his tenure in office. Alternatively, suppose that Serbia had another set of leaders (such as the reformers), who were known to be honest and would thus pursue peace. In both cases the spiral dynamic would not occur when C is cooperative.

The model therefore implies that the death of Tito did not plunge Yugoslavia into war, as some have claimed. Rather, the outbreak of ethnic violence required the presence of two sources of uncertainty and that C's actions "confirmed" M's exorbitant claims about them in the Bayesian sense of increasing P's estimation of the likelihood that the Croatians were aggressive.

Further Implications: Comparative Statics Results

The model yields a series of comparative statics results: that is, implications about how aspects of the equilibrium behavior change in response to changing environmental factors. The first result concerns the incentives for political leaders implied by the model. Return to the critical probability, q^*, triggering P's choice of M. Recall that the stakes, W-S, affect q^*. Letting the stakes be $\sigma = $ (W-S), we have $\partial q^*/\partial \sigma < 0$. As P's perception of the stakes σ rises, the critical probability q^* decreases: *the higher the perceived stakes, the lower the probability threshold* inducing P to support M and the ethnification of politics.

This result has a direct implication for the strategies of opportunistic political leaders. Leaders attempting to remain in power by playing the ethnic card have powerful incentives to raise the stakes. First, raising the stakes to potential ethnic opponents may induce them to react in ways that increase the pivotal supporter's subjective assessment that the leader's opponents represent a real threat to the pivot's security. Second, the greater the perceived stakes, the lower P's threshold for acting on its fears and, hence, the more likely that the leader's ethnic claims will be taken seriously.

This perspective helps to explain why ethnification of politics can be so explosive. Opportunistic leaders use ethnic politics to remain in power by raising the stakes. The comparative statics result about how rising stakes lowers q^* combines with the discontinuity in P's behavior when q crosses q^* to cause a spiral dynamic.

Political Opportunism and Genocide in Rwanda

In the previous case we presented a model of how ethnic insecurities were utilized by an opportunistic leader to maintain power. A similar explanation can be employed to understand the emergence of mass genocide in Rwanda in 1994.[16] As in our interpretation of ethnic conflict in Yugoslavia, our account of Rwanda incorporates political opportunism and gambling for resurrection by leaders who are losing power and willing to plunge their country into chaos and violence to improve their chances of remaining in power. Further, this case illustrates the diversity of mechanisms by which such opportunism can manifest itself.

We begin our discussion with a caveat: what follows is a provisional model. So much less is known about Rwanda than Yugoslavia that we must take our representations cautiously. Further, we focus on only one aspect of Rwanda's gruesome politics, albeit a critical one. The mechanism discussed in the Yugoslavia section may also be at work.

Jones's (1997) report provides the following outline of events. The Rwanda Patriotic Front's (RPF) surprisingly successful offensive in February

1993 granted the Tutsi minority a great military advantage. This afforded them a strong bargaining position, resulting in a favorable peace settlement in the Arusha protocols of 1992 and 1993. Forced to share power with the RPF, the incumbent regime lost power. Unfortunately for Rwandans, the accords were not immediately implemented and thus left the incumbent Hutu regime in power. A small UN force was deployed to maintain peace, but this soon proved wholly inadequate (see also Prunier 1995; Sellstrom and Wohlgemuth 1996).

The genocide began in April of 1994 with the assassination of President Juvenal Habyarimana. Government forces successfully attacked the UN force, causing them to pack their bags.

What was the purpose of the genocide? Jones emphasizes that genocide was designed to undermine the possibility of a stable RPF regime governing a peaceful Rwanda. But how did this work? Genocide per se does not undermine a new regime. One factor noted by Jones concerns the ensuing chaos and mass destruction of the country. This destruction led to far less infrastructure and fiscal resources for the new regime—but was this alone sufficient motivation for the Hutu leaders to induce violence?

Another aspect of the phenomenon to be explained is the mass participation in the genocide. Why did the regime engineer this? Further, what made moderate Hutus succumb to the regime's pressure?

Our approach suggests an additional factor—a deeply political purpose to the violence. As we will show, *by removing the possibility of domestic support for the new RPF regime, genocide reduced the probability that a new regime could survive.*

Implicit in this claim is an explanation of why moderates participated in the violence. Suppose that the extremist Hutus had not initiated genocide. A new RPF regime would have had two natural groups to whom to appeal for political support sufficient to sustain power. The first group was the domestic Tutsis, approximately one-tenth of the Rwandan population. In addition to their ethnic brethren, the RPF might be able to garner the support of moderate Hutus. Sufficient support would allow the new regime a basis to establish ethnic peace and, potentially, a modest degree of prosperity. These conditions gave it a reasonable chance at long-term stability.

Genocide undermined support for a new RPF regime in three fundamental ways. First, it eliminated the most natural support group of the new regime, the domestic Tutsis. Second, it eliminated a small fraction of the second support group, the moderate Hutus, and forced the rest into cooperating with the genocide. Third, it made impossible for the new regime to *commit not to undertaking reprisals*. This, in turn, had two effects. First, it would prevent most Hutus from supporting the regime. Second, by forcing moderate Hutus to participate in the genocide of Tutsis, it made it virtually impossible for the RPF regime to differentiate moderate Hutus from other Hutus. Moderate Hutus would not be safe from reprisals and thus would not support an RPF regime. By this account, extremist Hutu leaders initiated genocide because they were losing power. The genocide's diabolic, political purpose was to undermine the stability of the new RPF regime. This would allow the extremist Hutus a chance to regroup and, later, to challenge the RPF.

A Model of Genocide in Rwanda

The model of the emergence of genocide in Rwanda is a variant on that developed above. Although the means by which Hutu leaders manipulated the Rwandan pivot differed from those utilized by Milosevic, the end result was similar.

The Model

The sequence of interaction is given in figure 8.4. Nature has the first move and must choose a type for the RPF Tutsis (T). As in the previous model, this construction is used to represent uncertainty about the intentions of a Tutsi government. With probability p, T's type is retributive; with prob-

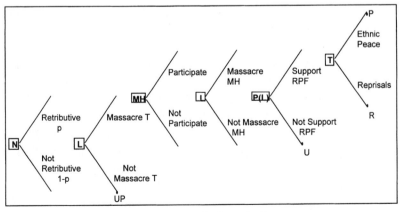

FIGURE 8.4. Sequence of Interaction in the Rwanda Game

ability 1-p, T is not retributive. The difference in types concerns their preferences, with retributive types preferring outcomes in which they have undertaken reprisals against perpetrators of an aggressive massacre. Nonretributive types prefer peaceful outcomes to retribution.

The incumbent Hutu leaders, L, make the next choice, choosing either to massacre or not to massacre the Tutsi minority. If they choose not to massacre the Tutsis, the game ends and the result is an uncontested RPF peace, an outcome we designate UP. If they choose genocide, the game continues to the next stage.

If the Hutu leaders have chosen a program of genocide against the Tutsis, the Hutu populace, signified by the moderate Hutus, MH, must decide whether or not to participate in the massacre of the Tutsis. The game's fourth choice is once again made by the Hutu leaders: they must choose whether or not to massacre the moderate Hutus.

The political pivot makes the game's next choice. One of the central features of genocide is that it truncates the distribution of the population in terms of support for the incoming RPF regime. As noted previously, if no genocide had occurred, both Tutsis and moderate Hutus would likely have supported the incoming RPF regime, honoring the Arusha accords. The elimination of the moderate Hutus and Tutsis, however, would change the pivotal player: the pivot of the smaller distribution would then be a Hutu. Thus, we use the notation P(L) to indicate that the identity of the pivot depends on the Hutu leaders' choice whether or not to massacre moderate Hutus. Recall that on this path of the game the genocide against the Tutsis will have occurred, with or without the participation of moderate Hutus. If the Hutu leaders, L, have chosen to massacre moderate Hutus, MH, then the political pivot, P(L), is H, a supporter of the Hutu regime. If L has chosen not to massacre MH, then P(L) is MH. Thus, we assume that the identity of the political pivot depends on the population that remains after genocidal (or nongenocidal) choices. The pivot (of whichever type) makes the game's next move, choosing whether or not to support the new RPF-dominated regime. If P(L) chooses not to support the new regime, the game ends and the outcome is an uncertain future, possibly allowing the previous Hutu leaders to regain power.[17] This outcome is labeled U. If, however, the pivot decides to support the RPF regime, T, then T decides whether to take reprisals or not. These outcomes are labeled R (for reprisals) and P (for ethnic peace).

Incomplete information is important in this game. The central risk facing the Hutu leaders and moderate Hutus concerns an incoming RPF regime's type. Neither the Hutu leaders nor the pivot knows the RPF's type when it makes its decisions.

Preferences over outcomes are summarized in figure 8.5. The RPF regime's preferences depend on its type. Both types would most prefer an uncontested peace, UP, and least prefer an uncertain future, U. The difference between the types is that while a retributive type prefers reprisals, R, to ethnic peace, P, a nonretributive type does not.

The pivot's preferences vary by whether or not the pivot has participated in the massacres. In this formulation there are three possible types. If the pivot's decision has been reached, it means that it is either a nationalist Hutu who has participated in the massacre, a moderate Hutu who has participated in the massacre, or a moderate Hutu who has not participated in the massacre. All the pivot types prefer UP to all other outcomes. If the pivot is a nationalist Hutu, H, then it prefers a Hutu regime, possible under an uncertain future, to a Tutsi regime, particularly a retributive one. If the pivot is a moderate Hutu, MH, who participated in the massacres, then it prefers a peaceful Tutsi regime to an uncertain future but is most fearful of reprisals against the earlier Tutsi massacres. If, however, the pivot has not participated in the massacre, then it will not be the object of retaliation and will continue to support the RPF regime; therefore, P is preferred to R, which is preferred

T's Type		Pivot Type			L
R	~R	H	MH_p	MH_n	
UP	UP	UP	UP	UP	U_T
R	P	U	P	P	U_{TMH}
P	R	P	U	R	UP
U	U	R	R	U	P_T
					P_{TMH}
					R_T
					R_{TMH}

Notes: Subscript (p,n) on MH pivot types indicates whether or not MH participated in massacres
Subscript on outcomes for L indicates whether or not the outcome was reached after L massacred Tutsis (T) or Tutsis and moderate Hutus (TMH)

FIGURE 8.5. Preferences of the Players in the Rwanda Game

to U. For obvious reasons, MH's least preferred outcome is any outcome in which it is massacred. Finally, we assume that, if they will be massacred, moderate Hutus prefer not to participate in a Tutsi massacre.

The Hutu leaders' preferences are a bit more complex. Under an RPF regime with sufficient support, they lose power for sure. Further, if the RPF regime undertakes reprisals, Hutu leaders will face sanctions. Under an uncertain future L has a chance to regain power. This implies that L orders the outcomes as U, UP, P, R. Further, incumbent Hutu leaders prefer not to massacre their own people. They suffer a disutility for massacring, making their preferences over outcomes dependent on whether or not MH has been massacred. We assume this disutility is small enough so that the preference order above is preserved.

Equilibrium Behavior

To determine the equilibrium of this game, we work backward through the tree, taking care to preserve information sets. At the second to last node if $P(\cdot)$, the conditional pivot, chooses to support a Tutsi regime, T, then the RPF has the last move of the game and must choose between peace, P, and reprisals, R. This choice is completely determined by T's type, which is determined by Nature in the game's first move. If T is retributive, it chooses R; if nonretributive, it chooses P.

Working back a stage, we come to the pivot's choice, which depends on its identity. Recall that the pivot's identity—and thus its preferences—depends on whether the leaders massacred the moderate Hutus, MH, and if not, whether MH participated in the massacre. If any of these pivot types chooses not to support the RPF regime, the outcome is U. If they choose to support the RPF regime, then they perceive the expected outcome as R with probability p and P with probability 1-p.

The pivot, irrespective of type, will support the RPF regime if and only if:

$$pR + (1-p)P > U. \tag{5}$$

As with the previous model, whether the left side of (5) is larger than the right side depends on p. Once again, we can solve (5) to find the critical minimum probability, p^*:

$$p > (P-U)/(P-R) = p^*. \tag{6}$$

Thus, if $p > p^*$, $P(\cdot)$ will choose to not support the RPF and the outcome will be U.

Based on these conditions the choice is clear for a pivot that is a moderate Hutu who did not participate in the genocide, MH_n, where the subscript p or n indicates whether or not MH participated in the massacre of Tutsis. In this case the pivot prefers both P and R to U, so condition (5) is always met, meaning that MH_n will always choose to support the RPF Tutsis.

The choice is also clear for a nationalist Hutu pivot since it prefers U to either P or R. This means that when the pivot is a nationalist Hutu, it will always choose not to support the RPF and the outcome will be U.

If $P(L) = MH_p$, the pivot is a moderate Hutu that has participated in the massacres, and the choice is not so clear. This pivot also will have participated in the massacre and, therefore, will be concerned about possible retribution. Since this pivot, however, prefers peace to an uncertain future, whether he supports the incoming RPF regime depends on condition (6). Here, support will be conditional on a low value of p (i.e., $p < p^*$). If the fear of retribution is low, then MH_p will be willing to support the RPF despite having participated in the massacre of Tutsis. Further, as with the previous model, the critical probability depends on the relative magnitude of the stakes. The higher the stakes, the lower is p^*. When reprisals involve subjugation of the participants in the genocide, the stakes are massive, involving possible retributive genocide against Hutus. The uncertain outcome resulting from not supporting the RPF may mean war, with some exile and deaths, but this is not likely to be as bad as retributive genocide. Hence, moderate Hutus who have participated in the genocide are likely to consider P-R much larger than P-U, implying that the critical probability, p^*, is much closer to 0 than to 1.

The next step in solving the game concerns the Hutu leaders' choice of whether or not to massacre moderate Hutus. This choice depends on whether MH participated in the genocide or not and the value of p. If MH participated, and $p > p^*$, then L will get U_T if it chooses not to massacre (where subscripts indicate whether or not the outcome was reached after the Hutu leaders massacred Tutsis only or Tutsis and moderate Hutus, subscripted as T and TMH respectively). If MH participated, and $p < p^*$, then the leaders will get R_T with probability p and P_T with probability 1-p by not massacring MH. If moderate Hutus participated in the massacre, and the Hutu leaders choose to massacre them, then the leaders obtain U_{TMH}. Comparing these values, we obtain the following condition: if moderates participated in the genocide, Hutu leaders will massacre MH if $p < p^*$, and will not massacre otherwise.

What if moderate Hutus, MH, did not participate in the massacre? If the Hutu leaders, L, do not massacre MH, it gets P_T with probability p and R_T with probability 1-p. If, alternatively, L massacres MH, then the pivot is a nationalist Hutu, which means the leaders will obtain a payoff of U_{TMH}. Since U_{TMH} is larger then either P_T or R_T, it is a dominant strategy for L to massacre a nonparticipating MH. Thus, the Hutu leaders can *credibly* threaten that they will massacre moderate Hutus if the moderates do not participate.

Given the Hutu leaders' best response, we can now consider moderate Hutus' choice to participate. Recall that MH's worst outcome is to be massacred, but if they are going to be massacred anyway, they prefer not to participate. Consider, then, MH's participation decision in equilibrium under two cases: when $p > p^*$ and when $p < p^*$. When $p > p^*$, if MH participates, they will not be massacred, and if they choose not to participate, they will be. Thus, for the moderates, the credible threat of massacre by Hutu extremists is sufficient to induce moderate participation in the massacre. When $p < p^*$, however, the moderates will be massacred whether or not they participate. Thus, given that they cannot influence their own fates, moderates will not participate. When p is small, then, the moderates cannot commit to supporting the Hutu leaders, even if they participate in the massacre, so that they can not guard their own livelihoods. In other words, the higher the chance of retribution, the greater the possibility that, given a genocide, the moderates will participate and will not be massacred themselves.

Finally, given the equilibrium strategies of the other players, we can consider the Hutu leaders', or L's, choice to initiate genocide. Notice that, depending on p, there are only two possible equilibrium outcomes if L massacres T. If $p > p^*$, then the outcome will be U_T, since moderates will participate in the massacre and not support the RPF. If $p < p^*$, then MH will participate in the massacre but still be massacred itself. In this case a nationalist Hutu becomes the pivot and will not support the RPF. Thus, if $p < p^*$, L will get U_{TMH}. If, alternatively, L chooses not to massacre the Tutsis, then the game ends and the outcome is an uncontested RPF peace. All this implies that, irrespective of p, massacring T is a dominant strategy for L, and it will always be in the leaders' interest to initiate genocide.

The above analysis indicates there are only two equilibria in the Rwandan genocide game, summarized in figure 8.6. The outcomes are conditional on the value of p. If $p > p^*$, L will massacre T, MH will participate in the massacre, L will not massacre MH, and P(L) = MH will not support the

RPF, so that the outcome is U_T. If $p < p^*$, L will choose to massacre T, supported by MH. Here, however, if $P(L) = MH$, $P(L)$ will choose to support the RPF, and L will choose to massacre MH, so that the pivot is H. In this case, then, H will choose again not to support the RPF and the outcome will be U_{TMH}.

Implications

The initiation of violence in Rwanda contrasts with that in Yugoslavia in interesting ways. In both cases the incumbent leaders incite violence as a means of preserving their power. Yet the mechanisms by which the leaders manipulate the pivot differ greatly. In Yugoslavia Milosevic manipulated the Serbian pivot in part by sabotaging the peace process. The result was a Serbian pivot more prepared to support Milosevic because of the perceived risk of genocide. When the guerrilla action in Croatia began, Milosevic had sufficient support to plunge the country into war. The incumbent Hutu leaders' manipulation of the Rwandan pivot was more direct than the process in Yugoslavia. Instead the genocide directly affected the pivot's identity, by murdering all potential pivots of one type and by forcing moderate Hutus into behavior that would mix them with all other Hutus. By engineering the possibility for reprisals and genocide, L ensured that Hutus must worry about a Tutsi reprisal.

Perhaps the most interesting case shows how uncertainty interacts with two mechanisms of resurrection. The key concern for the Hutu leaders is how to get the pivotal supporter to prefer uncertainty to a Tutsi regime. When the likelihood that there will be reprisals is large, the leaders can use fear of retribution to induce Hutus not to support the RPF. The problem, however, for the leaders is that if the moderate Hutus do not participate in the massacre, then the moderates need not fear reprisals: reprisals will be directed only at the Hutu extremists. The leaders use the threat of massacre to induce the moderates to participate in the genocide, thereby making the

Value of p	L's choice	MH's choice	L's choice	P(L)	P(L)'s choice
$p > p^*$	massacre T	participate	not massacre MH	MH	not support RPF
$p < p^*$	massacre T	participate	massacre MH	H	not support RPF

FIGURE 8.6. Equilibriums of the Rwanda Game

moderates share in the real fear of reprisals. Further, as with the Yugoslavian case, the grave stakes of either massacre by the Hutu extremists or reprisals from a Tutsi government have a critical implication for moderate Hutus. The high stakes mean that the likelihood that fears of Tutsi reprisals will be realized need not be too large for moderate Hutus to act to prevent them. As argued above, even a small probability of reprisals is enough to induce fear and mass participation in the genocide. This fact indicates why the game's most likely realized outcome—indeed the one that seems actually to have occurred—is the massacre of the Tutsis (only) by all Hutus and the downfall of the Arusha accords.

In contrast, when there is little threat that there will be reprisals, the mechanism whereby the Hutu leaders manipulate their constituents is different, and more direct. Here the Hutus' only recourse, given that there is very little fear of a Tutsi regime, is to eliminate all potential supporters of an RPF government. In the end the Hutus successfully retain a chance at power by massacring all of their opponents.[18]

The model has another important similarity with the case of Yugoslavia. Notably, as in the previous case, except for the Hutu leaders, all parties preferred peace over all other outcomes. Yet, despite this universal desire, ethnic war and massive casualties resulted. We provide an explanation of why this occurs. In particular, given the opportunity to initiate genocide, the leaders were able to manipulate both the population and the fears of the remainder to maximize their chances of retaining control. The gruesome incentives of a few extremists, then, interacting with both the time and means to initiate violence, allowed the leaders to exploit the fears of the general populace and plunge the country into a spiral of violence, destruction, and political chaos.

The model answers the two questions raised at the beginning of the section concerning how genocide directly undermined the possibility of a stable RPF regime. The incumbent Hutu regime initiated genocide to reduce the likelihood that their Tutsi opponents would survive in power. Further, our model shows why Hutu leaders engineered mass participation in the genocide. Mass participation raised the possibility of massive reprisals by Tutsis, greatly lowering the likelihood that moderate Hutus would support a Tutsi regime. Although the mechanisms differed in Yugoslavia and Rwanda, the end was the same: opportunistic politicians used massive violence as a gamble for resurrection to preserve their power.

Most observers consider ethnic conflict to be as irrational and senseless as it is brutal. We take a somewhat different view. In the lexicon of game theory, ethnic violence is a social dilemma because it makes virtually all citizens worse off. As the familiar prisoners' dilemma suggests, however, a *socially* irrational outcome does not imply *individual* irrationality. We argue that the eruption of ethnic violence is a social dilemma that can best be understood using the tools of rational analysis of individual behavior.

Fear and emotional reactions are central to the genesis of ethnic violence. Yet they are not automatic. As Fearon and Laitin (1996) observe, the lion's share of ethnic groups live in peace with one another. Madmen leaders, induced citizen fear, and the spiral dilemma may accompany every case of ethnic violence. But these elements cannot explain violence, because they cannot explain why violence occurs only sometimes.

Our paper provides a new approach for understanding the emergence of ethnic conflict. It rests on the paradoxical result of social dilemma caused by individually rational action. Average citizens, taking the actions of others as given, rationally pursue actions leading to violence that they would rather avoid.

Our approach shows that three factors combine to cause ethnic conflict: weak leaders who attempt to use ethnic violence to remain in power, fear of victimization among the citizenry, and uncertainty about leaders' intentions. Many students of ethnic conflict have observed the first two. What they fail to explain is how weak leaders induce either fear among citizens or support for the ethnic violence. Our approach provides a missing link by showing that weak leaders can exploit causal ambiguity and uncertainty.

The argument begins with weak leaders who, without concern about the consequences, gamble for resurrection as a means of maintaining power (Downs and Rocke 1995). But leaders alone cannot induce fear in their constituents or convince them to drop everything and fight; political opportunism is insufficient to generate fear. Leaders must somehow induce citizens to support the leader's attempts to transform politics into ethnic conflict.

In Yugoslavia Milosevic of Serbia charged that the Croatians were bent on violence against Serbs. Because most Serbians favored peace and reform, both of which Milosevic was not well equipped to provide, Milosevic's charges alone could not keep him in power. To convince the average citizen to support fighting the Croatians—and hence to support him—Milosevic sought to induce fear. Our model reveals part of the mechanism by which Milosevic accomplished this.

The model shows that inducing fear is not always possible. To succeed, Milosevic had to manufacture the causal ambiguity as to why Yugoslavia was falling apart, why peace was failing, and—at the moment just before war—why violent guerrilla warfare broke out between the Croatians and the

Croatian Serbs. Had it been clear that Milosevic and the Croatian Serbs were responsible for these actions, Milosevic could not have succeeded. Causal ambiguity meant that Serbian citizens simply could not tell whether Milosevic or the Croatians had manufactured these outcomes. Ambiguity worked in Milosevic's favor. The model shows how the Coatians' actions confirmed (in the Bayesian sense) Milosevic's views about them by raising the average Serbians' beliefs that Milosevic was correct. The Croatians' actions and the failure of peace ruled out the possibility of simultaneously benign Croatians and a nontreacherous Milosevic. Eliminating this combination of "good" types raised the subjective probability of the remaining types—in particular, that the Croatians were bent on violence.

Our model yields an important insight into this rational, fear-driven support of violence by average citizens. Consider the stakes. The model predicts that there is a critical probability surrounding Milosevic's claims with the following property: if the average citizen's assessment that Milosevic is correct falls above this critical probability, then she will support Milosevic. We also showed that the larger the stakes of being wrong about Milosevic's claims, relative to the costs of having him in power if his claims proved wrong, the lower the critical probability. These factors combine to imply that the critical probability triggering support for Milosevic would have been closer to 0 than to 1. On this account the average Serbian would have supported Milosevic, even though he did not have very much confidence that his claims about the Croatians were correct. The huge stakes—underpinning fear—drove Serbians to support Milosevic and violence. Further, without the manufactured causal ambiguity, the average citizen's assessment of the probability that Milosevic was correct would not have been high enough to support violence.

The Rwandan case also begins with weak leaders likely to lose power. As in the Yugoslavian case, fear induces moderate Hutus to participate. In this case, however, it is the moderates' fear that they will be annihilated by a still powerful interim Hutu regime. Because the Hutus were allowed to retain sufficient strength during the transition after Arusha, it meant that they could legitimately threaten moderates, to garner their support, and avoid having to engage an even larger-scale massacre.

Our approach provides an answer to the two *fundamental puzzles of ethnic violence*. The fundamental economic puzzle asks why individuals are willing to support violence when it is so costly. The answer is that they are driven by fear. Potential victimization implies that citizens do not view the choice as between peace and violence but between fighting and being a victim. Leaders cannot induce fear at will, however.

The fundamental political puzzle asks what explains the timing of a particular outbreak of an ethnic conflict. This question is important, especially because ethnic violence is typically infrequent and among groups that had previously lived in peace. Our answer is that it takes a combination of factors, namely, weak leaders with a particular ability to manipulate their citizens. The principal flaw of the Rwanda peace accords, obvious in retrospect, is that it left weak leaders in power, granting them the opportunity to raise the stakes and gamble for resurrection. In the Yugoslav case Milosevic also sought to raise stakes and gamble for resurrection. Critical to his success were the Croatians' confirming actions, helping to create causal ambiguity about why Yugoslavia was falling apart. Our approach therefore suggests that violence was not inevitable in Yugoslavia.

We end with two final observations. First, our view has considerable implications for issues of ethnic identity. The model reveals a principal mechanism underlying the transformation of a society from one in which ethnicity is one among many political dimensions of conflict to one in which it is the sole dimension of political conflict. It therefore suggests a set of conditions under which sudden transformations in identity occur.

Like many constructivists (e.g., Anderson 1991; Nagel 1986; Sollors 1989), our approach suggests that identity can be reinvented, indeed, that it is constructed. As with constructivists, we agree that circumstances do not compel a unique form of identity. In our account Milosevic helps construct a new Serbian identity. Had he not sought to do so, we argue, ethnic violence may not have erupted in the former Yugoslavia and thus no new Serbian identity would have emerged (see also Bates, de Figueiredo, and Weingast 1998).

Yet constructivists rarely address the issue of why one form of new identity emerges and not another. Our model suggests the nature of the compelling dynamic driving Serbians toward one identity in particular: the causal ambiguity combined with the huge stakes to cause large numbers of citizens to simultaneously revise their beliefs about the world. Lots of leaders propose new identities for their citizens. Most fail. Milosevic's new Serbian identity combined with both the causal ambiguity and fear that compelled citizens to give up their old understandings and beliefs and thus to take on new ones along with new identities.

Our second observation concerns journalists, political scientists, and historians who consider mass support for ethnic violence irrational. We have already observed that some confuse social irrationality with individual rationality. Even when these observers study individuals, they often ignore the calculus of those who face the consequences. Students of ethnic conflict often scrutinize the evidence for one group's claims that the opposing group is bent on violence. When they find it far more likely that the opposing group is not bent on violence, they conclude that there is no rational basis for citizens to support a leader bent on resisting the opposing group. This attempt at objectivity weighs solely the relative likelihoods of the competing claims.[19]

Our approach suggests that this "objective" assessment is irrelevant for citizen behavior, because it ignores the stakes. Rational citizens do not simply try to assess the likelihood of competing claims. They must instead weigh the likelihood of competing claims by the stakes. When the stakes are in high asymmetry, the critical probability necessary for rationally triggering violence may be far closer to 0 than to 1. In other words, when the stakes are highly asymmetric, citizens may well rationally choose to act on a claim whose likelihood is noticeably less than that of the competing claims.

We argue that ethnic violence is a social dilemma triggered by fear of victimization. Moreover, fear causes citizens to act on ideas and claims they believe are more likely to be false than true. This is not irrational, but a rational response to the huge costs of being wrong.

Appendix

In this appendix we discuss in greater detail how the assumptions we make about preferences lead to the set of outcomes in figure 8.3. In the full extensive form of the game there are thirty-two terminal nodes. We do not, however, fully specify the preferences of the players over all the nodes, instead making assumptions over classes of the outcomes.

The assumptions we make are

1. C and M of all types prefer outcomes in which they do not disarm unilaterally to ones in which they disarm unilaterally.
2. C of type A and NA both prefer outcomes in which P chooses R to ones in which P chooses M.
3. C of type A prefers outcomes in which no pact is reached to those in which a pact is reached.
4. C of type NA prefers outcomes in which both sides disarm to those in which neither does.
5. M of type T prefers all outcomes in which P chooses M to those in which P chooses R.

6. M of type NT prefers outcomes in which both sides disarm over all outcomes in which no peace is reached; conditional on disarmament, M prefers outcomes in which P chooses M over R.
7. P prefers M to R if, and only if, C is of type A.

Given these assumptions it is possible to prove the following:

Result:

A peace pact will be reached if and only if M is nontreacherous and C is cooperative.

Proof:

Notice first that by assumption (1), all action combinations in which one side disarms and the other does not are strictly dominated. Thus, by (3), if C is aggressive, no pact will be reached, meaning for the type combinations (T, A) and (NT, A), where the first argument is M's type and the second C's type, no pact will be reached in equilibrium. For the combination (NT, C), (4) and (6) imply that, irrespective of P's choice, both prefer to reach a pact. Finally, consider M's choice when the type combination is (T, C). In this case, if he allows a pact, then P will know C's type with certainty and, given (7), will choose R. Thus, given (5), sabotaging peace weakly dominates pursuing peace if the probability q exceeds q^*. Then, by (1), neither side will disarm. Thus, under (T, C), no pact will be reached.

NOTES

Haas School of Business and Department of Political Science, University of California, Berkeley; and Hoover Institution and Department of Political Science, Stanford University. The authors gratefully acknowledge Robert Bates, Francis Colaco, V.P. Gagnon, Brian Gaines, Tim Groseclose, David Holloway, Erin Jenne, Bruce Jones, David Laitin, Lisa McIntosh-Sundstrom, James Morrow, Norman Naimark, Roger Noll, Robert Powell, Scott Sagan, Alastair Smith, Jack Snyder, Steve Solnick, and Susan Woodward for helpful conversations.

1. Fearon and Laitin (1996) provide the following evidence. (1) In the former Soviet Union: (a) violence by titular groups against Russians in non-Russian republics occurred in only 10 percent of the cases (3 of 30); (b) violence between titular groups and other ethnic groups (constituting at least 1 percent of the

population) in the former union republics occurred in only 4.4 percent of the cases (2 of 45). (2) In Africa, from independence through 1979, they find the ratio of actual violence to potential cases is .0005, or less than 1/10 of 1 percent. Recent results of Parikh (1997) on India support a similar conclusion.

2. Gambling for resurrection has been applied to a range of topics; e.g., to leaders of states in international competition (Downs and Rocke 1995); and to leaders of ailing savings and loans during the S&L crisis (Romer and Weingast 1989).

3. In this sense we attempt to focus the Snyder and Ballentine (1996) argument even more sharply by discussing conditions when elite claims of security threats become *plausibile*. In other words, the communication between Milosevic and Serbs was a strategic process of information transmission, and for the messages to induce the behaviors (fear and voting in this case) coincident with Milosevic's interests, it was necessary for the Croatians to "confirm" the message Milsoevic was providing. Indeed, Snyder and Ballentine's discussion of the portrayal of Draskovic is a nice counterpoint. As they explain, the Serbian elite's claim that Draskovic was collaborating with Albanians and Croats was not credible to the Serb audience—Draskovic's history and actions simply did not support such a claim.

4. As Ignatieff (1993b) points out, although these Ustache symbols were reprehensible to the Serbs, for Croatians these relics did not carry the same connection to Nazi Germany. Instead, for Croatians these symbols represented *independence*, since they were remnants of the only period in the twentieth century during which Croatia had been sovereign.

5. According to Woodward (1995:102–3), the Croatian parliament revised its constitution, "redefining the essence of the republic's sovereignty as residing in the Croatian people. This replaced the concept, embodied in the previous two constitutions, that each republic was a community of the people of the republic, which, in the case of Croatia, read: 'the Croatian people in brotherly unity with the Serbs of Croatia.' For Serbs . . . this was a demotion in status of major consequence. They were to be granted the cultural and social rights of a minority but not the equal political status and full rights to self-determination that belonged constitutionally to nations in Yugoslavia. Croatia was the state of the Croatian nation, but the implication for rights of citizenship of those who were not Croat but who resided in Croatia, perhaps for many generations, became very uncertain."

6. "Serbs often complained that the expression, 'weak Serbia—strong Yugoslavia' embodied the attitude of their countrymen." Silber and Little (1996:34). See also Crnobrnja (1994:107).

7. As Woodward writes of the situation in the late 1980s, "Milosevic's political use of crowds in 1988 and 1989 was perceived by others as an aggression against the rest of Yugoslavia, but it did not reflect his political support among the Serb population or Serbian views on the fate of the country. *The majority still favored*

a liberal, Europeanist, and pro-Yugoslav option." (Woodward 1995:97; emphasis added)

8. Note that whether M or C moves first here is not relevant; players could move in any order or simultaneously with the same result.

9. Throughout the chapter we loosely refer to the pivotal Serbian citizen also as the "average" or "ordinary" Serb. This is not to say that Milosevic needed the support of a majority, only a subset of groups whose support he needed to retain power, which might have been less than a majority. Further, although we assume that there is a pivotal Serbian constituency, that is not to say that Milosevic required only the support of one constituency. Instead, since politics was focused on simply one dimension in Serbia at the time, reform and economic growth versus militarization, and politicians took positions at some location in that dimension, if Milosevic satisfied the group that was at once farthest away from his own views *and* necessary for his survival, the constituency we call P, then he would have satisfied all those who were closer to his own policies (Bates, de Figueiredo, and Weingast 1998).

10. Gagnon (1995:153–154) describes the insecurity Milosevic and his supporters felt about their own leadership position. He explains that there were two threats to Milosevic in the late 1980s and early 1990s, before the outbreak of war. First, the policies of the prime minister of Yugoslavia, Markovic, "were quite successful in lowering inflation and improving the country's economic situation, and he was very popular, especially in Serbia. Taking advantage of these successes, and looking ahead to multi-party elections, he pushed bills through the Federal Assembly legalizing a multi-party system in the entire country, and in July 1990 formed a political party to support his reforms." The second threat cam from within Serbia, where reformers were gaining ground as well. "The biggest challenge . . . came from within Serbia itself," Gagnon explains. "Encouraged by the fall of communist regimes in the rest of Eastern Europe and the victory of noncommunists in Croatia and Slovenia, opposition forces in Serbia began organizing and pressuring the regime for multiparty elections, holding massive protest rallies in May. Although Milosevic argued that elections could not be held until the Kosov issue was resolved, by June the Serbian regime recognized that elections were unavoidable."

11. A brief review of the events during the peace process is chronicled by Ramet (1992). She describes how Croations were simultaneously calling openly for peaceful confederalization in late 1990 and early 1991, arming themselves more vigorously, and rejecting proposals made by Milosevic. At the same time, Milosevic and the Yugoslav army led by General Kadijevic were proclaiming their attempts at peace while aggressively pursuing the disarmament of the Croats. One event in particular highlights the lack of clarity as to who was stalling the peace process. On January 30, 1991, Kadijevic, after repeated calls for the standing down of Croatian militias and reservists, ordered the arrest of the Croatian

defense minister, Martin Spegelj. Croatia and Tudjman refused to arrest the minister and promised the use of force to resist the order. Ultimately, outside observers were unable to assign blame. As Ramet (1992:247–254) comments, however, observers *could* see the ultimate dissolution of the peace process. "By the end of January 1991," she describes, "political talks between Croatian and federal leaders had broken down, with Croatia's Tudjman refusing to take part in any further meetings as long as the army was represented there."

12. This information structure draws on the work of Groseclose (1996). He shows how, in the context of American legislative politics, public officials utilize causal ambiguity over policy failure to avoid reprisals from voters. The model also has some similarities with that of Kydd (1997).

13. In some situations an unenforceable pact might take some time to fall apart. This is not likely to hold in the Yugoslav case. Because a pact would have involved constitutional and other restrictions, a militaristic leader could not long masquerade behind a pact.

14. The posterior is calculated as $p_2 / (p_1 + p_2 - p_1 p_2)$. In the numerical example, this translates to $.1 / [.5 + .1 - .05]$ or approximately .182.

15. A more complex model would reinforce this point. Suppose, for example, we add a step in the model for C to assert its independence from Yugoslavia, in part by raising its own army. C might choose this option because it knows M's type and therefore rationally seeks to defend itself against a potentially hostile Serbia. But it might also choose this option because it is aggressive. If the only circumstance under which C would choose *not* to assert its independence and build an army is when it is cooperative and M is honest, then P's observation of C's assertion of independence increases P's subjective probability that C is aggressive.

16. As an effort to integrate our models into the volume, our account of Rwanda draws directly on Jones (1997); and on Block (1994), Prunier (1995), and Sellstrom and Wohlgemuth (1996).

17. Note, here, that we embed gambling for resurrection in this outcome. In effect, the Hutu leaders can decide to attempt to force a lottery over leadership or lose power. This places a restriction on the preferences of H: the probability of winning must be sufficiently high and the benefits of winning sufficiently large, relative to the costs of pursuing genocide.

18. Notice that, perhaps ironically, this means that a sufficient threat of reprisals by the RPF actually served to restrict an even larger violence.

19. This is not to say that all fear is rational, in the sense of actual subjective stakes or beliefs *ex post*. Serbians might have "overestimated" the threat and potential costs of even an aggressive Croatian regime. Instead, we argue that, using the rational basis as a benchmark, it is possible to analyze the "irrational residual."

REFERENCES

Anderson, Benedict. 1991. *Imagined Communities: Reflections on the Origins and Spread of Nationalism.* Rev. ed. London: Verso.

Anderson, Charles W., Fred R. von der Mehden, and Crawford Young. 1967. *Issues of Political Development.* Englewood Cliffs, N.J.: Prentice-Hall.

Axelrod, Robert. 1984. *The Evolution of Cooperation.* New York: Basic.

Bates, Robert H., Rui J. P. de Figueiredo Jr., and Barry R. Weingast. 1998. "The Politics of Interpretation: Rationality, Culture and Transition," *Politics and Society,* vol. 26 (December), pp. 603–642.

Brown, Michael. 1996. *The International Dimensions of Internal Conflict.* Cambridge: MIT Press.

Burg, Steve L. 1983. *Conflict and Cohesion inq Socialist Yugoslavia: Political Decision Making Since 1966.* Princeton: Princeton University Press.

Burg, Steve L., and Michael L. Berbaum. 1989. "Community, Integration, and Stability in Multinational Yugoslavia," *American Political Science Review,* vol. 83 (June), pp. 535–554.

Crnobrnja, Mihailo. 1994. *The Yugoslav Drama.* Montreal and Kingston: McGill-Queens University Press.

David, Steven R. 1997. "Internal War: Causes and Cures," *World Politics,* vol. 49 (July), pp. 552–576.

Denitch, Bogdan D. *Ethnic Nationalism.* Minneapolis: University of Minnesota Press.

Diamond, Larry. 1987. "Ethnicity and Ethnic Conflict," *Journal of Modern African Studies,* vol. 25 (1987), pp. 117–128.

Djilas, Aleksa. 1991. *The Contested Country: Yugoslav Unity and Communist Revolution, 1919–1953.* Cambridge: Harvard University Press.

Downs, George W., and David M. Rocke. 1995. *Optimal Imperfection? Domestic Uncertainty and Institutions in International Relations.* Princeton: Princeton University Press.

Drakulic, Slavenka. 1993. *The Balkan Express: Fragments from the Other Side of War.*

Elster, Jon. 1989. *The Cement of Society.* New York: Cambridge University Press.

Fearon, James D. 1998. "Commitment Problems and the Spread of Ethnic Conflict," in David A. Lake and Donald S. Rothchild, eds., *The International Spread of Ethnic Conflict: Fear, Diffusion, and Escalation.* Princeton: Princeton University Press.

Fearon, James D., and David D. Laitin. 1996. "Explaining Interethnic Cooperation," *American Political Science Review,* vol. 90 (December), pp. 715–735.

Gagnon, V. P. 1995. "Ethnic Nationalism and International Conflict: The Case of Serbia," *International Security,* vol. 19, no. 3 (Winter), pp. 130–166.

Glenny, Misha. 1992. *The Fall of Yugoslavia: The Third Balkan War*. New York: Penguin.

Groseclose, Timothy. 1996. "Blame-Game Politics." Unpublished paper, Massachusetts Institute of Technology.

Gurr, Ted Robert. 1993. *Minorities at Risk: A Global View of Ethnopolitical Conflicts*. Washington, D.C.: United States Institute of Peace Press.

Hardin, Russell. 1995. *One for All: The Logic of Group Conflict*. Princeton: Princeton University Press.

Hechter, Michael. 1995. "Explaining Nationalist Violence," *Nations and Nationalism*.

Horowitz, Donald L. 1985. *Ethnic Groups in Conflict*. Berkeley: University of California Press.

Ignatieff, Michael. 1993a. "The Balkan Tragedy," *New York Review of Books*, May 13, pp. 3–5.

—— 1993b. *Blood and Belonging: Journeys Into the New Nationalism*. New York: Farrar, Straus and Giroux.

Jervis, Robert. 1976. *Perception and Misperception in International Relations*. Princeton: Princeton University Press.

—— 1978. "Cooperation Under the Security Dilemma," *World Politics*, vol. 30 (January), pp. 167–214.

Jones, Bruce D. 1997. "Military Intervention in Rwanda's 'Two Wars': Partisanship and Indifference," chapter 4 in this volume.

Kaplan, Robert D. 1993. *Balkan Ghosts: A Journey Through History*. New York: St. Martin's.

Kydd, Andrew. 1997. "Game Theory and the Spiral Model." *World Politics*, vol. 49 (April), pp. 371–402.

Laitin, David D. 1995. "Transitions to Democracy and Territorial Integrity," in Adam Przeworski, eds., *Sustainable Democracy*. New York: Cambridge University Press.

—— 1999. "Somalia: Civil War and International Intervention." [This volume.]

Lake, David A., and Donald S. Rothchild, eds., *The International Spread of Ethnic Conflict: Fear, Diffusion, and Escalation*. Princeton: Princeton University Press.

Lipjhart, Arend. 1967. *The Politics of Accommodation: Pluralism and Democracy in the Netherlands*. Berkeley: University of California Press.

Magas, Branka. 1993. *The Destruction of Yugoslavia: Tracking the Break-up, 1980–92*. London: Verso.

Mansfield, Edward D., and Jack Snyder. 1995. "Democratization and the Danger of War," *International Security* (Summer), vol. 20, no. 1.

Morrow, James D. 1994. *Game Theory for Political Scientists*. Princeton: Princeton University Press.

Moynihan, Daniel Patrick. 1993. *Pandaemonium: Ethnicity in International Politics*. Oxford: Oxford University Press.

Nagel, Joane. 1986. "Political Construction of Ethnicity," in Susan Olzak and Joane Nagel, eds., *Competitive Ethnic Relations*. Orlando: Academic Press.

Parikh, Sunita. 1997. "Caste, Religion, and the Politics of Violence in Contemporary India." Unpublished manuscript, Columbia University.

Posen, Barry R. 1993. "The Security Dilemma and Ethnic Conflict," in Michael E. Brown, ed., *Ethnic Conflict in International Politics*. Princeton: Princeton University Press.

Prunier, Gerard. 1995. *The Rwanda Crisis: History of a Genocide*. London: Hurst.

Przeworksi, Adam. 1991. *Democracy and the Market*. New York: Cambridge University Press.

Rabushka, Alvin, and Kenneth A. Shepsle. 1972. *Politics in Plural Societies*. Columbus, Mo.: Merrill.

Ramet, Sabrina P. 1992. *Nationalism and Federalism in Yugoslavia, 1962–1991*. Bloomington: Indiana University Press.

Romer, Thomas, and Barry R. Weingast. 1991. "Political Foundations of the Thrift Debacle," in Alberto Alesina and Geoffrey Carliner, eds., *Politics and Economics in the 1980s*. Chicago: University of Chicago Press.

Rogowski, Ronald. 1988. *Commerce and Coalitions*. Princeton: Princeton University Press.

Sellstrom, Tor, and Lennart Wohlgemuth. 1996. *The International Response to Conflict and Genocide: Lessons from the Rwanda Experience*. Copenhagen: Steering Committee of the Joint Evaluation of Emergency Assistance to Rwanda.

Silber, Laura, and Allan Little. 1996. *Yugoslavia: Death of a Nation*. New York: TV Books.

Snyder, Jack, and Karen Ballentine. 1996. "Nationalism and the Marketplace of Ideas." *International Security* (Fall), vol. 21, pp. 5–40.

Sollors, Werner. 1989. *The Invention of Ethnicity*. Oxford

Taylor, Michael. 1976. *Anarchy and Cooperation*. New York: Wiley.

Thompson, Mark. 1994. *Forging the War: The Media in Serbia, Croatia, and Bosnia-Hercegovina*. Article 19. London: International Centre Against Censorship.

Van Evera, Stephen. 1994. "Hypotheses on Nationalism and War." *International Security*, vol. 18, no. 4 (Spring), pp. 5–39.

Walter, Barbara F. "Negotiating Civil Wars: Why Bargains Fail." Unpublished manuscript, Columbia University.

Waltz, Kenneth. 1979. *Theory of International Politics*. New York: McGraw-Hill.

Weingast, Barry R. 1998. "Constructing Trust: The Politics and Economics of Ethnic and Regional Conflict," in Virginia Haufler, Karol Soltan, and Eric Uslaner, eds., *Institutions and Social Order*. Ann Arbor: University of Michigan Press.

Woodward, Susan L. 1995. *Balkan Tragedy: Chaos and Dissolution after the Cold War*. Washington: Brookings Institution.

—— 1997. "Intervention in Civil Wars: Bosnia and Herzegovina." Unpublished manuscript, Brookings Institution.

Conclusion

Barbara F. Walter

The preceding chapters have explored the extent to which uncertainty and fear can give rise to a civil war, hinder attempts to negotiate a settlement, and lead to the breakdown of agreements even when security is the paramount aim of all parties. Much of the volume has attempted to identify those conditions under which domestic groups will become suspicious of their neighbors and their neighbor's intentions, to explain why groups have difficulty communicating their peaceful intentions to each other at these times, and to describe how outside intervention can either help groups signal their desire for peace or make it impossible for groups to act opportunistically. The volume has also tried to identify when predatory aims rather than fear are more to blame for the decision to go to war. What follows is a short discussion of the lessons we have learned from this exercise and some suggestions on new avenues for future research.

What Have We Learned?

Most of the authors in this volume agreed that periods of great domestic change—whether a breakdown of government, an impending shift in the political balance of power, a redistribution of economic resources, or forced or voluntary demobilization—produced periods of equally great uncertainty: times when competing groups had difficulty ascertaining how each would respond to potential opportunities for advancement or decline. This uncertainty put stress on internal group relations and made a smooth transition difficult. The authors also agreed, however, that war was not inevitable during these times of upheaval. What mattered was not so much when the changes occurred or what type of change ensued, but the degree to which groups were able to assess how their rival would react to these changes. If competing domestic groups were able to assess—with a high level of confidence—that their opponent would not use these transitional periods to score quick and easy gains, they were likely to weather these changes in peace. If, however, they could not confidently assess how potential rivals would react, they were likely to approach them suspiciously and take precautions that steered them toward war. The outbreak of violence, therefore, seemed to hinge on the degree to which groups could assess how their neighbor would react to periods of what could be called "domestic anarchy."[1]

Domestic groups, however, often have great difficulty making quick and confident assessments of each other's intentions during these times, and it is this fact that tends to steer them toward violence. Assessment can be difficult for four reasons. First, security-driven individuals and predatory individuals often have incentives to act in similar, if not indistinguishable, ways when large domestic changes are imminent. Both will be tempted to retain whatever economic, political and military assets they control. Both will likely mobilize additional allies. Both might even prepare for a military confrontation. In El Salvador, for example, the rebels tried to hide a substantial arms cache soon after they signed the 1992 peace treaty as a hedge against government exploitation. Although the rebels did not intend to attack the government and wished to retain these reserves for defensive purposes only, this plan was not clear to a government whose own security seemed to suffer as a result. Outward behavior, therefore, does not necessarily offer the best clue to a rival's true intentions.

A second assessment problem is lack of time. Domestic groups are often forced to make hurried appraisals of what a neighbor intends to do, since the opportunity for aggression is often short and predators can be expected to act quickly. This short window of opportunity leaves groups little time to collect accurate information and forces them to rely on information that is sometimes inaccurate, misleading, and incendiary. This could explain the rapid escalation of hostilities between the Serbs and Croats in 1991. In the aftermath of Soviet collapse both groups acted quickly: the Croats declared independence and discriminated against Serbs living within their new borders; the Serbs appropriated military stocks from the former Yugoslav state. Both sides could have quietly observed the other and waited to use violence until they were sure that they knew what their neighbor would do. Instead, each took informational short-cuts: the Serbs assumed the Croats would act as brutally as they had in World War II; the Croats assumed that the Serbs would once again try to set up a greater Serbian state.[2]

The third assessment problem domestic groups face is lack of experience. Domestic groups are less accustomed to the problem of assessing potential adversaries than are independent states familiar with anarchy. Ordinarily, domestic groups need not worry about how their neighbor might behave since an effective government almost always exists to monitor behavior and enforce order for them. But once a government breaks down groups must learn to monitor behavior themselves, and they must do this with little or no intelligence apparatuses to aid them, and no baseline from which to measure what "normal" behavior under these conditions might be like.

Finally, assessment is made more difficult due to the potentially devastating consequences of mistakenly trusting an opponent. Independent states are accustomed to the absence of central order and have had time to establish fortifications and set up effective monitoring and surveillance systems. They are also unlikely to be eliminated if attacked. This is not the case with individual citizens sharing a single state. Because the repercussions of mistakenly trusting an opponent can be potentially deadly, groups will be more suspicious of information that paints a rival in a benevolent light and will require greater assurance that this information is true than information that paints their rival in a less flattering light. Less flattering portrayals are easier and safer to believe. This places even greater pressure on obtaining good information.

In short, domestic groups will sometimes have great difficulty assessing how their rival will react to periods of great domestic change because (1) security-driven and predatory-driven behaviors appear similar, (2) they have little time to collect accurate information, (3) they are information-gathering novices, or (4) because they are hesitant to trust any information that portrays a rival favorably. Domestic groups, therefore, are often unable to confidently assess whether or not their opponent truly wants peace. Knowing that misplaced trust could be fatal, groups may, in circumstances that our contributors have tried to specify, find it prudent to act as if neighboring groups are ruthless predators and in so doing propel the security dilemma forward.

Intervention

Outside intervention, however, can help solve these assessment problems in three important ways. First, outside states or international organizations can monitor and verify the behavior of competing domestic groups for them and serve to reassure each side that they are obtaining accurate and reliable information. Second, outsiders can choose to actively punish predators and thus eliminate any incentive groups might have to act opportunistically. Intervention, therefore, can further guarantee that if a scoundrel does pass through the cracks, the trusting side will be protected. Third, outside intervention provides important information about what type of opponent each side is facing, distinguishing predators from nonpredators. Domestic groups who are intent on aggression are unlikely to accept outside interference since this would jeopardize their ability to carry out any malicious plans. Peace-loving groups, on the other hand, should eagerly agree to such involvement and thus signal their benign intentions

Where Do We Go from Here?

This book was an effort in theory building rather than testing. Thus, it is only the first step on a much longer road toward a comprehensive understanding of civil wars, their causes and their resolution. This volume has identified some of the mechanisms that might account for why individuals channel their fear into war but has also left many important questions unanswered. For example, this volume does not attempt to understand all the reasons why groups might go to war; it simply attempts to highlight certain conditions that seem to encourage violence. It does not attempt to understand why individuals tend to mobilize along ethnic lines rather than along class-based, regional, or ideological lines. In addition, this volume assumes that individual leaders will initiate or end a civil war based on rational calculations of costs and benefits but offers no explanation for why some leaders refuse to negotiate under any circumstances. Why would Jefferson Davis consistently refuse to negotiate a solution to the American civil war even after it was clear that the South would eventually lose the war? And why would his constituents continue to support him in the face of an ongoing slaughter? Finally, this book stops short of answering what could be the most important question of all. Much research and scholarly attention has been devoted to studying the conditions under which civil war opponents will negotiate a settlement to their war rather than fight to the finish. But most of this literature, mine included, has not addressed a disturbing pattern associated with the durability of civil war peace settlements. Over time, civil war settlements frequently do not deliver the peace they promise. Since 1945 57 percent of civil war settlements failed to prevent the reemergence of conflict.[4] Negotiated settlements were signed in Colombia, Cyprus, India

(Kashmir), Lebanon, Sudan, and Zimbabwe but were unable to prevent renewed violence. Designed to incorporate competing factions into a shared government, restore law and order, and rebuild working state institutions, these settlements often dissolve into one-party dictatorships, corrupt and arbitrary governments, ineffective institutions, or renewed civil war.[5] They do not create the new domestic political order most people envision when they sign the original settlement. Our next big challenge, therefore, is to understand what *ultimately* brings lasting, stable peace.

NOTES

1. It is important to emphasize that not all civil wars are the result of assessment problems; in fact, most are not. Although fear did appear to play a role in the wars in Rwanda, Bosnia, Somalia, and Cambodia, most civil wars are not primarily the result of security dilemmas but rather the result of purposive strategies to reform a corrupt government, overthrow an oppressive regime, or win territory. It is important, therefore, not to analyze situations solely in terms of the security dilemma but to assess how security fears interact with, intensify, or are intensified by other reasons for civil conflict.

2. For an excellent explanation of the Serb/Croat war from this perspective, see Barry R. Posen, "The Security Dilemma and Ethnic Conflict," in Michael E. Brown, ed., *Ethnic Conflict and International Security* (Princeton: Princeton University Press, 1993).

3. This book says relatively little about how intervention can help prevent wars, but says much about how outside intervention can help resolve wars once they start. This is partly because the study was designed to look at war termination and intervention. Nonetheless, the kinds of institutional remedies that help settle ongoing conflicts (e.g., reassuring groups about their security from exploitation) should be at least part of the repertoire of methods for preventing their outbreak.

4. For data on the outcomes of civil war settlements, see Roy Licklider, "The Consequences of Negotiated Settlements in Civil Wars, 1945–1993," *American Political Science Review*, vol. 89, no. 3 (September 1995).

5. Settlements negotiated in China, Greece, Chad, Uganda, Laos, and Angola all broke down into renewed civil war. Lebanon's 1958 treaty lasted until 1976, when it too collapsed into renewed war. The settlements in Sudan and Rhodesia have evolved into one-party states, and settlements in Cambodia and Sudan have suffered coups d'état.

Index